Data Engine with Apache Spark, Delta Lake, and Lakehouse

Create scalable pipelines that ingest, curate, and aggregate complex data in a timely and secure way

Manoj Kukreja

BIRMINGHAM—MUMBAI

Data Engineering with Apache Spark, Delta Lake, and Lakehouse

Copyright © 2021 Packt Publishing

Group Product Manager: Kunal Parikh

Publishing Product Manager: Sunith Shetty

Senior Editor: Davud Sugarman

Content Development Editor: Joseph Sunil

Technical Editor: Sonam Pandey

Copy Editor: Safis Editing

Project Coordinator: Aparna Ravikumar Nair

Proofreader: Safis Editing

Indexer: Tejal Daruwale Soni

Production Designer: Prashant Ghare

First published: October 2021

Production reference: 1170921

Published by Packt Publishing Ltd.

Livery Place

35 Livery Street

Birmingham

B3 2PB, UK.

ISBN 978-1-80107-774-3

www.packt.com

In memory of my two fathers, my mother, and my father-in-law, whom I lost recently. Hope you keep showering your blessings from far and beyond. To my darling wife Roopika, a simple thank you is not good enough. To my daughter Saesha who inspired me to write this book, and to my other daughter Shagun who is living my other dream.

I love you all.

– Manoj Kukreja

Foreword

I don't think it is required anymore to explain the importance data plays in the modern world. Many of the online services we use today are powered by data systems of varying complexity. Machine learning emerged as a powerful tool for certain tasks in big part thanks to modern data platforms that can collect, process, and distribute large volumes of data. These data platforms also provide a strong foundation for data analytics and help drive real world decisions in healthcare, business, and education.

One of the challenges that I have faced when I have started working in data space, which I'm sure is familiar to many of you, is the lack of good books and other educational resources on the topic. There is a lot of documentation on specific tools that you can use, but knowledge of what good architectures look like and which patterns work in which specific cases only resides with a few experts who have done this type of work before. This is especially true when it comes to emerging cloud technologies.

Manoj is one of such experts since he has been implementing data platforms for companies in different industries for the last 10 years. In this book, he will share his knowledge and experience on architecting and implementing modern data platforms using Microsoft Azure, one of the leading cloud providers for data workloads. You will learn practical skills on implementing data lake architectures, implementing data pipelines, and running them in a production environment. Books like this are useful because they give you a download of the knowledge and experience that Manoj has accumulated over the years and you know that recipes and advice he gives will work in a real-life implementation because he has implemented similar systems many times before.

Getting practical data engineering skills is a great investment in your career and knowing patterns that you can rely on will spare you lots of trial and error and will help you get results much faster. Hope you enjoy it!

Danil Zburivsky,

Senior Consultant at Sourced Group

Data Engineering and Cloud Infrastructure specialist

Ottawa, Ontario, Canada

Contributors

About the author

Manoj Kukreja is a Principal Architect at Northbay Solutions who specializes in creating complex Data Lakes and Data Analytics Pipelines for large-scale organizations such as banks, insurance companies, universities, and US/Canadian government agencies. Previously, he worked for Pythian, a large managed service provider where he was leading the MySQL and MongoDB DBA group and supporting large-scale data infrastructure for enterprises across the globe. With over 25 years of IT experience, he has delivered Data Lake solutions using all major cloud providers including AWS, Azure, GCP, and Alibaba Cloud. On weekends, he trains groups of aspiring Data Engineers and Data Scientists on Hadoop, Spark, Kafka and Data Analytics on AWS and Azure Cloud.

About the reviewers

Rajeesh Punathil is currently a Data Architect with a prominent energy company based in Canada. He leads the digital team in building cloud data analytics solutions aimed to help businesses arrive at right questions and answers.In prior roles he has designed data analytics pipelines in AWS and Azure stack for major companies like Sunlife, CIBC , City National bank, Hudsons Bay etc. He holds a B Tech in Electronics and Telecom Engineering from University of Calicut and has over 15 Years of IT experience. He consider himself as a forever student, and his constant striving for knowledge has made him an expert and leader in the field of data analytics and big data. He has completed AWS Big Data Analytics certification to his credit.

Dang Trung Anh is a principal engineer and software architect with over 15 years of experience in delivering big software systems for various customers across many areas. He has spent most of his career writing many software systems that support millions of users. He has had various roles from an ordinary full-stack developer, through software architect, to director of engineering. He is the author of many viral articles related to software engineering on Medium.

Table of Contents

Preface

Section 1:
Modern Data Engineering and Tools

1
The Story of Data Engineering and Analytics

The journey of data	4	computing	8
Exploring the evolution of data analytics	5	Adoption of cloud computing	10
		Data storytelling	11
Core capabilities of storage and compute resources	7	**The monetary power of data**	**13**
Availability of varying datasets	7	Organic growth	13
The paradigm shift to distributed		**Summary**	**17**

2
Discovering Storage and Compute Data Lakes

Introducing data lakes	20	Discovering data lake architectures	33
Exploring the benefits of data lakes	21	The CAP theorem	34
Adhering to compliance frameworks	24		
Segregating storage and compute in a data lake	26	**Summary**	**51**

3

Data Engineering on Microsoft Azure

Introducing data engineering in Azure	53	Data processing services in Microsoft Azure	65
Performing data engineering in Microsoft Azure	56	Data engineering as a service (SaaS)	68
Self-managed data engineering services (IaaS)	56	Data cataloging and sharing services in Microsoft Azure	75
Azure-managed data engineering services (PaaS)	59	Opening a free account with Microsoft Azure	76
		Summary	77

Section 2: Data Pipelines and Stages of Data Engineering

4

Understanding Data Pipelines

Exploring data pipelines	82	Development phase	92
Components of a data pipeline	82	Deployment phase	93
Process of creating a data pipeline	85	Running a data pipeline	93
		Sample lakehouse project	95
Discovery phase	86	Summary	96
Design phase	88		

5

Data Collection Stage – The Bronze Layer

Architecting the Electroniz data lake	98	Configuring data sources	106
The cloud architecture	100	Data preparation	106
The pipeline design	103	Configuring data destinations	117
The deployment strategy	104	Building the ingestion pipelines	119
Understanding the bronze layer	105	Building a batch ingestion pipeline	119
		Testing the ingestion pipelines	141

Building the streaming
ingestion pipeline   155

Summary   160

6

Understanding Delta Lake

Understanding how Delta
Lake enables the lakehouse   162

Understanding Delta Lake   163

Preparing Azure resources   164

Creating a Delta Lake table   174

Changing data in
an existing Delta Lake table   180

Performing time travel   181

Performing upserts of data   184

Understanding isolation levels   191

Understanding
concurrency control   193

Cleaning up Azure resources   194

Summary   195

7

Data Curation Stage – The Silver Layer

The need for curating raw data   198

Unstandardized data   198
Invalid data   199
Non-uniform data   201
Inconsistent data   202
Duplicate data   203
Insecure data   204

The process of curating
raw data   205

Inspecting data   205
Getting approval   205
Cleaning data   206
Verifying data   206

Developing a data
curation pipeline   206

Preparing Azure resources   207
Creating the pipeline
for the silver layer   215

Running the pipeline for
the silver layer   220

Verifying curated data
in the silver layer   226

Verifying unstandardized data   226
Verifying invalid data   229
Verifying non-uniform data   232
Verifying duplicate data   236
Verifying insecure data   238

Cleaning up Azure resources   240

Summary   240

8
Data Aggregation Stage – The Gold Layer

The need to aggregate data 242
The process of
aggregating data 243
Developing a data
aggregation pipeline 245
Preparing the Azure resources 246
Creating the pipeline for
the gold layer 251
Running the
aggregation pipeline 263

Understanding data
consumption 264
Accessing silver layer data 266
Accessing gold layer data 267
Verifying aggregated
data in the gold layer 268
Meeting customer
expectations 273
Summary 281

Section 3: Data Engineering Challenges and Effective Deployment Strategies

9
Deploying and Monitoring Pipelines in Production

The deployment strategy 286
Developing the
master pipeline 288
Testing the master pipeline 295
Scheduling the
master pipeline 296

Monitoring pipelines 300
Adding durability features 301
Dealing with failure conditions 303
Adding alerting features 306
Summary 315

10
Solving Data Engineering Challenges

Schema evolution 318
Sharing data 334
Preparing the Azure resources 337
Creating a data share 338
Data governance 352

Preparing the Azure resources 353
Creating a data catalog 355
Cleaning up Azure resources 365
Summary 365

11
Infrastructure Provisioning

Infrastructure as code	368	Deploying ARM templates containing secrets	379
Deploying infrastructure using Azure Resource Manager	369	Deploying multiple environments using IaC	383
Creating ARM templates	369	Cleaning up Azure resources	386
Deploying ARM templates using the Azure portal	373	Summary	387
Deploying ARM templates using the Azure CLI	378		

12
Continuous Integration and Deployment (CI/CD) of Data Pipelines

Understanding CI/CD	390	Creating the Electroniz infrastructure CI/CD pipeline	406
Traditional software delivery cycle	390	Creating the Electroniz code CI/CD pipeline	421
Modern software delivery cycle	391	Creating the CI/CD life cycle	432
Designing CI/CD pipelines	393	Summary	442
Developing CI/CD pipelines	397		
Creating an Azure DevOps organization	397		

Other Books You May Enjoy

Index

Preface

In the world of ever-changing data and ever-evolving schemas, it is important to build data pipelines that can auto-adjust to changes. This book will help you build scalable data platforms that managers, data scientists, and data analysts can rely on.

Starting with an introduction to data engineering, along with its key concepts and architectures, this book will show you how to use Microsoft Azure cloud services effectively for data engineering. You'll cover data lake design patterns and the different stages through which the data needs to flow in a typical data lake. Once you've explored the main features of Delta Lake to build data lakes with fast performance and governance in mind, you'll advance to implementing the lambda architecture using Delta Lake. Packed with practical examples and code snippets, this book takes you through real-world examples based on production scenarios faced by the author in his 10 years of experience working with big data. Finally, you'll cover data lake deployment strategies that play an important role in provisioning cloud resources and deploying data pipelines in a repeatable and continuous way.

By the end of this data engineering book, you'll have learned how to effectively deal with ever-changing data and create scalable data pipelines to streamline data science, ML, and **artificial intelligence (AI)** tasks.

Who this book is for

This book is for aspiring data engineers and data analysts who are new to the world of data engineering and are looking for a practical guide to building scalable data platforms. If you already work with PySpark and want to use Delta Lake for data engineering, you'll find this book useful. Basic knowledge of Python, Spark, and SQL is expected.

What this book covers

Chapter 1, The Story of Data Engineering and Analytics, introduces the core concepts of data engineering. It introduces you to the two data processing architectures in big data – Lambda and Kappa.

Chapter 2, Discovering Storage and Compute Data Lake Architectures, introduces one of the most important concepts in data engineering – segregating storage and compute layers. By following this principle, you will be introduced to the idea of building data lakes. An understanding of this key principle will lay the foundation for your understanding of the modern-day data lake design patterns discussed later in the book.

Chapter 3, Data Engineering on Microsoft Azure, introduces the world of data engineering on the Microsoft Azure cloud platform. It will familiarize you with all the Azure tools and services that play a major role in the Azure data engineering ecosystem. These tools and services will be used throughout the book for all practical examples.

Chapter 4, Understanding Data Pipelines, introduces you to the idea of data pipelines. This chapter further enhances your knowledge of the various stages of data engineering and how data pipelines can enhance efficiency by integrating individual components together and running them in a streamlined fashion.

Chapter 5, Data Collection Stage – The Bronze Layer, guides us in building a data lake using the Lakehouse architecture. We will start with data collection and the development of the bronze layer.

Chapter 6, Understanding Delta Lake, introduces Delta Lake and helps you quickly explore the main features of Delta Lake. Understanding Delta Lake's features is an integral skill for a data engineering professional who would like to build data lakes with data freshness, fast performance, and governance in mind. We will also be talking about the Lakehouse architecture in detail.

Chapter 7, Data Curation Stage – The Silver Layer, continues our building of a data lake. The focus of this chapter will be on data cleansing, standardization, and building the silver layer using Delta Lake.

Chapter 8, Data Aggregation Stage – The Gold Layer, continues our building a data lake. The focus of this chapter will be on data aggregation and building the gold layer.

Chapter 9, Deploying and Monitoring Pipelines in Production, explains how to effectively manage data pipelines running in production. We will explore data pipeline management from an operational perspective and cover security, performance management, and monitoring.

Chapter 10, Solving Data Engineering Challenges, lists the major challenges experienced by data engineering professionals. Various use cases will be covered in this chapter and a challenge will be offered. We will deep dive into the effective handling of the challenge, explaining its resolution using code snippets and examples.

Chapter 11, Infrastructure Provisioning, teaches you the basics of infrastructure provisioning using Terraform. Using Terraform, we will provision the cloud resources on Microsoft Azure that are required for running a data pipeline.

Chapter 12, Continuous Integration and Deployment of Data Pipelines, introduces the idea of **continuous integration and deployment (CI/CD)** of data pipelines. Using the principles of CI/CD, data engineering professionals can rapidly deploy new data pipelines/changes to existing data pipelines in a repeatable fashion.

To get the most out of this book

You will need a Microsoft Azure account.

Software/hardware covered in the book	Operating system requirements
Azure	Windows, macOS, or Linux

If you are using the digital version of this book, we advise you to type the code yourself or access the code from the book's GitHub repository (a link is available in the next section). Doing so will help you avoid any potential errors related to the copying and pasting of code.

Do ensure that you close all instances of Azure after you have run your code, so that your costs are minimized.

Download the example code files

You can download the example code files for this book from GitHub at `https://github.com/PacktPublishing/Data-Engineering-with-Apache-Spark-Delta-Lake-and-Lakehouse`. If there's an update to the code, it will be updated in the GitHub repository.

We also have other code bundles from our rich catalog of books and videos available at `https://github.com/PacktPublishing/`. Check them out!

Download the color images

We also provide a PDF file that has color images of the screenshots and diagrams used in this book. You can download it here: `https://static.packt-cdn.com/downloads/9781801077743_ColorImages.pdf`.

Conventions used

There are a number of text conventions used throughout this book.

Code in text: Indicates code words in text, database table names, folder names, filenames, file extensions, pathnames, dummy URLs, user input, and Twitter handles. Here is an example: "In the case of the `financial_df` DataFrame, the index was auto-generated when we downloaded the dataset with the `read_csv` function."

A block of code is set as follows:

```
const df = new DataFrame({...})
df.plot("my_div_id").<chart type>
```

When we wish to draw your attention to a particular part of a code block, the relevant lines or items are set in bold:

```
...
var config = {
          displayModeBar: true,
          modeBarButtonsToAdd: [
...
```

Any command-line input or output is written as follows:

```
npm install @tensorflow/tfjs
```

Bold: Indicates a new term, an important word, or words that you see onscreen. For instance, words in menus or dialog boxes appear in **bold**. Here is an example: "In Microsoft Edge, open the **Edge** menu in the upper right-hand corner of the browser window and select **F12 Developer Tools**."

> **Tips or important notes**
> Appear like this.

Get in touch

Feedback from our readers is always welcome.

General feedback: If you have questions about any aspect of this book, email us at customercare@packtpub.com and mention the book title in the subject of your message.

Errata: Although we have taken every care to ensure the accuracy of our content, mistakes do happen. If you have found a mistake in this book, we would be grateful if you would report this to us. Please visit www.packtpub.com/support/errata and fill in the form.

Piracy: If you come across any illegal copies of our works in any form on the internet, we would be grateful if you would provide us with the location address or website name. Please contact us at copyright@packt.com with a link to the material.

If you are interested in becoming an author: If there is a topic that you have expertise in and you are interested in either writing or contributing to a book, please visit authors.packtpub.com.

Share Your Thoughts

Once you've read , we'd love to hear your thoughts! Scan the QR code below to go straight to the Amazon review page for this book and share your feedback.

https://packt.link/r/1-801-07774-6

Your review is important to us and the tech community and will help us make sure we're delivering excellent quality content.

Section 1: Modern Data Engineering and Tools

This section introduces you to the world of data engineering. It gives you an understanding of data engineering concepts and architectures. Furthermore, it educates you on how to effectively utilize the Microsoft Azure cloud services for data engineering.

This section contains the following chapters:

- *Chapter 1, The Story of Data Engineering and Analytics*
- *Chapter 2, Discovering Storage and Compute Data Lake Architectures*
- *Chapter 3, Data Engineering on Microsoft Azure*

1
The Story of Data Engineering and Analytics

Every byte of data has a story to tell. The real question is whether the story is being narrated accurately, securely, and efficiently. In the modern world, data makes a journey of its own—from the point it gets created to the point a user consumes it for their analytical requirements.

But what makes the journey of data today so special and different compared to before? After all, **Extract, Transform, Load (ETL)** is not something that recently got invented. In fact, I remember collecting and transforming data since the time I joined the world of **information technology (IT)** just over 25 years ago.

In this chapter, we will discuss some reasons why an effective data engineering practice has a profound impact on data analytics.

In this chapter, we will cover the following topics:

- The journey of data
- Exploring the evolution of data analytics
- The monetary power of data

> **Remember:**
> the road to effective data analytics leads through effective data engineering.

The journey of data

Data engineering is the vehicle that makes the journey of data possible, secure, durable, and timely. A **data engineer** is the driver of this vehicle who safely maneuvers the vehicle around various roadblocks along the way without compromising the safety of its passengers. Waiting at the end of the road are **data analysts**, **data scientists**, and **business intelligence (BI) engineers** who are eager to receive this data and start narrating the **story of data**. You can see this reflected in the following screenshot:

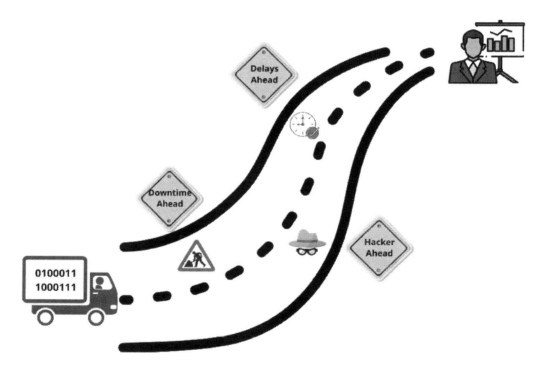

Figure 1.1 – Data's journey to effective data analysis

Traditionally, the journey of data revolved around the typical ETL process. Unfortunately, the traditional ETL process is simply not enough in the modern era anymore. Due to the immense human dependency on data, there is a greater need than ever to streamline the journey of data by using cutting-edge architectures, frameworks, and tools.

You may also be wondering why the journey of data is even required. Gone are the days where datasets were limited, computing power was scarce, and the scope of data analytics was very limited. We now live in a fast-paced world where decision-making needs to be done at lightning speeds using data that is changing by the second. Let's look at how the evolution of data analytics has impacted data engineering.

Exploring the evolution of data analytics

Data analytics has evolved over time, enabling us to do bigger and better. For many years, the focus of data analytics was limited to **descriptive analysis**, where the focus was to gain useful **business insights** from data, in the form of a report. This type of analysis was useful to answer question such as "*What happened?*". A hypothetical scenario would be that the sales of a company sharply declined within the last quarter.

Very quickly, everyone started to realize that there were several other indicators available for finding out *what happened*, but it was the *why it happened* that everyone was after. The core analytics now shifted toward **diagnostic analysis**, where the focus is to identify anomalies in data to ascertain the reasons for certain outcomes. An example scenario would be that the sales of a company sharply declined in the last quarter because there was a serious drop in inventory levels, arising due to floods in the manufacturing units of the suppliers. This form of analysis further enhances the decision support mechanisms for users, as illustrated in the following diagram:

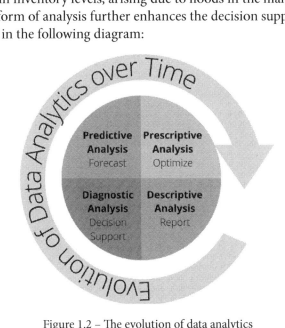

Figure 1.2 – The evolution of data analytics

> **Important note**
>
> Both descriptive analysis and diagnostic analysis try to impact the decision-making process using factual data only.

Since the advent of time, it has always been a core human desire to look beyond the present and try to forecast the future. If we can predict future outcomes, we can surely make a lot of better decisions, and so the era of **predictive analysis** dawned, where the focus revolves around "*What will happen in the future?*". Predictive analysis can be performed using **machine learning** (**ML**) algorithms—let the machine learn from existing and future data in a repeated fashion so that it can identify a pattern that enables it to predict future trends accurately.

Now that we are well set up to forecast future outcomes, we must use and optimize the outcomes of this predictive analysis. Based on the results of predictive analysis, the aim of **prescriptive analysis** is to provide a set of prescribed actions that can help meet business goals.

> **Important note**
>
> Unlike descriptive and diagnostic analysis, predictive and prescriptive analysis try to impact the decision-making process, using both factual and statistical data.

But how can the dreams of modern-day analysis be effectively realized? After all, data analysts and data scientists are not adequately skilled to collect, clean, and transform the vast amount of ever-increasing and changing datasets.

The data engineering practice is commonly referred to as the **primary support** for modern-day data analytics' needs.

The following are some major reasons as to why a strong data engineering practice is becoming an absolutely unignorable necessity for today's businesses:

- Core capabilities of compute and storage resources
- Availability of varying datasets
- The paradigm shift to distributed computing
- Adoption of cloud computing
- Data storytelling

We'll explore each of these in the following subsections.

> **Important note**
> Having a strong data engineering practice ensures the needs of modern analytics are met in terms of durability, performance, and scalability.

Core capabilities of storage and compute resources

25 years ago, I had an opportunity to buy a Sun Solaris server—128 **megabytes** (**MB**) **random-access memory** (**RAM**), 2 **gigabytes** (**GB**) storage—for close to $ 25K. The intended use of the server was to run a client/server application over an Oracle database in production. Given the high price of storage and compute resources, I had to enforce strict countermeasures to appropriately balance the demands of **online transaction processing** (**OLTP**) and **online analytical processing** (**OLAP**) of my users. One such limitation was implementing strict timings for when these programs could be run; otherwise, they ended up using all available power and slowing down everyone else.

Today, you can buy a server with 64 GB RAM and several **terabytes** (**TB**) of storage at one-fifth the price. The extra power available can do wonders for us. Multiple storage and compute units can now be procured just for data analytics workloads. The extra power available enables users to run their workloads whenever they like, however they like. In fact, it is very common these days to run analytical workloads on a continuous basis using data streams, also known as **stream processing**.

The installation, management, and monitoring of multiple compute and storage units requires a well-designed data pipeline, which is often achieved through a data engineering practice.

Availability of varying datasets

A few years ago, the scope of data analytics was extremely limited. Performing data analytics simply meant reading data from databases and/or files, denormalizing the joins, and making it available for descriptive analysis. The structure of data was largely known and rarely varied over time.

We live in a different world now; not only do we produce more data, but the variety of data has increased over time. In addition to collecting the usual data from databases and files, it is common these days to collect data from social networking, website visits, infrastructure logs' media, and so on, as depicted in the following screenshot:

Figure 1.3 – Variety of data increases the accuracy of data analytics

> **Important note**
> More variety of data means that data analysts have multiple dimensions to perform descriptive, diagnostic, predictive, or prescriptive analysis.

Naturally, the varying degrees of datasets injects a level of complexity into the data collection and processing process. On the flip side, it hugely impacts the accuracy of the decision-making process as well as the prediction of future trends. A well-designed data engineering practice can easily deal with the given complexity.

The paradigm shift to distributed computing

The traditional data processing approach used over the last few years was largely singular in nature. To process data, you had to create a program that collected all required data for processing—typically from a database—followed by processing it in a single thread. This type of processing is also referred to as **data-to-code** processing. Unfortunately, there are several drawbacks to this approach, as outlined here:

- Since vast amounts of data travel to the code for processing, at times this causes heavy network congestion. Since a network is a shared resource, users who are currently active may start to complain about network slowness.

- Being a single-threaded operation means the execution time is directly proportional to the data. Therefore, the growth of data typically means the process will take longer to finish. This could end up significantly impacting and/or delaying the decision-making process, therefore rendering the data analytics useless at times.

- Something as minor as a network glitch or machine failure requires the entire program cycle to be restarted, as illustrated in the following diagram:

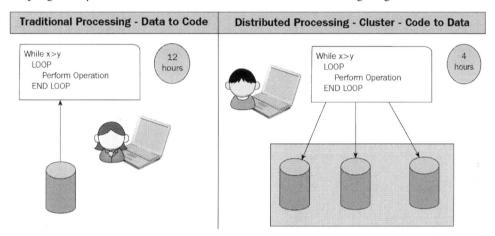

Figure 1.4 – Rise of distributed computing

The distributed processing approach, which I refer to as the **paradigm shift**, largely takes care of the previously stated problems. Instead of taking the traditional data-to-code route, the paradigm is reversed to **code-to-data**.

In a distributed processing approach, several resources collectively work as part of a cluster, all working toward a common goal. In simple terms, this approach can be compared to a team model where every team member takes on a portion of the load and executes it in parallel until completion.
If a team member falls sick and is unable to complete their share of the workload, some other member automatically gets assigned their portion of the load.

Distributed processing has several advantages over the traditional processing approach, outlined as follows:

- The **code-to-data** paradigm shift ensures the network does not get clogged. The entire idea of distributed processing heavily relies on the assumption that data is stored in a distributed fashion across several machines, also referred to as nodes. At the time of processing, only the code portion (usually a much smaller footprint as compared to actual data) is sent over to each node that stores the portion of the data being processed. This ensures that the processing happens locally on the node where the data is stored.

- Since several nodes are collectively participating in data processing, the overall completion time is drastically reduced.

- Program execution is immune to network and node failures. If a node failure is encountered, then a portion of the work is assigned to another available node in the cluster.

> **Important note**
>
> Distributed processing is implemented using well-known frameworks such as Hadoop, Spark, and Flink. Modern **massively parallel processing** (**MPP**)-style data warehouses such as Amazon Redshift, Azure Synapse, Google BigQuery, and Snowflake also implement a similar concept.

Since distributed processing is a multi-machine technology, it requires sophisticated design, installation, and execution processes. That makes it a compelling reason to establish good data engineering practices within your organization.

Adoption of cloud computing

The vast adoption of cloud computing allows organizations to abstract the complexities of managing their own data centers. Migrating their resources to the cloud offers faster deployments, greater flexibility, and access to a pricing model that, if used correctly, can result in major cost savings.

In the previous section, we talked about distributed processing implemented as a cluster of multiple machines working as a group. For this reason, deploying a distributed processing cluster is expensive.

In the pre-cloud era of distributed processing, clusters were created using hardware deployed inside on-premises data centers. Very careful planning was required before attempting to deploy a cluster (otherwise, the outcomes were less than desired). You might argue why such a level of planning is essential. Let me address this:

- Since the hardware needs to be deployed in a data center, you need to physically procure it. The real question is how many units you would procure, and that is precisely what makes this process so complex.

- Order more units than required and you'll end up with unused resources, wasting money.

- Order fewer units than required and you will have insufficient resources, job failures, and degraded performance.

To order the right number of machines, you start the planning process by performing benchmarking of the required data processing jobs.

- The results from the benchmarking process are a good indicator of how many machines will be able to take on the load to finish the processing in the desired time. You now need to start the procurement process from the hardware vendors. Keeping in mind the cycle of procurement and shipping process, this could take weeks to months to complete.

- Once the hardware arrives at your door, you need to have a team of administrators ready who can hook up servers, install the operating system, configure networking and storage, and finally install the distributed processing cluster software—this requires a lot of steps and a lot of planning.

I hope you may now fully agree that the *careful planning* I spoke about earlier was perhaps an understatement. The complexities of on-premises deployments do not end after the initial installation of servers is completed. You are still on the hook for regular software maintenance, hardware failures, upgrades, growth, warranties, and more.

This is precisely the reason why the idea of cloud adoption is being very well received. Having resources on the cloud shields an organization from many operational issues. Additionally, the cloud provides the flexibility of automating deployments, scaling on demand, load-balancing resources, and security.

> **Important note**
> Many aspects of the cloud particularly scale on demand, and the ability to offer low pricing for unused resources is a game-changer for many organizations. If used correctly, these features may end up saving a significant amount of cost. Having a well-designed cloud infrastructure can work miracles for an organization's data engineering and data analytics practice.

Data storytelling

I started this chapter by stating *Every byte of data has a story to tell*. Data storytelling is a new alternative for non-technical people to simplify the decision-making process using narrated stories of data. Traditionally, decision makers have heavily relied on visualizations such as bar charts, pie charts, dashboarding, and so on to gain useful business insights. These visualizations are typically created using the end results of data analytics. The problem is that not everyone views and understands data in the same way. Let me give you an example to illustrate this further.

Here is a BI engineer sharing stock information for the last quarter with senior management:

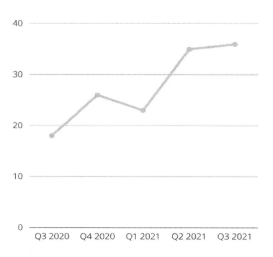

Figure 1.5 – Visualizing data using simple graphics

And here is the same information being supplied in the form of data storytelling:

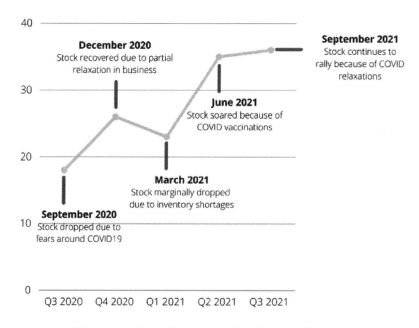

Figure 1.6 – Storytelling approach to data visualization

> **Important note**
> Visualizations are effective in communicating why something happened, but the storytelling narrative supports the reasons for it to happen.

Data storytelling tries to communicate the analytic insights to a regular person by providing them with a narration of data in their natural language. This does not mean that data storytelling is only a narrative. It is a combination of narrative data, associated data, and visualizations. With all these combined, an interesting story emerges—a story that everyone can understand.

As data-driven decision-making continues to grow, data storytelling is quickly becoming the standard for communicating key business insights to key stakeholders.

There's another benefit to acquiring and understanding data: *financial*. Let's look at the monetary power of data next.

The monetary power of data

Modern-day organizations are immensely focused on revenue acceleration. Traditionally, organizations have primarily focused on increasing sales as a method of revenue acceleration… but is there a better method?

Modern-day organizations that are at the forefront of technology have made this possible using **revenue diversification**. Here are some of the methods used by organizations today, all made possible by the *power of data*.

Organic growth

During my initial years in data engineering, I was a part of several projects in which the focus of the project was beyond the usual. On several of these projects, the goal was to increase revenue through traditional methods such as increasing sales, streamlining inventory, targeted advertising, and so on. This meant collecting data from various sources, followed by employing the good old descriptive, diagnostic, predictive, or prescriptive analytics techniques.

But what can be done when the limits of sales and marketing have been exhausted? Where does the revenue growth come from?

Some forward-thinking organizations realized that increasing sales is not the only method for revenue diversification. They started to realize that the real wealth of data that has accumulated over several years is largely untapped. Instead of solely focusing their efforts entirely on the growth of sales, why not tap into the power of data and find innovative methods to grow organically?

This innovative thinking led to the revenue diversification method known as **organic growth**. Subsequently, organizations started to use the power of data to their advantage in several ways. Let's look at several of them.

Customer retention

Data scientists can create **prediction models** using existing data to predict if certain customers are in danger of terminating their services due to complaints. Based on this list, customer service can run targeted campaigns to retain these customers. By retaining a loyal customer, not only do you make the customer happy, but you also protect your bottom line.

Fraud prevention

Banks and other institutions are now using data analytics to tackle financial fraud. Based on key financial metrics, they have built prediction models that can detect and prevent fraudulent transactions before they happen. These models are integrated within case management systems used for issuing credit cards, mortgages, or loan applications.

Using the same technology, credit card clearing houses continuously monitor live financial traffic and are able to flag and prevent fraudulent transactions before they happen. Detecting and preventing fraud goes a long way in preventing long-term losses.

Problem detection

I was part of an **internet of things** (**IoT**) project where a company with several manufacturing plants in North America was collecting metrics from **electronic sensors** fitted on thousands of machinery parts. The sensor metrics from all manufacturing plants were streamed to a common location for further analysis, as illustrated in the following diagram:

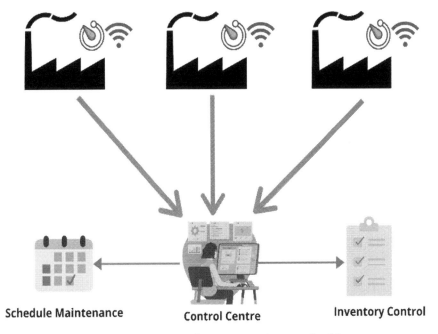

Figure 1.7 – IoT is contributing to a major growth of data

These metrics are helpful in pinpointing whether a certain consumable component such as rubber belts have reached or are nearing their **end-of-life** (**EOL**) cycle. Collecting these metrics is helpful to a company in several ways, including the following:

- The data indicates the machinery where the component has reached its EOL and needs to be replaced. Having this data on hand enables a company to schedule preventative maintenance on a machine before a component breaks (causing downtime and delays).

- The data from machinery where the component is nearing its EOL is important for inventory control of standby components. Before this system is in place, a company must procure inventory based on guesstimates. Buy too few and you may experience delays; buy too many, you waste money. At any given time, a data pipeline is helpful in predicting the inventory of standby components with greater accuracy.

The combined power of IoT and data analytics is reshaping how companies can make timely and intelligent decisions that prevent downtime, reduce delays, and streamline costs.

Data monetization

Innovative minds never stop or give up. They continuously look for innovative methods to deal with their challenges, such as revenue diversification. Organizations quickly realized that if the correct use of their data was so useful to themselves, then the same data could be useful to others as well.

As per Wikipedia, **data monetization** is the "*act of generating measurable economic benefits from available data sources*".

The following diagram depicts data monetization using **application programming interfaces (APIs)**:

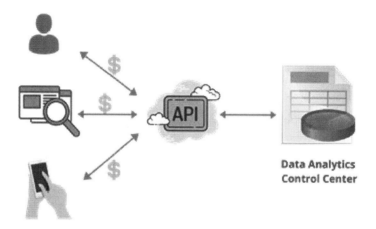

Figure 1.8 – Monetizing data using APIs is the latest trend

In the latest trend, organizations are using the power of data in a fashion that is not only beneficial to themselves but also profitable to others. In a recent project dealing with the health industry, a company created an innovative product to perform medical coding using **optical character recognition (OCR)** and **natural language processing (NLP)**.

Before the project started, this company made sure that we understood the real reason behind the project—data collected would not only be used internally but would be distributed (for a fee) to others as well. Knowing the requirements beforehand helped us design an event-driven API frontend architecture for internal and external data distribution. At the backend, we created a complex data engineering pipeline using innovative technologies such as Spark, Kubernetes, Docker, and microservices. This is how the pipeline was designed:

- Several microservices were designed on a self-serve model triggered by requests coming in from internal users as well as from the outside (public).

- For external distribution, the system was exposed to users with valid paid subscriptions only. Once the subscription was in place, several frontend APIs were exposed that enabled them to use the services on a per-request model.

- Each microservice was able to interface with a backend analytics function that ended up performing descriptive and predictive analysis and supplying back the results.

The power of data cannot be underestimated, but the monetary power of data cannot be realized until an organization has built a solid foundation that can deliver the right data at the right time. Data engineering plays an extremely vital role in realizing this objective.

Summary

In this chapter, we went through several scenarios that highlighted a couple of important points.

Firstly, the importance of data-driven analytics is the latest trend that will continue to grow in the future. Data-driven analytics gives decision makers the power to make key decisions but also to back these decisions up with valid reasons.

Secondly, data engineering is the backbone of all data analytics operations. None of the magic in data analytics could be performed without a well-designed, secure, scalable, highly available, and performance-tuned data repository—a **data lake**.

In the next few chapters, we will be talking about data lakes in depth. We will start by highlighting the building blocks of effective data—storage and compute. We will also look at some well-known architecture patterns that can help you create an effective data lake—one that effectively handles analytical requirements for varying use cases.

2
Discovering Storage and Compute Data Lakes

In the previous chapter, we discussed the immense power that data possesses, but with immense power comes increased responsibility. In the past, the key focus of organizations has been to detect trends with data, with the goal of revenue acceleration. Very commonly, however, they have paid less attention to vulnerabilities caused by inconsistent data management and delivery.

In this chapter, we will discuss some ways a data lake can effectively deal with the ever-growing demands of the analytical world.

In this chapter, we will cover the following topics:

- Introducing data lakes
- Segregating storage and compute in a data lake
- Discovering data lake architectures

Introducing data lakes

Over the last few years, the markers for effective data engineering and data analytics have shifted. Up to now, organizational data has been dispersed over several internal systems (silos), each system performing analytics over its own dataset.

Additionally, it has been difficult to interface with external datasets for extending the spectrum of analytic workloads. As a result, it has been difficult for these organizations to get a **unified** view of their data and gain **global insights**.

In a world where organizations are seeking revenue diversification by fine-tuning existing processes and generating organic growth, a globally unified repository of data has become a core necessity. Data lakes solve this need by providing a unified view of data into the hands of users who can use this data to devise innovative techniques for the betterment of mankind.

The following diagram outlines the characteristics of a data lake:

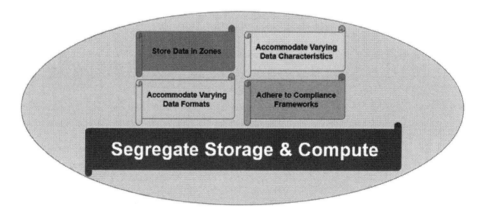

Figure 2.1 – Characteristics of a data lake

You will find several varying definitions of a data lake on the internet. Instead of defining what a data lake is, let's focus on the benefits of having a data lake for a modern-day organization.

We will also see how the storage and computations process in a data lake differs from traditional data storage solutions such as databases and data warehouses.

> **Important note**
> In the modern world, the typical **extract, transform, load** (ETL) process (collecting, transforming, and analyzing) is simply not enough. There are other aspects surrounding the ETL process—such as security, orchestration, and delivery—that need to be equally accounted for.

Exploring the benefits of data lakes

In addition to just being a simple repository, a data lake offers several benefits that make it stand out as a strong data management solution for modern data analytic needs.

Accommodating varying data formats

The most advertised benefit of a data lake is its ability to store **structured**, **semi-structured**, and **unstructured** data on a large scale. The increasing variety of data sources that participate in the data analytics process has introduced a new challenge. Since there has not been an accepted standard around **data exchange formats**, it is pretty much up to the discretion of the **data provider** to choose one for you. Some commonly used data exchange formats and their common uses are listed as follows:

- **Structured**—Database rows

- **Semi-Structured**—**Comma-separated values (CSV)**, **Extensible Markup Language (XML)**, and **JavaScript Object Notation (JSON)**.

- **Unstructured**—**Internet of things (IoT)**, logs, and emails

These can be better represented as follows:

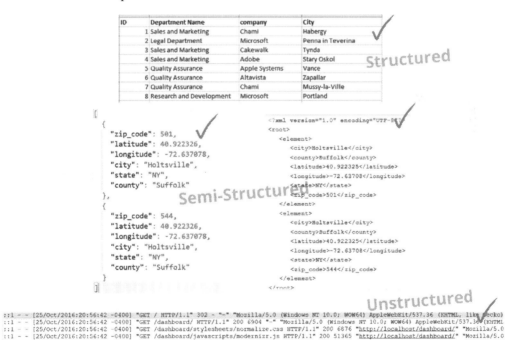

Figure 2.2 – Support for varying formats in a data lake

> **Important note**
> Data lakes do not differentiate data based on its structure, format, or size.

The **flexibility** of a data lake to store and process varying data formats makes it a one-stop shop for data analytics operations capable of dealing with a variety of data sources in one place. Without a data lake in place, you would need to deal with silos of data, resulting in dispersed analytics without a unified view of data.

Storing data in zones

A data lake is a repository of data that stores data in various zones. Although there are no limits or rules for how many zones are ideally required, three zones are generally considered the best practice: **raw**, **curated**, and **transformed**, as illustrated in the following diagram:

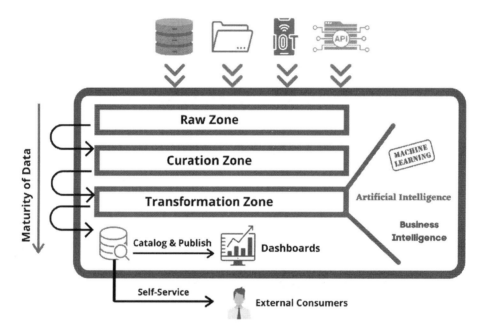

Figure 2.3 – Data lake zones and maturity of data

As data moves through each zone, it increases in maturity, becomes a lot cleaner, and finally achieves its true purpose for which it was originally collected: **data analytics**.

Once data gets ingested from a variety of sources such as databases, files, **application programming interfaces** (**APIs**), and IoT in the raw zone, it passes through a wrangling (cleaning) process to validate, standardize, and harmonize it—in short, bring all data to a common level in terms of format and organizational standards. After cleansing, data is saved to the curation zone.

The next phase of processing is done in a **self-service model**. Various sub-groups within the analytics group—such as data analysts, data scientists, **machine learning** (**ML**) engineers, and **artificial intelligence** (**AI**) engineers—start transforming data as per requirements.

> **Important note**
>
> Each sub-group has different requirements and views data a little differently from the others, but a data lake gives everyone the opportunity to use a unified set of data (in the curation zone) but reach different conclusions.

A typical set of transform operations include a combination of joining datasets, data aggregation, and data modeling. Finally, the results of the transformations are stored in the transformation zone. Now, data is ready to make the final leg of its journey.

Once data is in the transformation zone, it needs to be properly cataloged and published. Very frequently, data gets published in a **data warehouse** where it can be queried by **business intelligence** (**BI**) engineers for creating visualizations—dashboarding, charting, and reporting. The data has now met its final purpose.

Accommodating varying data characteristics

Data lakes can support varying characteristics of data, outlined as follows:

- **Volume**—In the early days of big data, everyone was focused on dealing with the growing size of data. Due to the immense growth of data, resource limits of databases and processing platforms were being tested to the limits. It was at this time that **Hadoop** originated as a distributed storage (**Hadoop Distributed File System**, or **HDFS**) and distributed processing (**MapReduce**) platform capable of dealing with large amounts of data at scale.

- **Variety**—Once organizations started to use Hadoop, the need to store and process large data volumes started to slowly diminish. This was the phase when dealing with large varieties of data—structured, semi-structured, and unstructured—became the top priority. The Hadoop framework was quickly able to deal with this because of its ability to store any format of data in HDFS, and MapReduce was able to read/write data using a variety of **serializers/deserializers (SerDes)**.

- **Velocity**—The rise of modern data sources such as IoT, logs, and social networking has created the challenge of dealing with incoming data at high speeds. During this phase, the Hadoop framework started to fall short due to its inability to deal with streaming data effectively, and other frameworks such as Spark, Kafka, and Flink started to take its place. We still seem to be in this phase, where a lot of work is going into the adoption of frameworks that are capable of accommodating batch and streaming workloads.

- **Veracity**—As we continue to ingest, store, and process big data, a lot of organizations are getting concerned about the quality of data, asking: *Is my data precise, out-of-date, or biased?* While the other characteristics of data highlighted here are well defined, this one is a little more complex to handle. Organizations are looking for innovative methods to fix data quality, both at technical and operational levels.

> **Important note**
>
> While a *data lake* is a globally accepted term/concept, it may be implemented using a range of tools, services, and frameworks. It can be created using on-premises hardware, but the true power is realized when a data lake is created in the cloud.

Adhering to compliance frameworks

It is becoming a standard practice to incorporate security in every layer of a data lake. It is safe to assume these days that a typical organization is likely to fall under at least one compliance framework or another, such as the **General Data Protection Regulation (GDPR)**, **Health Insurance Portability and Accountability Act (HIPAA)**, **Payment Card Industry (PCI)**, or the **Sarbanes-Oxley Act (SOX)**.

The three pillars of data security are depicted in the following screenshot:

Figure 2.4 – The three pillars of data security

During a brief period of my career, I was heavily focused on data security audits. I still remember something that one of the customers jokingly said over 15 years ago, as his words have resonated several times since. He held a sales report in his hand and said:

"There will come a time when people will care less about the correctness of data but will care more that it was processed securely."

Quite honestly, the sentence did not make too much sense to me at the time, but today, I can fully relate to it.

> **Important note**
> For any organization that deals with data, security is no longer a luxury—it is a core requirement.

As per the **CIA** triad, the key pillars of security are **integrity**, **confidentiality**, and **availability**. Following these principles, security in a data lake should be implemented in layers: the greater number of layers, the more protection. Data lakes can comply with the core requirements of most compliance frameworks using the following techniques to cover the key pillars of the CIA triad:

- **Perimeter security**—Access to data lake resources can be limited using a combination of site-to-site **virtual private networks** (**VPNs**), filtering **Internet Protocol** (**IP**) addresses, and blocking access to the internet.

- **Access control**—User access in a data lake can be controlled by a combination of **role-based access control** (**RBAC**), policies, **access control lists** (**ACLs**), **multi-factor authentication** (**MFA**), and **single-sign-on** (**SSO**).

- **Encryption**—A key method of protecting **data-in-motion** (traveling from one point to another) and **data-at-rest** (in storage) is using encryption. Encryption can be implemented not only at the file level in the storage, but also any **personally identifiable information** (**PII**) data within a file can be encrypted.

- **Authorization**—Extreme caution is desired during data distribution. The task becomes even more complex if data distribution includes external users. A data lake can comply with authorization needs by implementing a role-based access mechanism (RBAC) using a combination of table-, row-, and column-based security and data masking.

> **Important note**
> The CIA triad is simply a guideline for an organization's security program. The strength of security is directly proportional to the number of layers implemented within it.

Next, we'll see how storage and compute can be segregated within a data lake.

Segregating storage and compute in a data lake

We saved the best for last. The ability of a data lake to segregate (decouple) the storage and compute layers is perhaps one of its most desirable features. But why is decoupling storage and computation such a big deal? To understand why, we should first understand the storage and compute layers.

Storage

The fundamental function of storage is to store data. Briefly, this is how storage has evolved over the last few years:

- **Direct-attached storage** (**DAS**)—As the name suggests, a storage device (**hard disk drive/solid-state drive**, or **HDD/SSD**) is physically attached to the computer. This type of storage mostly exists in personal computers and laptops.

- **Network-attached storage** (**NAS**)—Centralized storage using multiple hard drives connected as an array. NAS allows quick and easy sharing of data between computers using regular ethernet.

- **Storage area network** (**SAN**)—High-performance shared storage using fiber-optic connectivity. A SAN allows for the fast sharing of data between computers.

- **Cloud storage**—Cloud storage is a relatively recent addition to this list. In this case, the storage physically exists on the cloud-provider servers. Cloud storage allows users the flexibility to access it from anywhere, as well as an assurance that data is highly available and safe because multiple copies are maintained on the backend.

> **Important note**
>
> Azure Blob storage, Amazon **Simple Storage Service** (**S3**), and Google Cloud Storage are some of the best-known cloud storage solutions.

Block storage

All storage types in the preceding list (except cloud storage) are categorized as file and block storage. This means data is stored on the storage device in small-sized blocks, usually 512 bytes in size. A group of contiguous blocks is deemed a file, and that is how humans relate to data.

Object storage

Cloud storage is categorized as object storage. Object storage does not work like a traditional filesystem. Unlike block storage, every object contains the following:

- **Identifier (id)**—A **globally unique identifier** (**GUID**) for each object in storage

- **Data**—Stored as blobs all in one location (not broken into multiple blocks)

- **Metadata**—Data about the data, such as author, permissions, and timestamps

The differences between block and object storage are better illustrated as follows:

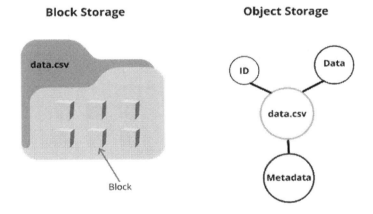

Figure 2.5 – Block storage versus object storage

Object storage is quickly becoming the standard for data engineering and analytics operations due to certain key advantages, listed here:

- Object storage is highly scalable, which means the storage can grow as per the growing data demands within an organization.

- You save money because there is no requirement to book storage capacity in advance.

- The feature of embedding metadata within the object facilitates data classification and analytics workloads.

- Data can easily be accessed via **HyperText Transfer Protocol** (**HTTP**) or APIs.

- Very suitable for storing large files such as video, audio, images, and backups of data.

- Suitable for write-once, read-many-times scenarios such as data analytics.

However, there are a few drawbacks as well, as outlined here:

- Performance of object storage is slower compared to block storage, particularly writing.

- Data cannot be **appended** to objects; any change to data simply amounts to deleting the existing object and recreating it.

- Suitable for workloads that require relatively static data.

Important note

Since each change to an object amounts to deleting it and creating a new version, object storage is unsuitable for **online transaction processing** (**OLTP**) operations where data changes are very frequent. However, it is very suitable for **online analytical processing** (**OLAP**) operations because data changes infrequently.

Compute

In the context of a data lake, compute is the ability to process (read and write) data for analytical operations such as wrangling, joining, and aggregating. In analytical computations, two resources are very critical for smooth operations, outlined as follows:

- **Central processing unit** (**CPU**)—On any given computer, all calculations are performed in the CPU. The speed of the CPU is measured in clock speed—2.8 **gigahertz** (**GHz**), for example. This means that this CPU can perform 2.8 billion computations per second. The greater the CPU speed, the more the computational power. In the world of virtualization, this term is referred to as a **virtual CPU** (**vCPU**).

- **Random-access memory** (**RAM**)—RAM stores active data that is required for any currently ongoing computations. This is done to prevent repeated read and write operations from hard drives, which are typically a lot slower (a ratio of 1:50) to respond compared to RAM. Therefore, it is generally preferred to possess as much RAM as possible.

Containers

In analytical processing terms, resources are allocated to jobs in container units. The idea of a container was introduced in **Yet Another Resource Negotiator** (**YARN**), the distributed processing framework in Hadoop.

In simple terms, a container is a logical grouping of the two key physical resources—a vCPU and RAM. Since YARN works in a cluster, it maintains the total tally of RAM and the vCPU across the cluster.

At processing time, YARN allocates containers based on the requirements of the job(s). If a cluster has enough resources to meet the demand of the job, it starts it immediately, else it puts it in wait mode until the resources free up. The different-sized containers are depicted in the following screenshot:

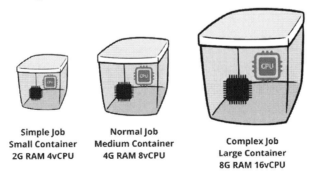

Figure 2.6 – Varying container sizes

The modern era's distributed frameworks are extremely resource-hungry. Apache Spark and Apache Flink perform computations in memory, so at times, you need a lot of it. In the big data world, understanding the internals of how job resources are allocated and managed in a cluster goes a long way in improving the completion times and performance of jobs.

> **Important note**
> The balancing act of allocating the optimal required resources to your jobs is a core skill that every data engineer should carry.

You might be wondering, *Why should I be bothered by all this? The cloud allows us to use practically endless amounts of resources anyway...* However, I assure you that I do have a point here, and a huge one...just wait for it.

Storage is cheap; compute is expensive

Here it is: *Storage is cheap, yet compute is expensive*. Now, what is that supposed to mean?

A few pages ago, I started this section by stating that the ability of a data lake to segregate (**decouple**) the storage and compute layers is perhaps one of the most desirable features—particularly if an organization's infrastructure is in the cloud.

I am going to support this theory by doing a very high-level estimate on **Microsoft Azure**. Please note that the estimate that I am going to present here is just an example to highlight the preceding point.

The assumptions are as follows:

- **Storage**—10 **terabytes** (**TB**)/month of hot tier Data Lake Storage Gen2 in the East-US region

- **Compute**—Azure Synapse Analytics for 500 **data warehouse units** (**DWU**)/month in the East-US region

We'll use the Microsoft Azure calculator available at `https://azure.microsoft.com/en-ca/pricing/calculator/` to make this estimate, shown in the following screenshot:

Real-Time Analytics

⌄ Azure Synapse Analytics ⓘ	Tier: Compute Optimized Gen2, Dedicated SQL Pool... 🗑	Upfront: US$0.00		Monthly: US$5,592.05
⌄ Storage Accounts ⓘ	Data Lake Storage Gen2, Standard, GRS Redundancy... 🗑	Upfront: US$0.00		Monthly: US$571.07

Figure 2.7 – Comparison of storage and compute costs

I hope that proves the point that I have been trying to make—**compute is almost 10 times more expensive than storage**.

Now, let me ask you a question. Put yourself in the shoes of the data engineer. Which layer would you try to optimize the most to keep the costs in check? If your answer is *compute*, then I have managed to get my point across.

> **Important note**
>
> As a data engineer, while choosing storage and compute resources, it is very important to keep cost optimization in mind. It is a rare skill to have but is something that your customers will thank you for the most.

In the pre-cloud era, big data platforms such as Hadoop were mostly installed on physical machines/**virtual machines (VMs)**. In this case, the storage layer was tightly coupled with the compute layer, as illustrated in the following diagram:

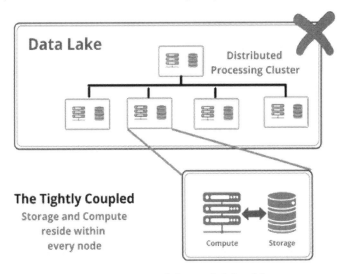

Figure 2.8 – A tightly coupled data lake

There are a few drawbacks with this setup, outlined as follows:

- The required capacity for compute and storage needs to be **pre-purchased**. The purchased capacity is typically based on the requirements for the most complex job. Assuming the most complex job only runs for a fraction of time during the day, the unused capacity is underutilized for the rest of the day.

- You need the cluster to stay up 24/7 (whether you are actively using it or not). Costs to keep the cluster operational, such as air conditioning, real estate, electricity, and administrative costs, all add up.

In short, you are paying for something that you are not using… and no one likes to do that.

In many respects, moving toward cloud computing has been a game-changer. Having a data lake in the cloud allows us to achieve something that was not possible before: we can finally decouple storage and compute!

The following diagram shows a loosely coupled data lake:

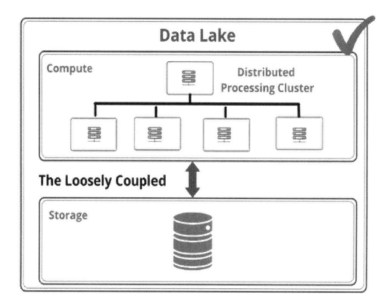

Figure 2.9 – A loosely coupled data lake

Decoupling storage from compute offers several advantages, outlined as follows:

With a **loosely coupled** data lake, the cheap (storage) layer is **permanent**, whereas the expensive (compute) layer is **temporary**. How does it work this way?

Typically, during batch processing, computations are performed only for a brief period each day (usually just a few hours). Having your infrastructure on the cloud allows you to create a distributed processing cluster (Hadoop/Spark/Flink) every day, just before batch processing starts; all the jobs are then run and, finally, the cluster is deleted right after all the jobs finish. Since the storage portion exists outside the compute cluster, there is no data loss if the cluster is destroyed. This process is depicted in the following diagram:

Figure 2.10 – Preserving compute costs

By doing this, you make sure that the compute costs are fully optimized… you **only pay for what you use**.

In *Chapter 1*, *The Story of Data Engineering and Analytics*, we discussed the journey of data and the reasons why a data engineering practice is becoming a core necessity for organizations that are serious about data analytics. The question is, how should they start this journey? In the next section, we will deep dive into the planning stages of creating a data lake, starting with understanding some well-known data lake architectures.

Discovering data lake architectures

Before we start the journey of data lake creation, it is important to understand how we undertake a normal journey in real life. Before taking a journey—a vacation, for instance —we often start by doing some preparations, such as these:

- **Plan**—Shortlist destinations that we want to visit during our trip.
- **Reserve**—Book the best airlines and hotels that fall within our **budget**.
- **Visit**—Hopefully, our preparations will make the trip both **comfortable** and **secure**.

Preparing for the journey of data lake creation is no different, as we can note here:

- **Plan**—Choose the correct data lake architecture that meets the objectives of the organization's analytical needs (**destination**).
- **Reserve**—Procure resources (computer and human) required to create a data lake within the financial restrictions (**budget**).

- **Create**—Create the necessary infrastructure and data pipelines based on a chosen architecture that helps decision makers (**comfort**) and distributes as per individual clearances (**security**).

I hope it is evident from this comparison that without the correct choice of data lake architecture, all subsequent steps will not meet the objectives of the organization.

A properly designed architecture should be capable of meeting the diverse needs of data storage and data processing, including aggregating, joining, and querying—not only in a batch mode but, more importantly, in a streaming mode as well.

> **Important note**
>
> In batch processing, analysis is performed using data that has been collected and stored over a large period (typically a few hours), whereas in stream processing, analysis is performed using data as soon as it is collected. After processing, this data may or may not be permanently stored.

In this section, we will focus on four well-known data lake architectures that are very commonly used in the data lake world, listed as follows:

- Traditional architecture

- Lambda architecture

- Kappa architecture

- Lakehouse architecture

Before we understand the various architecture types, we should know about a famous theorem applicable to distributed computing platforms.

The CAP theorem

In the era prior to distributed computing reaching maturity, the **scalability** of a system was increased by adding more hardware resources. This is likely done by adding more memory, disk, and CPU (or a combination of) to the pre-existing nodes. This type of scaling is commonly referred to as **vertical scalability**, as shown in *Figure 2.11*. But there are a couple of huge drawbacks with this type of scaling, as detailed here:

- Adding new hardware is limited to the maximum expandable in the node—for example, there are only a limited number of slots available on the motherboard for expanding memory.

- An existing node will eventually reach its expiration period and may need to be replaced entirely. Therefore, the cost of adding new hardware may not be justified.

In the modern era of computing, commonly referred to as **distributed computing**, the scalability of the system is achieved laterally, as shown in *Figure 2.12*. This type of scaling is commonly referred to as **horizontal scalability**. It works on the principle of *just keep adding nodes*.

Vertical scalability can be depicted as follows:

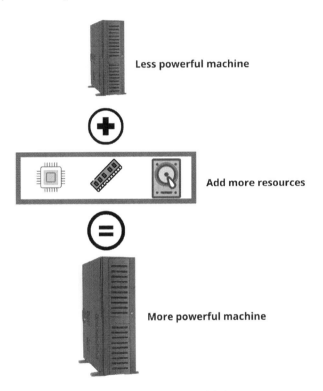

Figure 2.11 – Vertical scalability

Important note

Horizontal scaling is not achieved by adding hardware to existing nodes but by adding new nodes whenever more power is required.

Horizontal scalability can be depicted as follows:

Less powerful cluster   More powerful cluster

Figure 2.12 – Horizontal scalability

The CAP theorem is based on three key characteristics of a distributed computing system, outlined as follows:

- **Consistency**—All nodes should contain the same data. This means that a write request should successfully propagate data to all other replicated nodes before it becomes available for read requests. In other words, a read request should receive the same data irrespective of which node served it.

- **Availability**—Users should be able to access the system even if a node goes down. This means they should always receive a **success** response to their read/write requests. However, this does not mean that the data that has been read is indeed the most recent.

- **Partition tolerance**—The system should be able to tolerate network delays and interruptions. This means that the data replication arrangement in the distributed system should be done taking network failures in mind. In Hadoop, this concept is implemented using rack awareness.

As per the CAP theorem, it is impossible for a distributed computing system to simultaneously provide all three guarantees at the same time. It can provide a maximum of two—you need to sacrifice the third. The concept is illustrated in the following diagram:

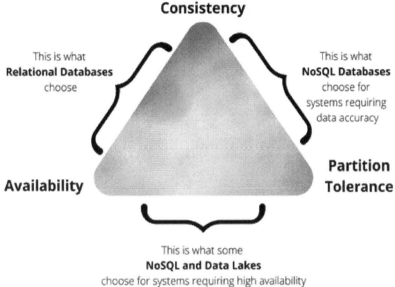

Figure 2.13 – The CAP theorem

The CAP theorem is important to understand in the data lake world because it makes you aware of trade-offs that you may need to make in your case scenarios.

The trade-offs

As per *Figure 2.13*, for data lake operations we usually opt for **AP** (**availability** and **partition** tolerance) and sacrifice consistency. This choice covers most data analytics scenarios where data accuracy can be sacrificed for the greater good. If the data is aggregated over a large period, a few inconsistent/incorrect values are not going to affect the correctness to a greater degree.

However, consider a case in IoT analytics where we are trying to monitor the temperature of a room using sensors in the possibility of a fire event. In this case, a missing or incorrect reading from a sensor could be catastrophic. Therefore, it may be advisable to choose **CP** (**consistency** and **partition** tolerance) for this situation. This is the reason why using a NoSQL database is a better choice for mission-critical streaming analytics.

Traditional architecture

Several years ago, Hadoop was the most popular engine for distributed data storage and processing systems—it was the phase of **batch processing**. Using Hadoop, a typical batch workflow functioned like this:

- **Orchestration**—Using preconfigured tools such as **Oozie** to invoke workflows (pipelines) that perform the following set of operations.

- **Batch collection**—Collecting and ingesting data every few hours. Initially, a window of 24 hours was the norm, but due to growing demands for real-time data, the windows started to get smaller. Data collection was performed using a variety of Hadoop ecosystem tools such as **Sqoop** and **Flume**. The incoming data was stored in HDFS for further processing. Every time new data was collected, it was appended to the previous dataset, usually by creating a timestamp partition.

- **Batch processing**—Once the data had been saved to HDFS, processing was performed using the **MapReduce** engine (distributed processing framework). This was done using a variety of methods such as writing programs in languages such as **Java**, **Python**, or **Perl**, or by using frameworks such as **Pig** and **Hive**.

I must admit that in those times, my customers were simply thrilled by the fact that I managed to ingest and process their data from various sources in Hadoop, even though it came with **high latency**.

The following diagram represents the state of **SALES** data 24 hours apart:

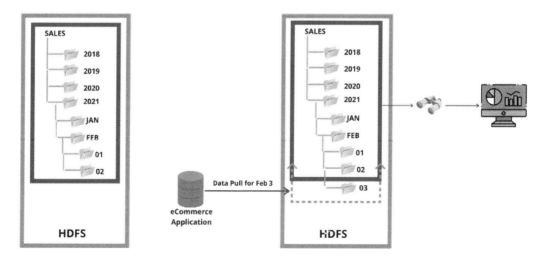

Figure 2.14 – State of data 24 hours apart

Sales report created on February 2—Includes all data from start (2018) until February 2, 2021.

Sales report created on February 3—Includes all data from start (2018) until February 3, 2021.

Now, here is the problem with traditional architecture:

If the sales report is produced somewhere between the usual scheduled report generation times on February 2 and February 3, the report will be missing sales that are happening on February 3. In other words, no matter what a report generated during an interim period, this will always only be partially inaccurate. To address this problem, we started to bring the batch window down to 12/8/4 hours, but no matter what, there would always be a fraction of data missing in the report.

As times changed, customers started to request data analytics over near-real-time data, paving the way for a better architecture that could address their growing demands.

> **Important note**
> The inability of MapReduce to process data in real time paved the way for other distributed frameworks such as Spark and Flink to come into existence.

Lambda architecture

Lambda architecture came into existence to address the need for hybrid processing that can account for both batch and streaming data at the same time. Lambda architecture was introduced by **Nathan Marz**, who created the famous real-time processing engine named **Apache Storm**. Lambda architecture is comprised of three layers, detailed next.

Batch layer

The batch layer stores the master dataset. The master dataset includes all historical data collected since the collection process started. In the example that we covered previously, the dataset in the screenshot represents the **SALES** master dataset.

These are some of the characteristics of the master dataset:

- It is immutable. Immutability of data means that existing data cannot be changed, and new data can only be appended.
- It can be used by the serving layer to publish data.
- It can incrementally merge changed data on a regular basis.

You can see the file structure of the master dataset here:

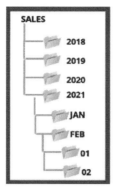

Figure 2.15 – Master dataset

Let's now have a brief introduction to the term **change data capture**, or **CDC** in short. Successfully capturing and processing changing data over time makes it one of the top three challenges that I have faced in my career. We will dedicate a whole section to CDC in a future chapter, titled *Solving Data Engineering Challenges*.

A few well-known tools of the trade for creating the batch layer are **Apache Hadoop**, **Apache Flink**, and **Apache Spark**.

Serving layer

The serving layer makes the master data available to the query process using batch views. The batch views are often the results of precomputed aggregations. Due to the data being largely precomputed, these views provide low latency access to the users.

The following screenshot shows a batch view that aggregates **SALES** by quarters. In this view, the aggregations of quarters in 2018 till 2020 will be accurate, because the data is not changing for those partitions anymore. However, data for **2021 > Q1** is still evolving and changing by the second due to currently ongoing sales:

Figure 2.16 – Aggregated batch view

Here is how we can achieve an accurate result for 2021-Q1:

2021-Q1 from batch view + Aggregate (February 3 SALES)

The latter summation of data is missing, and this is where the speed layer will help us.

The tools of the trade for the serving layer are **Apache Hive** and **Presto**.

Speed layer

The speed layer stores the most recent dataset (**incremental**) that has not yet been merged to batch views due to the latency of the merge process. This data is made available to the query process as **real-time views**, often created using stream processing. You can see a depiction of a real-time view here:

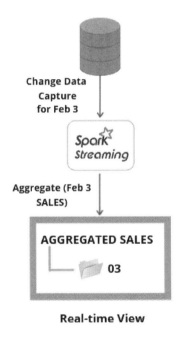

Figure 2.17 – Aggregated real-time view

In traditional architecture, this is exactly the layer that could not be handled by Hadoop MapReduce, and therefore advancement to newer frameworks was required.

The tools of the trade for the speed layer are **Apache Spark Streaming**, **Apache Storm**, and **Apache Flink**.

This is how everything comes together in Lambda architecture:

- Incremental data from the source is concurrently pushed to the batch and speed layers.

- The batch layer keeps accumulating the data over a certain period and refreshes the batch view after the period expires.

You can see the various layers of a Lambda architecture here:

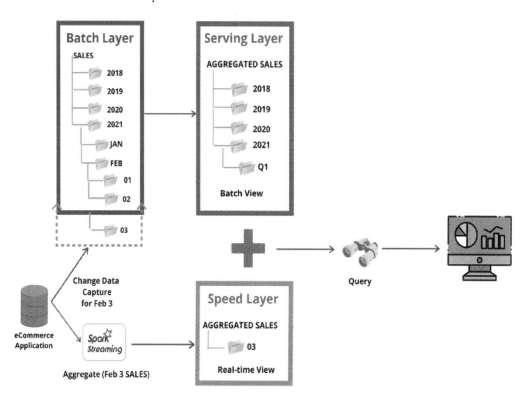

Figure 2.18 – Various layers of a Lambda architecture

- Incremental data is pushed to the speed layer where it is aggregated in a streaming fashion as a real-time view.

- At query time, the results from the batch view are consolidated with the results from the real-time view to get the most recent and accurate figures.

Lambda architecture has several benefits, including low latency due to precomputed views, and data accuracy due to near-real-time access to data.

Here are some case scenarios where you might use a Lambda architecture with great success:

- **Access to near-real-time data**—There are scenarios in which the decision-making process is detrimentally impacted if access to the latest data is not available.

- **Large historical datasets**—There are situations in which the historical data is extremely large, so aggregations can take a long time to finish and cannot be performed frequently.

- **Dynamic nature of analytics (ad hoc)**—There are cases in which the case scenarios for data analytics are very dynamic and vary quite frequently. In this case, the batch and real-time views can be created or adjusted without affecting the underlying master data.

> **Important note**
>
> A particular strength of the Lambda architecture is its strength to be easily migrated from traditional architecture. I have done several of these migrations in the past with great success.

Lambda architecture provides a nice balance of performance and data freshness. But in recent times, requirements for streaming analytics have grown quite sharply. Use cases such as IoT monitoring and anomaly detection require a fast real-time analytics engine able to support millions of incoming requests per second.

Despite all the advantages that Lambda architecture has, there are a few drawbacks, as outlined here:

- In a few cases, it is sometimes complex to implement due to the multiple layers. More layers also translate to more costs, in resources, administration, and monitoring.

- Each layer requires a different set of tools, services, and programming. Therefore, infrastructure and code management become a challenge.

- In some scenarios, implementing a Lambda architecture may be overkill due to the nature of the analytics.

Quite recently, a simpler architecture was introduced, the Kappa architecture, which many call the simplified version of the Lambda architecture.

Kappa architecture

The Kappa architecture was introduced in 2014 by **Jay Kreps**. This architecture eliminates the need for the batch layer altogether. Instead, all data is stored in a real-time layer that maintains an immutable stream of events stored in a stream-processing platform.

The major components of the Kappa architecture are described in the following subsections.

Streaming layer

The **streaming layer** stores all raw data in the form of sequential events (messages) sorted by the creation timestamp. Since data is not stored on a regular filesystem, the chosen streaming platform should include built-in features such as **fault tolerance (FT)** and **high availability (HA)**.

The tools of the trade for the streaming layer storage are **Apache Kafka**, **Azure Event Hubs**, **Amazon Kinesis**, and **Google Pub/Sub**.

The stream-processing engine reads event data, performs required computations, and publishes the transformed data as views in the serving layer.

The tools of the trade for streaming-layer processing are **Apache Spark Streaming**, **Apache Flink**, and **Kafka Streams**.

Serving layer

The serving layer makes event data available to the query process using precomputed views. These views can be recomputed at regular intervals by relaunching the view build code.

The tools of the trade for the serving layer are **relational databases** and **data warehouses**, **cloud data warehouses**, and **cloud data storage**.

Here is how the Kappa architecture functions:

The stream-processing engine performs aggregations and publishes the results to the serving layer as precomputed views. As per *Figure 2.19*, at time **t**, the stream-processing code computes data from 2018 until the latest event in the sales topic.

The computed data is published as the **AGGREGATED SALES** view, which is then queried for analysis.

You can see a diagram of the process here:

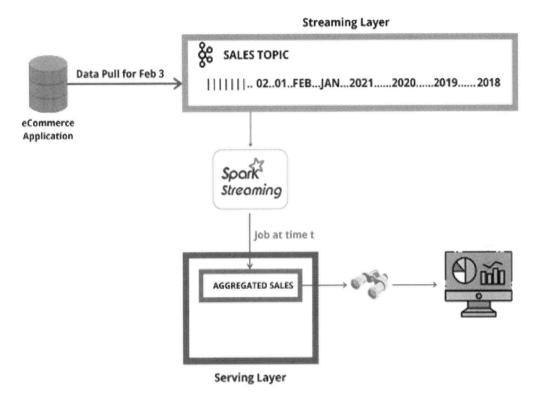

Figure 2.19 – State of aggregate view at time t

At time **t + 1**, the stream-processing code recomputes data from 2018 up to the most recent event within the sales topic. Notice that new events have been added to the queue since the last time the computations were performed. The recomputed data is published as follows:

- The previous version of the **AGGREGATED SALES** view is dropped.

- A new version of the **AGGREGATED SALES** view is computed to take its place.

- Queries are pointed to the recomputed view.

You can see a diagram of the process here:

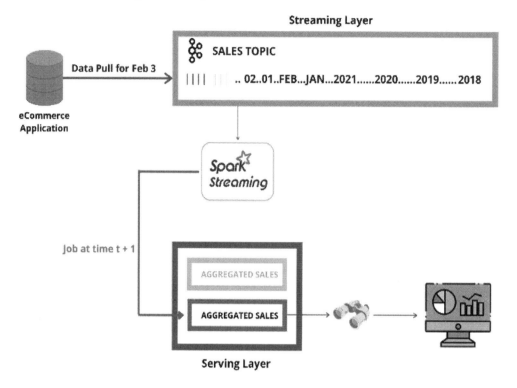

Figure 2.20 – State of aggregate view at time t+1

Now we know how the Kappa architecture generally functions, let's outline some of the pros and cons of it, as follows:

- The Kappa architecture works extremely well for use cases around IoT monitoring and real-time analytics with limited dependency on historical data.

- Unlike Lambda architecture, a single code base is sufficient for data processing. This hugely simplifies infrastructure deployment and management requirements.

- Since Kappa stores all data in the streaming layer for larger datasets, typically in the TB range, the architecture becomes extremely expensive.

Let's compare the costs at a very high level, as follows:

- Storing 32 TB of data on Microsoft Azure Premium SSD Managed Disks will cost you roughly **US dollars** (**USD**) $4,194/month.

- Storing 32 TB of data on Microsoft Azure Blob storage will cost you just $682/month.

Many experts feel the Kappa architecture is a substitute for the Lambda architecture, although I see things a bit differently. To me, each one of these architectures solves a different purpose. Here are some case scenarios where I have used the Kappa architecture with great success:

- **Real-time monitoring**—Monitoring of IoT sensors is a perfect use case for the Kappa architecture. In almost all monitoring cases, having access to historical data is not required.

- **Live dashboarding**—I am sure you have seen dashboards that visualize data in a live fashion. The visual is refreshed every few seconds based on incoming data.

- **Real-time ML**—Many companies are now exposing their ML models as microservices for use cases such as fraud detection.

- **Real-time data monetization**—We previously discussed data monetization as a means for revenue diversification. More and more companies are now exposing their data to external companies for consumption in real time.

> **Important note**
> Before choosing a suitable architecture, data engineers should carefully evaluate the strength of each one based on customer requirements, the urgency of near-real-time analysis, and resource costs.

Both Lambda and Kappa architectures are layered—data is collected in the storage/ streaming layer, processed, and finally published to a warehouse. I have done several projects in the past using these architectures but, truthfully, implementing either one of them comes with a few challenges, such as the following:

- Keeping data fresh and up to date in each tier is difficult. Ever-changing data requires a carefully designed merge process.

- Infrastructure costs in both architectures can be steep at times.

- More layers mean more chances of failure. Dealing with a failure is not only costly but also untimely because it delays the ongoing data analytics.

- If the data is being published externally for data monetization purposes, any failures or inaccuracies can cause revenue loss and customer dissatisfaction.

Some of the previously mentioned deficiencies of the Lambda and Kappa architectures have forced the experts to find a new way of thinking.

Generally, in any data lake operation, we ingest data to storage, process it as per requirements, and finally publish the aggregated data to a warehouse so that it is available for analytics.

Lately, a new architecture is being adopted at a fast rate that combines the power of a data lake and a data warehouse in one, as illustrated in the following diagram:

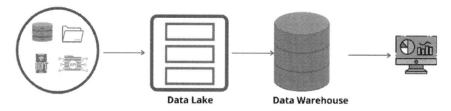

Data Lake and Data Warehouse are Decoupled

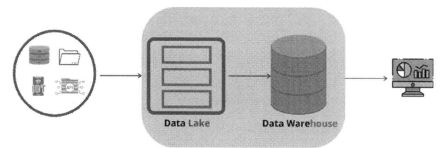

Data Lake and Data Warehouse are Merged

Figure 2.21 – Rise of the Lakehouse architecture

In this section, we learned about the Kappa and Lambda architecture, and the rise of the Lakehouse architecture.

Lakehouse architecture

Before we discuss the **Lakehouse** architecture, it is important to understand what I refer to as the power struggle between traditional and modern data processing systems.

The give-and-take struggle

There was a card game that I used to play when I was younger. In this game, to advance to the next level, you were required to sacrifice your best card.

Through many years in the data processing world, I have seen the same give-and-take struggle between the traditional method of data processing (database/data warehouses) versus the modern one (data lakes).

You can see this power struggle depicted in the following diagram:

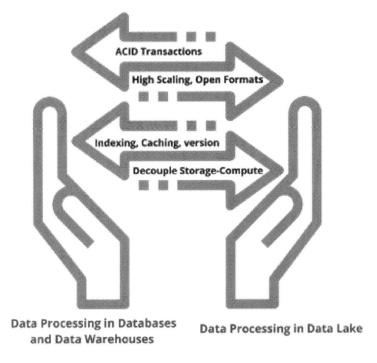

Figure 2.22 – The power struggle

The decision to move toward modern data processing platforms has forced us to make some sacrifices; you gain some and you lose some. Let me highlight some of these give-and-take situations in which you must move from traditional to modern methods, as follows:

- Sacrifice durability and consistency features such as **atomicity, consistency, isolation, and durability (ACID)** transactions but gain the ability to process on a highly scalable platform.

- Sacrifice performance features such as indexing and caching but gain the ability to process data in multiple formats.

- Sacrifice security features such as versioning and auditing but gain the ability to decouple storage and compute.

The Lakehouse architecture, as depicted in the following diagram, merges the low-cost storage of a data lake with the **massively parallel processing (MPP)** power of a warehouse to serve the diverse and ever-evolving requirements of modern-era analytics:

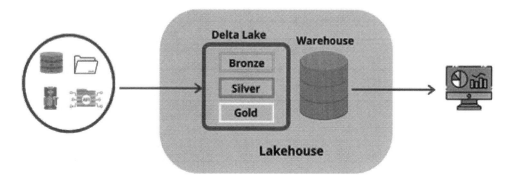

Figure 2.23 – Lakehouse architecture

Here are a few important features of the Lakehouse architecture:

- **Supports low-cost storage**—The Lakehouse architecture carries forward the support for using low-cost storage. Data can be structured, semi-structured, or unstructured over open formats such as Parquet.

- **Supports ACID transactions**—Now, this one is big. An absence of transaction support hugely impacts the data integrity and quality in a data lake. Over the years, dealing with duplicated and deleted data has been a huge challenge. In the early days, I remember going through a multi-step process in Hive to deal with this. A few years later, Spark took over, but the challenge stayed the same. But the struggle is finally over…. long live **Databricks Delta Lake**!

> **Important note**
>
> Since its introduction, Delta Lake has proved to be a lifesaver for data engineers, not only to resolve the CDC challenge but many other ones, such as schema evolution and time travel. The Lakehouse architecture assumes the use of an open source storage engine such as Delta Lake for ACID transactions, metadata management, governance, and many other features.

- **Metadata management**—The Lakehouse architecture offers strong metadata management features such as schema enforcement and evolution. Once again, the absence of such features in the past has forced us to perform similar checks using code.

- **Segregation of storage and compute**—The Lakehouse architecture preserves the idea of decoupling storage and compute for massive scalability and cost-saving.

- **Support for BI tools**—Lakehouse architecture supports connectivity to all major BI tools using standard **Java Database Connectivity (JDBC)/Open Database Connectivity (ODBC)** connectivity.

- **Native support for Structured Query Language (SQL)**—Users can easily utilize the power of the SQL language for performing analytics.

> **Important note**
>
> In Azure, the Lakehouse architecture is implemented using Synapse Analytics. In addition to using Synapse SQL for performing analysis, it provides support for Apache Spark.

- **Supports streaming workloads**—The Lakehouse architecture supports real-time analytics and reporting using streaming data.

The tools of the trade for the Lakehouse architecture include **Azure Synapse Analytics**, **Amazon Redshift Spectrum**, **Google BigQuery**, and **Snowflake**.

These sections should explain how a Lakehouse architecture provides a nice blend of traditional, Lambda, and Kappa architectures. The way I see it, the Lakehouse is the right recipe for creating a data lake—one that not only works but also provides the correct balance between **user experience** (**UX**), scalability, and cost.

Summary

In this chapter, we learned about a data lake and its various characteristics, such as multiple zones, the ability to deal with multiple formats, governance, and—most importantly—its ability to decouple storage and compute.

We also learned about four key data lake architectures: traditional, Lambda, Kappa, and Lakehouse. We analyzed each one from their applicability to certain case scenarios, costing, and overall management.

In the next chapter, I will highlight various tools and services available in Microsoft Azure required to build a data lake using the Lakehouse architecture.

3
Data Engineering on Microsoft Azure

In the previous chapter, we discussed how cloud adoption offers greater flexibility and faster deployments for data engineering and analytical workloads. In this chapter, we'll discuss the major tools and services in Microsoft Azure that may help us implement such a solution.

In this chapter, we will cover the following topics:

- Introduction to data engineering in Azure
- Performing data engineering in Azure
- How to open a free account with Azure

Introducing data engineering in Azure

In recent years, Microsoft Azure has added several powerful services to its arsenal that seamlessly collect, store, process, and publish data for both batch and streaming workloads. Gone are the days where choices for storage and compute were severely limited among cloud vendors. As a user, you simply needed to conform with the supplied tools and services: now, your options are more extensive.

Today, the cloud ecosystem looks very different from what it did previously. The growth of cloud services allows users to choose from a variety of storage, compute, and deployment options. As an example, if I want to run a Spark program, I can choose from at least four different options in **Microsoft Azure**. The real question is, if all four options are running **Apache Spark**, then why are these options even required?

> **Important Note**
> The array of options available on the cloud are not limited to compute only: the same variety exists for data collection, infrastructure deployments, and pipeline orchestration services.

Here are some of the reasons why several options for performing similar kinds of operations in data engineering are available on Microsoft Azure:

- **Ease of use**: The ease of use of a service is a key factor in deciding which option to use. As a data engineer, you may code the entire **ETL** program yourself or opt for a service that can auto-generate and invoke the code for you after creating a visual workflow.

- **Data engineering team skills**: The skill level of the data engineering team plays a very important role in deciding which option to choose. Teams with skilled data engineers typically tend to choose services where data workflows need to be coded from scratch. Doing so offers engineers complete control over their programs, as well as any other dependencies.

- **The desired level of administration and monitoring**: Having a skilled data engineering team does not automatically mean that the same team will be involved in administering and monitoring the operations. The choice of service may need to be adjusted, depending on who will be managing it in production.

- **Self-serve analytics**: These days, the concept of self-serve analytics is on the rise. This means that end users are getting more and more involved in creating ETL/ELT workflows. For this specific set of users, the ability to create a drag-and-drop workflow in a few clicks is extremely desirable.

> **Important Note**
> The idea of self-serve analytics is gaining a lot of popularity these days. Self-serve analytics enables fast-paced delivery of end user analytical goals.

- **Level of control that's desired over the infrastructure**: The level of control that's desired over the infrastructure is an important factor that impacts the choice of service. In some cases, the cloud-provided service may lack some desired functionality and does not permit changing the underlying infrastructure. In this case, the data engineers may want to choose a service that offers complete control of the infrastructure.

- **Complete data isolation**: Some stringent compliance frameworks do not permit the use of multi-tenant services. In such cases, complete data isolation is mandatory, thus impacting the choices that may be suitable.

> **Important Note**
>
> There is an ongoing debate around whether cloud services are truly compliant with well-known frameworks such as HIPAA. The multi-tenancy nature of cloud storage is a huge roadblock in making that claim. It is fair to say that cloud storages support compliance frameworks but are not truly compliant.

- **Prior familiarity with certain frameworks**: This is an extremely important factor for organizations migrating their analytics from on-premises to the cloud. Since they are already familiar with a certain tool or framework, they tend to choose the closest option available in the cloud.

- **Cost**: Finally, the cost of the service is a major factor that impacts what choice should be made. Typically, the easier the usage and management of a particular service, the higher its cost. Therefore, before choosing a service, careful cost analysis is deemed necessary.

> **Important Note**
>
> As a data engineer, it is understandable to have a bias toward specific tools, languages, and frameworks. But once you leave, it becomes the customer's responsibility to manage this. Try to keep your bias aside and provide the customer with a solution that uses technologies that the customer feels comfortable with.

Performing data engineering in Microsoft Azure

Data engineering in Microsoft Azure can be performed using the following three options:

- Self-managed data engineering services (**IaaS**)
- Azure-managed data engineering services (**PaaS**)
- Data engineering as a service (**SaaS**):

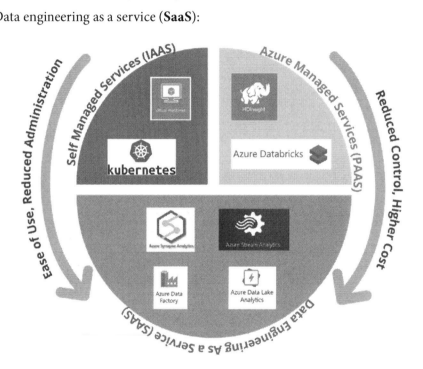

Figure 3.1 – Data engineering option in Microsoft Azure

Self-managed data engineering services (IaaS)

In the early phases of data engineering, using well-known distributed frameworks such as **Hadoop**, **Spark**, and **Kafka** rose sharply. As a result, many organizations were deploying Hadoop/Spark/Kafka using on-premises infrastructures. Since Hadoop/Spark/Kafka are multi-node frameworks, this meant the installations were performed using physical and virtual machines hosted on either the organization's owned or co-located data centers.

Then came the period when the cloud started to become a reality and organizations started to move their Hadoop/Spark/Kafka clusters to the cloud. In the very early stages of the cloud evolution, using a self-managed service was perhaps the only option available for data engineering.

IaaS use case

Here are a few use cases where using an IaaS layer is warranted:

- An organization that has heavily **customized** Hadoop/Spark/Kafka clusters. This means they are tied to specific versions that are unavailable on the cloud PaaS equivalent service.

- The organization has developed its own libraries for data engineering and data science that can't easily be deployed on PaaS or SaaS offerings on the cloud.

- An organization where security regulations do not permit the use of multi-tenant cloud services. This forces them to use single-tenant dedicated cloud resources.

- An organization that cannot tolerate variability in the compute power of the use of shared services.

Let's take a look at how a typical Hadoop/Spark/Kafka deployment is performed using self-managed services that use the **Infrastructure as a Service (IaaS)** layer on Microsoft Azure.

Azure Virtual Machines (Azure VMs) allows you to create on-demand compute resources for data processing. The following list describes some of the features available using Azure VMs:

- Take the inventory of the on-premises Hadoop/Spark/Kafka nodes – the total number of nodes, aggregated CPU, and aggregated memory.

- Shortlist virtual machines on Microsoft Azure that offer similar aggregated CPU and memory as the on-premises inventory. This step requires careful planning and calculations. It is not necessary to procure the same number of nodes on Microsoft Azure, so long as the aggregated CPU and memory meet or exceed the on-premises deployment. In distributed computing, horizontal scalability of nodes is preferable. It is highly recommended to compare different classes of virtual machines on Microsoft Azure; in many cases, you may be able to procure smaller class virtual machines that are cheaper than higher class ones, both offering the same aggregated CPU and memory.

- Procure virtual machines on Microsoft Azure.

- Configure networking among nodes, open required firewall ports, and install operating system prerequisites.

- Install and configure Hadoop/Spark/Kafka and any other ecosystem tools, such as Sqoop, Oozie, Hive, and so on. These steps need to be performed on multiple nodes.

- Install and configure administration and monitoring software.

Here are a few pros and cons of self-managed services:

- Performing deployments using virtual machines provides the data engineer with complete freedom to choose any framework and any version, and have complete control over its dependencies.

- It should be evident from the deployment process outlined previously that choosing self-managed services requires careful planning, design, and execution.

- Due to the vast variety of touchpoints, the data engineering team in charge of the deployment needs to be skilled in several areas, including cloud deployments, networking, administration, and monitoring. Note that all these skills are above and beyond the usual expectations of a data engineering team, which would normally involve things such as pipeline development and data orchestration.

- Scaling a cluster using a self-managed service can become a challenge.

As we mentioned previously, deploying a Hadoop/Spark/Kafka cluster using self-managed services is not optional. However, there are ways you can minimize the effects of the limitations we have just discussed.

Hadoop/Spark/Kafka distributions

The deployment process of Hadoop/Spark/Kafka clusters using VMs involves multiple nodes. A simpler way to deal with installing, upgrading, administrating, and monitoring these clusters is by using distributions such as **Cloudera**, **Hortonworks**, and **MapR**. Each of these distributions include software that enables cluster provisioning using a minimal setup. **Ambari** enables users to easily create, administer, and monitor a Hadoop cluster, whereas **Cloudera Manager** enables users to provision **Hadoop** and **Spark** clusters.

Infrastructure as Code

Infrastructure as Code (**IaC**) is a practice of deploying cloud resources such as VMs using configuration files. Using this practice, you may either create the entire infrastructure or make modifications to it. Using IaC significantly decreases manual effort for reoccurring tasks while maintaining a high level of consistency and accuracy. We will discuss this practice in greater detail in *Chapter 11, Infrastructure Provisioning*.

Azure Resource Manager (**ARM**) centralizes IaC deployments using resource templates.

Containerization

Containerization is the practice of abstracting application code from the underlying infrastructure. Using containerization provides several benefits, including segregating the host environment, choosing a software version, and dependency management. This means the cluster nodes can now run in their own isolated environment called containers. These containers can be orchestrated using the well-known orchestration engine known as **Kubernetes**. **Azure Kubernetes Service** (**AKS**) allows you to easily deploy and manage containerized applications.

> **Important Note**
> In the cloud era, a lot of organizations are adopting technologies that keep them cloud-agnostic. Who knows which vendor will drop their prices and when? Containerizing their applications keeps them open to moving between cloud vendors as desired.

Azure-managed data engineering services (PaaS)

Right after the big data wave started to gain momentum, cloud vendors such as Microsoft Azure started to create managed services to provide customers with fast deployments and easy management. Before we go into the specifics of the services, let's focus on what an Azure-managed service that uses the **platform as a service** (**PaaS**) layer on Azure means:

- The resource is deployed with minimal configuration and user input.
- Azure takes care of monitoring the resource for downtime and recovers it automatically in case a failure is detected.
- Globally available.
- Well integrated with other Azure services.
- Automatically provides data redundancy.
- Contains built-in security mechanisms for data protection.

PaaS use case

Here are a couple of use cases where using the PaaS layer is warranted:

- An organization has on-premises Hadoop/Spark/Kafka clusters and quickly wants to migrate to the cloud.

- An organization has limited cloud skills, so they want to use services with low operational requirements.

- An organization where security regulations permit the use of multi-tenant cloud services and can tolerate variability in compute power.

Here are a few of the Azure-managed PaaS services.

Data storage services in Microsoft Azure

During the big data wave, cloud vendors, including Microsoft Azure, started to launch storage solutions specifically targeted at storing vast volumes and varieties of data. To meet the high demand of storing large files at scale, object-level storage has become a unanimous choice among all cloud vendors. Let's take a look at the storage types in Microsoft Azure that are deemed suitable for data lakes.

Azure Blob storage

Azure Blob storage is an object storage solution that is highly optimized for storing large amounts of text and binary data. Azure Blob storage was built with a huge focus on scalability, high availability, and security. It stores data in three tiers: hot, cool, and archive. The hot tier is used for frequently accessed data, cool for infrequently accessed data, and archive for rarely accessed data. Depending on usage, you can choose between two performance tiers: standard and premium.

Data in Azure Blob storage is protected by several authentication mechanisms such as **Azure Active Directory**, shared keys, and **shared access signatures** (**SASes**). You can also protect your blobs using **role-based access control** (**RBAC**). You may turn versioning on for extra protection against accidental changes and deletes. This feature maintains the previous version of the blob in case you need to recover it.

Blobs in Azure Blob storage are automatically encrypted and redundant. Multiple copies of data are stored – three copies are stored within a single physical location by default, and several options exist for storing copies across zones and regions.

Azure Blob storage organizes data as follows:

- **Storage account**: The storage account holds your data. A unique namespace for your account is allocated in Azure. An example namespace address is `https://mydataanalytics.blob.core.windows.net`.

- **Containers**: A container organizes a group of blobs. A container should have a valid DNS name such as `https://mydataanalytics.blob.core.windows.net/mydatacontainer`.

- **Blobs**: Actual data that is stored in the containers:

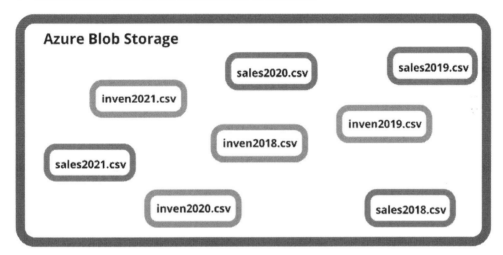

Figure 3.2 – Storing blobs in Azure Blob storage

Important Note

A particular drawback of object storage is its slow search performance.
In Azure Blob storage, you can speed up searches using index tags.

Azure Data Lake Storage Gen2

Azure Data Lake Storage offers a significant edge over Azure Blob storage when it comes to suitability for analytical workloads. But before we proceed with the reasons why, let me make one clarification: Azure Data Lake Storage is a layer built on top of Azure Blob storage.

Azure Data Lake Storage is compatible with Apache ecosystem tools such as Hadoop and Spark. It brings together all the great features offered by Azure Blob storage, plus more:

- **Hierarchical namespace**: Compared to Azure Blob storage, which has a flat namespace, Azure Data Lake Storage organizes blobs in a hierarchy of directories. This method of blob organization greatly enhances the performance of search operations.

- **Access control lists**: Azure Data Lake Storage supports the fine-grained security of blobs by using **POSIX**-style permissions.

- **Designed for analytics**: Azure Data Lake Storage provides excellent support for major open source platforms such as Hadoop and Spark. Using the Azure Blob filesystem driver, the open source platforms can easily access the object storage without the need for explicit code:

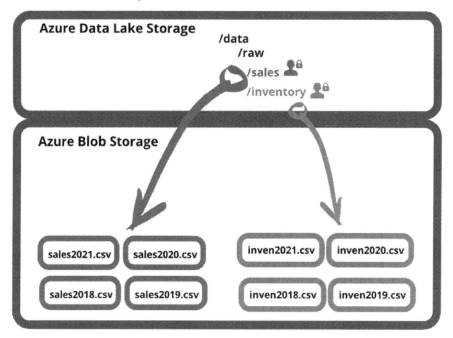

Figure 3.3 – Storing blobs in a hierarchy in Azure Data Lake Storage

- **Tight integration with Azure services**: Azure Data Lake Storage integrates seamlessly with Azure services such as Azure Data Factory, Azure HDInsight, and Azure Stream Analytics.

Azure Event Hubs

Azure Event Hubs is a data streaming platform used for ingesting event data. The source of the event data that's collected is usually application logs, clickstreams, and IoT. Azure Event Hubs can be deployed with minimal configuration.

You can use Azure Event Hubs for both batch and real-time processing. For batch processing, data from Event Hubs can be captured in Azure Blob storage or Azure Data Lake Storage so that it can be processed later. For real-time processing, you may have to send data to Azure Functions, which could take further action based on events:

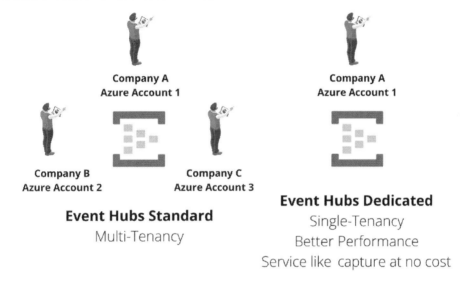

Figure 3.4 – Multi-tenancy and single-tenancy in Azure Event Hubs

Data in Azure Event Hubs is not stored permanently. By default, the queue is 1 day, but this can be increased to 7 days in the standard edition and 90 days in the dedicated edition.

Event data is stored in partitions – the higher the number of partitions, the higher the read and write throughput. The capacity of Azure Event Hubs is pre-purchased using throughput limits once the throughput limit equates to a write process (1 MB/1,000 events) or a read process (2 MB/4,096 events). The auto-inflate feature can be used to automatically scale your throughput units based on peak demands.

Azure Event Hubs replicates data within the primary data center with **automated failure detection** and recovery enabled. For extra protection, replication across availability zones can also be enabled.

Azure Cosmos DB

Azure Cosmos DB is a highly available and low latency NoSQL class database. Being a managed service, the usual administration challenges around installation, patching, and upgrades are taken care of by Azure. Cosmos DB stores data on SSD and the data is encrypted by default.

Azure Cosmos DB is globally distributed, making it extremely suitable for applications requiring high responsiveness. In a globally distributed deployment, **Azure Traffic Manager** can successfully route the application request to the closest Azure region, all without any changes needing to be made to the code. This way, the application can archive fast response times for both read and write operations:

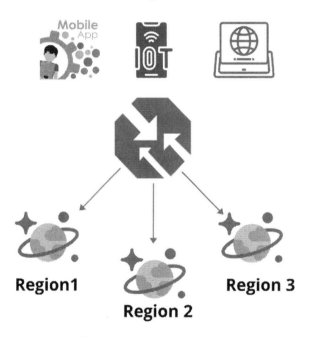

Figure 3.5 – Global distribution with Azure Cosmos DB

Due to its schema-less design, it is easy to store semi-structured and unstructured data at scale. Here is what the resource model of Azure Cosmos DB looks like:

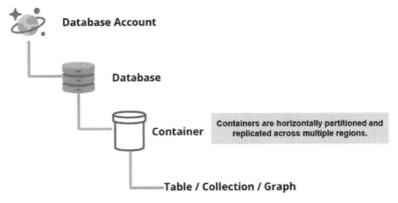

Figure 3.6 – Azure Cosmos DB resource model

Under an Azure Cosmos DB account, you can create databases, containers, and items. Multiple APIs are supported in Azure Cosmos DB and the API you choose impacts the item's type. Items store data in a container and have variable schemas based on the following mappings:

- **Table API and SQL API**: Table
- **Cassandra API**: Row
- **MongoDB API**: Document
- **Gremlin API**: Node

Partitioning is an important aspect of getting the best performance out of Azure Cosmos DB. Based on a partition key, data is stored in subsets called **logical partitions**. Storing data in partitions hugely improves performance since all the items in a logical partition have the same key value.

> **Important Note**
> Choosing the correct partition key is an extremely important skill for data engineers since it affects your application's performance in both negative and positive ways.

Data processing services in Microsoft Azure

Right after the big data wave started to gain momentum, cloud vendors started to package popular open source frameworks such as Hadoop, Spark, and Kafka and offer them as vendor-managed services. Let's look at a few Azure-managed data processing services.

Azure HDInsight

Azure HDInsight is a managed service for cloud distribution for Hadoop and its ecosystem. It embeds popular open source frameworks such as **Hadoop**, **Spark**, **Kafka**, **Hive**, and **Storm**. Azure HDInsight allows you to spin up clusters with ease and greater efficiency. Azure HDInsight embeds the popular **Hortonworks Data Platform (HDP)**. It has several benefits compared to self-managed Hadoop/Spark/Kafka clusters, as outlined in the following list:

- **Fully managed**: Azure HDInsight clusters are fully managed by Azure. This means the deployment cycle is seamless and highly accelerated. A new cluster can be spun up literally in a matter of minutes with minimal deployment steps.

- **Managed resources**: Azure HDInsight shields users from issues arising from underlying infrastructure problems. Underlying hardware and software components are monitored regularly and are self-healing.

- **Azure cloud-native security**: Azure HDInsight can leverage Azure cloud-native security services such as VNETs, transparent encryption, and **Azure Active Directory** integration for RBAC.

- **Azure cloud-native monitoring**: Azure HDInsight can leverage Azure cloud-native monitoring tools such as **Azure Monitor**.

- **Seamless integration with other Azure services**: Azure HDInsight can seamlessly integrate with Azure services such as **Azure Data Lake Storage Gen 2**, **Azure Data Factory**, **Azure CosmosDB**, and **Azure Synapse**.

- **Decouples storage and compute**: Azure HDInsight truly segregates storage and compute by providing options to store data that's external to the cluster on services such as **Azure Blob Storage** and **Azure Data Lake Storage Gen 2**.

- **Auto-scalability**: Azure HDInsight can auto-scale nodes up and down based on preset triggers that are based on scheduled or, more likely, performance metrics.

- **Azure marketplace extensibility**: Azure HDInsight can use several marketplace extensions that can further extend its power and functionality.

Azure Databricks

For those of you not familiar, **Databricks** is a company that was founded by the original creators of **Apache Spark**, **Delta Lake**, and **MLFlow**. Databricks Spark can only be run on a cluster that's been deployed on the cloud.

> **Important Note**
>
> **Databricks Community Edition** offers a free version that can be very useful if you are trying to learn Spark. Here is the link: `https://community.cloud.databricks.com`.

Azure Databricks is a data engineering and analytics platform for performing large-scale distributed computing on Microsoft Azure. Azure Databricks uses the Apache Spark framework for high-performance data processing. You may be wondering what is so special about the Azure Databricks version of Spark that makes it widely recognized as the leader in distributed computing. Here are a few reasons why:

- **Performance enhanced runtime**: Azure Databricks has added several performance enhancements over the open source version of Apache Spark. As per a few benchmarks, Databricks Spark performs up to eight times better than the open source version.

- **Collaborative environment**: Azure Databricks supports a collaborative environment between the data engineering, data analysis, and data science teams. Data engineers can easily share resources such as workspaces and jobs.

- **Interactive development**: Azure Databricks provides an **interactive development environment** (IDE) using notebooks. Data engineers can manage their Spark code (notebooks) using popular source control tools such as GitHub and Bitbucket.

- **Decouples storage and compute**: Azure Databricks decouples storage from compute by storing data on **Azure Blob Storage** and **Azure Data Lake Storage Gen2**.

- **Seamless integration with other Azure services**: Azure Databricks can seamlessly integrate with other Azure services, including **Azure Data Factory**, **Azure Event Hub**, and **Azure Synapse**.

- **Active Directory integration**: Azure Databricks integrates well with **Azure Active Directory**.

- **Auto-scalability**: Azure Databricks supports autoscaling by adding or removing worker nodes based on workloads.

- **Support for GPU instances**: Azure Databricks supports high-performance computing required for deep computing using **graphics processing units** (GPUs).

Azure Databricks offers a couple of environments for data engineering and analytics workloads.

Azure Databricks SQL Analytics

Azure Databricks SQL Analytics is a platform for performing data analytics using SQL. Azure Databricks uses **SQL endpoints** for computations. SQL endpoints vary by the size of the cluster chosen at the start of the installation. In addition to large-scale data processing, this service includes some other useful features such as alerts, which can trigger messages to tools such as **Slack** and **PagerDuty** based on the conditions that have been configured. Additionally, you can create visualizations such as bar and pie charts.

Azure Databricks workspace

An Azure Databricks workspace is an interactive environment for data engineers, data scientists, and machine learning engineers to collaboratively process batch and real-time data. An Azure Databricks workspace contains objects such as notebooks, libraries, and experiments that can be shared among team members.

Even though Azure and Databricks are two separate companies, they have provided a collaborative and unified data platform by structuring services in a way that they integrate seamlessly and securely. Azure Databricks operates using a **control plane** and a **data plane**:

- **Control plane**: Backend services managed by Azure. Single sign-on is integrated with Azure Active Directory. This plane consists of management layer components such as cluster manager, metadata, and web UI.

- **Data plane**: This plane resides in the customer's Azure account. For data processing, compute resources are created within the customer's VNET. This plane also stores customer data that's been collected from external sources, streaming, and IoT.

> **Important Note**
> Having data in the data plane ensures that you have full control over and access to your data. Importantly, it gives you the flexibility to use any cloud vendor or service in the future.

Data engineering as a service (SaaS)

In modern times, organizations want to be less bothered about maintaining infrastructure and more focused on doing things that matter. This is the reason why the concept of offering **software as a service** (**SaaS**) has gained immense popularity. In a typical SaaS solution infrastructure deployment, load balancing, high availability, and scalability are handled by the vendor. This gives their customers peace of mind to use the service without worrying about the underlying hardware or software.

SaaS use case

Here are a couple of use cases where using an SaaS layer is warranted:

- An organization that wants to focus on data engineering and analytics without going through the hassle of managing infrastructure or code.

- An organization where security regulations permit the use of multi-tenant cloud services and can tolerate variability in compute power.

Microsoft Azure offers several SaaS products via its pay-per-use model. Since the list of Azure-offered SaaS products is long, we will focus on the ones that are commonly used in the world of data engineering and analytics.

Azure Data Factory

Azure Data Factory is a managed data integration and transformation service. You can use over 90 built-in connectors to collect data from a vast variety of data sources, including databases (relational and non-relational), APIs, filesystems, and other SaaS applications.

Azure Data Factory is built to handle data integration workflows using the classical approach of **Extract, Transform, Load** (ETL) or the modern approach of **Extract, Load, Transform** (ELT). An Azure Data Factory workflow is referred to as a **pipeline**. A pipeline is a collection of activities that are units of work that perform actions on datasets. An activity uses a **linked service** to connect to external sources such as storage, databases, and clusters:

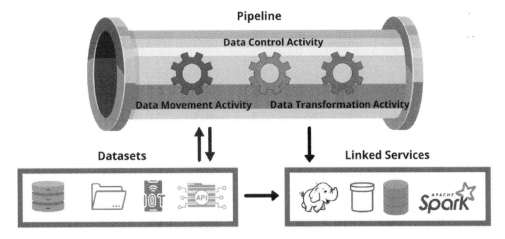

Figure 3.7 – Interaction between the Azure Data Factory components

An activity in Azure Data Factory can be one of the following three types:

- **Data movement activity**: A data movement activity is used for copying data from a source data store to a sink data store. The data movement activity is executed on an **integration runtime** that acts as a compute environment that facilitates running the activity. An integration runtime can be Azure-hosted (runs on Azure infrastructure), self-hosted (runs on customer infrastructure), or Azure-SSIS (runs on an Azure-managed SSIS cluster).

- **Data transformation activity**: A data transformation activity allows data engineers to build curation and transformation logic and execute it on a variety of computing environments, such as **Azure HDInsight** and **Azure Databricks**.

- **Data control activity**: A data control activity allows data engineers to build a data workflow using programmatic operations such as if-else, parameterization, and iterations.

Using Azure Data Factory, you can build, run, and monitor data-driven workflows without the need to write code. The following are the components of the Azure Data Factory service:

- **Ingest**: You can ingest data from over 90 data sources from on-premises, Azure cloud, or other cloud vendors.

- **Control flow**: You can generate code-free flows to control the execution of workflows using programmatic operations.

- **Data flow**: You can generate code-free transformations that execute in Spark or use pre-existing Spark clusters.

- **Schedule**: You can schedule pipelines using manual, event-based, or scheduled triggers.

- **Monitor**: You can view the pipeline's run history and create alerts/notifications.

Azure Data Factory replicates pipeline metadata across paired regions to protect against failures. It also implements RBAC for authoring, editing, and monitoring pipelines.

Azure Data Lake Analytics

Azure Data Lake Analytics is a fully managed analytics job service for large-scale data processing. It can run massively parallel data transformation jobs. Azure Data Lake Analytics dynamically provisions resources based on demand.

Azure Data Lake Analytics uses a **U-SQL** runtime engine that's submitted as jobs. A job in Azure Data Lake Analytics executes in four phases, as follows:

- **Preparing**: In this phase, the U-SQL script is uploaded to Azure and optimized for further execution.

- **Queued**: A job is queued until resources are made available that can run the job.

- **Running**: The job is started.

- **Finalizing**: The job has been completed.

Azure Data Lake Analytics divides the job into multiple sub-jobs, also known as **vertexes**. A vertex represents a parallelly executing portion of the job on the same data. The degree of parallelism is measured in **analytics units**. 1 AU = 1 Azure VM with 2 vCPUs and 6 GB of RAM:

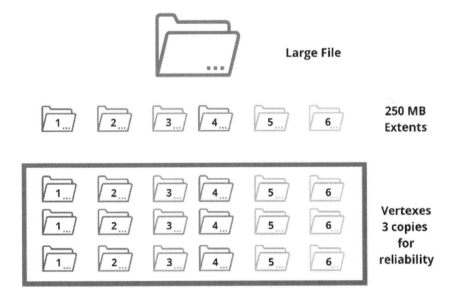

Figure 3.8 – Distribution of Azure Data Lake Analytics Jobs using vertexes

Azure Stream Analytics

Azure Stream Analytics is a fully managed real-time data analysis service. It is used to process high-velocity streaming data from data sources such as IoT sensors, logs, and social media. Here are some use case scenarios for Azure Stream Analytics:

- Real-time decision-making such as fraud detection and predictive analysis
- IoT anomaly detection of IoT sensor data
- Monitoring infrastructure and application logs
- To facilitate dashboarding
- Invoking workflows based on conditions
- Identifying patterns and aggregating data across several data sources
- Alerting based on threshold values
- Performing sentiment analysis for social media posts

An Azure Stream Analytics job is set up with an **input**, **query**, and **output**. The job input can stream data from Azure Event Hubs, Azure IoT Hub, or Azure Blob storage.

The query engine is based on SQL and can be used in combination with **JavaScript** and **C#** user-defined functions to perform operations such as filtering, sorting, and aggregating. Finally, the output can be sent to several locations, including Power BI, Azure Synapse, and Azure Data Lake Storage.

During the input and output operations, there is a chance that the Azure Stream Analytics job will connect to sources outside your Azure VNET. This can be securely accomplished using private endpoints or by setting up trusted networking services.

By default, Azure Stream Analytics is a **multi-tenant** service. For extremely security-conscious organizations, there is another option called **Azure Stream Analytics Cluster**. Azure Stream Analytics Cluster works in **single-tenant** mode using isolated and dedicated hardware.

The capacity of an Azure Stream Analytics cluster is measured in **streaming units** (**SUs**). You may scale your SUs up and down based on traffic demands:

> **Important Note**
> The multi-tenancy nature of SaaS and PaaS may be a roadblock for highly regulated organizations due to compliance issues with shared infrastructure. Using a dedicated IaaS layer may be the only choice in those cases.

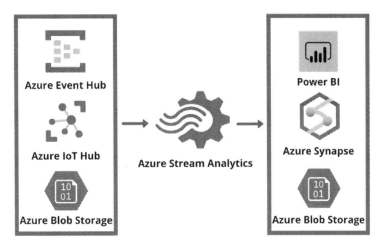

Figure 3.9 – Input and output of Azure Stream Analytics

Since Azure Stream Analytics is a fully managed service, it has built-in recovery mechanisms for fault tolerance. It works on the principle of at least once delivery, so events are never lost in case of failures. Azure Stream Analytics encrypts all incoming/outgoing communication and performs all computations in memory.

Azure Synapse Analytics

Azure Synapse Analytics is an enterprise-grade data engineering and analytics service. Synapse analytics implements the lakehouse architecture by embedding a unique mixture of data processing services, as follows:

- **Synapse SQL**: This implements a SQL-based data massively parallel processing data warehouse. Synapse SQL employs a couple of models:

  - **Dedicated SQL pools**: In the dedicated model, a set of resources is provisioned based on the chosen **data warehouse units** (**DWUs**). A dedicated SQL pool uses a node-based architecture for computations. At the lowest denomination, the DW100c (single-node cluster) stores 60 distributions of data on a single node. At the highest denomination, the DW30000c (60-node cluster) stores one distribution of data per node. The **performance** and **concurrency** of queries increase lineary as more DWUs get added, and so does the cost. The cost of storage is charged separately based on usage.

  The compute nodes store tables in a distributed fashion in Azure Storage and uses the **data movement service** (**DMS**) to run queries in parallel. Table distribution can be of three types: **hash**, **round robin**, and **replicated**.

The compute and storage layers are fully decoupled. To save on costs, you can pause the compute layer, at which time the billing stops for the allocated DWUs. On the other hand, the storage cost is permanent, regardless of whether the compute layer is active or has been paused.

- **Serverless SQL pools**: In the serverless model, there is no need to provision resources or copy data to compute nodes. Instead, you can query data in Azure Blob storage using an external data source. Using this method, you can query data in several formats, including **CSV**, **JSON**, and **parquet**. For files in parquet format, you can infer the schema automatically. Querying data from Azure Cosmos DB is also supported using **Azure Synapse Link**.

Serverless SQL pools automatically scale the resources based on the demands of the query. For faster execution, they utilize a **distributed query processing** (**DQP**) engine to split the query into multiple smaller queries. The cost of a serverless SQL pool is based on the data that's processed by queries.

> **Important Note**
>
> Dedicated and serverless pools follow different costing methods. While the dedicated pool is charged by the number of DWUs, the serverless model is based on data processed. Generally, serverless pools will cost less than dedicated pools. But there may be cases involving large data scans, in which case you may be better off using a dedicated pool. It is highly recommended that the data engineer performs a benchmark test before choosing the appropriate pool.

- **Synapse Spark**: Synapse Spark implements the Apache Spark engine for distributed computing. This process involves creating a Spark pool in Azure Synapse. A Spark pool is simply the definition of the resource, such as node size, autoscaling behavior, and the number of nodes. The actual Spark instance gets created when a job is submitted to the pool. To save on costs, you can use the **automatic pause** mechanism, which can release the Spark resources after a configurable idle time.

  Using a Synapse Studio notebook, a data engineer can manage data **wrangling**, **transformations**, and **visualizations**. Azure Synapse Analytics is compatible with the Delta Lake framework, which acts as the core storage component for implementing the lakehouse architecture.

> **Important Note**
> The ability of Azure Synapse to share table metadata across computational engines, namely serverless SQL pools and Spark pools, hugely simplifies data engineering tasks. The principle of cataloging data once and using it multiple times also establishes strong master data management strategies.

Data cataloging and sharing services in Microsoft Azure

Data catalogs and data sharing services are redefining the data distribution strategies of modern organizations. Data catalogs represent the trusted view of the data deemed worthy of consumption by internal and external users. Couple this with an easy and secure method of sharing data, and you are well on your way to providing your user base with a self-serve analytics platform.

Azure Purview

Azure Purview is a fully managed service that's used to discover, catalog, and consume data in a unified fashion. Azure Purview helps producers define a single source of truth for data that consumers may use in their downstream processes. It is important to understand that once the data source has been registered, only the metadata is stored in the data catalog; the actual data says in its original location. Azure Purview does not give you access to the data itself; it simply helps users discover data sources and their related information so that users can gauge their utility for their own use.

> **Important Note**
> Azure Purview also supports features such as data classification and end-to-end data lineage, which are extremely critical for data governance purposes.

Azure Purview uses a data source registration tool to extract the following metadata information:

- Details of the data source's location.

- Schema; that is, the structure of the table.

- Data profile (object and columns); that is, the number of rows, whether it contains null values, the size of the table, and the last updated timestamps.

In addition to the discovered metadata, users can add their own metadata manually.

Azure Purview supports a variety of data sources, including Azure Blob, Azure Synapse, Hive, MySQL, Oracle, and many more.

Azure Data Share

In *Chapter 1*, *The Story of Data Engineering and Analytics*, we had a section called *The monetary power of data*. In that section, we talked about modern methods of revenue diversification, including data monetization through sharing data. An organization can realize this dream by using **Azure Data Share**. Azure Data Share facilitates securely sharing data to other parties, including customers and partners. Traditionally, data sharing securely using mediums such as SFTP or APIs has been very expensive.

Using Azure Data Share, organizations can add datasets and invite customers/partners to safely access your shared data. Azure Data Share can be performed in a couple of ways:

- **Snapshot-based sharing**: Once shared, data moves to the consumer's Azure subscription.

- **In-place sharing**: Once shared, a data link is created that can be accessed by the consumer.

Azure Data Share access is protected with managed identities using Azure Active Directory. In addition to that, data shares are protected by usual data-at-rest and data-in-motion mechanisms.

> **Important Note**
>
> For organizations that are migrating to the cloud, the sudden idea of adopting SaaS is sometimes quite far-fetched. Not everyone likes to lose control over the infrastructure and one-off customizations.

Opening a free account with Microsoft Azure

In the upcoming chapters, we will be using the services you have just been reading about to build a data lake using the lakehouse architecture. Therefore, it is time to open a free Azure account that gives you 12 months of free services, plus a one-time $260 credit. Please note that not all – but most – services are free. To open a free account and browse through the free services, please visit the following link: `https://azure.microsoft.com/en-ca/free/`.

Here is some valuable advice:

- It is always a good idea to remove the compute resources once you've used them.
- You get 5 GB of **locally redundant data** (**LRS**) data for free. There is no need to remove data that's stored during future exercises since we will not be exceeding this limit.
- While using the free services in Azure, please keep a strict eye on your billing using the following link: `https://portal.azure.com/#blade/Microsoft_ Azure_Billing/BillingMenuBlade/Overview`.

  It is always a good idea to be extra cautious about billing. You can also set budgets in Azure to monitor costs over time. Azure will send you a notification if the set budget has been exceeded: `https://docs.microsoft.com/en-us/azure/ cost-management-billing/costs/tutorial-acm-create-budgets`.

Summary

In this chapter, we learned about the IaaS, PaaS, and SaaS services in Azure that can help a data engineer build a data lake. We also discussed that cloud vendors provide many different options to perform similar operations. It is up to the data engineer to choose the right service that provides the customer with benefits based on their usage patterns, in-house skills, and budget.

The modern-day data pipeline requires careful planning, design, development, and deployment. In the next chapter, we will learn about the life cycle of a data pipeline and effective strategies for each phase of data pipeline creation.

Section 2: Data Pipelines and Stages of Data Engineering

This section provides you with advanced knowledge about data pipelines and various stages of data engineering. We will focus our learning on the Lakehouse architecture.

This section contains the following chapters:

- *Chapter 4, Understanding Data Pipelines*
- *Chapter 5, Data Collection Stage – The Bronze Layer*
- *Chapter 6, Understanding Delta Lake*
- *Chapter 7, Data Curation Stage – The Silver Layer*
- *Chapter 8, Data Aggregation Stage – The Gold Layer*

4

Understanding Data Pipelines

In the previous chapter, we discussed the various services that can be used to build a data lake in Microsoft Azure. We will now focus on how to kick-start the process of building a data lake using data pipelines.

As a data engineer, the process of laying out a data pipeline should be extremely well planned. This chapter will educate data engineers regarding the various phases of a data pipeline creation, with a list of recommended actions and tasks that need to be accounted for during each phase. Better planning results in better execution.

In this chapter, we will cover the following topics:

- Exploring data pipelines
- Process of creating a data pipeline
- Running a data pipeline
- Sample lakehouse project

Exploring data pipelines

In *Chapter 1, The Story of Data Engineering and Analytics*, we talked about the journey of data. We equated data engineering to a vehicle that makes the journey of data possible through sharp turns and roadblocks to ultimately reach its destination as securely and timely as possible. If data engineering is a vehicle, then a data pipeline is the engine that makes the journey possible. The engine is simply a collection of components, each performing a specialized operation. Ultimately, all the parts and components working together can maneuver the vehicle in the desired direction.

In simple terms, a data pipeline is an engine that can move data through various stages of collection, curation, and aggregation to reach its analytics destination. As with the various parts and components of an engine, the data pipeline uses a series of actions to complete its work. Each action performs a specialized task (once or repeatedly) to contribute toward the end goal.

Data engineers are responsible for assembling the actions in a series of steps in the most effective fashion to ultimately address the demands of analytics. This series of steps, illustrated in the following diagram, is collectively referred to as a **data pipeline**:

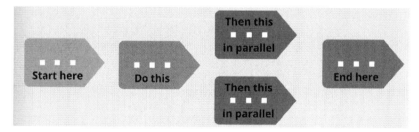

Figure 4.1 – Series of actions in a data pipeline

> **Important note**
> This is the age of options. It is the job of the data engineer to choose the most appropriate tool/service that can address the action most effectively.

Components of a data pipeline

A data pipeline is a collection of components. Each component performs a specialized operation contributing to the overall success of the journey of data. It is commonly seen that data engineers typically pay a lot of attention to the overall development of a pipeline but commonly neglect the operational aspects. While it is important to focus on the actual building of the various components, it is equally important to focus on how these components will be assembled, deployed, and monitored in the future. To understand data pipelines a little better, let's focus next on the core components of a data pipeline.

Source

Data sources are locations that store data required for data analytics. Some well-known sources of data are listed here:

- Databases and data warehouses
- Files
- **Application programming interfaces** (**APIs**)
- Sensor data from **internet of things** (**IoT**) devices
- Social networking and other **software-as-a-service** (**SaaS**) sites

Ingestion

A typical pipeline starts by ingesting data from one or more data sources. Over the years, data engineers have employed both push and pull mechanisms for accomplishing this action. Depending on the source of data, data engineers may need to choose between batch ingestion or streaming ingestion.

The complexity of ingesting from a data source is directly dependent on whether the nature of data is static or dynamic. Ingesting from a static data source is simple—the real complexity in data engineering arises when dealing with dynamic data sources. Data engineers need to employ effective **change data capture** (**CDC**) techniques to ingest data in an incremental fashion.

> **Important note**
>
> **Azure Data Factory** (**ADF**) loads incremental (delta) data using the watermark technique. A watermark is the last updated timestamp of data that was fetched in the last iteration.

Transformation

Before the ingested data is put to real use, it needs to pass through several maturity-gaining operations such as **curation**, **standardization**, **declassification**, **deduplication**, and—finally—**aggregation**. This process is collectively referred to as **data transformation**. In other words, the process of data transformation matures data to such a level that it can be readily and easily consumed for analytical operations.

Depending on the use case, data transformation can be a very complex operation. The complexity depends on several factors, including the following:

- Number and variety of data sources
- Complexity of business logic required for cleaning, declassification, and aggregation operations
- Frequency of data ingestion and subsequent data transformations
- Size of ingested data and how far back in time the data gets aggregated—days, weeks, months, or years

Destination

A data destination is a location that stores the results of the transformations. A data destination can be one of the following two types:

- **Final**—This destination type stores the end results of the transformations. In traditional architecture, it is referred to as the transformation layer, and in lakehouse architecture, it is called the gold layer.
- **Intermediate**—This destination type stores the intermediate results of the transformations. In traditional architecture, it is referred to as the raw or curation layer and in lakehouse architecture, it is called the bronze or silver layer.

Workflow

A workflow can be best described as a unit of work that has a sequence of actions. A workflow is designed in such a way that it can function in a repeatable fashion, usually triggered by a pre-defined schedule or event-based. A typical workflow is a collection of the following actions:

- **Input and output (I/O) actions**—Actions that perform data ingestion from data sources and storing data in destinations
- **Transformation actions**—Actions that perform data transformations
- **Control actions**—Actions that control the exception of the workflow including chaining, forking, joining, decision-making, and looping

Monitoring

After a workflow has been triggered, each action in the workflow needs to be closely monitored. Monitoring should be set up and configured in such a way that it stores the state of each action for every pipeline run in the form of logs. The operational team should be alerted if any action failed so that corrective actions can be performed.

Monitoring data pipelines has several benefits, including the following:

- It helps to establish the overall health of the data pipeline running, and its success or failure.

- It helps establish the total runtime for the data pipeline. This information is critical for calculating the miss rate for **service-level agreements** (SLAs).

- It helps identify performance bottlenecks. Having this information helps data engineers fine-tune code and manage resources.

> **Important note**
> In a data pipeline monitoring system, some key metrics to look out for are latency, throughput, and errors.

The understanding of what each component does in isolation, and how it contributes to the overall success of the data pipeline helps data engineers conceptualize, design, and develop components with a great degree of efficiency.

In the following sections, we will describe the various phases of the data pipeline creation process. In addition to the overall understanding of each phase, we will additionally learn about recommended tasks and actions that need to be accounted for. This list will hopefully give readers a solid baseline that can be further enhanced and built upon during real projects.

Process of creating a data pipeline

In analytics-centric organizations, it is very common to have multiple data pipelines, each one addressing a different use case. To make matters worse, each use case may be owned by a different sub-group within the organization and require a different dataset. In such cases, it becomes extremely important to carefully plan and design the data pipeline operation so that efficiencies can be discovered and repetitive work can be avoided. The creation of data pipelines is done in phases. In the subsequent sections, we will learn about each phase separately.

Before we deep dive into the details, the following diagram is important to highlight how each phase stacks on top of the other. The most important thing to notice in this diagram is that if data engineers diligently follow the recommended actions for each phase, the workload for each phase significantly decreases, and success is virtually guaranteed:

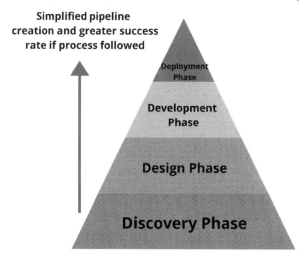

Figure 4.2 – Various phases of data pipeline creation

Let's explore the steps that can help data engineers kick-start the pipeline design process.

Discovery phase

The process of creating a data pipeline should start with a discovery phase. This phase not only gives data engineers an opportunity to know the team better, identify key stakeholders, and shortlist use cases but, more importantly, enables them to identify potential roadblocks and loopholes that could be detrimental to the overall success of a project.

Identifying a product owner

A product owner is someone who has ultimate authority over the overall success of a project. The product owner should have direct access to senior management for matters related to goal setting and for keeping them up-to-date on overall progress. Additionally, the product owner should be able to able to answer or gather information around some key questions relating to the following areas:

- Current and future state connectivity of connectivity to cloud
- Security regulations that the organization needs to comply with

- Any SLAs that need to be met
- End-user locations—on-prem, remote, or a combination of these
- How much automation is desired for infrastructure and code deployment
- Whether the deployment needs to be cloud vendor-agnostic

Shortlisting use cases

Create a list of individual use cases that need to be addressed by talking to each sub-group separately within the organization. Make sure that each use case has a designated owner who will act as the designated **knowledge champion** and has authority over matters relating to data access.

Conducting discovery sessions

Data engineers should conduct discovery sessions with each sub-group to collect the following information:

- Use-case description and end goals.
- Identification of data sources—location, connectivity information, any challenges with establishing connectivity such as **multi-factor authentication** (**MFA**), tokens, and firewall issues.
- Identification of datasets—list of tables, files, or APIs with corresponding data type and schema.
- What is the frequency of schema changes?
- The approximate data size of historical and incremental data for each data source.
- What is the approximate size of incremental data?
- What is the tolerable data lag between **online transaction processing** (**OLTP**) and **online analytical processing** (**OLAP**)? Is it a day, a few hours, or near real time?
- Details regarding data consumers—data analysts/data scientists.
- Is the intended use case brand new or did the **extract, transform, load** (**ETL**) code previously exist?
- If the use case did previously exist, ask for the existing ETL code. Also, ask for any supporting dashboards and reports.
- If the use case is brand new, ask for a written document explaining the intended joins, aggregations, and filters.
- Does **personally identifiable information** (**PII**) need to be masked?

- Are there any data classification rules?

- What are the requirements for table-level, row-level, and column-level security?

- Will data be encrypted using cloud-vendor encryption keys or client-supplied encryption keys?

- What **information technology** (**IT**) skills does the team currently carry? Is the team willing to invest time in learning modern frameworks such as Spark?

- Are there any data science, ad hoc reporting, and **business intelligence** (**BI**) tools that the users prefer?

I know you must be thinking that the requirement gathering list is awfully long. I assure you that all this is time well spent. The more prepared you are, the better the design, development, and deployment will be. I strongly suggest making it a habit to address items in the preceding list before starting any data lake project. You can keep adding more items to the list as you gain more experience in your career.

The deliverables of the discovery phase should be as follows:

- An understanding document (one per use case) that summarizes every piece of information gathered in detail

- List of gaps, loopholes, and roadblocks with designated owners

It is advisable that the understanding document be reviewed and accepted by the product owner before proceeding with the next steps. However, it is acceptable to proceed without resolving all gaps, loopholes, and roadblocks but with an understanding that they will be addressed before the development of the data pipeline is started.

> **Important note**
> The discovery process not only establishes a baseline but also provides you with a clear future direction. Most importantly, this phase gives you the opportunity to discover gaps, pinpoint loopholes, and identify roadblocks. This is an opportunity for data engineers to properly address these before they become serious issues down the road.

Design phase

Now the discovery phase has been completed, it is time to design the data pipeline. The information collected by data engineers in the discovery phase should be used to formulate the baseline for the design. The pipeline design process should address the items discussed next.

Shortlisting common datasets

Collect all use-case documents created during the discovery phase and shortlist common datasets. This is an extremely important step, so extra focus is warranted. Identifying common datasets across all sub-groups helps promote data reusability and enforce **master data management** (**MDM**) strategies.

The following diagram highlights a multi-pipeline design approach. Every use case discovered previously is represented as an individual pipeline without any dependencies to others. The result is that the same dataset may get ingested multiple times in different pipelines. Unfortunately, even though this approach seems simple and workable, due to unnecessary repetitions it significantly increases the storage and compute costs of an organization. As a result, a multi-pipeline design approach strategy is not recommended:

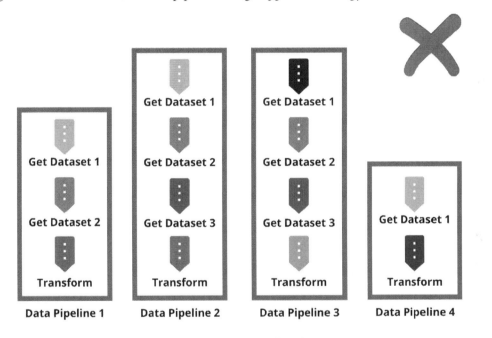

Figure 4.3 – A multi-pipeline design

Designing a pipeline using a parent-child approach – common datasets

You may recall that in *Chapter 1, The Story of Data Engineering and Analytics*, we learned that *storage is cheap, yet compute is expensive*. Here is an opportunity to put to good use something that you learned previously. With some extra overhead in the design phase, data engineers can provide a solution that follows best practices, promotes reusability, and minimizes both compute and costs.

Note in the following diagram how all datasets have been moved to a parent pipeline, and each use case discovered previously has been created as a child pipeline. This approach offers several benefits over a multi-pipeline approach and is therefore highly recommended:

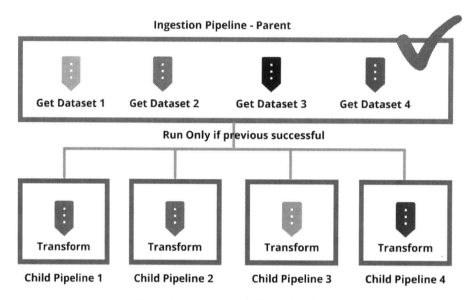

Figure 4.4 – A parent-child pipeline design

A parent-child pipeline design offers several benefits, including the following:

- Each dataset is ingested only once, and every subsequent child pipeline can use it.

- Saves on storage and compute costs.

- Provides better execution control over child pipelines by enforcing dependencies with the parent.

> **Important note**
> Some data engineers argue that designing a well-architected solution at a low price is simply not possible. I think it is—you just need to go that extra mile.

Designing a cloud architecture

Based on the agreed-upon discovery documents, data engineers should create a visual diagram that outlines the cloud resources that will be used for building the data pipeline. This should include services such as the network, the connection to on-premises and external locations, storage, compute, and orchestration.

Designing automation and monitoring

Based on the desired level of automation, data engineers should design **continuous integration/continuous deployment (CI/CD)** pipelines for infrastructure and code deployment on the cloud. Additionally, data engineers should also design the data pipeline's monitoring and notification mechanisms.

Costing

Once the high-level design has been completed, data engineers should create a rough estimate of cloud resources, as follows:

- Estimate the monthly cost of cloud resources for various environments during development. Remember that the requirement for storage and compute costs in development is usually less than in production, therefore it is important to adjust your resources accordingly.

- Estimate the monthly cost of cloud resources required in production. This estimate should factor in costs resulting from auto-scalability during peak demands.

> **Important note**
> When creating the costing, data engineers should properly research the variability of cost based on on-demand and reserved resources. There can be significant cost savings if a resource is reserved for several years.

The deliverable of the design phase is a document that summarizes the following:

- Cloud architecture

- Detailed description about parent and child pipelines

- How does the pipeline design address key compliance requirements?

- How does the pipeline design address incremental data, data lag, and schema evolution?

- How will the final data be published to end users?

- How will end users be notified regarding pipeline runs?

- Development strategy—development language, tools, and environments

- Which cloud layer will be used: **infrastructure as a service (IaaS)**, **platform as a service (PaaS)**, or SaaS?

- How will the infrastructure and code pipelines be deployed?

- How will the pipelines be monitored in production?
- Costing information

Data engineers should submit the design document to the client and arrange for a few walkthrough sessions. These sessions should be conducted with every sub-group that participated in the discovery sessions and the IT group, which will be responsible for deploying and managing the pipelines.

It is advisable that the design document be reviewed and formally accepted by the product owner before proceeding with the next steps.

> **Important note**
> Having walkthrough sessions with the IT group and gaining their confidence is extremely important. Ultimately, they will be deploying and managing the pipelines, so they need to be on board with the proposed design.

Development phase

If you have reached this point, chances are that the design document has been formally accepted by the product owner. Congratulations! I can safely tell you that the job is more than half done at this point. Now is the time to start the development phase, as follows:

- Start with the focus on the **parent** pipeline.
- Start by testing **connectivity** to each data source and familiarize yourself with the data formats and schema.
- Find out how **incremental** data will be provided.
- Develop a strategy to **merge** incremental data in the data lake.
- Develop strategies to deal with schema **evolution** in the data lake.
- Plan the intermediate and final storage **destinations**.
- Develop the parent pipeline.
- Pay special attention to data **security** at every step.
- Once the parent pipeline has been completed, then focus on individual **child** pipelines.
- For each child pipeline, develop the transformations in such a way that they minimize compute **repetitions** and promote dataset **reuse**.

Deployment phase

Assuming the use of an agile development approach, newly created data pipeline code is merged into a shared code repository and promptly deployed to different environments. Since this process could happen several times during the development life cycle, a repeatable and automated process is desired.

This is exactly where CI/CD fits in. Using such an approach, pipeline code is seamlessly merged, tested, and deployed automatically. We will be focusing in greater detail on these topics in *Chapter 11*, *Infrastructure Provisioning*, and *Chapter 12*, *Continuous Integration and Deployment (CI/CD) of Data Pipelines*.

> **Important note**
>
> These days, deployments are considered an integral part of the development life cycle. Instead of dealing with deployment issues after completing the development of a project, it is becoming a standard practice to adopt CI/CD where deployment is done in short cycles.

Running a data pipeline

Once the development and deployment have succeeded, it is time to orchestrate the data pipeline. Data pipeline runs are typically instantiated using the following three methods:

- **Manually**—The simplest way to invoke a data pipeline is by doing this manually. This means that action needs to be taken by either using the control panel, command-line tools, or **REpresentational State Transfer** (**REST**) APIs. This method is suitable for development/testing or one-off executions but is unsuitable for production. As an example, data engineers may choose to run a pipeline manually while performing unit testing or may need to perform a one-off execution of the pipeline because the scheduled run failed.

- **Scheduled**—In this method, the data pipeline is invoked using a scheduler. The scheduler can either be operating system-based—using schedulers in orchestration tools—or built into the ETL tool itself. This is the most common method of invoking data pipelines in production. Based on case scenarios, data pipelines are scheduled to run daily or hourly if more frequent data refreshes are desired. In financial systems, you may additionally schedule monthly runs for accounting batches.

> **Important note**
>
> Over the years, data pipelines have been primarily invoked using operating system schedulers such as `cron` in Linux and Task Scheduler in Windows. In the last few years, orchestration tools such as Oozie and Apache Airflow have taken over. These tools come with built-in schedulers.

- **Event-based**—There are cases where schedule-based invocations do not work well. This is true where the data pipeline has dependencies on something else, such as the availability of data or the completion of another pipeline. In many cases, the pipeline cannot be run until the data has been fully ingested. Since it is difficult to time the completion of such a process, an event-based mechanism is a better fit. Very frequently, curation pipelines are triggered using an event-based mechanism after the ingestion pipeline has been successfully completed. Similarly, an aggregation pipeline is triggered after a curation pipeline signals completion.

> **Important note**
>
> A parent-child pipeline is a good example to understand suitable invocations mechanisms. Typically, a parent pipeline should be invoked using a **schedule**, whereas child pipelines on **event-based** mechanisms run the child pipeline only if the parent is successful.

Finally, once the pipeline has been run, data engineers need to make sure that data pipeline monitoring is enabled and functional. For the first few days, it is a good idea for a data engineer to be part of the pipeline notification group. Many a time, simply by looking at the run logs, the data engineer will catch what others may miss. The final deliverable of this phase is the runbook, which will help the team with operational and administrative issues in the following areas:

- Running CI/CD pipelines
- Monitoring data pipelines
- How to deal with failures and re-evoking data pipelines after failures
- Changing data pipeline schedules
- Disabling data pipelines

Sample lakehouse project

Thus far, we have discussed the theoretical aspects of data engineering. The theory often teaches us *why it happens*; now, it's time to shift our focus to the practical aspects of *how it happens*. In the following chapters, we will build a data lake using a lakehouse architecture.

We will conduct the practical learning process as if we were part of a live project. You have been hired as a data engineer at a leading big-box store named **Electroniz**, which sells electronic goods. Electroniz wants to formulate a modern business strategy to diversify revenue by streamlining its data engineering and analytics operations. On the first day on your job, the **chief technology officer (CTO)** has shared their vision of the future in the form of the following diagram:

Figure 4.5 – Future Electroniz platform

He has also provided some high-level details that may help you kick-start the process, as follows:

- Electroniz sells electronic goods in several brick-and-mortar stores throughout the **United States** (**US**) and on their e-commerce site. Goods sold over the e-commerce site can be shipped to Canada, the **United Kingdom** (**UK**), and Germany.

- Shipping is handled using external vendors such as DHL, Purolator, and **United Parcel Service** (**UPS**).

- Electroniz's current analytics platform is using an on-prem SQL Server database.

- Using the sales data, Electroniz is planning to streamline its inventory, shipping, accounting, and advertising.

- Electroniz must abide by **Payment Card Industry** (**PCI**) regulations, so all PII data needs to be properly masked and encrypted.

- Currently, ETL is performed once a day, which creates a 24-hour lag for updating shipping and inventory. In some cases, items sold on the internet were out of stock, but the website was unaware of it because of the lag. This has caused severe delays in shipping and many order cancellations. Due to customer dissatisfaction, Electroniz has seen a drop in sales.

- Electroniz is aiming for a near-real-time sales analytics platform that can serve its customer needs faster and better. The maximum permissible data lag is 1 hour.

- Electroniz wants to streamline its budget allocations for advertising and marketing using intelligent analytics based on user traffic on its e-commerce website.

In the future chapters, we will be going on a journey of data. On this journey, you will be in the driving seat, maneuvering Electroniz through all the roadblocks to their destination.

Summary

In this chapter, we learned about the data pipeline life cycle. Hopefully, I was able to highlight the fact that the discovery sessions and pipeline design are more important than the development itself. Similarly, it is very important to keep the stakeholders in the loop with everything that is happening. It is important that data engineers conduct regular checkpoints, demonstrations, and code review sessions with the stakeholders.

It is time to put the cloud services that we learned about during *Chapter 3, Data Engineering on Microsoft Azure,* to work. In the next chapter, we will start to use the Azure services and highlight the various stages of data engineering.

5
Data Collection Stage – The Bronze Layer

In the previous chapters, we discussed many theories involving data lakes, their architectures, and pipelines as a method in which to create data lakes. Now that you have a fair understanding of these topics, it is the perfect time to begin creating our actual data lakehouse.

In this chapter, we will cover the following topics:

- Architecting the Electroniz data lake
- Understanding the bronze layer
- Configuring data sources
- Configuring data destinations
- Building the ingestion pipelines
- Testing the ingestion pipelines

Architecting the Electroniz data lake

In the previous chapter, *Chapter 4, Understanding Data Pipelines*, we introduced the sample lakehouse project for a leading big-box store named **Electroniz** that sells electronic goods. We are going to assume that the final contract has been awarded, so the next step is to start building the data lakehouse. Now, it's time to put the skills that we learned in *Chapter 4, Understanding Data Pipelines*, to good use. Since our company is big on following best practices, the data engineering team has decided to diligently follow all of the steps in the *Process of creating a data pipeline* section.

As efficient data engineers, we will kick-start the process by conducting discovery sessions with customer groups. Often, conducting discovery sessions and extracting useful information from a customer can be very challenging. At times, you should expect to encounter varying personalities and pushbacks since everyone might not be on board with the global ideas of the management. Additionally, consider that team members from the customer side might be involved in other activities that are related to their normal job, or they might need to extract the required information for other team members. It is important that you learn to anticipate some delays and factor them into your project timelines.

> **Important**
>
> One simple way of minimizing pushbacks, delays, and follow-ups is to involve the product owner at every stage of the process.

In some cases, you might need to conduct several discovery sessions and follow up multiple times before you are able to extract the required information. I do understand that this might be frustrating at times. But for several reasons, the discovery phase is extremely critical for the overall success of the project.

> **Important**
>
> Before starting the discovery sessions, let the product owner know the anticipated number of sessions so that they can appropriately plan any timelines and resources on their end.

At this point, we are going to assume that the discovery sessions were a huge success. Although there were some challenges, you were, finally, able to sufficiently extract all of the required information from the customer. As part of the process, you have documented your findings in the form of a document that has been reviewed and finalized by **Electroniz**.

The following is a list of several important findings that were discovered during those sessions:

- There are five data sources that need to be ingested, as follows:

  - **Sales database**: This database stores data for sales that happen in brick-and-mortar stores throughout the US. The sales database is a **Microsoft SQL server** hosted on **Azure SQL**.

  - **E-commerce transactions**: **Electroniz** also does the online selling of its products. Every time a transaction occurs on the online store, an event will be streamed to a central resource. The sales data is in a structured format.

  - **Currency conversion data**: **Electroniz** sells products in varying currencies on the online store. The currency conversion data is required to convert all sales into USD. The conversion data is available using **REST API** calls. The currency conversion data is in a semi-structured format.

  - **E-commerce website tracking**: All visitors to the **Electroniz** online store are tracked on the web server. This information is instrumental in tracking users by country and helps the advertising team perform targeted advertising. The website log is available as a file that can be downloaded from **Azure Blob storage**. The website tracking data is in an unstructured format.

  - **Geo-location data**: Geo-location data is necessary to map the IP addresses from the web server logs to the country of origin. This data can be downloaded from an **HTTP** source. The geo-location data is in a structured format.

- Transactions in the sales database and online store happen very frequently throughout the day. The lakehouse needs to be kept up to date with a maximum delay of 1 hour.

- The consumers of data are data analysts, business intelligence developers, and data scientists. The preferred analytical tool for data analysts and business intelligence groups is **SQL**, whereas data scientists prefer to use **Apache Spark**.

- All PII data, including credit cards, addresses, and phone numbers, needs to be masked.

- All data needs to be encrypted at rest and in motion.

- Using the new lakehouse, the **Electroniz** team is looking for aggregated metrics for sales and inventory. They would like to streamline their shipping operations and the intelligent distribution of advertising budgets based on available metrics.

> **Important**
>
> A key recipe for the success of any project is to keep the customer involved in all of the major decisions. After all, they will be responsible for managing the solution after you leave.

So far so good. Based on the preceding findings, we need to design some key components of the data lakehouse:

- The cloud architecture
- The pipeline design
- The deployment strategy

The cloud architecture

After carefully reviewing the requirements, it is evident that **Electroniz** will truly benefit from a data lakehouse. Recall that we discussed the benefits of the lakehouse in *Chapter 2, Discovering Storage and Compute Data Lake Architectures*. A lakehouse provides a nice balance of low-cost storage and compute layers that natively support ACID transactions, SQL, schema evolution, and many other features.

This is what the architecture of the **Electroniz** lakehouse will look like.

Raw data – the bronze layer

Raw data from five data sources will be ingested into the bronze layer, as follows:

- Datasets from the sales database, currency conversion, geo-location, and website tracking will be ingested using **Azure Data Factory** into **Azure Data Lake Storage**.
- The e-commerce transactions will be streamed to Azure Event Hubs as events. Azure Event Hubs Capture will save events within **Azure Data Lake Storage**.

> **Important**
>
> It is customary to store data in the bronze layer in the exact shape and form as it was ingested from the source. This not only helps to preserve the exact state of data as ingested but also goes a long way in establishing a clear **data lineage**.

Curated data – the silver layer

After data has been ingested within the bronze layer, it will be curated and standardized using **Azure Databricks**. This layer will merge the incremental data from the data sources using **Delta Lake**. Curated tables will be visible to users using **Azure Synapse**. The curated (Delta) tables can be readily consumed for the purposes of data analytics, machine learning, and artificial intelligence. Access to the curated tables enables users to have the option to analyze/aggregate data beyond the standard set of aggregations provided in the gold layer.

> **Important**
>
> Provisioning a unified layer for both batch and streaming data is a key component of the lakehouse architecture. The silver layer is the "bring it all together" zone, where data from varying types, sources, and formats is unified within one single location and in a common format, called **delta**.

Aggregated data – the gold layer

Finally, data from the silver layer will be aggregated using **Azure Synapse**. Aggregated results will be stored in **Azure Data Lake Storage**. Aggregated tables will be visible to users using **Azure Synapse**. Aggregated tables in the gold layer can be consumed for data analytics, machine learning, and artificial intelligence purposes. This is better illustrated in the following diagram:

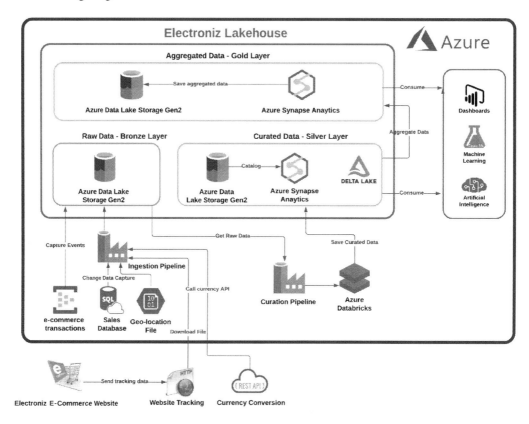

Figure 5.1 – The Electroniz cloud architecture

> **Important**
>
> Automated infrastructure provisioning helps organizations spin up cloud infrastructures quickly and reliably. A recommended career progression for a data engineer is to gain DevOps skills.

The pipeline design

This is what the data pipeline design for the **Electroniz** lakehouse looks like. We will have four pipelines, as follows:

- The batch ingestion pipeline – the **bronze layer**
- The streaming ingestion pipeline – the **bronze layer**
- The curation pipeline – the **silver layer**
- The aggregation pipeline – the **gold layer**

These pipelines can be viewed in the following diagram:

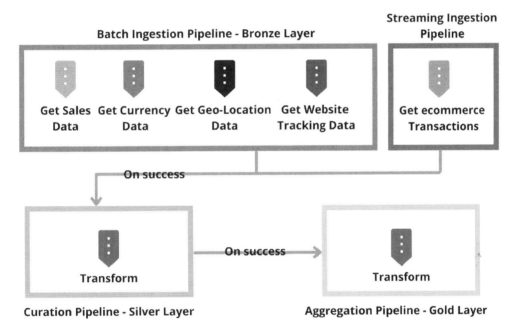

Figure 5.2 – The Electroniz pipeline design

We will explore all of the preceding components in more detail, as follows:

- **The batch ingestion pipeline**: The batch pipeline will ingest data for four data sources – the sales database, currency conversion, geo-location, and website tracking. This pipeline is created and invoked using **Azure Data Factory**.

- **The streaming ingestion pipeline**: The streaming pipeline is a continuously running pipeline that continuously watches for new events in the messaging layer. New events are promptly saved to **Azure Data Lake Storage** every 2 minutes using capture events. This pipeline is created and invoked using **Azure Event Hubs**.

- **The curation pipeline**: The curation pipeline will trigger automatically depending on the success of the batch ingestion pipeline. When invoked, it will merge data collected over the last hour from the batch and streaming pipelines into delta tables. In the same process, **data standardization** and data masking rules will be applied to the data to make it ready for consumption purposes. **Data masking** is essential in order to satisfy **PCI** compliance requirements.

- **The aggregation pipeline**: The aggregation pipeline will be triggered automatically depending on the success of the curation pipeline. When invoked, it will aggregate data available in the silver layer for sales and inventory purposes.

The deployment strategy

Following best practices, the deployment of the **Electroniz** lakehouse will be performed using CI/CD pipelines. Deployments are done using **Azure Pipelines** and **Azure Resource Manager** templates. At a high level, the CI/CD process will function as follows:

- Developers will author and unit test the data factory pipelines in their respective feature branches.

- On completion of the coding, the developer will generate a pull request for a code review by the team.

- After the code review and approval by the team, the developer's code branch is merged with the main branch.

- When ready for deployment, the main branch is deployed in the development environment. This initiates the creation of the Azure Data Factory artifact branch (`adf_publish`). This branch is automatically created by the **Azure Data Factory** service.

- To deploy code in UAT, a **release** is created in Azure Pipelines using the `adf_publish` branch. This release is deployed in the UAT environment.

- After successful verification and testing, the same release is pushed to the production environment.

From the looks of things, over the last few days, we have made some pretty good progress. At this stage, we are going to assume that Electroniz has reviewed all of the design and architecture documents that have been submitted to them. The product owner has advised us that Electroniz is happy with the proposed design and architecture of the lakehouse. They are eager to move ahead with the next steps of the lakehouse creation life cycle. This means that we are ready to kick off the development cycle.

The journey of data has started. We have some serious work ahead of us, so let's get started.

> **Important**
>
> While you are waiting for final approvals from the customer regarding the design and architecture documents, it is a good use of your time to set up code repositories, test cloud connectivity, and set up development environments.

Before we initiate the development, I want to make sure that we clearly understand what the bronze layer means in a lakehouse architecture.

Understanding the bronze layer

Inside a lakehouse, the bronze layer stores raw data exactly in the same shape, form, and format as it was collected from the data sources. The following is a list of some of the features of the data within the bronze layer:

- **Unclean and non-standardized**: This is deemed unsuitable for consumption by analytical workloads.

- **Support for multiple formats and types**: Data in the bronze layer might be structured, semi-structured, or unstructured. It can also be a combination of text and binary types.

- **Immutable**: By definition, data in the bronze layer should not be editable. If data changes over time, it is stored as duplicate copies.

- **Stored forever**: Data in the bronze layer is never deleted. This is less of a concern due to the low cost of storage. However, to save costs, some portions of data might be archived.

Having data in the native format offers several advantages, as follows:

- **Replayed**: Often, analysts and data scientists discover mistakes and oversights in coding. This requires data in the silver and gold layers to be rebuilt from scratch. Since original data is available, future transformations can be regenerated by replaying data from start to finish.

- **Repurposed**: As new requirements trickle in, having access to original data helps data engineers create new transformations.

- **Audit**: Having data in a native format is extremely important for data lineage and accuracy.

> **Important**
>
> Here, lineage refers to the traceability of the journey that data has taken over time. Many compliance frameworks look at data lineage as solid proof of whether an organization has followed the best practices regarding data usage or not.

Now that we have learned about the different layers of the lakehouse, let's move on to configure the data sources that will be used to ingest data.

Configuring data sources

We're all set and ready to roll! We will build the Electroniz lakehouse one layer at a time starting with the bronze layer. The problem is that we do not have any data. Since this is a learning exercise, we will generate our own data; however, most likely, data will preexist for you when you work on actual customer projects.

Data preparation

To proceed with the lakehouse creation, we will create the following data sources with sample data:

- **The stores database**: This is stored in Microsoft SQL Server.

- **E-commerce transactions**: These are pushed to Azure Event Hubs.

- **The e-commerce website tracking**: This is downloaded from an Azure Blob storage location.

There is no need to generate data for the following datasets because they are downloaded in real time from external sources:

- **Currency conversion data**: This is downloaded from a REST API.

- **Geo-location data**: This is downloaded from an HTTP source.

Preparing source data for the stores database

We'll start preparing source data using the following steps:

1. Log in to the Azure portal using the URL `https://portal.azure.com/`.

2. To create a new SQL database, browse to `https://portal.azure.com/#create/Microsoft.AzureSQL`, as follows:

Figure 5.3 – The Azure SQL deployment options

Click on the **Create** button underneath **SQL databases**:

- In **Subscription**, select the **Free Tier** or **Paid** subscription.

- In **Resource group**, click on the **Create new** link.

- For the name of the resource group, enter `training_rg`.

- In **Database name**, enter `salesdb`.

- In **Server**, click on the **Create new** link.

A new window will open with the title of **New server**:

- In **Server name**, enter a unique name that is globally available, such as `salesdb100`.

- In the **Server admin** login, enter `salesadmin`.

- In **Password** and **Confirm Password**, enter a password as per the policy and remember it for future steps.

- In **Location**, select **(US) East US**.

Click on **Configure database**.

Choose **Standard S0, 10 DTUs,** and a maximum data size of **250 GB**:

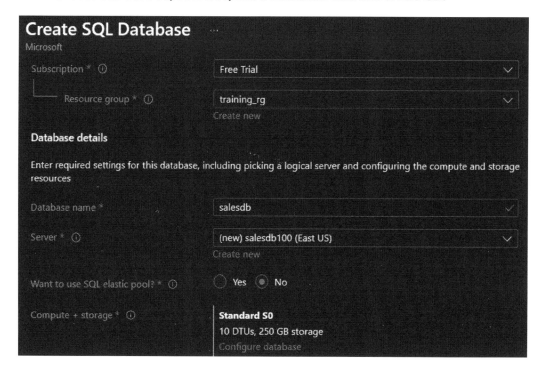

Figure 5.4 – The Azure SQL create options

3.   Click on **Apply**. Then, click on **Next: Networking**:

- Choose **Public endpoint**.

- To allow Azure services and resources to access this server, select **Yes**.

- To add a current client IP address, select **Yes**.

- Click on **Review + create**.

Click on **Create**. You should be able to view the **Deployment is in progress** window, as follows:

Figure 5.5 – Azure SQL deployment progress

4. Once the deployment is complete, click on **Go to resource**. You should now see the newly created SQL database:

Figure 5.6 – Azure SQL database deployment confirmation

5. To connect to the newly created database, click on **Query editor (preview)** in the pane on the left-hand side. Log in as `salesadmin`:

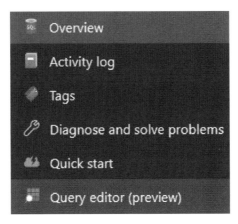

Figure 5.7 – Azure SQL database deployment confirmation

6. Copy the contents of the following file within the training Git repository:
    `https://raw.githubusercontent.com/PacktPublishing/Data-Engineering-with-Apache-Spark-Delta-Lake-and-Lakehouse/main/project/prep/stores/sql/history/storedb_history.sql`.

7. Paste the contents inside the **Query editor** window. Click on **Run**:

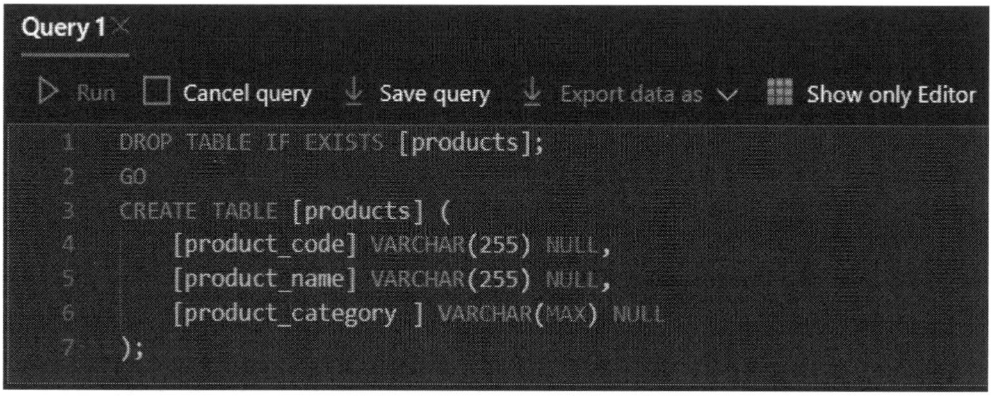

Figure 5.8 – The Azure SQL query editor

8. After a few seconds, the **Messages** pane should display a success message similar to the following:

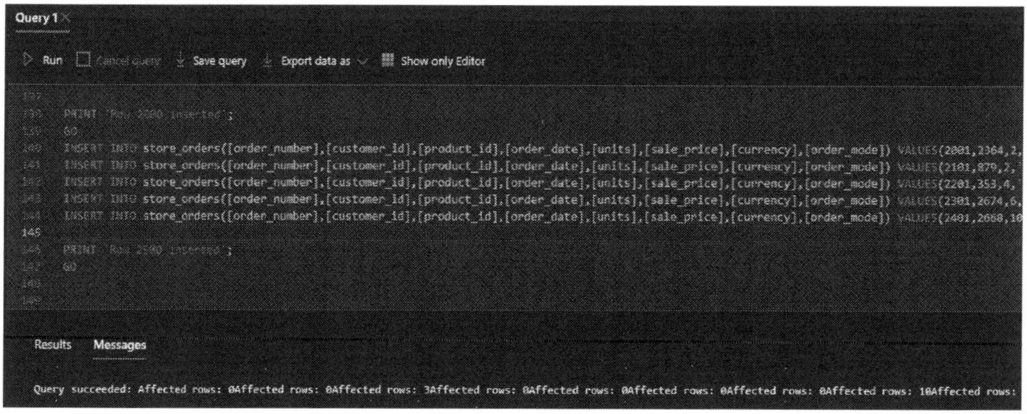

Figure 5.9 – The Azure SQL query editor success message

9. On the pane on the left-hand side, select the **refresh** icon (the rounded arrow), then click on **Tables**. Now click on the **three dots** and choose **Select Top 1000 Rows**:

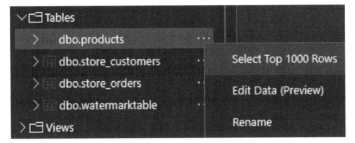

Figure 5.10 – Selecting rows in the Azure SQL query editor

10. You should be able to view the rows in the products table, as follows:

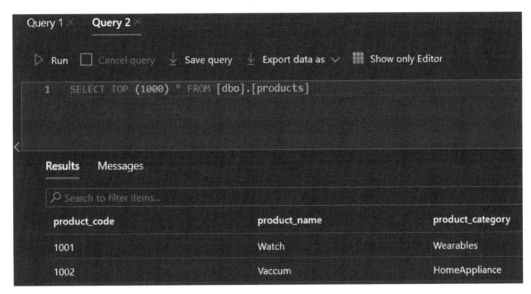

Figure 5.11 – The Azure SQL query editor results

All done. You are all set to proceed with the next steps.

Preparing the source data for e-commerce transactions

In order to generate e-commerce transactions, we will register an **Azure event grid** and create an **Azure event hub**. This time, the Azure portal will not be used to create the resources. Instead, we will invoke shell commands that will create the resource for us. For this exercise, we will use **Azure Cloud Shell**. Cloud Shell is interactive and can be accessed using a browser. The shell experience is available either as **Bash** or **PowerShell**:

> **Important**
>
> When creating Azure resources, data engineers should not only limit themselves to the Azure portal. They should learn how to use command-line tools such as the Azure CLI for deployments. Using shell commands to create resources is quicker and less error-prone in comparison to the interactive method using the portal.

1. Open Cloud Shell using the **Cloud Shell** icon that is available from the top menu of the Azure portal:

Figure 5.12 – The Cloud Shell icon in the Azure portal

2. A welcome window will open asking you to choose between two options: **Bash** or **PowerShell**. Choose **Bash**:

Welcome to Azure Cloud Shell

Select Bash or PowerShell. You can change shells any time via the environment selector in the Cloud Shell toolbar. The most recently used environment will be the default for your next session.

Figure 5.13 – The choice of shells in Azure Cloud Shell

3. In the next window, choose **Create storage**. Please do not confuse Cloud Shell storage with Azure Data Lake Storage. Cloud Shell uses this storage account to persist internal files. We will **not** be using this storage to store Electroniz lakehouse data:

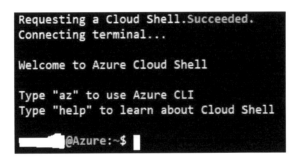

Figure 5.14 – Cloud Shell storage

4. You should now be connected to the Bash shell with a window that appears similar to the following:

```
Requesting a Cloud Shell.Succeeded.
Connecting terminal...

Welcome to Azure Cloud Shell

Type "az" to use Azure CLI
Type "help" to learn about Cloud Shell

         @Azure:~$
```

Figure 5.15 – The Cloud Shell screen

5. Throughout this book, we will be using the **Packt Publishing** Git repository to download code files and sample data. This is a good time to clone the Git repository so that we can access the required files. Invoke the following command inside the Bash shell:

```
git clone https://github.com/PacktPublishing/Data-
Engineering-with-Apache-Spark-Delta-Lake-and-Lakehouse.
git
```

If the cloning was successful, you should expect to see an output similar to the following:

```
Azure> git clone https://github.com/PacktPublishing/Data-Engineering-with-Apach
Cloning into 'Data-Engineering-with-Apache-Spark-Delta-Lake-and-Lakehouse'...
remote: Enumerating objects: 22, done.
remote: Counting objects: 100% (22/22), done.
remote: Compressing objects: 100% (17/17), done.
remote: Total 22 (delta 2), reused 9 (delta 0), pack-reused 0
Unpacking objects: 100% (22/22), done.
```

Figure 5.16 – The Git clone output

6. Now, let's create an Azure event grid. **Azure Event Grid** allows you to easily build applications based on event-based architectures. Azure Event Grid connects event sources to the event handlers. The event grid topic provides an endpoint where the source sends events. The e-commerce website tracking logs are stored in an **Azure Blob storage account**:

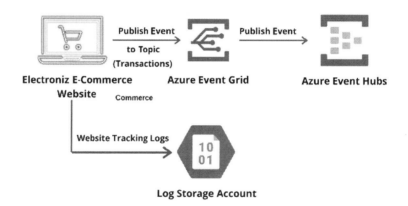

Figure 5.17 – Publishing events to Azure Event Hubs

Copy each of the following commands, line by line, and paste them inside the Cloud Shell window. Then, press *Enter*:

```
RESOURCEGROUPNAME="training_rg"
LOCATION="eastus"
TOPIC="esales"
EVENTHUB_NAMESPACE="esalesns"
EVENTHUB_NAME="esaleshub"
EVENT_SUBSCRIPTION="esalesevent"
az provider register --namespace Microsoft.EventGrid
az provider show --namespace Microsoft.EventGrid --query
```

```
"registrationState"
```
```
az eventgrid topic create --name $TOPIC -l $LOCATION -g
$RESOURCEGROUPNAME
```

7. Create the Azure event hub and Azure event hub namespace. An Azure hub namespace provides a **DNS**-integrated network endpoint. Finally, you need to subscribe to the event grid topic that we created previously. This tells the event grid which events will be tracked and where to send those events. Copy each of the following commands, line by line, and paste them inside the Cloud Shell window. Then, press *Enter*:

```
az eventhubs namespace create --name $EVENTHUB_NAMESPACE
--resource-group $RESOURCEGROUPNAME
```
```
az eventhubs eventhub create --name $EVENTHUB_NAME
--namespace-name $EVENTHUB_NAMESPACE --resource-group
$RESOURCEGROUPNAME
```
```
sh Data-Engineering-with-Apache-Spark-Delta-Lake-and-
Lakehouse/project/prep/ecommerce/eventhub/eventhub.
sh  -e $EVENTHUB_NAME -n $EVENTHUB_NAMESPACE -r
$RESOURCEGROUPNAME -s $EVENT_SUBSCRIPTION -t $TOPIC
```

If the preceding commands are successful, you can confirm whether the Azure event hub has been created by navigating to the Azure portal.

Navigate to **Home | All Resources | esalesns**, and you'll be redirected to the following:

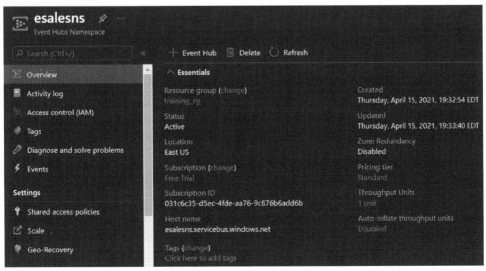

Figure 5.18 – Publishing events to Azure Event Hubs

8. Next, create the data source for the e-commerce website tracking logs and upload a sample website tracking file. Copy each of the following commands, line by line, and paste them inside the Cloud Shell window. Then, press *Enter*:

```
LOGSTORAGEACCOUNTNAME="ecommercetracking"

LOGSCONTAINER="ecommercelogs"

RESOURCEGROUPNAME="training_rg"

LOCATION="eastus"

az storage account create --name $LOGSTORAGEACCOUNTNAME
--resource-group $RESOURCEGROUPNAME --kind StorageV2
--location $LOCATION --sku Standard_LRS --tags owner=data
engineering project=lakehouse environment=development

KEY=`az storage account keys list -g $RESOURCEGROUPNAME
-n $LOGSTORAGEACCOUNTNAME | jq .[0].value`

az storage container create -n $LOGSCONTAINER --account-
name $LOGSTORAGEACCOUNTNAME --account-key $KEY

az storage blob upload --container-name $LOGSCONTAINER
--account-name $LOGSTORAGEACCOUNTNAME --name electroniz_
access_log_1.json --file ~/Data-Engineering-with-Apache-
Spark-Delta-Lake-and-Lakehouse/project/prep/ecommerce_
logs/electroniz_access_log_1.log --account-key $KEY
```

> **Note**
>
> Storage account names in Azure need to be globally unique. If you get a *The storage account named ecommercetracking is already taken* error, you will need to change the account name in the instructions in the next section.

We have now successfully created data sources for the stores database and e-commerce transactions. Now we will create the data destinations using the steps outlined in the next section.

Configuring data destinations

Once the batch and streaming ingestion pipelines have been invoked, they will fetch data from the data sources and dump the results into the data destination. The data destination for the bronze layer is **Azure Data Lake Storage Gen2**:

1. We will now use the Azure client to create an Azure Data Lake Storage account. Copy each of the following commands, line by line, and paste them inside the Cloud Shell window. Then, press *Enter*:

```
STORAGEACCOUNTNAME="traininglakehouse"
RESOURCEGROUPNAME="training_rg"
LOCATION="eastus"
az storage account create --name $STORAGEACCOUNTNAME
--resource-group $RESOURCEGROUPNAME --kind StorageV2
--location $LOCATION  --hns true --sku Standard_
LRS --tags owner=data engineering project=lakehouse
environment=development
```

If the preceding commands are successful, you should see an output that looks like this:

```
Azure> STORAGEACCOUNTNAME="traininglakehouse"
Azure> RESOURCEGROUPNAME="training_rg"
Azure> LOCATION="eastus"
Azure> az storage account create --name $STORAGEACCOUNTNAME --reso
owner=data engineering project=lakehouse environment=development
{| Finished ..
  "accessTier": "Hot",
  "allowBlobPublicAccess": null,
  "allowSharedKeyAccess": null,
  "azureFilesIdentityBasedAuthentication": null,
  "blobRestoreStatus": null,
  "creationTime": "2021-04-15T22:53:56.415458+00:00",
  "customDomain": null,
  "enableHttpsTrafficOnly": true,
  "enableNfsV3": null,
  "encryption": {
    "encryptionIdentity": null,
    "keySource": "Microsoft.Storage",
```

Figure 5.19 – Output of the creation of the Data Lake Storage account

2. You can confirm whether the Azure Data Lake Storage account has been created by going to the Azure portal.

Navigate to **Home | All Resources | traininglakehouse**:

Figure 5.20 – The Azure Data Lake Storage account on the Azure portal

3. Azure Data Lake Storage will store data in blobs. In Azure Data Lake Storage, blobs are organized in a filesystem hierarchy. To enable the hierarchy, we need to create a namespace for the bronze layer. Copy each of the following commands, line by line, and paste them inside the Cloud Shell window. Then, press *Enter*:

```
NAMESPACE="bronze"
```
```
az storage fs create -n $NAMESPACE --account-name
$STORAGEACCOUNTNAME --metadata project=lakehouse
environment=development layer=bronze --only-show-errors
```

If the preceding commands are successful, you should see an output that looks like this:

```
Azure> NAMESPACE="bronze"
Azure> az storage fs create -n $NAMESPACE --account-name $STORA
{
  "client_request_id": "9b6cac78-9e3d-11eb-ba35-0a580af4d008",
  "date": "2021-04-15T22:54:59+00:00",
  "error_code": null,
  "etag": "\"0x8D900617FA8E463\"",
  "last_modified": "2021-04-15T22:55:00+00:00",
  "request_id": "465e9179-f01e-0021-034a-3281de000000",
  "version": "2020-02-10"
}
```

Figure 5.21 – Output of the creation of the Data Lake Storage namespace

At this point, we have successfully prepared the data sources and data destinations for the Electroniz lakehouse's bronze layer. In the next section, we will begin building the ingestion pipeline that will fetch data from the sources and store it in the destinations.

Building the ingestion pipelines

You might recall from previous sections that we decided to create two ingestion pipelines – batch ingestion and streaming ingestion. Each one of these pipelines will be built using a different set of Azure services. For batch ingestion, we will use Azure Data Factory, and for streaming ingestion, we will use Azure Event Hubs Capture. So, let's get going, as we still have a long way to go.

Building a batch ingestion pipeline

Before proceeding with the actual creation of the batch pipeline, let me remind you of a key requirement of the Electroniz lakehouse. Previously, Electroniz stated that the transactions within the sales database and online store happen very frequently throughout the day. They wanted the lakehouse to be kept up to date with the newly created data with a maximum delay of 1 hour.

To satisfy this requirement, we will need to structure the pipeline using the **watermark** approach. Simply put, a watermark is a column that can be used to identify the last point until which data was ingested in the previous ingestion run. Typically, the choice of the watermark column is between an incremented key column or a timestamp column:

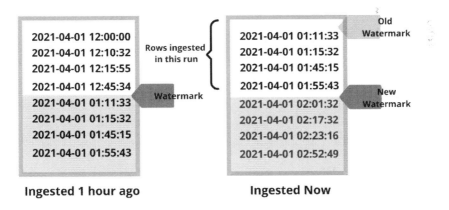

Figure 5.22 – Watermark updates at every ingestion run

The batch pipeline will need to be created in such a way that it can load changed data between an old watermark and a new watermark. At every ingestion run, a new watermark will be created that will be used as the **marker** for the next run:

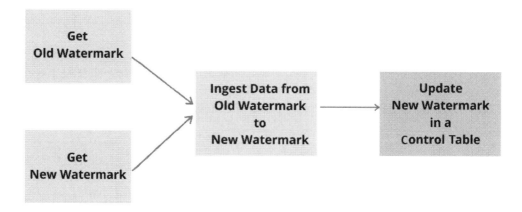

Figure 5.23 – The watermark approach for incremental data ingestion

With the incremental ingestion approach in mind, let's start building the batch ingestion pipeline:

1. We will start with the creation of the **Azure data factory**. Browse to **Home** on the Azure portal. Using the search box at the top of the screen, search for data factories. Click on **Data factories** underneath **Services**:

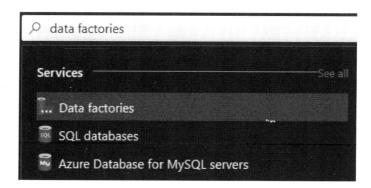

Figure 5.24 – Searching for the Data Factory service on the Azure portal

2. Click on the **Create data factory** button and input the following:

    *   Resource group: **training_rg**
    *   Region: **East US**

- Name: `traininglakehousedf`
- Version: **V2**

Then, click on **Next: Git configuration**:

- Configure Git later: **Checked**
- Click on **Review + create**. You should get a **Validation passed** message.

    Finally, click on **Create**. Once the deployment is complete, click on **Go to resource**:

Figure 5.25 – The Data Factory service on the Azure portal

3. During the creation of the pipeline, one of the steps will require you to connect to a REST API that will download currency conversion data from the internet. To do this, we will use a free service. You can source the API from `https://free.currencyconverterapi.com/`. Choose the **Get Your Free API** button. Once you receive an email, replace the value of **XXXXXXXXXXX** in **API_KEY** with it.

    Additionally, we will also store the Azure Data Lake account key in the **secrets manager** of **Azure Key Vault**. Invoke the following commands on Azure Cloud Shell. Make sure you replace the value of `ADLS_KEY` with the value of **key1** that was fetched previously:

```
RESOURCEGROUPNAME="training_rg"
LOCATION="eastus"
KEYVAULTNAME="trainingkv100"
ADLS_SECRETNAME="ADLSKEY"
```

```
ADLS_KEY="XXXXXXXXXXXXXXXXXXXXXXXXXXXXXXXXX"

API_SECRETNAME="CURRAPIKEY"

API_KEY="XXXXXXXXXXXXXXXXXXXXXXXXXXXXXXXXX"

az config set extension.use_dynamic_install=yes_without_
prompt

az keyvault create --location $LOCATION --name
$KEYVAULTNAME --resource-group $RESOURCEGROUPNAME

az keyvault secret set --name $ADLS_SECRETNAME --vault-
name $KEYVAULTNAME --value $ADLS_KEY

az keyvault secret set --name $API_SECRETNAME --vault-
name $KEYVAULTNAME --value $API_KEY
```

This results in the following output:

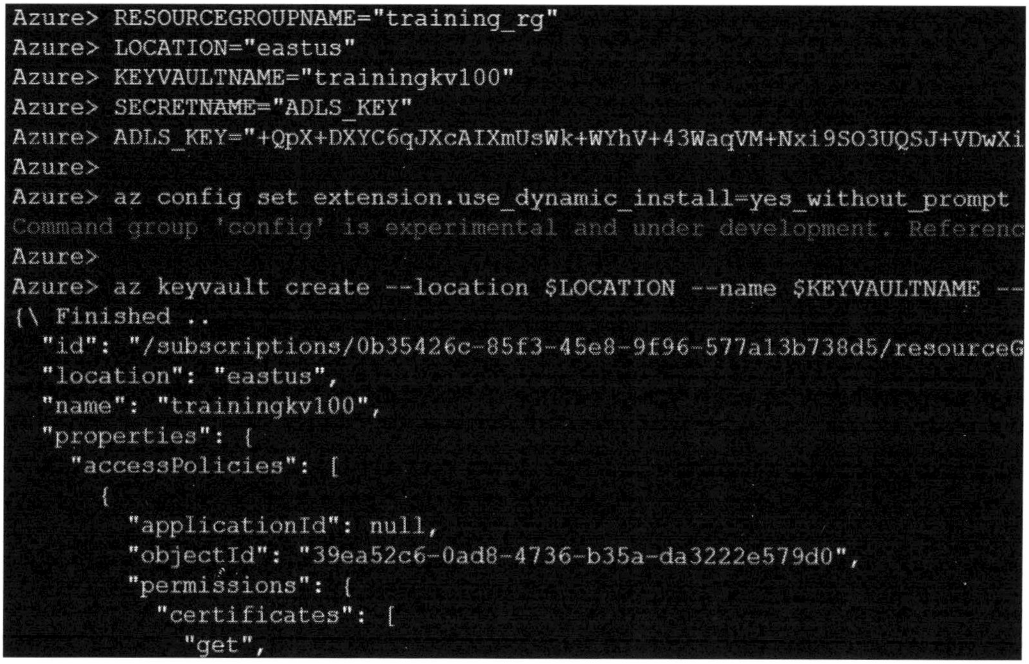

```
Azure> RESOURCEGROUPNAME="training_rg"
Azure> LOCATION="eastus"
Azure> KEYVAULTNAME="trainingkv100"
Azure> SECRETNAME="ADLS_KEY"
Azure> ADLS_KEY="+QpX+DXYC6qJXcAIXmUsWk+WYhV+43WaqVM+Nxi9SO3UQSJ+VDwXi
Azure>
Azure> az config set extension.use_dynamic_install=yes_without_prompt
Command group 'config' is experimental and under development. Referenc
Azure>
Azure> az keyvault create --location $LOCATION --name $KEYVAULTNAME --
{\ Finished ..
  "id": "/subscriptions/0b35426c-85f3-45e8-9f96-577a13b738d5/resourceG
  "location": "eastus",
  "name": "trainingkv100",
  "properties": {
    "accessPolicies": [
      {
        "applicationId": null,
        "objectId": "39ea52c6-0ad8-4736-b35a-da3222e579d0",
        "permissions": {
          "certificates": [
            "get",
```

Figure 5.26 – Azure Key Vault creation

4. To validate the creation of the Azure key vault, navigate to the Azure portal.

    Navigate to **Home | All Resources | trainingkv100**.

    Then, click on **Secrets | ADLSKEY**. Now click on the entry underneath **CURRENT VERSION**.

Click on **Show Secret Value** and validate that it shows the Azure Data Lake Storage key:

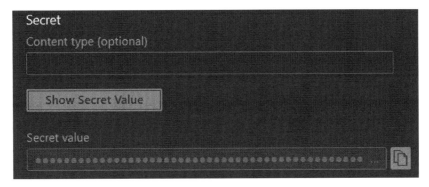

Figure 5.27 – Creating a new secret in Azure Key Vault

Note down the value of the **secret identifier**. You will need this later.

5. Finally, we want to provide Azure Data Factory access to read the secrets.

    Navigate to **Home | All Resources | trainingkv100 | Access Policies**.

    Then, click on **Add Access Policy**.

    For Key permissions, choose **Get** and **List**.

    For Secret permissions, choose **Get** and **List**.

    For Select Principal, click on **None Selected**. For **Principal,** find the name of your Azure data factory created earlier:

Figure 5.28 – Choose a principal for access to a new secret

Click on **Select**. Then, click on **Add**. Finally, click on **Save**:

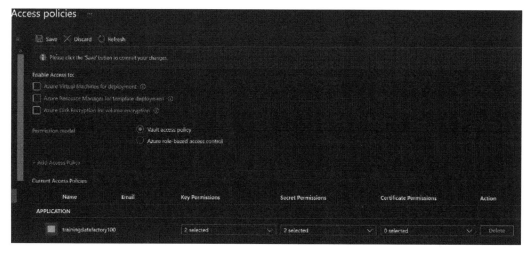

Figure 5.29 – Providing access to new secret for the data factory

6. It is time to build the ingestion pipeline. Click on **Open** underneath the **Open Azure Data Factory Studio** section. In some cases, you might get the following window. If so, click on **Continue**:

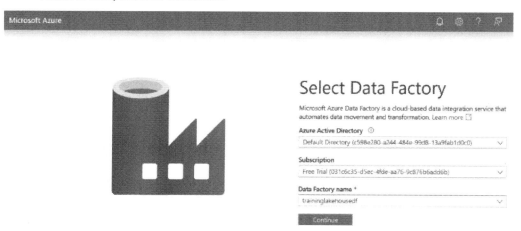

Figure 5.30 – The Select Data Factory screen

7. Using the panel on the left-hand side, click on **Manage**. We will start by creating the source- and destination-linked services.

8. To create the source-linked service, click on **Create linked service**. In the **New linked service** window, choose the icon for **Azure SQL Database**. Then, click on **Continue**. A new window will open with the title of **New linked service (Azure SQL Database)**:

- Name: `salesdbsource`

- Account selection method: **From Azure subscription**

- Azure subscription: **Free Tier or Paid Subscription**

- Server name: `salesdb100`

- Database name: `salesdb`

- Authentication type: **SQL authentication**

- Username: `salesadmin`

- Password: **<PASSWORD SET PREVIOUSLY>**

Finally, click on **Test connection**. If the connection is successful, click on **Create**:

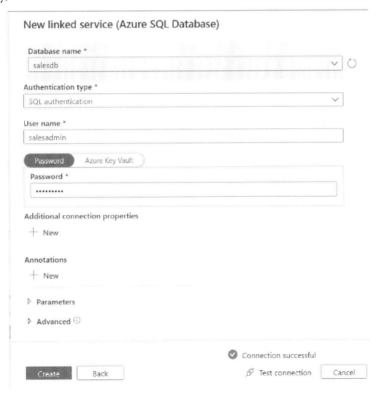

Figure 5.31 – The Data Factory-linked service options for Azure SQL

9. To create the destination-linked service, click on **New**. In the **New linked service** window, choose the icon for **Azure Data Lake Storage Gen2**. Then, click on **Continue**. A new window will open with the title of **New linked service (Azure Data Lake Storage Gen2)**:

*   Name: `traininglakehouse`

*   Account selection method: **From Azure subscription**

*   Azure subscription: **Free Tier or Paid Subscription**

*   Storage account name: **traininglakehouse**

Finally, click on **Test connection**. If the connection is successful, click on **Create**:

New linked service (Azure Data Lake Storage Gen2)

Connect via integration runtime * ⓘ

AutoResolveIntegrationRuntime	⌄

Authentication method

Account key	⌄

Account selection method ⓘ

(●) From Azure subscription   ( ) Enter manually

Azure subscription ⓘ

Free Trial (031c6c35-d5ec-4fde-aa76-9c876b6add6b)	⌄

Storage account name *

traininglakehouse	⌄	↻

Test connection ⓘ

(●) To linked service   ( ) To file path

Annotations

+ New

▷ Parameters

⊘ Connection successful

| Create | Back | 🖉 Test connection | Cancel |

Figure 5.32 – The Data Factory-linked service options for Azure Data Lake Storage

10. The two linked services are now ready for use. They should appear in the Azure portal as follows:

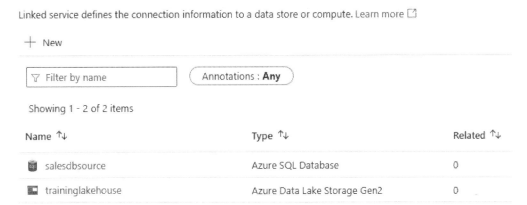

Figure 5.33 – Confirmation regarding the creation of the two linked services

11. Using the panel on the left-hand side, from the menu, click on **Author**. From the **Factory resources** panel, click on the **three dots** on the right-hand side of **Pipelines** and choose **New pipeline**.

    In the **Properties** panel, input the following:

    - Name: `electroniz_batch_ingestion_pipeline`

    - Description: `This pipeline will ingest data from sales database, currency conversion, geo-location, and ecommerce website tracking`

12. In the **Activities** panel, search for **Web**. Now, drag the **Web** activity to the panel on the right-hand side:

    - Name: `Get Secret`.

    - Click on **Settings**.

    - For the URL, enter the **secret identifier** from the Azure Key Vault secret that we created previously. You can find this by navigating to **Home | trainingkv100 | CURRAPIKEY**.

    - Add `?api-version=7.0` to the end of the URL, as follows: `https://trainingkv100.vault.azure.net/secrets/CURRAPIKEY/f167b5eb b4f440ca93421610dbe731aa?api-version=7.0`.

- Authentication: **Managed Identity**.
- Resource: `https://vault.azure.net:`

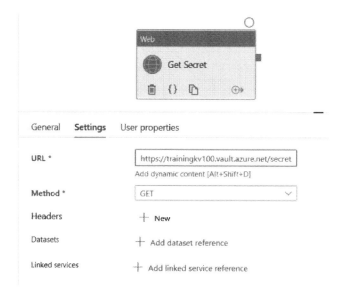

Figure 5.34 – Creating a Get Secret activity in electroniz_ingestion_pipeline

13. We will now create the activities for downloading **Geo-location** data.

On the pane on the left-hand side, click on **Manage**.

Now, click on **New**.

From the **New linked service** pane, click on **File**. Then, click on **HTTP**.

Click on **Continue**. Input the following:

- Name: `httpsource`
- Base URL: `https://raw.githubusercontent.com/`
  `PacktPublishing/Data-Engineering-with-Apache-Spark-`
  `Delta-Lake-and-Lakehouse/main/project/prep/iplocation/`
  `IP2LOCATION-LITE-DB1.CSV`
- Authentication type: **Anonymous**

Click on **Test connection**. If the **Connection successful** message has been received, click on **Create**:

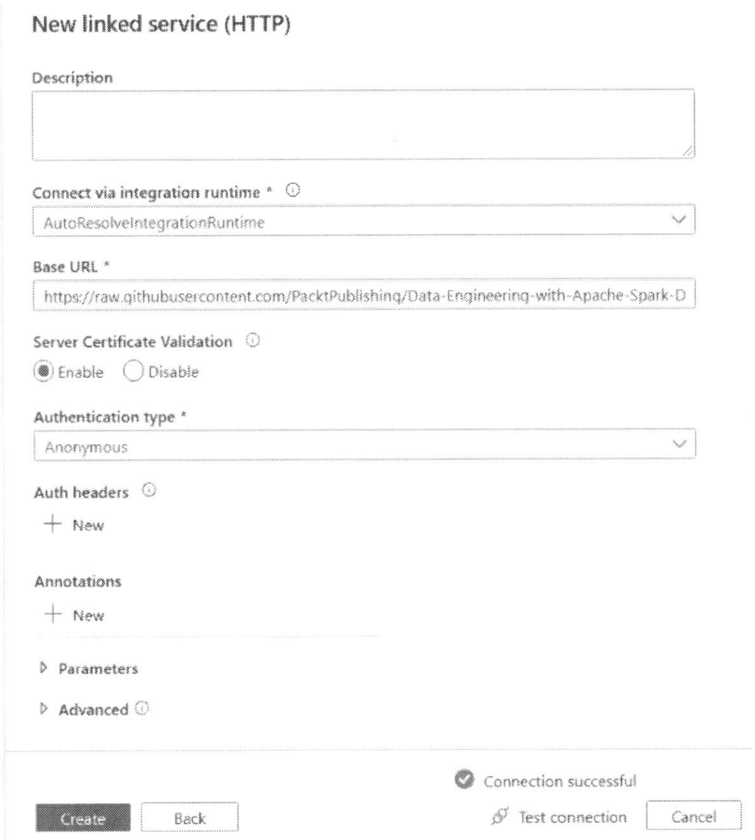

Figure 5.35 – New linked service for geo-location data

In the **Activities** pane, search for **Copy data**.

Drag the copy data activity to the pane on the right-hand side. Input the following:

- Name: `Get Geo-location Mapping`

Click on **Source**. For the source dataset, click on **New**. Inside the **New dataset** pane, click on **File**. Now click on **HTTP**.

Click on **Continue**. Then, click on **DelimitedText**. Input the following:

- Name: `GeoDelimitedTextSource`
- Linked service: **httpsource**

Click on **OK**. Then, click on **Sink**.

For the **Sink** dataset, click on **New**.

In the new dataset pane, click on **Azure data Lake storage Gen 2**.

Click on **Continue**. Then, click on **DelimitedText**. Input the following:

- Name: `GeoDelimitedTextSync`

- Linked service: **traininglakehouse**

- File path: `bronze`

Click on **OK**. Then, click on **Open** next to the **Sink** dataset. Input the following:

- Directory: `geolocation/@{formatDateTime(utcnow(),'yyyy')}/@{formatDateTime(utcnow(),'MM')}/@{formatDateTime(utcnow(),'dd')}/@{formatDateTime(utcnow(),'HH')}`

Using the tabs, click on the **electroniz_batch_ingestion_pipeline** tab. Chain the two activities together by dragging the arrow from **Get Secret** to **Get Geo-location Mapping**.

14. Now click on **Publish all** from the top menu followed by the **Publish** button.

    Once published, the pipeline should look like this:

Figure 5.36 – The geo-location pipeline

15. Now, let's move on to the activities for downloading **store sales** data.

    In the **Activities** panel, search for **Lookup**. Now, drag the **Lookup** activity to the panel on the right-hand side. Select the following:

- Name: **Find SalesDB Tables**

- Click on **Settings**.

    In **Source** dataset, click on **New**. In the **New dataset** panel, click on **Azure SQL Database**. Click on **Continue**. In the **Set properties** panel, enter the following details:

- Name: `salesdbds`

- Linked service: **salesdbsource**

Click on **OK**. You should now be back in the **Settings** tab of **Find SalesDB Tables**. Input the following:

- Use query: **Choose Query**

- Query: `SELECT QUOTENAME(table_schema)+'.'+QUOTENAME(table_name) AS Table_Name FROM information_Schema.tables WHERE table_name not in ('watermarktable', 'database_firewall_rules')`

Notice that the preceding dynamic select statement generates a list of tables that will be ingested inside the lakehouse. If you want to exclude some tables from the list, you can use the **NOT IN** clause.

For the first row only, uncheck the boxes.

16. From the top menu, click on **Publish all**. You should have two changes that are ready to be published. Click on **Publish**:

Publish all

You are about to publish all pending changes to the live environment. Learn more [

Pending changes (2)

NAME	CHANGE	EXISTING
▲ Pipelines		
▥ electroniz_batch_ingestion... (Edited)		electroniz_batch_ingestion_pipeline
▲ Datasets		
⊞ salesdbds	(New)	-

Figure 5.37 – The Publish all screen for the batch ingestion pipeline

17. In the **Activities** panel, search for **ForEach**. Now, drag the **ForEach** activity to the panel on the right-hand side.

The **ForEach** activity will loop through the list of tables supplied by the **Find SalesDB Tables** activity. For each iteration, it will perform the following operations:

Look up the old watermark and set the new watermark, ingest the table from the old watermark to the new watermark, and finally, update the watermark in the control table.

- Name: **For Each Table**

Click on **Settings**. Input the following:

- Items: `@activity('Find SalesDB Tables').output.value`

Notice the use of **@activity**. At runtime, each activity returns a general response JSON with items such as `output` and `status`. You can read the response of the items using the preceding convention. In the preceding example, we are reading the output of the **Find SalesDB Tables** activity. This will output the list of tables, which, in turn, is the output from the preceding SQL.

Chain both activities together by dragging the arrow from **Find SalesDB Tables** to **For Each Table**. Chaining ensures that the output of the previous activity becomes the input of the next activity:

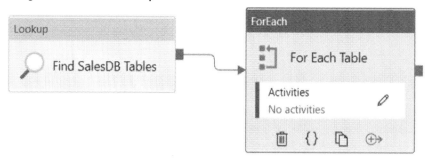

Figure 5.38 – Chaining the two sales activities together

18. Click on the **pencil** icon in the **Activities** section of **For Each Table**.

In the **Activities** panel, search for **Lookup**. Now, drag the **Lookup** activity to the panel on the right-hand side.

Name: `Lookup Old Watermark`

Click on **Settings**.

For the **Source** dataset, choose **salesdbds**.

Use Query: **Query**

Query: `SELECT * FROM [dbo].[watermarktable] AS WatermarkValue WHERE table_name='@{item().Table_Name}'`

Notice that the dynamic select statement selects the old watermark of the table being ingested from the previous iteration of the ingestion run.

In the **Activities** panel, search for **Lookup**. Now, drag the **Lookup** activity to the panel on the right-hand side.

Name: `Lookup New Watermark`

Click on **Settings**.

For the **Source** dataset, choose **salesdbds**.

Use Query: **Query**

Query: `SELECT MAX(updated_at) as NewWatermarkvalue FROM @{item().Table_Name}`

Notice that the dynamic creates a new watermark of the table being ingested.

19. In the **Activities** panel, search for **Copy data**. Now, drag the **Copy data** activity to the panel on the right-hand side.

    Name: `Copy Table Data`

    Click on **Source**.

    For the **Source** dataset, choose **salesdbds**.

    Use query: **Query**

    Query: `SELECT * FROM @{item().Table_Name} WHERE updated_at > '@{activity('Lookup Old Watermark').output.firstRow.watermark_value}'`

    Notice this SQL is selecting records that are greater than the old watermark of the table being ingested. We have chosen **updated_at** as the watermark column.

    Click on **Sink**.

    A sink is a destination to which the output of the preceding SQL will be stored.

    In the **Sink** dataset, click on **New**. Then, click on **Azure Data Lake Storage Gen 2**. Finally, click on **Continue**.

    In Select Format, click on **DelimitedText**. Then, click on **Continue**.

    In the **Set properties** pane, input the following:

    Name: `SalesDelimitedText`

    Linked service: **traininglakehouse**

    In **File path**, input the following:

    Filesystem: `bronze`

    Click on **OK**. Next to the **Sink** dataset, click on **Open**.

Directory: `sales/@{activity('Lookup Old Watermark').output.firstRow.table_name}/@{formatDateTime(utcnow(),'yyyy')}/@{formatDateTime(utcnow(),'MM')}/@{formatDateTime(utcnow(),'dd')}/@{formatDateTime(utcnow(),'HH')}`

Notice that we are storing the output in a date and hour folder, as follows:

File: `@concat(dataset().FileTime,'.',dataset().FileExt)`

Click on **Parameters**. Then, add the following parameters:

Name: `FileExt`   Type: `String`   Value: `csv`

Name: `FileTime`   Type: `String`   Value: `@pipeline().TriggerTime`

20. Using tabs, click on the **electroniz_batch_ingestion_pipeline** tab. Chain the three activities together.

    You can do this by dragging the arrow from **Lookup Old Watermark** to **Copy Table Data** and dragging the arrow from **Lookup New Watermark** to **Copy Table Data**.

21. In the **Activities** panel, search for **Stored procedure**. Now, drag the **Stored procedure** activity to the panel on the right-hand side.

    Name: `Update Watermark`

    Click on **Settings**. Input the following:

    Linked Service: **salesdbsource**

    Stored procedure name: `[dbo].[usp_write_watermark]`

    Underneath the **Stored procedure** parameters, add two parameters. Then, click on **New**. Input the following:

    Name: `LastModifiedtime`   Type: `Datetime`

    Value: `@{activity('Lookup New Watermark').output.firstRow.NewWatermarkvalue}`

    Name: `TableName`   Type: `String`

    Value: `@{activity('Lookup Old Watermark').output.firstRow.table_name}`:

General   **Settings**   User properties

Linked service * ⓘ   ▣ salesdbsource   ∨   ✐ Test connection   ✐ Edit   ＋ New

Stored procedure name *   [dbo].[usp_write_watermark]   ∨   ◌ Refresh
                           ☐ Edit ⓘ

▲ Stored procedure parameters ⓘ

←⊣ Import   ＋ New   🗑 Delete

☐	Name	Type	Value	
☐	LastModifiedtime	Datetime ∨	@{activity('Lookup New Watermark').out...	☐ Treat as null
			Add dynamic content [Alt+P]	
☐	TableName	String ∨	@{activity('Lookup Old Watermark').out...	☐ Treat as null

Figure 5.39 – The parameters for the stored procedure

Now chain **Copy Table Data** to **Update Watermark**.

22. Using the top menu, click on **Publish all**. Then, click on **Publish**.

    Once published, the pipeline should look like this:

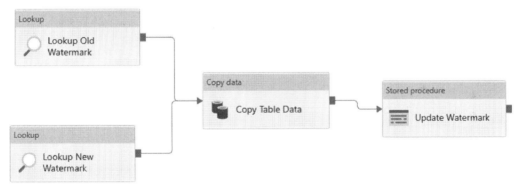

Figure 5.40 – The pipeline for the sales database incremental ingestion

23. We have completed the incremental ingestion pipeline for the sales database. The
    pipeline should now look like this:

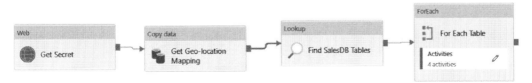

Figure 5.41 – The pipeline for the store sales ingestion

24. We have completed the ingestion of the **store sales** data. Let's move on to the next data source on our list, that is, **currency conversion**. Start by creating a linked service for the currency conversion data.

On the pane on the left-hand side, click on **Manage**.

Next, click on **New**.

From the **New linked service** pane, click on **Generic Protocol**. Now click on **REST**.

Click on **Continue**. Input the following:

Name: `restsource`

Base URL: `https://free.currconv.com/api/v7/convert?`

Authentication type: **Anonymous**

Click on **Test connection**. If the **Connection successful** message is received, click on **Create**:

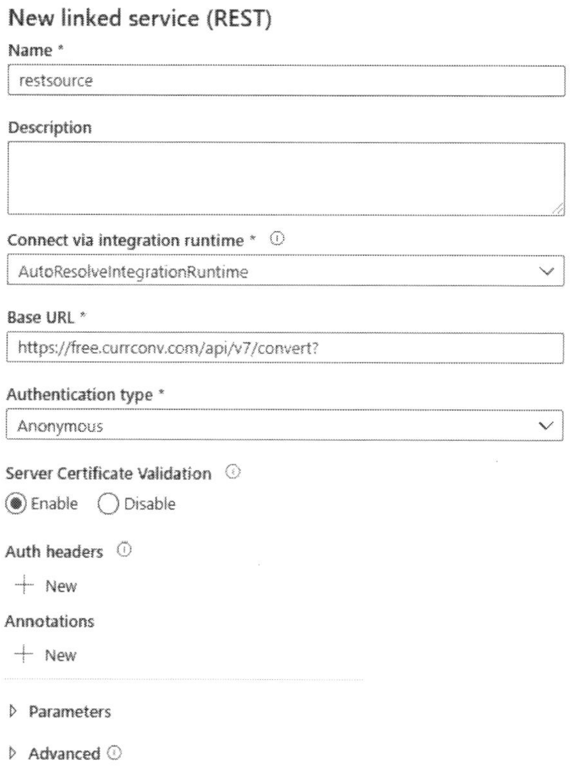

Figure 5.42 – New linked service for currency conversion data

25. Now click on **Publish all** in the top menu followed by the **Publish** button.

26. Using the pane on the left-hand side, click on **Author**. Click on the previously created pipeline, **electroniz_batch_ingestion_pipeline**, underneath **Pipelines**. You should now be at the level of **Find SalesDB Tables**.

In the **Activities** panel, search for **Lookup**. Now drag the **Lookup** activity to the panel on the right-hand side.

Name: `Find Currencies`

Click on **Settings**.

For the **Source** dataset, choose **salesdbds**.

Use Query: **Query**

Query: `SELECT DISTINCT currency FROM [dbo].[store_orders] WHERE currency <> 'USD'`

In the first row only, select the **Uncheck** boxes.

In the **Activities** panel, search for **ForEach**. Now drag the **ForEach** activity to the right-hand side panel.

The **ForEach** activity will loop through the list of tables supplied by the **Find Currencies** activity. For each iteration, it will perform the following operations:

Name: `For Each Currency`

Click on **Settings**.

Items: `@activity('Find Currencies').output.value`

Chain both activities together by dragging the arrow from **Find Currencies** to **For Each Currency**. Chaining ensures that the output of the previous activity becomes the input of the next activity:

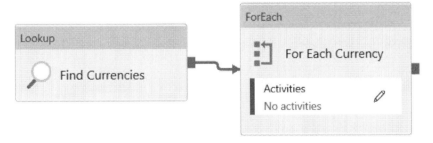

Figure 5.43 – Chaining two currency activities together

27. Click on the **pencil** icon in the **Activities** section of **For Each Currency**.

    In the **Activities** panel, search for **Copy data**. Now, drag the **Copy data** activity to the panel on the right-hand side.

    Name: `Get Currency Value`

    Click on **Source**. Click on **New**. In the **New dataset** panel, click on **Generic Protocol**.

    Click on **REST**. Then, click on **Continue**. Next to the **Source** dataset, click on **Open**.

    In **Connection**, input the following:

    Linked service: **restsource**

    Relative URL: `convert?q=USD_@{item().`
    `Currency}&compact=ultra&apiKey=XXXXXXXXXXX`

    Click on the previously created pipeline, **electroniz_batch_ingestion_pipeline**, under **Pipelines**. Click on **Sink**.

    In the **Sink** dataset, click on **New**. Then, click on **Azure Data Lake Storage Gen 2**. Finally, click on **Continue**.

    In **Select Format**, click on **DelimitedText**. Then, click on **Continue**.

    In the **Set properties** pane, input the following:

    Name: `CurrencyDelimitedText`

    Linked service: **traininglakehouse**

    In **File path**, input the following:

    Filesystem: `bronze`

    Click on **OK**. Next to the **Sink** dataset, click on **Open**.

    Directory: `currency/@{item().Currency}/@`
    `{formatDateTime(utcnow(),'yyyy')}/@`
    `{formatDateTime(utcnow(),'MM')}/@`
    `{formatDateTime(utcnow(),'dd')}/@`
    `{formatDateTime(utcnow(),'HH')}`

    Notice that we are storing the output in a date and hour folder.

28. Click on the previously created pipeline, **electroniz_batch_ingestion_pipeline**, underneath **Pipelines**. You should now be at the level of **Find Currencies**.

Chain the activities together by dragging the arrow from **For Each Table** to **Find Currencies**.

Now, click on **Publish all** from the top menu followed by the **Publish** button.

Once published, the pipeline should look like this:

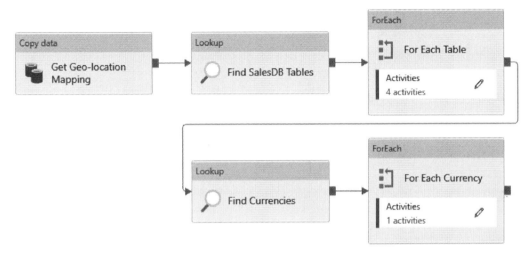

Figure 5.44 – The Electroniz batch ingestion pipeline with currency data

29. The last data source to go now is **ecommerce website tracking**. To create the e-commerce website tracking source linked service, perform the following steps:

On the left-hand side pane, click on **Manage**.

Now, click on **New**.

In the new linked service pane, click on **Azure Blob Storage**. Now, click on **Continue**:

Name: `websitetrackinglogs`

Account selection method: **From Azure susbscription**

Azure subscription: **Free Tier or Paid Subscription**

Storage account name: **ecommercetracking**

Finally, click on **Test connection**. If the connection is successful, click on **Create**.

30. Using the pane on the left-hand side, click on **Author**. Click on the previously created pipeline, **electroniz_batch_ingestion_pipeline**, underneath **Pipelines**. You should now be at the level of **Find SalesDB Tables**.

In the **Activities** panel, search for **Copy data**. Now, drag the **Copy data** activity to the panel on the right-hand side:

Name: `Copy Website Tracking Data`

Click on **Source**.

In the **Source** dataset, click on **New**. Then, click on **Azure Blob Storage**. Finally, click on **Continue**.

Select **Format**. Click on **JSON**. Then, click on **Continue**.

In the **Set properties** pane, input the following:

Name: `TrackingJSON`

Linked service: **websitetrackinglogs**

File path: `ecommercelogs`

Click on **OK**. Go back to the **Copy Website Tracking Data** activity.

For **File path type**, carry out the following:

Choose **Prefix**.

Prefix: `electroniz_access`

Click on **Sink**.

In the **Sink** dataset, click on **New**. Then, click on **Azure Data Lake Storage Gen 2**. Finally, click on **Continue**.

Select **Format** and click on **JSON**. Then, click on **Continue**.

In the **Set properties** pane, input the following:

Name: `TrackingJSONSync`

Linked service: **traininglakehouse**

In **File path**, input the following:

Filesystem: `bronze`

Click on **OK**. Next to the **Sink** dataset, click on **Open**.

Select the following directory: `logs/@{formatDateTime(utcnow(),'yyyy')}/@{formatDateTime(utcnow(),'MM')}/@{formatDateTime(utcnow(),'dd')}/@{formatDateTime(utcnow(),'HH')}`

31. Click on the previously created pipeline, **electroniz_batch_ingestion_pipeline**, under **Pipelines**. Chain the activities together by dragging the arrow from **For Each Currency** to **Copy Website Tracking Data**. Additionally, drag the arrow from **Copy website tracking data** to **Delete Website Tracking Logs**.

Finally, we want to clean up the e-commerce website tracking logs that have been successfully ingested. In the **Activities** panel, search for **Delete**. Now, drag the **Delete** activity to the right-hand side panel:

Name: `Delete Website Tracking Logs`

Click on **Source**:

Dataset: **TrackingJSON**

File path type: **File path in dataset**

In the logging settings, in Enable logging, select **Unchecked**.

32. Now click on **Publish all** from the top menu followed by the **Publish** button.

Once published, the pipeline should now look like this:

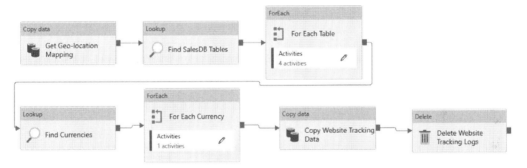

Figure 5.45 – The final Electroniz batch ingestion pipeline

All done! It is time to check whether the newly created **electroniz_batch_ingestion_ pipeline** pipeline works. Proceed with the next steps to unit test the pipeline.

Testing the ingestion pipelines

We will now test the **electroniz_batch_ingestion_pipeline** pipeline. You might recall that Electroniz wanted to have a maximum lag of 1 hour between their sales database and the lakehouse. In the future, we will configure a trigger that will run the **electroniz_batch_ ingestion_pipeline** pipeline every hour. For now, we will invoke this pipeline manually a few times to test the outcome.

Testing the batch ingestion pipeline for historical data

Perform the following steps:

1. To invoke the pipeline, invoke the following commands on the Azure Cloud Shell:

```
PIPELINENAME="electroniz_batch_ingestion_pipeline"
DATAFACTORYNAME="trainingdatafactory100"
RESOURCEGROUPNAME="training_rg"
az datafactory pipeline create-run --factory-name
$DATAFACTORYNAME --name $PIPELINENAME --resource-group
$RESOURCEGROUPNAME
```

2. Now click on **Pipeline runs**. After some time, the **Status** will change to **Succeeded**. This indicates a successful run:

Figure 5.46 – The status of the Electroniz batch ingestion pipeline on completion

3. Underneath **Pipeline name**, click on the **electroniz_batch_ingestion_pipeline** pipeline. Notice that each activity has succeeded. If you place your cursor over the activity name, you will be able to see that there is an input and output log for each activity. Spend as much time as you can familiarizing yourself with these outputs. If the pipeline runs into an error, it will be reported underneath the **Error** column:

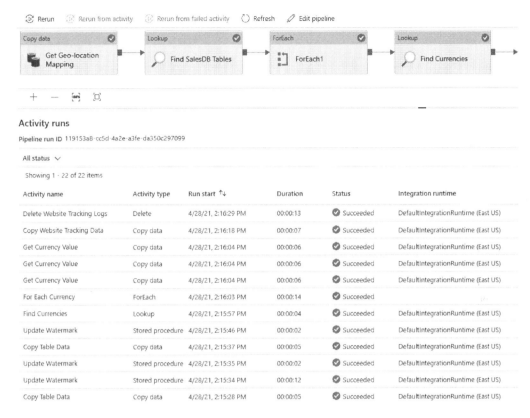

Figure 5.47 – The Electroniz batch ingestion pipeline run details

> **Important**
>
> From an operational aspect, a data engineer should be very familiar with
> pipeline logging mechanisms. Due to several reasons, you should expect
> your pipeline will fail one day in production, and that day, your debugging
> techniques will come to your rescue.

4. Let's validate whether the data has been correctly ingested. In the Azure portal, navigate to **Home | All resources | traininglakehouse**.

   Click on **Containers | Bronze**. You should expect to see four folders as follows:

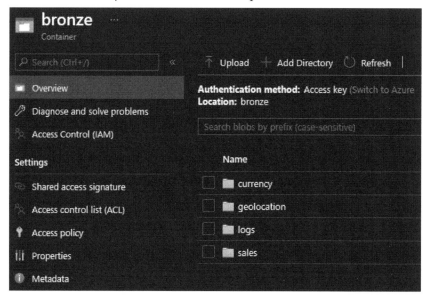

Figure 5.48 – The data ingested using the Electroniz batch pipeline

5. Spend some time clicking through the preceding folders, and verify whether the data looks as expected.

   Since you will be running this on different data compared to when this pipeline was run, the dates and hours of the various folders might not exactly match the following screenshot:

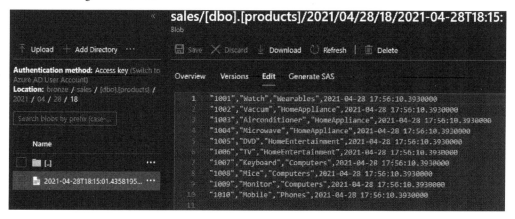

Figure 5.49 – Delimited data for the sales.product table as ingested by the Electroniz batch pipeline

From the looks of things, the **electroniz_batch_ingestion_pipeline** pipeline worked as expected for the first run.

Testing the batch ingestion pipeline for incremental data

We will now check how the pipeline reacts to incremental data inside the stores database. To do that, we will emulate changes to the database, including inserts, updates, and deletes. Following this, we will retrigger **electroniz_batch_ingestion_pipeline** three more times and validate that the newly added data has made its way through to the lakehouse.

The second run of the pipeline – inserts

Currently, the first hour after the initial ingestion is taking place. We are going to assume that, at this time, the sales database is fully operational and new customers and orders are being inserted. To emulate the insert activity, let's insert some data into the sales database:

1. Return to the Azure SQL database and check the latest watermarks.

    Navigate to **Home | All Resources | salesdb | Query Editor**. Run the following query:

    ```
    SELECT TOP (1000) * FROM [dbo].[watermarktable]
    ```

    Notice the watermark value for each table. This timestamp represents the last time data was ingested by **electroniz_batch_ingestion_pipeline**:

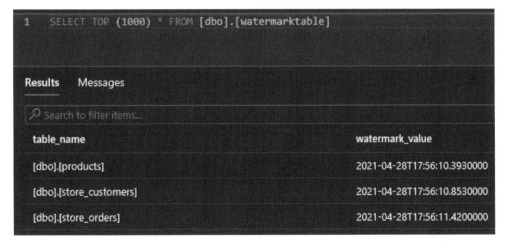

Figure 5.50 – The watermark values after the first run of the batch ingestion pipeline

2. Copy the contents of the following file in the training Git repository:
    `https://raw.githubusercontent.com/PacktPublishing/Data-Engineering-with-Apache-Spark-Delta-Lake-and-Lakehouse/main/project/prep/stores/sql/incremental/1/storedb_incremental_1.sql`.

    Paste the contents into the **Query Editor** window. Select **Run**. This will **insert** 100 new rows in the **store_customers** table and 200 rows in the **store_orders** table:

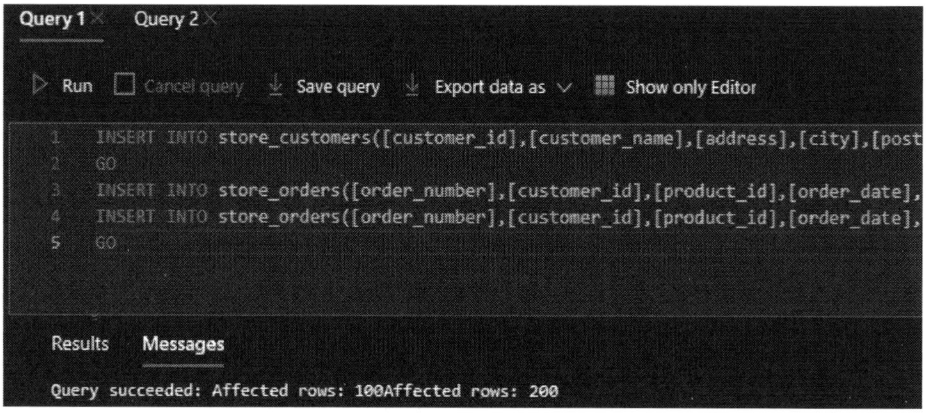

Figure 5.51 – Inserting new data into the stores_customers and stores_orders tables

3. Additionally, we have received a new website tracking log that needs to be ingested. Copy each of the following commands, line by line, and paste them into the Cloud Shell window. Then, press *Enter*:

```
LOGSTORAGEACCOUNTNAME="ecommercetracking"

LOGSCONTAINER="ecommercelogs"

RESOURCEGROUPNAME="training_rg"

LOCATION="eastus"

KEY=`az storage account keys list -g $RESOURCEGROUPNAME -n $LOGSTORAGEACCOUNTNAME | jq .[0].value`

az storage container create -n $LOGSCONTAINER --account-name $LOGSTORAGEACCOUNTNAME --account-key $KEY

az storage blob upload --container-name $LOGSCONTAINER --account-name $LOGSTORAGEACCOUNTNAME --name electroniz_access_log_2.json --file ~/Data-Engineering-with-Apache-Spark-Delta-Lake-and-Lakehouse/project/prep/ecommerce_logs/electroniz_access_log_2.log --account-key $KEY
```

4. Go back to Azure Data Factory and wait until the current hour expires. In the next iteration, the pipeline will only pull incremental data from the sales database. When the next hour arrives, rerun the pipeline using the following command:

```
PIPELINENAME="electroniz_batch_ingestion_pipeline"
DATAFACTORYNAME="trainingdatafactory100"
RESOURCEGROUPNAME="training_rg"
az datafactory pipeline create-run --factory-name
$DATAFACTORYNAME --name $PIPELINENAME --resource-group
$RESOURCEGROUPNAME
```

5. Now, click on **Pipeline runs**. After some time, **Status** will change to **Succeeded**. This indicates a successful run:

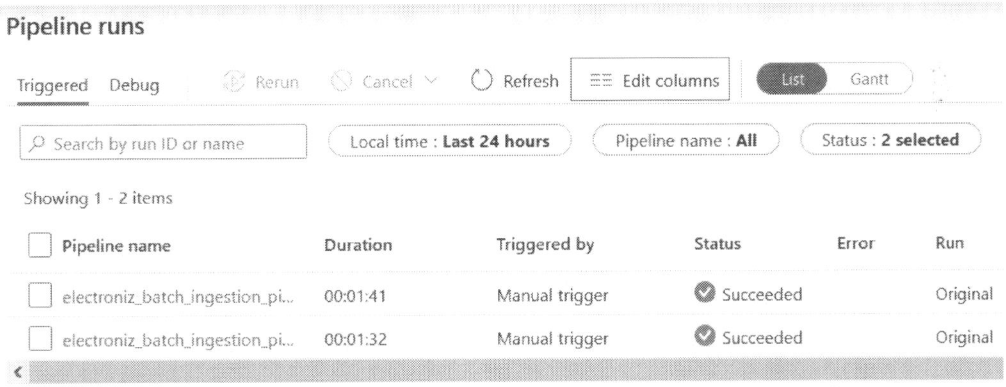

Figure 5.52 – The status of the Electroniz batch ingestion pipeline for the second iteration

6. From the preceding screenshot, it looks like the pipeline has been successfully completed for the second iteration. Let's check whether the watermark was updated. Run the following watermark query one more time:

```
SELECT TOP (1000) * FROM [dbo].[watermarktable]
```

Notice that the watermark value for the **store_customers** and **store_orders** tables have been updated:

table_name	watermark_value
[dbo].[products]	2021-04-28T17:56:10.3930000
[dbo].[store_customers]	2021-04-28T18:25:40.9270000
[dbo].[store_orders]	2021-04-28T18:25:41.1300000

Figure 5.53 – The edited watermark values after the second run of the batch ingestion pipeline

7. Let's validate whether the incremental data was correctly ingested. From the Azure portal, navigate to **Home | All resources | traininglakehouse**.

    Then, navigate to **Containers | Bronze | sales**. Browse to the newly created folder from the last hour.

    You should expect a new hour folder in the **[dbo].[store_customers]** and **[dbo].[store_orders]** folders as follows:

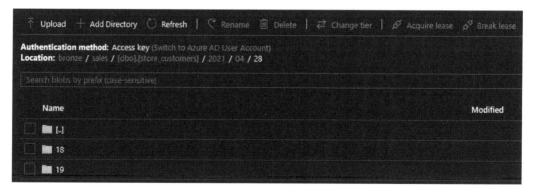

Figure 5.54 – New hourly folder for the second iteration

8. Click on the new hour folder. It should contain a new file that has 100 rows for the **store_customers** table and 200 rows in the **store_orders** table:

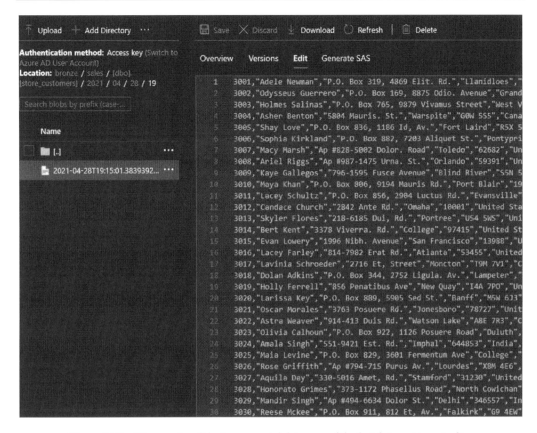

Figure 5.55 – The results of the incremental data run of the batch ingestion pipeline

The third run of the pipeline – updates

Currently, the second hour after the initial ingestion is taking place. Once again, we are going to assume that, at this time, the sales database is still fully operational, but the database activity in this hour amounted to five customers calling the help desk to **update** their orders:

1. Before the next run happens, let's show some `update` activity in the sales database. Copy the contents of the following file in the training Git repository: `https://raw.githubusercontent.com/PacktPublishing/Data-Engineering-with-Apache-Spark-Delta-Lake-and-Lakehouse/main/project/prep/stores/sql/incremental/2/storedb_incremental_2.sql`.

Paste the contents inside the **Query Editor** window. Click on **Run**. This will **update** five orders in the **store_orders** table:

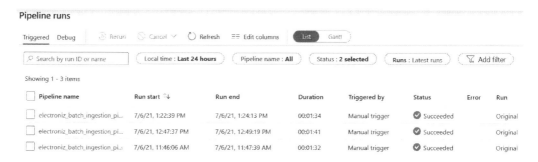

Query 1 ×   Query 2 ×

▷ Run   ☐ Cancel query   ⬇ Save query   ⬇ Export data as ∨   ▦ Show only Editor

```
1   UPDATE [store_orders] SET [sale_price] =      , [currency] =      , [order_mode]
2   UPDATE [store_orders] SET [sale_price] =      , [currency] =      , [order_mode]
3   UPDATE [store_orders] SET [sale_price] =      , [currency] =      , [order_mode]
4   UPDATE [store_orders] SET [sale_price] =      , [currency] =      , [order_mode]
5   UPDATE [store_orders] SET [sale_price] =      , [currency] =      , [order_mode]
6   GO
```

Results   **Messages**

Query succeeded: Affected rows: 5

Figure 5.56 – Updating data in the stores_orders table

2. In the next iteration, the pipeline will only pull incremental data from the sales database. When the next hour arrives, rerun the pipeline using the following command:

```
PIPELINENAME="electroniz_batch_ingestion_pipeline"
DATAFACTORYNAME="trainingdatafactory100"
RESOURCEGROUPNAME="training_rg"
az datafactory pipeline create-run --factory-name
$DATAFACTORYNAME --name $PIPELINENAME --resource-group
$RESOURCEGROUPNAME
```

3. Now click on **Pipeline runs**. After some time, **Status** will change to **Succeeded**. This indicates a successful run:

Pipeline runs

Triggered   Debug   ⟳ Rerun   ⊘ Cancel ∨   ○ Refresh   ☰☰ Edit columns   (List) Gantt

🔍 Search by run ID or name   (Local time : **Last 24 hours**) (Pipeline name : **All**) (Status : **2 selected**) (Runs : Latest runs) ▽ Add filter

Showing 1 - 3 items

☐ Pipeline name	Run start ↑↓	Run end	Duration	Triggered by	Status	Error	Run
☐ electroniz_batch_ingestion_pi...	7/6/21, 1:22:39 PM	7/6/21, 1:24:13 PM	00:01:34	Manual trigger	✅ Succeeded		Original
☐ electroniz_batch_ingestion_pi...	7/6/21, 12:47:37 PM	7/6/21, 12:49:19 PM	00:01:41	Manual trigger	✅ Succeeded		Original
☐ electroniz_batch_ingestion_pi...	7/6/21, 11:46:06 AM	7/6/21, 11:47:39 AM	00:01:32	Manual trigger	✅ Succeeded		Original

Figure 5.57 – The status of the Electroniz batch ingestion pipeline for the third iteration

4. From the preceding screenshot, it looks like the pipeline has been successfully completed for the third time. Let's validate whether the incremental data was correctly ingested. From the Azure portal, navigate to **Home | All resources | traininglakehouse**.

    Then, navigate to **Containers | Bronze | sales**. Browse to the newly created folder from the last hour.

    You should expect a new hour folder in the **[dbo].[store_customers]** and **[dbo].[store_orders]** folders, as follows:

Figure 5.58 – New hourly folder for the third iteration

5. Click on the new hour folder for **store_orders**. It should contain a new file that has five rows. Notice that each row has been marked as **EDIT**, signaling an updated row:

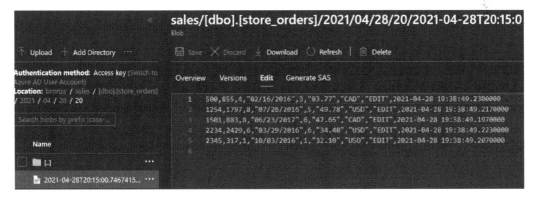

Figure 5.59 – The results of the incremental data run of the batch ingestion pipeline

The fourth run of the pipeline – inserts

Currently, the third hour after the initial ingestion is taking place. In this run, we will assume that some customers have called to cancel (**delete**) their orders:

1. Before the next scheduled run occurs, let's show some activity in the sales database. Copy the contents of the following file in the training Git repository: `https://raw.githubusercontent.com/PacktPublishing/Data-Engineering-with-Apache-Spark-Delta-Lake-and-Lakehouse/main/project/prep/stores/sql/incremental/3/storedb_incremental_3.sql`.

    Paste the contents inside the **Query Editor** window. Select **Run**. Notice that **order_mode** shows the orders have been deleted:

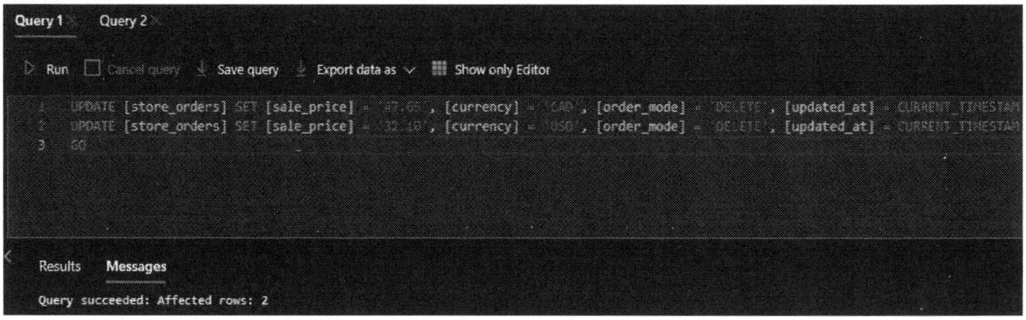

    Figure 5.60 – Deleted data in the stores_orders table

2. In the next iteration, the pipeline will only pull incremental data from the sales database. When the next hour arrives, rerun the pipeline using the following command:

```
PIPELINENAME="electroniz_batch_ingestion_pipeline"
DATAFACTORYNAME="trainingdatafactory100"
RESOURCEGROUPNAME="training_rg"
az datafactory pipeline create-run --factory-name
$DATAFACTORYNAME --name $PIPELINENAME --resource-group
$RESOURCEGROUPNAME
```

3. Now click on **Pipeline runs**. After some time, **Status** will change to **Succeeded**. This indicates a successful run:

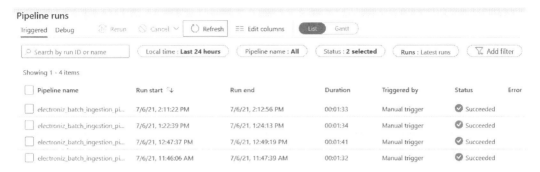

Figure 5.61 – The status of the Electroniz batch ingestion pipeline for the fourth iteration

4. Let's validate whether the incremental data was correctly ingested. From the Azure portal, navigate to **Home | All resources | traininglakehouse**.

Navigate to **Containers | Bronze | sales**. Browse to the newly created folder from the last hour.

You should expect a new hour folder in the **[dbo].[store_orders]** folder, as follows:

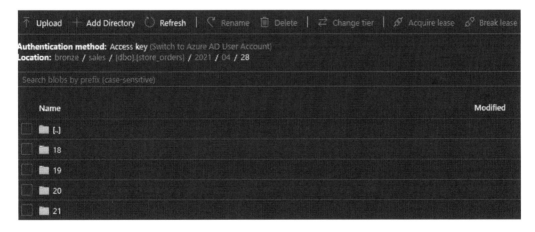

Figure 5.62 – New hourly folder for the fourth iteration

5. Click on the new hour folder for **store_orders**. It should contain a new file that has five rows. Notice that each row has been marked as **DELETE**, signaling an updated row:

Figure 5.63 – The results of the incremental data run of the batch ingestion pipeline

Everything seems to have worked as expected. It is a good idea to rebuild and test the pipeline a few times to build up your practice. However, there is one last thing remaining before you start to build the **Electroniz** streaming ingestion pipeline. Once you are comfortable that **electroniz_batch_ingestion_pipeline** is working as expected, export the code of the pipeline from **Azure Data Factory** so that you can check it in your source control system, such as **Git**.

6. Go back to the **Azure data factory** window. Using the top menu, click on **Save as template**.

Now click on **Export template**. This will download a file named **electroniz_batch_ ingestion_pipeline.zip** to your computer. You can check this file inside your source control system. I have provided a sample of the same file in the training Git repository:

```
https://github.com/PacktPublishing/Data-Engineering-with-
Apache-Spark-Delta-Lake-and-Lakehouse/tree/main/project/
ingestion/batch
```

Building the streaming ingestion pipeline

Now we will move on to the streaming ingestion pipeline for **Electroniz**. During the discovery sessions, we found out that the **Electroniz** e-commerce website continuously sends new sales transactions to **Azure Event Hubs**. In a previous section, we had successfully created the **Electroniz** streaming source components – an **Azure event grid**, an **Azure event hub**, and an **Azure event hub namespace**:

1. Let's start by sending some data to the previously created Azure event hub. Please review the following file: `https://github.com/PacktPublishing/Data-Engineering-with-Apache-Spark-Delta-Lake-and-Lakehouse/blob/main/project/prep/ecommerce/eventhub/ecomm_orders_1.txt`.

   There are a few transactions that will allow us to test the delivery of events to storage using Azure Event Hubs Capture. Copy each of the following commands, line by line, and paste them inside the Cloud Shell window. Then, press *Enter*:

   ```
   RESOURCEGROUPNAME="training_rg"
   LOCATION="eastus"
   TOPIC="esales"
   EVENTHUB_NAMESPACE="esalesns"
   EVENTHUB_NAME="esaleshub"
   EVENT_SUBSCRIPTION="esalesevent"
   sh Data-Engineering-with-Apache-Spark-Delta-Lake-and-
   Lakehouse/project/prep/ecommerce/eventhub/sendevent_1.
   sh -e $EVENTHUB_NAME -n $EVENTHUB_NAMESPACE -r
   $RESOURCEGROUPNAME -s $EVENT_SUBSCRIPTION -t $TOPIC
   ```

   After invoking the preceding commands, your Azure Cloud Shell should look like this:

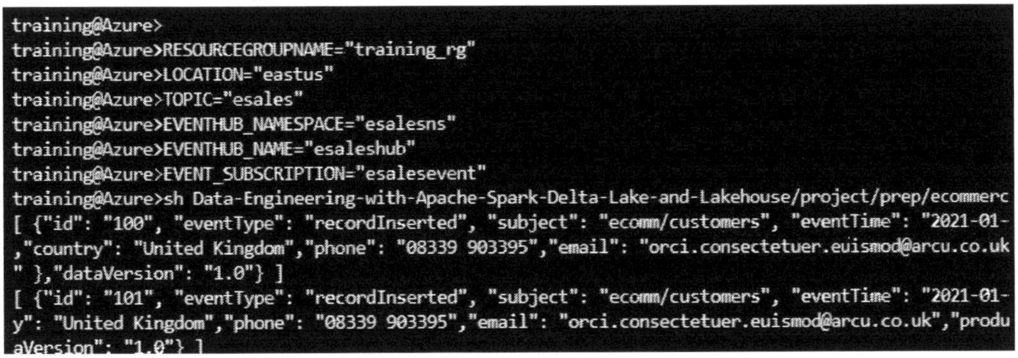

Figure 5.64 – Confirmation of the sample events sent to Azure Event Hubs

2. To make sure we received the sample events, navigate to **Home | All Resources | esalesns**.

Using the pane on the left-hand side, click on **Event Hubs**. On the pane on the right-hand side, click on **esaleshub**.

To make sure that Azure Event Hubs is receiving events, click on **Process data**. Using the data generated by the Azure Event Hubs process, you can preview the data in your stream:

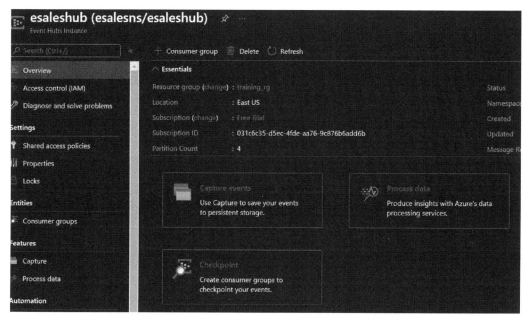

Figure 5.65 – The Azure Event Hubs screen showing the process data and capture events

3. Click on **Explore**. From the **Query** window, notice the message regarding permissions. Click on **Create**:

Figure 5.66 – The Azure Event Hubs process data permissions screen

The window should now refresh itself. Alternatively, you can select **Test query**:

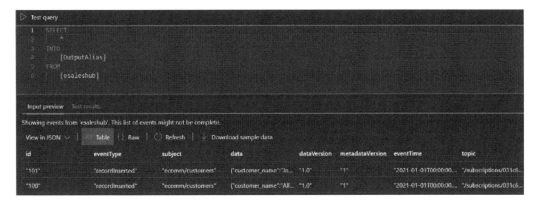

Figure 5.67 – The Azure Event Hubs process data permissions screen

4. Close the **Query** window. Using the pane on the left-hand side, click on **Capture**. Input the following:

- Capture: **On**

- Time window: `2 minutes`

- Size Window: `10 MB`

Do not emit empty files when no events occur during the Capture time window: **Checked**

Click on **Select Container**. Navigate to **traininglakehouse | bronze.** Then, click on **Select**.

Finally, click on **Save changes**:

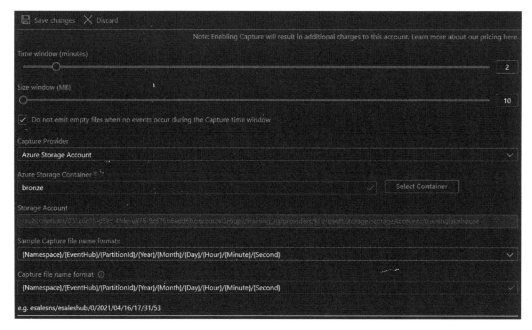

Figure 5.68 – The Azure Event Hubs Capture data screen

5. To check whether the events are being successfully captured in Azure Data Lake Storage, navigate to **Home | All Resources | traininglakehouse**.

Then, click on **Containers**. Finally, click on **bronze**. After a few minutes, you should see the events captured in this container. Navigating through the directories will take you to events that are stored in **Avro** format:

Figure 5.69 – Sample e-commerce transactions saved as Avro files

> **Important**
>
> Avro format uses JSON to define a schema and serialize data in a compact binary row format. Avro is well known for seamless schema evolution – adapting to schema changes over time.

If you see the preceding Avro files, this means you have successfully tested both batch and streaming pipelines. From the preceding testing, it appears that the data pipelines are reacting well to existing data, but that is not it.

6. Finally, let's push a few more e-commerce transactions. Copy each of the following commands, line by line, and paste them into the Cloud Shell window. Then, press *Enter*:

```
RESOURCEGROUPNAME="training_rg"
LOCATION="eastus"
TOPIC="esales"
EVENTHUB_NAMESPACE="esalesns"
EVENTHUB_NAME="esaleshub"
EVENT_SUBSCRIPTION="esalesevent"
sh Data-Engineering-with-Apache-Spark-Delta-Lake-and-
Lakehouse/project/prep/ecommerce/eventhub/sendevent_2.
sh -e $EVENTHUB_NAME -n $EVENTHUB_NAMESPACE -r
$RESOURCEGROUPNAME -s $EVENT_SUBSCRIPTION -t $TOPIC
```

Based on the results of the preceding test cases, we can safely infer that both the batch and streaming ingestion pipelines for **Electroniz** are working as desired. We now have the raw data in the bronze layer, which means we are ready to move our focus to the silver layer.

The next chapter is extremely important for many reasons. Before we start creating the silver layer, we need to understand the foundational framework that the lakehouse architecture is built upon – **Delta Lake**.

> **Cost-saving tip**
>
> Although the cost of the Azure resources should be covered under your Free Tier, it is still a good idea to remove any non-required resources. At this point, feel free to delete all of the resources except the storage accounts. A quick way to check which resources are currently running is to go to **Home | Resource groups | training_rg**. Choose the resources you want to drop, and press the **Delete** button in the menu. Once again, do not delete the storage accounts because we will need the data that is stored on them for the next chapters.

Summary

In this chapter, we learned how to kick-start data pipeline development by reflecting on the user requirements in the form of a cloud architecture diagram and pipeline design document. In the pipeline design document, we decided to create ingestion, curation, and aggregation pipelines that could build the bronze, silver, and gold layers of the lakehouse.

We also learned about the bronze layer in greater detail and how it relates to the overall lakehouse architecture. We followed up on our understanding of the bronze layer with the actual development of the **Electroniz** batch and streaming ingestion pipelines. Now that we have the raw data from the various data sources available in the bronze layer, we will move on to *Chapter 6, Understanding Delta Lake,* and learn about **Delta Lake**. Understanding how Delta Lake works is essential for building the silver layer of the lakehouse.

6
Understanding Delta Lake

In the previous chapter, we created the bronze layer of the lakehouse. The bronze layer stores raw data in the native form as collected from the data sources. The problem is that raw data is not in a shape that can be readily consumed for analytical operations.

As a data engineer, it is your responsibility to convert raw data into a shape and form that becomes ready for use analytical workloads. In this chapter, we will further advance our learning to cleanse raw data. The process of cleansing data involves applying the logic that cleans and standardizes data followed by writing it to the silver layer of the lakehouse.

But that is not all – the silver layer should store data in an open format that supports **ACID (atomicity**, **consistency**, **isolation**, and **durability**) transactions. This is done by using the **Delta Lake** engine. Before we start building the silver layer, we need to completely understand some critical features of Delta Lake and how they relate to the lakehouse architecture.

In this chapter, we will cover the following topics:

- Understanding how Delta Lake enables the lakehouse
- Understanding Delta Lake
- Creating a Delta Lake table
- Performing upserts of data
- Understanding isolation levels
- Understanding concurrency control

Understanding how Delta Lake enables the lakehouse

In *Chapter 2, Discovering Storage and Compute Data Lake Architectures*, we talked about the give-and-take struggle between traditional warehouse systems versus data lakes. In the last few years, many organizations have modernized their data engineering and analytics platforms by moving away from traditional data warehouses to data lakes. The move to the data lake has undoubtedly given them the flexibility to store and compute any format of data at a large scale. However, these advantages did not come without a few sacrifices along the way. The biggest one is the reliability of data. Like data warehouses, there is no transactional assurance available in a data lake. This need led to the launch of an open source storage layer known as Delta Lake.

After its launch, experts came up with the idea of mixing the power of resilient data warehouses with the flexibility of data lakes and they called it a **lakehouse**. The combined power of a data lake and data warehouse provides a unique and powerful mix of features, as follows:

- Data can be analyzed in multiple formats – structured, semi-structured, or unstructured.
- Preserves the idea of low-cost storage and compute on demand.
- Supports a variety of use cases including analysis, data science, machine learning, and artificial intelligence.
- Preserves the sanity of data using effective techniques such as curation, standardization, and deduplication.
- Provides a secure way to store and share data while maintaining compliance.

The following diagram shows the data layers:

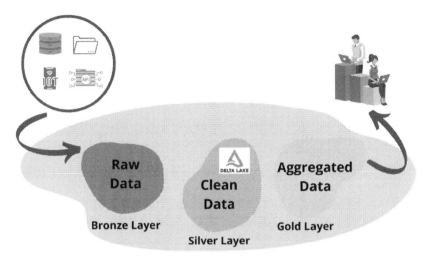

Figure 6.1 – Lakehouse data layers

In *Chapter 5, Data Collection Stage – The Bronze Layer*, we discussed the bronze layer of the lakehouse in greater detail. We are now moving our focus to the silver layer. While the bronze layer stores data that constantly trickles from various data sources in native formats, the silver layer stores data from all data sources in a common open format after the curation phase.

Data curation is a combined term for the **cleanup**, **sanitization**, **standardization**, and **deduplication** of data. As per the preceding figure, the Delta Lake engine sits at the heart of the silver layer. It is responsible for managing and exposing a layer of data that is not only clean but most importantly trustworthy. It's a common layer that data consumers such as data analysts, scientists, and machine learning engineers can freely access and use with confidence.

Understanding Delta Lake

As mentioned before, modern data lakes lack some critical features such as **ACID transactions**, **indexing**, and **versioning**, which can negatively affect the reliability, quality, and performance of data.

> **Important Note**
> In data warehouse terms, ACID is the short form for atomicity, consistency, isolation, and durability of data. These properties are intended to make database transactions accurate, reliable, and permanent.

The following diagram depicts the properties:

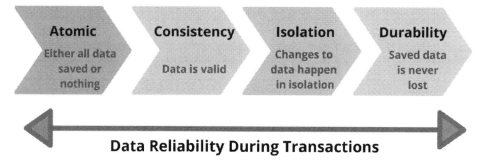

Figure 6.2 – ACID properties in Delta Lake

Delta Lake functions as a layer on top of the distributed computing framework **Apache Spark**. By design, Apache Spark lacks the following key principles of transaction management:

- It does not lock previous data during edit transactions, which means data may become unavailable during overwrites for a very brief period.

- During data overwrites, there is a chance where the old data gets deleted yet the new data fails the save operation. This could leave data in an inconsistent state.

- Apache Spark does not protect against two separate transactions writing data to the same location at the same time.

We are going to learn about some key features of Delta Lake through a series of live examples. Let's get started by preparing the environment that will be used for this exercise.

Preparing Azure resources

Before we deep dive into the workings of Delta Lake, we need to spin up a few resources as follows:

1. To save data in the delta format, we will use a temporary Azure data lake storage namespace for this exercise. Invoke the following commands in the Azure Cloud Shell.

   I had mentioned earlier that storage account names in Azure are globally unique. Throughout this exercise, we are using the storage account name `traininglakehouse`. You will need to edit it as per the account name that you created:

   ```
   SCRATCH_NAMESPACE="scratch"
   STORAGEACCOUNTNAME="traininglakehouse"
   ```

```
RESOURCEGROUPNAME="training_rg"
LOCATION="eastus"
az storage fs create -n $SCRATCH_NAMESPACE --account-
name $STORAGEACCOUNTNAME --metadata project=lakehouse
environment=development layer=bronze --only-show-errors
```

This results in the following output:

```
training@Azure>SCRATCH_NAMESPACE="scratch"
training@Azure>STORAGEACCOUNTNAME="traininglakehouse"
training@Azure>RESOURCEGROUPNAME="training_rg"
training@Azure>LOCATION="eastus"
training@Azure>az storage fs create -n $SCRATCH_NAMESPACE --account-name $
{
  "client_request_id": "b3a9a6c6-ac1e-11eb-a5c9-0a580af459e5",
  "date": "2021-05-03T14:49:02+00:00",
  "error_code": null,
  "etag": "\"0x8D90E4297ED9BCC\"",
  "last_modified": "2021-05-03T14:49:02+00:00",
  "request_id": "4362a4cd-a01e-0058-4c2b-407462000000",
  "version": "2020-02-10"
}
```

Figure 6.3 – Container for Delta Lake exercises

2. If the preceding command is successful, you should be able to see the newly
    created container on the Azure portal by browsing to **Home** > **All Resources** >
    traininglakehouse:

Figure 6.4 – Scratch namespace in traininglakehouse

3. For this exercise, we will use **Azure Databricks** to read and write data from the Azure data lake storage created previously. To read and write data, Azure Databricks requires the storage account keys for Azure Data Lake storage. Invoke the following commands on the Azure Cloud Shell:

```
STORAGEACCOUNTNAME="traininglakehouse"

az storage account keys list --account-name
$STORAGEACCOUNTNAME
```

If the preceding commands worked as desired, you should see two storage keys as follows. Take note of the value for `key1` from the output for the command. We will need it later in the Databricks workspace configuration.

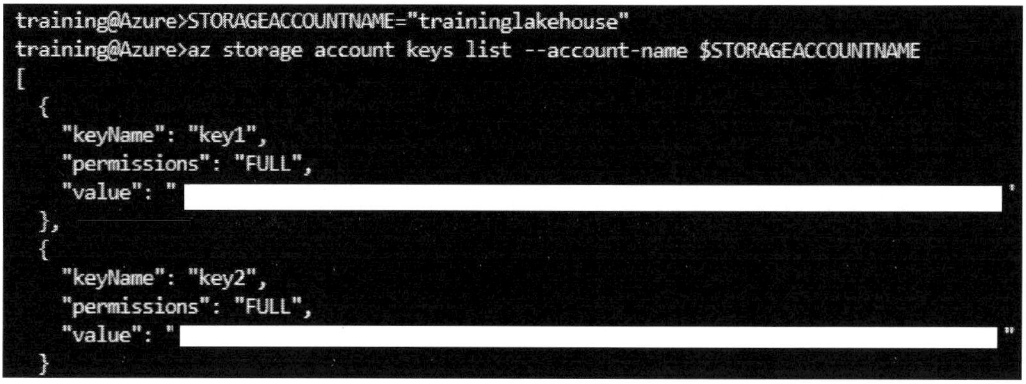

```
training@Azure>STORAGEACCOUNTNAME="traininglakehouse"
training@Azure>az storage account keys list --account-name $STORAGEACCOUNTNAME
[
  {
    "keyName": "key1",
    "permissions": "FULL",
    "value": "                                                  ',
  },
  {
    "keyName": "key2",
    "permissions": "FULL",
    "value": "                                                  "
  }
]
```

Figure 6.5 – traininglakehouse keys

4. Since Delta Lake works on top of Apache Spark, we need to create the Azure Databricks workspace using instructions as shown in the next code example. Invoke the following commands on the Azure Cloud Shell. Azure Databricks workspace names are globally unique, so please edit the WORKSPACE name accordingly:

```
RESOURCEGROUPNAME="training_rg"

LOCATION="eastus"

WORKSPACE="trainingdatabricks"

az config set extension.use_dynamic_install=yes_without_
prompt

az databricks workspace create --resource-group
$RESOURCEGROUPNAME --name $WORKSPACE --location $LOCATION
--sku trial
```

If you do not have an Azure trial account, you need to use the `sku` standard.

```
training@Azure>RESOURCEGROUPNAME="training_rg"
training@Azure>LOCATION="eastus"
training@Azure>WORKSPACE="trainingdatabricks"
training@Azure>az config set extension.use_dynamic_install=yes_without_prompt
Command group 'config' is experimental and under development. Reference and support le
training@Azure>az databricks workspace create --resource-group $RESOURCEGROUPNAME --na
{| Finished ..
  "authorizations": [
    {
      "principalId": "9a74af6f-d153-4348-988a-e2672920bee9",
      "roleDefinitionId": "8e3af657-a8ff-443c-a75c-2fe8c4bcb635"
    }
  ],
  "createdBy": {
    "applicationId": "c44b4083-3bb0-49c1-b47d-974e53cbdf3c",
    "oid": "09a48665-df3d-42cd-b4d4-5b314a4cc3d4",
    "puid": "000300003AA12A41"
```

Figure 6.6 – Azure Databricks workspace creation

5. To validate the creation of the Azure Databricks workspace, navigate to the Azure portal.

    Click on **Home** > **All Resources** > **trainingdatabricks**.

    Click on **Launch Workspace**:

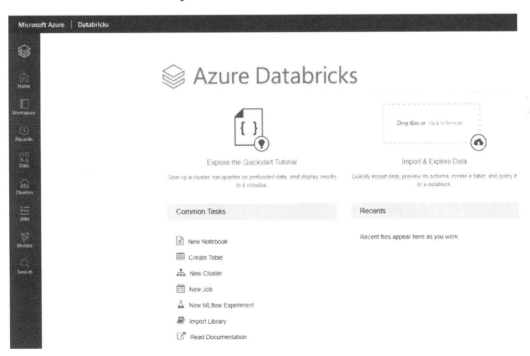

Figure 6.7 – Azure Databricks workspace on the Azure portal

6. We are now ready to create an Azure Spark cluster. Using the menu on the left, click on **Compute**, then click on **Create Cluster**.

    - Cluster name: `trainingcluster`.

    - Cluster mode: `Single node`.

    - Leave everything else as default and press the **Create Cluster** button. This will spin up a small Apache Spark cluster that we will be used for invoking Spark and Delta Lake commands. Once the cluster creation has been completed, you should see a window that looks like this:

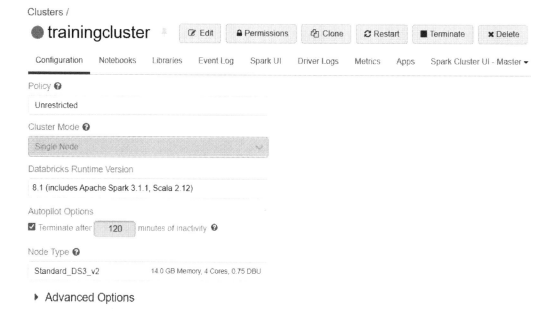

Figure 6.8 – Azure Databricks cluster creation

If the cluster creation fails unexpectedly due to the following error:

Cluster terminated Reason: Cloud Provider Launch Failure

Complete the troubleshooting steps as follows:

- On the Azure portal, navigate to **Home** > **Subscriptions** > **<Your Subscription Name>**.

- Using the menu on the left, click on **Resource Providers**.

- In the list, search for **Microsoft.Compute** and make sure that the provider is **Registered**. If not, select it and click on **Register** at the top of the search bar.

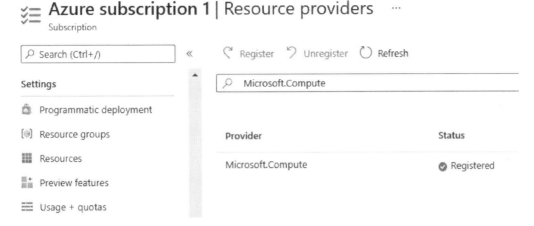

Figure 6.9 – Registering Microsoft.Compute in your Azure subscription

7. We now need a notebook that will serve as our **interactive development environment (IDE)** for the exercise. A notebook is a web-based interface to type and run **PySpark** code, as well as create visualizations. Now we have two choices for developing the notebook:

- The first choice is to use a pre-existing notebook loaded on the **Packt Git repo**. Use this option if you have prior exposure to PySpark and **SQL** and want to save yourself the hassle of typing commands.

- On the Databricks workspace, click on **Workspace**, then click on **Users**.

- Click on the arrow beside your username, and click on **Import**.

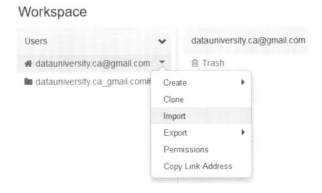

Figure 6.10 – Import a notebook in Azure Databricks workspace

- Choose **URL** and use the following URL: `https://github.com/` `PacktPublishing/Data-Engineering-with-Apache-Spark-Delta-` `Lake-and-Lakehouse/blob/main/project/curation/delta_lake/` `sales_orders_notebook.ipynb`.

- Click on **Import**.

- Now, click on the cluster dropdown and choose **trainingcluster**.

sales_orders_notebook (Python)

Figure 6.11 – Choose a spark cluster for the notebook

Before running the notebook cells, make sure you edit `STORAGE_ACCOUNT` and `ADLS_KEY` as per your Azure account. For `ADLS_KEY`, use `key1` (fetched previously).

The second choice is suitable for beginners, as it forces you to type commands and review each code instruction carefully. This enables better learning.

Using the menu on the left, click on the **Databricks** icon, which is on top of **Home**. Now click on **New Notebook**:

- Name: `sales_orders_notebook`.

- Default language: `Python`.

- Cluster: `trainingcluster`.

- Click on **Create**. You will now see a new notebook created as follows:

Figure 6.12 – Azure Databricks notebook

If you are new to using notebooks, it is highly recommended to visit the following link to get used to some common notebook commands.

```
https://docs.microsoft.com/en-us/azure/databricks/
notebooks/notebooks-use
```

From here onwards, we will assume that you chose the second option for developing the notebook. If you chose the first one, then there is no need to hand-type the commands that follow.

8. In the first cell of your notebook, copy the commands that follow. This first line imports the Delta Lake module and the second one imports the PySpark SQL Types class.

```
from delta.tables import *
from pyspark.sql.types import StructType, StructField,
IntegerType, StringType, array, ArrayType, DateType,
TimestampType, FloatType
```

Press *Shift* + *Enter* to run the preceding commands in your notebook.

9. Copy the following commands in the second cell of the notebook. Replace the Xs with the Azure data lake value of `key1` (fetched earlier) and make sure the other parameters match the bronze layer in the Azure data lake you created in *Chapter 5, Data Collection Stage – The Bronze Layer*.

The **ADLS_FOLDER** is the hour when **electroniz_batch_ingestion_pipeline** was run the very first time. For example, when we ran the pipeline in *Chapter 5, Data Collection Stage – The Bronze Layer*, the folder structure looked like the following screenshot. The hour **2021/04/28/18** folder was the first iteration.

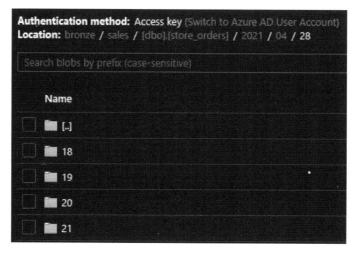

Figure 6.13 – Folder structure of the sales_orders table in the bronze layer

We'll now run the following commands:

```
STORAGE_ACCOUNT="traininglakehouse"
ADLS_KEY="XXXXXXXXXXXXXXXXXXXXXXXXXXXXXXXX"
BRONZE_LAYER_NAMESPACE="bronze"
SCRATCH_LAYER_NAMESPACE="scratch"
STORE_SALES_FOLDER="sales"
TABLE="store_orders"
ADLS_FOLDER="2021/04/28/18"
BRONZE_TABLE_PATH="wasbs://"+BRONZE_LAYER_
NAMESPACE+"@"+STORAGE_ACCOUNT+".blob.core.windows.
net/"+STORE_SALES_FOLDER+"/\[dbo\].\["+TABLE+"\]/"+ADLS_
FOLDER
spark.conf.set("fs.azure.account.key."+STORAGE_ACCOUNT+".
blob.core.windows.net", ADLS_KEY)
```

Press *Shift* + *Enter* to run the commands.

10. We are now ready to read the `store_orders` table from the Azure data lake storage. You may recall that we had previously ingested this table using `electroniz_batch_ingestion_pipeline`. Copy the following commands into the third cell of the notebook:

```
ORDERS_SCHEMA = [
      ('order_number', IntegerType()),
      ('customer_id', IntegerType()),
      ('product_id', IntegerType()),
      ('order_date', StringType()),
      ('units', IntegerType()),
      ('sale_price', FloatType()),
      ('currency', StringType()),
      ('order_mode', StringType()),
      ('updated_at', TimestampType())
]
fields = [StructField(*field) for field in ORDERS_SCHEMA]
schema = StructType(fields)
df_read_data_hour1 = spark.read.csv(BRONZE_TABLE_PATH,
schema=schema )
display(df_read_data_hour1)
```

Notice how the schema for the `store_orders` table is being defined before reading its data in a Spark DataFrame.

This results in the following output:

```
1   ORDERS_SCHEMA =[
2       ('order_number', IntegerType()),
3       ('customer_id', IntegerType()),
4       ('product_id', IntegerType()),
5       ('order_date', StringType()),
6       ('units', IntegerType()),
7       ('sale_price', FloatType()),
8       ('currency', StringType()),
9       ('order_mode', StringType()),
10      ('updated_at', TimestampType())
11  ]
12  fields = [StructField(*field) for field in ORDERS_SCHEMA]
13  schema = StructType(fields)
14  df_read_data_hour1 = spark.read.csv(BRONZE_TABLE_PATH, schema=schema )
15  display(df_read_data_hour1)
16
```

▸ (1) Spark Jobs

▸ ▦ df_read_data_hour1: pyspark.sql.dataframe DataFrame = [order_number: integer, customer_id: integer ... 7 more fields]

	order_number	customer_id	product_id	order_date	units	sale_price	currency	order_mode	updated_at
1	1	212	5	02/03/2019	10	11.6	USD	NEW	2021-04-28T17:56:11.053+0000
2	2	1940	10	06/24/2020	8	72.31	USD	NEW	2021-04-28T17:56:11.053+0000
3	3	60	6	02/11/2019	4	24.82	INR	NEW	2021-04-28T17:56:11.053+0000
4	4	2776	6	05/20/2018	4	20.91	USD	NEW	2021-04-28T17:56:11.053+0000
5	5	409	9	07/05/2019	5	98.41	INR	NEW	2021-04-28T17:56:11.053+0000
6	6	978	6	12/16/2020	1	6.9	USD	NEW	2021-04-28T17:56:11.053+0000
7	7	2904	6	01/04/2021	1	71.56	EURO	NEW	2021-04-28T17:56:11.053+0000

Showing the first 1000 rows.

Figure 6.14 – DataFrame of the sales_orders table in the bronze layer

If you see an output that shows `store_orders` data, then we are looking pretty good. If not, revalidate your settings and reinvoke this cell again. We will now move on to creating a Delta Lake table that shows us how it works.

Creating a Delta Lake table

With the environment set up, we are ready to understand how Delta Lake works. In our Spark session, we have a Spark DataFrame that stores the data of the `store_orders` table that was ingested at the first iteration of the `electroniz_batch_ingestion_pipeline` run:

> **Important Note**
>
> A Spark DataFrame is an immutable distributed collection of data. It contains rows and columns like a table in a relational database.

1. At this point, you should be comfortable running instructions in notebook cells. New cells can be created using *Ctrl + Alt + N*. After each command, you need to press *Shift + Enter* to run the command.

From here onwards, I will simply ask you to run the instructions with the assumption that you know how to create new cells and run commands. Invoke the following instructions to write the `store_orders` delta table:

```
SCRATCH_LAYER_NAMESPACE="scratch"
```
```
DELTA_TABLE_WRITE_PATH="wasbs://"+SCRATCH_LAYER_
NAMESPACE+"@"+STORAGE_ACCOUNT+".blob.core.windows.
net/"+STORE_SALES_FOLDER+"/"+TABLE
```
```
PARTITION_COLUMN="currency"
```
```
df_read_data_hour1.write.format("delta").option("path",
DELTA_TABLE_WRITE_PATH).partitionBy(PARTITION_COLUMN).
saveAsTable(TABLE)
```

Note the use of `format=delta`. Delta Lake uses versioned **Parquet** files to store data. Using the `partitionBy` clause, we are asking data to be written in folders partitioned by the `currency` column.

Also, we are asking the table to be saved as `store_orders` in the Delta Lake metastore.

> **Important Note**
>
> All Databricks deployments include a built-in **Hive** metastore to persist table definitions.

2. To check if the Delta Lake table got written to storage, click on the following:

Home > **All Resources** > **traininglakehouse** > **scratch** > **sales** > **store_orders**

The folder structure for the table should look like the following:

Figure 6.15 – Checking the sales_orders table folder structure using the Azure portal

3. Alternatively, you can also invoke the following command to look at the folder structure directly from the notebook itself:

```
display(dbutils.fs.ls(DELTA_TABLE_WRITE_PATH))
```

This results in the following output:

```
1    display(dbutils.fs.ls(DELTA_TABLE_WRITE_PATH))
```

▶ (2) Spark Jobs

	path	name	size
1	wasbs://scratch@traininglakehouse.blob.core.windows.net/sales/store_orders/_delta_log/	_delta_log/	0
2	wasbs://scratch@traininglakehouse.blob.core.windows.net/sales/store_orders/currency=CAD/	currency=CAD/	0
3	wasbs://scratch@traininglakehouse.blob.core.windows.net/sales/store_orders/currency=EURO/	currency=EURO/	0
4	wasbs://scratch@traininglakehouse.blob.core.windows.net/sales/store_orders/currency=INR/	currency=INR/	0
5	wasbs://scratch@traininglakehouse.blob.core.windows.net/sales/store_orders/currency=USD/	currency=USD/	0

Figure 6.16 – Checking the sales_orders table folder structure using the notebook

In the preceding output, take note of a few key items as follows:

- The _delta_log folder is referred to as the Delta Lake transaction log (**DeltaLog**). DeltaLog is the central repository to store and track every transaction that happens on a table. By checking the transaction log each time before posting any new changes, Delta Lake can ensure consistency between data in the user's session compared to stored data.

- DeltaLog uses the principle of *If the transaction does not exist in the log, you may assume it never happened*. Using this principle can ensure atomicity.

- Registering only the successful transactions in DeltaLog establishes a level of trust in the data. Successful transactions are persisted in Parquet files on storage ensuring durability.

- Delta Lake performs concurrent transactions in such a way that they occur serially and in isolation from each other.

The actual data has been written to storage partitioned by the currency column. column=key is a Hive partitioning convention that correlates folders to partitions.

> **Important Note**
>
> In Hive, the partition column is not stored in the data files. Instead, it exists as a virtual column deciphered at runtime using the folder structure. The correct choice of the partition column can hugely enhance the performance of queries.

1. Go back to the Azure portal and click on the `_delta_log` folder. Click on **00000000000000000000.json**, then **Edit**.

   Delta Lake writes committed transactions to **JSON** files starting with `00000000000000000000.json`. Notice `operation=CREATE TABLE AS SELECT`. The first transaction was written to the transaction log when we wrote the `store_orders` table. In the bronze layer, we had 2,500 records in the `store_orders` file. Notice how `numrecords` varies for all partitions that have the same value.

Figure 6.17 – The sales_orders table transaction log

2. Dive a step further into the folder structure. Browse to **scratch** > **sales** > **store_orders** > **currency=EURO**:

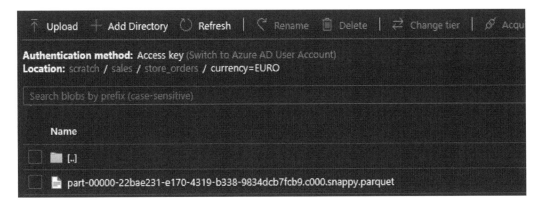

Figure 6.18 – The sales_orders table data in Parquet format

The data for the `currency=EURO` partition has 623 records but is stored as a single Parquet file in storage.

> **Important Note**
> Apache Parquet is an open source columnar storage format. Parquet is extremely efficient for querying because of its smaller footprint and efficient I/O utilization.

3. Navigate back to the notebook. Now, let's read the delta table from storage. Invoke the following instructions to read the `store_orders` delta table directly from the notebook. The following command reads the delta table:

```
spark.read.format("delta").load(DELTA_TABLE_WRITE_PATH).
show()
```

This results in the following output:

```
1    spark.read.format("delta").load(DELTA_TABLE_WRITE_PATH).show()
```

▶ (1) Spark Jobs

```
+------------+-----------+----------+----------+-----+----------+--------+---------+--------------------+
|order_number|customer_id|product_id|order_date|units|sale_price|currency|order_mode|          updated_at|
+------------+-----------+----------+----------+-----+----------+--------+---------+--------------------+
|          13|       2681|         1|05/12/2017|    3|      7.69|     CAD|      NEW|2021-04-28 17:56:...|
|          15|       2550|         6|08/14/2020|    4|      5.51|     CAD|      NEW|2021-04-28 17:56:...|
|          19|       1819|         2|02/26/2021|    2|     52.88|     CAD|      NEW|2021-04-28 17:56:...|
|          21|       1031|         6|12/21/2019|    8|     15.68|     CAD|      NEW|2021-04-28 17:56:...|
|          26|        311|         8|07/12/2019|    6|     94.06|     CAD|      NEW|2021-04-28 17:56:...|
|          29|        827|         9|06/29/2019|    8|     50.45|     CAD|      NEW|2021-04-28 17:56:...|
|          37|        988|         2|06/12/2020|    2|      8.03|     CAD|      NEW|2021-04-28 17:56:...|
|          39|       2034|         6|08/28/2019|    8|     86.06|     CAD|      NEW|2021-04-28 17:56:...|
|          40|       1751|         3|09/15/2017|    3|     18.81|     CAD|      NEW|2021-04-28 17:56:...|
|          41|       1317|         7|01/21/2021|   10|     41.28|     CAD|      NEW|2021-04-28 17:56:...|
|          43|       2265|         9|04/15/2017|    8|     71.35|     CAD|      NEW|2021-04-28 17:56:...|
|          45|       1008|         5|10/12/2017|    6|     55.83|     CAD|      NEW|2021-04-28 17:56:...|
|          51|        987|         7|08/05/2020|    7|     69.25|     CAD|      NEW|2021-04-28 17:56:...|
|          52|       1426|         9|04/17/2018|    7|     21.35|     CAD|      NEW|2021-04-28 17:56:...|
|          66|       1498|         4|08/25/2018|    9|     93.04|     CAD|      NEW|2021-04-28 17:56:...|
|          69|       1131|         7|06/21/2017|    7|     45.89|     CAD|      NEW|2021-04-28 17:56:...|
|          70|       1675|         2|04/26/2017|    5|     14.77|     CAD|      NEW|2021-04-28 17:56:...|
|          74|       2027|         6|01/28/2020|   10|     83.58|     CAD|      NEW|2021-04-28 17:56:...|
```

Figure 6.19 – Checking the data in the sales_orders table using PySpark

Alternatively, you can also read the delta table with SQL commands by using the following instructions:

```
%sql
SELECT * FROM store_orders;
```

This results in the following output:

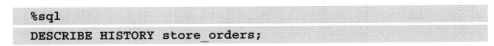

	order_number	customer_id	product_id	order_date	units	sale_price	currency	order_mode	updated_at
1	13	2681	1	05/12/2017	3	7.69	CAD	NEW	2021-04-28T17:56:11.053+0000
2	15	2550	6	08/14/2020	4	5.51	CAD	NEW	2021-04-28T17:56:11.053+0000
3	19	1819	2	02/26/2021	2	52.88	CAD	NEW	2021-04-28T17:56:11.053+0000
4	21	1031	6	12/21/2019	8	15.68	CAD	NEW	2021-04-28T17:56:11.053+0000
5	26	311	8	07/12/2019	6	94.06	CAD	NEW	2021-04-28T17:56:11.053+0000
6	29	827	9	06/29/2019	8	50.45	CAD	NEW	2021-04-28T17:56:11.053+0000
7	37	988	2	06/12/2020	2	8.03	CAD	NEW	2021-04-28T17:56:11.053+0000

Showing the first 1000 rows

Figure 6.20 – Checking the data in the sales_orders table using SQL

4. Remember that Delta Lake stores transaction histories in JSON files starting with 00000000000000000000.json. You can check the transaction history of the store_orders table using the following SQL instructions:

```
%sql
DESCRIBE HISTORY store_orders;
```

This results in the following output:

	version	timestamp	userId	userName	operation	operationParameters
1	0	2021-05-03T19:48:24.000+0000	2180993539918818		CREATE TABLE AS SELECT	["isManaged": "false", "description": null, "partitionBy": "[\"currency"

Showing all 1 rows

Figure 6.21 – Transaction history of the sales_orders table

Using the preceding instructions, we were able to create a delta table. That's a good start, but data evolves over time. Let's see how to change existing data in an existing delta table.

Changing data in an existing Delta Lake table

In the previous section, we saw how new data can be written to a Delta Lake table. But transactions in Delta Lake are not only about new data – we may also need to update and delete data as well. In this section, we will find out how the data lake reacts to changes in existing data:

1. To highlight the effect of changes to Delta Lake tables, we will work with a sample row in the `store_orders` table as follows:

   ```
   %sql
   SELECT * FROM store_orders WHERE order_number=5;
   ```

   This results in the following output:

Figure 6.22 – Checking the data in the sales_orders table for the sample row

2. Now, we will update this row and change the `sale_ price` value from `98.41` to `90.50`:

   ```
   %sql
   UPDATE store_orders SET sale_price=90.50 WHERE order_
   number=5;
   ```

3. Check if the `sale_ price` value got updated in the `store_orders` table:

   ```
   %sql
   SELECT * FROM store_orders WHERE order_number=5;
   ```

   This results in the following output:

Figure 6.23 – Checking the data in the sales_orders table for the sample row

4. Invoke the following instructions to check the history of the `store_orders` table:

```sql
%sql
DESCRIBE HISTORY store_orders;
```

This results in the following output:

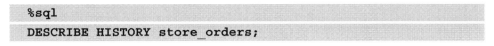

```
1    %sql
2    DESCRIBE HISTORY store_orders;
```

▸ (1) Spark Jobs

	version	timestamp	userId	userName	operation
1	1	2021-05-03T23:48:04.000+0000	2180993539918818		UPDATE
2	0	2021-05-03T23:46:30.000+0000	2180993539918818		CREATE TABLE AS SELECT

Figure 6.24 – Transaction history of the sales_orders table after an update operation

Note how the history has advanced and each transaction is allocated a new version. Version **1** was created because of issuing the update statement (operation=UPDATE). The atomic update to the table resulted in creating a new transaction log file named `00000000000000000001.json`.

The beauty of Delta Lake is that it stores previous versions of data over time. Now, let's learn how to retrieve previous versions using **time travel**.

Performing time travel

A unique feature of Delta Lake is its ability to perform time travel. By using this feature, you can query and restore previous snapshots of your table. Access to previous snapshots is granted by using the `versionAsOf` option.

> **Important Note**
>
> The time travel functionality in Delta Lake implements **data lineage**. Data lineage is an extremely critical tool for data audits and compliance purposes. The same feature comes in handy for data engineers who are trying to trace data anomalies.

1. This is how you can query previous versions of the delta table. In this example, we are querying `version 0` of the table – in other words, when it was created:

```sql
%sql
SELECT * FROM store_orders VERSION AS OF 0 WHERE order_
number=5;
```

This results in the following output:

```
1   %sql
2   SELECT * FROM store_orders  VERSION AS OF 0 WHERE order_number=5;

▸ (2) Spark Jobs
```

order_number	customer_id	product_id	order_date	units	sale_price	currency	order_mode	updated_at
5	409	9	07/05/2019	5	98.41	INR	NEW	2021-04-28T17:56:11.053+0000

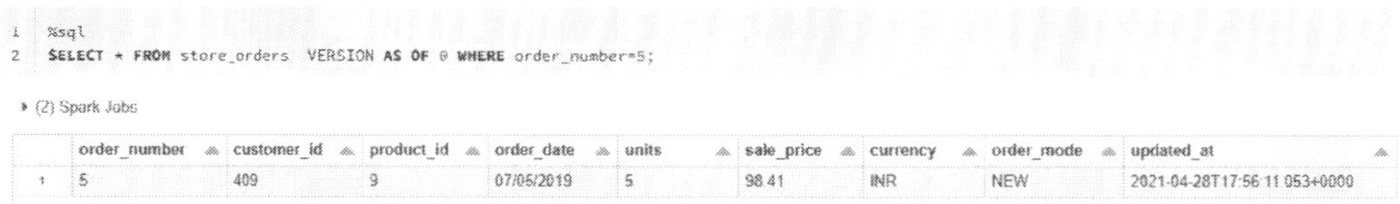

Figure 6.25 – Checking the data in the sales_orders table for the sample row for version 0

Notice how the previous version of the table shows the `sale_ price` value as `98.41`.

2. This time we will delete this order from the `store_orders` table:

```
%sql
DELETE FROM store_orders WHERE order_number=5;
SELECT * FROM store_orders WHERE order_number=5;
```

This results in the following output:

```
1   %sql
2   DELETE FROM store_orders WHERE order_number=5;
3
4   SELECT * FROM store_orders WHERE order_number=5;
```

```
▸ (8) Spark Jobs
Query returned no results
```

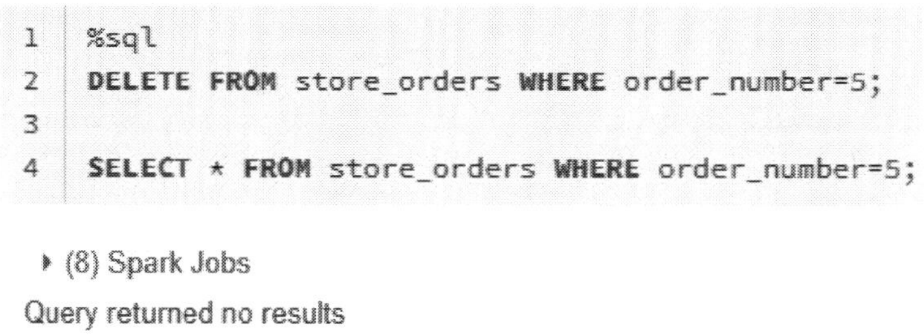

Figure 6.26 – Checking the data in the sales_orders table after the delete operation

Notice how the `SELECT` query for the rows comes back with zero results, indicating that the record indeed got deleted.

3. It would be interesting to check the history of the `store_orders` table now:

```
%sql
DESCRIBE HISTORY store_orders;
```

This results in the following output:

Figure 6.27 – Transaction history of the sales_orders table after the delete operation

Notice that version 2 of the table shows the operation=DELETE.

4. We may find out later that the operator who deleted the order had done it by mistake. Luckily, Delta Lake is very forgiving and supports restoring the table to any previous version. In the following example, we are going back in time to version 1 and recovering the snapshot:

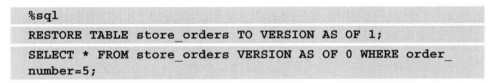

This results in the following output:

Figure 6.28 – Checking the data in the sales_orders table after the restore operation

5. Once again, it would be interesting to check how the history of the store_orders table looks now:

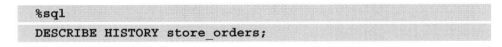

This results in the following output:

```
1  %sql
2  DESCRIBE HISTORY store_orders;
```

▸ (1) Spark Jobs

	version	timestamp	userId	userName	operation
1	3	2021-05-04T15:09:30.000+0000	2180993539918818		RESTORE
2	2	2021-05-04T15:09:14.000+0000	2180993539918818		DELETE
3	1	2021-05-04T15:09:09.000+0000	2180993539918818		UPDATE
4	0	2021-05-04T15:09:03.000+0000	2180993539918818		CREATE TABLE AS SELECT

Showing all 4 rows

Figure 6.29 – Transaction history of the sales_orders table after the restore operation

Notice that version **3** of the table shows the `operation=RESTORE`, indicating that the table was restored to a previous state.

During the scheduled ingestion process, data is inserted and updated repeatedly. Delta Lake provides a convenient way of merging data in existing tables using **upserts**.

Performing upserts of data

Delta Lake also supports the upsert operation using the `MERGE` clause. The idea of the upsert is simply to merge data in the existing table with new data originating from the source. It is very common in a lakehouse to ingest incremental data and merge it with the pre-existing table in Delta Lake. The `MERGE` process is repeated each time new data gets ingested and is instrumental in creating the single truth of data in the silver layer of the lakehouse.

> **Important Note**
>
> An UPSERT operation is a mix of updates and inserts in the same operation. Using the MERGE clause, you can perform an insert in a table if it does not exist or simply update existing data if it does.

1. Before we start the `MERGE` process, let's find out the current number of rows in the `store_orders` table:

```
%sql
SELECT count(*) FROM store_orders;
```

This results in the following output:

```
1  %sql
2  SELECT count(*) FROM store_orders;
```

▸ (3) Spark Jobs

	count(1) ▲
1	2500

Showing all 1 rows.

Figure 6.30 – Checking the count of rows in sales_orders

2. Now, we will read the incrementally ingested data on the second iteration of the `electroniz_batch_ingestion_pipeline` run. For example, when we ran the pipeline in *Chapter 5, Data Collection Stage – The Bronze Layer*, the `2021/04/28/19` folder structure stored the incremental data for the second run. This folder contains data for 200 new rows in the `sales_orders` table that are ready to be merged in the delta table:

```
ADLS_FOLDER="2021/04/28/19"

BRONZE_TABLE_PATH="wasbs://"+BRONZE_LAYER_
NAMESPACE+"@"+STORAGE_ACCOUNT+".blob.core.windows.
net/"+STORE_SALES_FOLDER+"/\[dbo\].\["+TABLE+"\]/"+ADLS_
FOLDER

df_read_data_hour2 = spark.read.csv(BRONZE_TABLE_PATH,
schema=schema )

display(df_read_data_hour2)
```

This results in the following output:

```
1  ADLS_FOLDER="2021/04/28/19"
2
3  BRONZE_TABLE_PATH="wasbs://"+BRONZE_LAYER_NAMESPACE+"@"+STORAGE_ACCOUNT+".blob.core.windows.net/"+STORE_SALES_FOLDER+"/\[dbo\].\["+TABLE+"\]/"+AD
4
5  df_read_data_hour2 = spark.read.csv(BRONZE_TABLE_PATH, schema=schema )
6  display(df_read_data_hour2)
```

▸ (1) Spark Jobs
▸ ▦ df_read_data_hour2: pyspark.sql.dataframe.DataFrame = [order_number: integer, customer_id: integer ... 7 more fields]

	order_number ▲	customer_id ▲	product_id ▲	order_date ▲	units ▲	sale_price ▲	currency ▲	order_mode ▲	updated_at ▲
1	2501	568	3	04/05/2020	10	68.07	USD	EDIT	2021-04-28T18:25:41.120+0000
2	2502	825	4	03/29/2017	7	50.44	INR	EDIT	2021-04-28T18:25:41.120+0000
3	2503	616	10	07/27/2019	6	82.61	USD	EDIT	2021-04-28T18:25:41.120+0000
4	2504	606	10	12/05/2018	9	77.29	EURO	EDIT	2021-04-28T18:25:41.120+0000
5	2505	550	2	06/30/2020	8	98.87	INR	EDIT	2021-04-28T18:25:41.120+0000
6	2506	848	3	10/28/2018	2	41.32	USD	EDIT	2021-04-28T18:25:41.120+0000
7	2507	810	8	11/08/2020	7	89.12	EURO	EDIT	2021-04-28T18:25:41.120+0000

Showing all 200 rows.

Figure 6.31 – Incremental data for the second iteration of electroniz_batch_ingestion_pipeline

Notice that the new DataFrame, `df_read_data_hour2`, has 200 rows in it.

3. At this point, we are ready to merge the existing `sales_orders` table with the incremental data, using the following code:

```
1  deltaTable = DeltaTable.forPath(spark, DELTA_TABLE_WRITE_PATH)
2  deltaTable.alias("store_orders").merge(
3      df_read_data_hour2.alias("store_orders_new"),
4                  "store_orders.order_number = store_orders_new.order_number")           \
5              .whenMatchedUpdate(set = {"order_number":    "store_orders_new.order_number",   \
6                                        "customer_id":     "store_orders_new.customer_id",    \
7                                        "product_id":      "store_orders_new.product_id",     \
8                                        "order_date":      "store_orders_new.order_date",     \
9                                        "units":           "store_orders_new.units",          \
10                                       "sale_price":      "store_orders_new.sale_price",     \
11                                       "currency":        "store_orders_new.currency",       \
12                                       "order_mode":      "store_orders_new.order_mode",     \
13                                       "updated_at":      "store_orders_new.updated_at" } )  \
14             .whenNotMatchedInsert(values =                                                  \
15                 {                                                                           \
16                                        "order_number":   "store_orders_new.order_number",   \
17                                        "customer_id":    "store_orders_new.customer_id",    \
18                                        "product_id":     "store_orders_new.product_id",     \
19                                        "order_date":     "store_orders_new.order_date",     \
20                                        "units":          "store_orders_new.units",          \
21                                        "sale_price":     "store_orders_new.sale_price",     \
22                                        "currency":       "store_orders_new.currency",       \
23                                        "order_mode":     "store_orders_new.order_mode",     \
24                                        "updated_at":     "store_orders_new.updated_at"      \
25                 }                                                                           \
26             ).execute()
```

▶ (11) Spark Jobs

Command took 5.56 seconds -- by roopikakukreja@gmail.com at 5/4/2021, 10:36:17 AM on trainingcluster

Figure 6.32 – Merge data from the second iteration of electroniz_batch_ingestion_pipeline

Note how the PySpark command has been structured for the upsert operation.

- `sales_orders` – The existing delta table (2000 rows).

- `sales_orders_new` – The temporary table that stores incremental data (200 rows).

- `sales_orders` and `sales_orders_new` are joined together using the `order_number` column.

- `whenMatchedUpdate` – Clause indicates rows that pass the above join condition, which means they pre-exist in the delta table and therefore should simply be updated using new data from the incremental dataset.

- `whenNotMatchedInsert` – Clause indicates rows that do not pass the preceding join condition, which means they are new and therefore should be inserted using the incremental dataset.

4. After completion, let's find out the change in the number of rows in the `store_orders` table after the merge:

    ```
    %sql
    SELECT count(*) FROM store_orders;
    ```

    This results in the following output:

    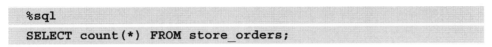

    Figure 6.33 – Checking the count of rows in sales_orders after the merge of the second iteration

    The number of rows has incremented by 200. I am sure you have guessed by now that the incremental rows were merged using the `whenNotMatchedInsert` clause.

5. Due to the recent merge, the history of the `store_orders` table will have advanced as well:

    ```
    %sql
    DESCRIBE HISTORY store_orders;
    ```

    This results in the following output:

    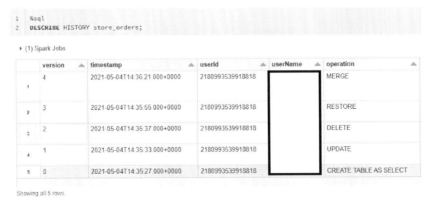

    Figure 6.34 – Transaction history of the sales_orders table after
    the merge operation of the second iteration

Notice that version **4** of the `store_orders` table shows `operation=MERGE`. I am sure that, by this point, you relate well to the ACID compliance in delta tables.

6. You may recollect that `electroniz_batch_ingestion_pipeline` runs every hour. After the third iteration, more incremental data was ingested and this time my folder structure after the third iteration looked like `2021/04/28/20`. This folder contains data for five rows that were edited in the source database. Most likely, this may have happened due to price adjustments.

   To maintain the consistency of data, we want the adjusted prices from the `stores` database to be correctly reflected in the lakehouse. We can start by reading the incremental data as follows:

```
ADLS_FOLDER="2021/04/28/20"
BRONZE_TABLE_PATH="wasbs://"+BRONZE_LAYER_
NAMESPACE+"@"+STORAGE_ACCOUNT+".blob.core.windows.
net/"+STORE_SALES_FOLDER+"/\[dbo\].\["+TABLE+"\]/"+ADLS_
FOLDER
df_read_data_hour3 = spark.read.csv(BRONZE_TABLE_PATH,
schema=schema )
display(df_read_data_hour3)
```

   This results in the following output:

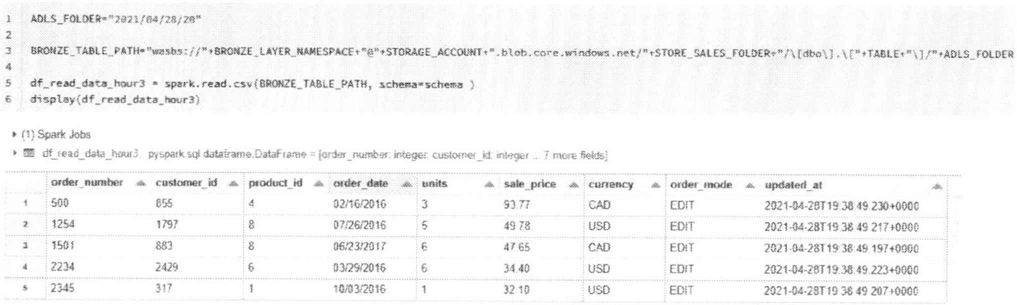

```
ADLS_FOLDER="2021/04/28/20"

BRONZE_TABLE_PATH="wasbs://"+BRONZE_LAYER_NAMESPACE+"@"+STORAGE_ACCOUNT+".blob.core.windows.net/"+STORE_SALES_FOLDER+"/\[dbo\].\["+TABLE+"\]/"+ADLS_FOLDER

df_read_data_hour3 = spark.read.csv(BRONZE_TABLE_PATH, schema=schema )
display(df_read_data_hour3)
```

▸ (1) Spark Jobs

▸ df_read_data_hour3: pyspark.sql.dataframe.DataFrame = [order_number: integer, customer_id: integer ... 7 more fields]

	order_number	customer_id	product_id	order_date	units	sale_price	currency	order_mode	updated_at
1	500	855	4	02/16/2016	3	93.77	CAD	EDIT	2021-04-28T19:38:49.230+0000
2	1254	1797	8	07/26/2016	5	49.78	USD	EDIT	2021-04-28T19:38:49.217+0000
3	1501	883	8	06/23/2017	6	47.65	CAD	EDIT	2021-04-28T19:38:49.197+0000
4	2234	2429	6	03/29/2016	6	34.40	USD	EDIT	2021-04-28T19:38:49.223+0000
5	2345	317	1	10/03/2016	1	32.10	USD	EDIT	2021-04-28T19:38:49.207+0000

Figure 6.35 – Incremental data for the third iteration of electroniz_batch_ingestion_pipeline

   Notice the file contains five rows with `order_mode=EDIT`.

7. Compare the same rows in the `store_orders` table. Notice the `sale_price` value for these rows differs compared to the incremental data read in the preceding Spark DataFrame, `df_read_data_hour3`:

```
%sql
SELECT * FROM store_orders WHERE order_number IN (500,
1254, 1501, 2234, 2345);
```

This results in the following output:

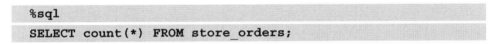

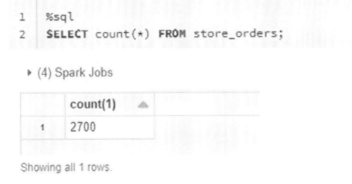

Figure 6.36 – Checking the data in the sales_orders table before
the merge operation of the third iteration

8. Invoke the merge for the `sales_orders` table one more time. Notice that this
    time the Spark DataFrame, `df_read_data_hour3`, is being merged. You can find
    the complete code block on GitHub for this chapter.

9. You may recall that the rows merged this time are price adjustments, therefore,
    they should pre-exist in the delta table. This means the number of rows in the
    `store_orders` table should remain unaffected after the merge:

```
%sql
SELECT count(*) FROM store_orders;
```

This results in the following output:

```
1  %sql
2  SELECT count(*) FROM store_orders;
```

▶ (4) Spark Jobs

	count(1)
1	2700

Showing all 1 rows.

Figure 6.37 – Checking the count of rows in sales_orders after the merge of the third iteration

Surely enough, the count of the `store_orders` table is the same as before.

10. Check if the rows in the `store_orders` table have been edited:

```sql
%sql
SELECT * FROM store_orders WHERE order_number IN (500,
1254, 1501, 2234, 2345);
```

This results in the following output:

```
1   %sql
2   SELECT * FROM store_orders WHERE order_number IN (500, 1254, 1501, 2234, 2345);
```

▶ (3) Spark Jobs

	order_number	customer_id	product_id	order_date	units	sale_price	currency	order_mode	updated_at
1	1254	1797	8	07/26/2016	5	49.78	USD	EDIT	2021-04-28T19:38:49.217+0000
2	2234	2429	6	03/29/2016	6	34.4	USD	EDIT	2021-04-28T19:38:49.223+0000
3	2345	317	1	10/03/2016	1	32.1	USD	EDIT	2021-04-28T19:38:49.207+0000
4	500	855	4	02/16/2016	3	93.77	CAD	EDIT	2021-04-28T19:38:49.230+0000
5	1501	883	8	06/23/2017	6	47.65	CAD	EDIT	2021-04-28T19:38:49.197+0000

Showing all 5 rows

Figure 6.38 – Checking the data in the sales_orders table after the merge operation of the third iteration

Notice the `sale_price` value now reflects the latest prices after adjustments.

11. The history of the `store_orders` table should have advanced due to the recent merge:

```sql
%sql
DESCRIBE HISTORY store_orders;
```

This results in the following output:

```
1   %sql
2   DESCRIBE HISTORY store_orders;
```

▶ (1) Spark Jobs

	version	timestamp	userId	userName	operation	operationParameters
1	5	2021-05-04T14:42:30.000+0000	2180993539918818	roopikakukreja@gmail.com	MERGE	▶ {"predicate": "(store_orders.`order_number` = store_orders_new.`order_numbe` [{\"actionType\":\"update\"}]", "notMatchedPredicates": "[{\"actionType\": \"insert\"
2	4	2021-05-04T14:36:21.000+0000	2180993539918818	roopikakukreja@gmail.com	MERGE	▶ {"predicate": "(store_orders.`order_number` = store_orders_new.`order_numbe` [{\"actionType\":\"update\"}]", "notMatchedPredicates": "[{\"actionType\": \"insert\"
3	3	2021-05-04T14:35:55.000+0000	2180993539918818	roopikakukreja@gmail.com	RESTORE	▶ {"version": "1", "timestamp": null}
4	2	2021-05-04T14:35:37.000+0000	2180993539918818	roopikakukreja@gmail.com	DELETE	▶ {"predicate": "[\"(spark_catalog.default.store_orders.`order_number` = 5)\"]"}
5	1	2021-05-04T14:35:33.000+0000	2180993539918818	roopikakukreja@gmail.com	UPDATE	▶ {"predicate": "(order_number#5975 = 5)"}
6	0	2021-05-04T14:35:27.000+0000	2180993539918818	roopikakukreja@gmail.com	CREATE TABLE AS SELECT	▶ {"isManaged": "false", "description": null, "partitionBy": "[\"currency\"]", "propert

Showing all 6 rows

Figure 6.39 – Transaction history of the sales_orders table after the merge operation of the third iteration

Notice that version 5 of the `store_orders` table also shows the `operation=MERGE`.

Now that we understand upserts, we will deep dive into other important features of Delta Lake.

Understanding isolation levels

In Delta Lake, the isolation level of a table defines the degree to which the transaction must be isolated from modifications that are being made by concurrent transactions. There are two isolation levels, as follows:

- The `Serializable` isolation level is strong, which means the write and read operations exist in a serial sequence.

- The `WriteSerializable` isolation level is the default. In this isolation level, only the write operations exist in a serial sequence.

We will check them out as follows:

1. The isolation level can be queried for every transaction in history:

```sql
%sql
SELECT version, operation, isolationLevel
  from (DESCRIBE HISTORY store_orders);
```

This results in the following output:

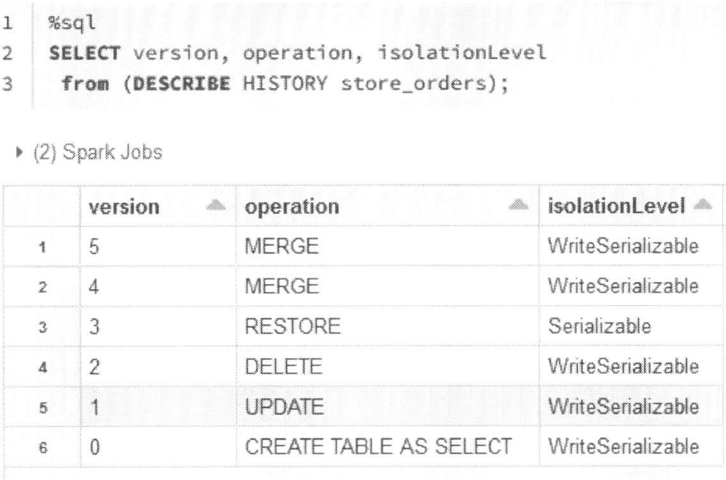

```
1   %sql
2   SELECT version, operation, isolationLevel
3     from (DESCRIBE HISTORY store_orders);
```

▸ (2) Spark Jobs

	version	operation	isolationLevel
1	5	MERGE	WriteSerializable
2	4	MERGE	WriteSerializable
3	3	RESTORE	Serializable
4	2	DELETE	WriteSerializable
5	1	UPDATE	WriteSerializable
6	0	CREATE TABLE AS SELECT	WriteSerializable

Figure 6.40 – Transaction history isolationLevel

2. Although the default isolation level for delta tables is `WriteSerializable`, it can be changed as desired. We can alter the isolation of the `store_orders` table to the `Serializable` isolation level:

```sql
%sql
ALTER TABLE store_orders SET TBLPROPERTIES ('delta.
isolationLevel' = 'Serializable')
```

This results in the following output:

```
1   %sql
2   ALTER TABLE store_orders SET TBLPROPERTIES ('delta.isolationLevel' = 'Serializable')
```

▸ (4) Spark Jobs

OK

Figure 6.41 – Changing the isolation level of the store_orders table

3. From here onwards, all transactions on the `store_orders` table will use `isolationlevel=Serializable`. We are going to update a row in the table to check if the isolation was appropriately altered:

```
%sql
UPDATE store_orders SET sale_price=100.00 WHERE order_
number=500;
```

4. Now, check the isolation level for the latest transaction in history:

```
%sql
SELECT version, operation, isolationLevel
  from (DESCRIBE HISTORY store_orders);
```

This results in the following output:

```
1   %sql
2   SELECT version, operation, isolationLevel
3     from (DESCRIBE HISTORY store_orders);
4
```

▸ (2) Spark Jobs

	version	operation	isolationLevel
1	7	UPDATE	Serializable
2	6	SET TBLPROPERTIES	SnapshotIsolation
3	5	MERGE	WriteSerializable
4	4	MERGE	WriteSerializable
5	3	RESTORE	Serializable
6	2	DELETE	WriteSerializable
7	1	UPDATE	WriteSerializable

Showing all 8 rows.

Figure 6.42 – Transaction history isolationLevel after the override

Notice that the latest transaction was performed using the `Serializable` isolation level. We will now check out what concurrency control is all about.

> **Important Note**
>
> The `Serializable` isolation level offers strong consistency, whereas `WriteSerializable` offers the correct balance of availability and consistency of data.

Understanding concurrency control

By now, hopefully, we have a good understanding of ACID compliance in a Delta Lake using the transaction log. Up until now, all operations during this exercise were performed using the same user. However, in a real case scenario, you can have multiple users trying to read and write to the same delta table at the same time. This is how concurrency controls are implemented in Delta Lake.

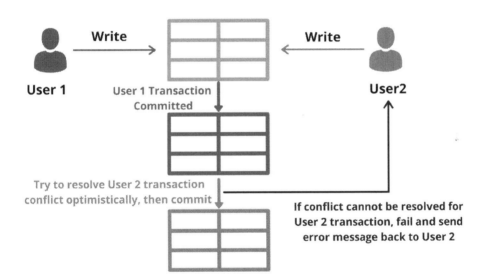

Figure 6.43 – Concurrency control in Delta Lake

This is better represented as follows:

- Assume User 1 and User 2 perform a write operation to a delta table at the same time.

- Delta Lake records the version of the table before any change has been made to the delta table.

- The write from User 1 commits successfully, and a success message is sent back.

- The write from User 2 does not fail. Instead, Delta Lake tries to silently resolve conflicts from User 2's transaction against the previously committed data. If no conflicts are discovered, the transactions are committed, else an error message is sent back to User 2.

This type of concurrency control is also known as **optimistic concurrency control**. Now that we are done with most of the work here, we will go ahead and clean up the Azure resources that we used in the following section.

Cleaning up Azure resources

For this training exercise, we created a `scratch` namespace in Azure Data Lake storage. This namespace is not required for the rest of the book, so you may delete i:

1. Invoke the following commands in the Cloud Shell to delete the `scratch` namespace:

```
SCRATCH_NAMESPACE="scratch"
STORAGEACCOUNTNAME="traininglakehouse"
az storage fs delete -n $SCRATCH_NAMESPACE --account-name
$STORAGEACCOUNTNAME --yes
```

2. Invoke the following commands in the Cloud Shell to delete the Azure Databricks workspace:

```
RESOURCEGROUPNAME="training_rg"
WORKSPACE="trainingdatabricks"
az config set extension.use_dynamic_install=yes_without_
prompt
az databricks workspace delete --resource-group
$RESOURCEGROUPNAME --name $WORKSPACE
```

The resources have now been deleted and we should be good to go!

Summary

In this chapter, we learned about Delta Lake, known to be the driving force behind the modern lakehouse architecture – it truly enables the lakehouse. We learned in detail about some key features of Delta Lake, such as ACID compliance and open standards. After that, we performed common data lake table operations and showed how Delta Lake controls data isolation and concurrency levels.

In *Chapter 7, Data Curation Stage – The Silver Layer*, we will put the knowledge gained in this chapter to good use. Using Delta Lake, we will create the silver layer of the Electroniz lakehouse. You may recall from previous chapters that the silver layer in the lakehouse stores the curated, deduplicated, and standardized data. The silver layer represents the single source of truth of data, stored in a state that is readily consumable by diverse data analytics workloads.

7
Data Curation Stage – The Silver Layer

The journey of data is now at a very critical stage. In this stage, the driver (data engineer) needs to carefully plan and maneuver the vehicle (data pipeline) around several roadblocks in such a way that the sanity, durability, and security of the data are preserved.

In the previous chapter, we performed a deep dive into Delta Lake. Understanding the Delta Lake functionality is a critical skill, as it enables the data engineer to design and develop the silver layer of the lakehouse. In this chapter, we will advance our understanding of how to cleanse raw data. We will start by learning the need for data curation, followed by building a data curation pipeline that can perform the cleaning work consistently and regularly.

In this chapter, we will cover the following topics:

- The need for curating raw data
- The process of curating raw data
- Developing a data curation pipeline
- Running the pipeline for the silver layer
- Verifying curated data in the silver layer

The need for curating raw data

Data in the bronze layer is raw by nature in that it gets collected from several distinct and diverse data sources. Due to the diverse sources, it is natural for data to be delivered in unstandardized, invalid, inconsistent, non-uniform, duplicate, or insecure forms. In some other cases, raw data may have **PII** data in clear text, which should be properly masked before analytical consumption.

> **Important note**
>
> In big data, one of the hotly debated topics is veracity – that is, can the organization put trust in the data that is being collected? And if yes, then how much?

Let's try to understand some characteristics of unclean data so that we can properly justify the reasons for curating data.

Unstandardized data

These days, typically, data is collected using **online transaction processing (OLTP)** applications. The problem is that OLTP applications, such as web applications and mobile applications created in different countries, follow varying standards. During user input, some applications may accept first and last names as two separate fields, whereas other applications may have just one field for both. In the US, it is common to follow the MM/DD/YYYY format for dates, whereas many other countries prefer to use DD/MM/YYYY.

Let me quote some examples from the Electroniz data that falls into this category.

The `store_orders` data has a column named `order_date` that uses the MM/DD/YYYY format:

order_date ▲
05/12/2017
08/14/2020
02/26/2021
12/21/2019
07/12/2019
06/29/2019
06/12/2020

Figure 7.1 – Store_orders data in the MM/DD/YYYY date format

And the e-commerce transactions have the `order_date` column that uses DD/MM/
YYYY format:

Figure 7.2 – E-commerce transaction data in the DD/MM/YYYY date format

In another scenario, the `store_customers` data has a column named `email` with
a mix of lowercase and uppercase characters. Ideally, emails should be stored in lowercase.

Figure 7.3 – Customer emails in mixed case

Before making this data available to end users, it needs to be properly standardized as per
agreed-upon organizational policies.

Invalid data

Invalid data does not conform to constraints. These constraints can be of several types:

- **Types**: Columns should be of a specific data type, such as numeric, date, or floats.

- **Ranges**: The data in a column needs to fall within a range of values.

- **Uniqueness**: The data in the column should have unique values.

- **Relational**: The column should not be an orphan – the parent should mandatorily
  exist in the parent table.

Here is the **entity-relationship diagram (ERD)** for the Electroniz `stores` database:

> **Important note**
>
> ERDs are an important tool for data engineers to visualize database structures and gain knowledge of the business domain under consideration. These diagrams also contain important information regarding data types that will be useful later in the development of the curation code.

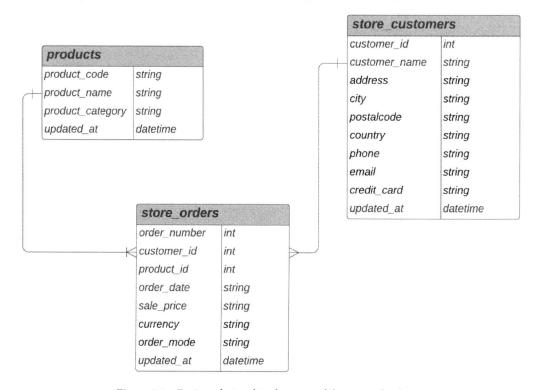

Figure 7.4 – Entity-relationship diagram of the stores database

Unfortunately, a careful study of the ERD will reveal that this dataset is short on many levels. Several problems need to be highlighted with this dataset:

- The `products` table has a `product_code` column that is the parent column for the `product_id` column in the `store_orders` table. As per best practices, the name of the columns in the parent and child tables should be the same.

- Notice that the `products.product_code` column is of the *string* data type, yet it is supposed to join with `store_orders.product_id`, which is of an *integer* type.

> **Important note**
>
> Having different data types of columns that join with each other can lead to a serious performance drag during querying. The curation stage is an ideal phase to trace and fix these kinds of issues.

- After careful review of the data, it was discovered that the following two orders reference `product_id` rows that do not exist in the `products` table. In other words, they are *orphan* rows.

order_number	customer_id	product_id
1001	2840	20
1002	907	13

Figure 7.5 – Orphan rows in store_orders

Before making it available to end users, we should either exclude or fix invalid data.

Non-uniform data

Non-uniform data exists in varying forms across different datasets. We have found a couple of instances of non-uniform data in the bronze layer:

- In the Electroniz `stores` database, the `country` column exists in the `store_customers` table as follows:

country
United States
United Kingdom

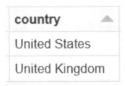

Figure 7.6 – Country data in store_customers

Whereas it exists like this in the `e-commerce` transactions:

country
USA
UK

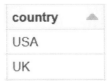

Figure 7.7 – Country data in e-commerce transactions

- Additionally, we noticed that the `store_orders` and `e-commerce` transactions are done in varying currencies – USD, CAD, EUR, and INR. Ideally, we should convert all transactions to a uniform currency.

Before making this data available to end users, we should make it uniform across all data consumption layers.

Inconsistent data

Inconsistent data means having different values of the same data in two separate datasets. As an example, the following customer in the Electroniz `stores` database lives in a city named `Crewe`:

Figure 7.8 – Data for a customer in the stores database

The same customer bought products on the e-commerce store but claimed to live in a different city named `Milton Keynes`.

Figure 7.9 – Data for the same customer in the e-commerce transactions

Before making this data available to end users, we should make it consistent across all data consumption layers.

> **Important note**
> Before implementing the curation logic in the pipelines, a data engineer should seek the organization's approval regarding the rules that make data uniform, consistent, valid, and standard.

Duplicate data

In the fast-changing world, data evolves all the time, from customers changing demographic data such as addresses and phone numbers to orders being bought and returned. Capturing and processing changed data is also referred to as **change data capture** (CDC) and has been an ongoing challenge in the data lake world. Let me try to explain this using a couple of examples:

- A new customer was created in the `stores` database at 17:56 on April 4, 2021. The record was ingested in the bronze layer using the `electroniz_batch_ingestion_pipeline` run at 18:00 on April 4, 2021:

customer_id	email	customer_name	address	city	updated_at
501	Phasellus.vitae@vitae.co.uk	Prescott Barnes	960-5386 Vel, Road	Pangnirtung	2021-04-28T17:56:10.520+0000

Figure 7.10 – New customer record ingested into the electroniz lakehouse

- The customer discovered that his name was not properly input into the system, so requested the store clerk to make the change at 18:30 on April 4, 2021. The edited record was ingested into the bronze layer using the `electroniz_batch_ingestion_pipeline` run at 19:00 on April 4, 2021:

customer_id	email	customer_name	address	city	updated_at
501	Phasellus.vitae@vitae.co.uk	Prescott Barnes Jr.	960-5386 Vel, Road	Pangnirtung	2021-04-28T18:25:40.927+0000

Figure 7.11 – Edited customer record ingested into the electroniz lakehouse creating duplicates

Now, here is the problem. In the store's database, the above record exists *only once*, yet there are *two* records of the same person in the data lake bronze layer. These are referred to as *duplicate* records.

- A similar kind of issue exists with `store_orders`. The following orders were placed in stores and were ingested into the bronze layer using the `electroniz_batch_ingestion_pipeline` run at 18:00 on April 4, 2021:

order_number	order_date	sale_price	order_mode	updated_at
500	02/16/2016	99.63	NEW	2021-04-28T17:56:11.093+0000
1254	07/26/2016	33.70	NEW	2021-04-28T17:56:11.220+0000
1501	06/23/2017	46.69	NEW	2021-04-28T17:56:11.273+0000
2234	03/29/2016	72.15	NEW	2021-04-28T17:56:11.387+0000
2345	10/03/2016	40.10	NEW	2021-04-28T17:56:11.410+0000

Figure 7.12 – New orders ingested into the electroniz lakehouse

- After some price adjustments were performed, the same records were ingested in the bronze layer as follows using the `electroniz_batch_ingestion_pipeline` run at 20:00 on April 4, 2021.

order_number	order_date	sale_price	order_mode	updated_at
500	02/16/2016	93.77	EDIT	2021-04-28T19:38:49.230+0000
1254	07/26/2016	49.78	EDIT	2021-04-28T19:38:49.217+0000
1501	06/23/2017	47.65	EDIT	2021-04-28T19:38:49.197+0000
2234	03/29/2016	34.40	EDIT	2021-04-28T19:38:49.223+0000
2345	10/03/2016	32.10	EDIT	2021-04-28T19:38:49.207+0000

Figure 7.13 – Edited orders ingested into the electroniz lakehouse creating duplicates

Like customers, orders are duplicated in the bronze layer as well. Before this data can be used, it needs to be properly deduplicated in such a fashion that only the latest version of the record is visible to the end users.

Insecure data

In *Chapter 4, Understanding Data Pipelines*, during the discovery phase, Electroniz mentioned that the lakehouse must abide by PCI regulations, so all PII data needs to be properly masked and encrypted. Following careful review of the data, we found out that all PII columns are visible as clear text in the bronze layer, as follows:

customer_id	email	customer_name	address	phone	credit_card
1	amet.metus@Nullatinciduntneque.net	Ariel Hale	Ap #660-3260 Pellentesque St	1-973-833-9836	5124442517412973
2	sollicitudin@enimmitempor.ca	Aubrey Norris	Ap #943-1347 Imperdiet Avenue	07672 321093	5103696625359419
3	Donec.non@dapibusrutrum.com	Bruno Hebert	8566 Nisi Avenue	02794 010514	5132188470727440
4	nec@lectus.net	Ira Lucas	936-3011 Convallis Road	1-117-676-2784	5164946381862809
5	nec@orciluctuset.co.uk	Hannah Ferrell	P.O. Box 755, 7941 Aenean St	1 (867) 533-2852	5256394502723692
6	egestas@Sedeueros.edu	May Bentley	P.O. Box 507, 7752 A Street	1 (581) 785-4024	5553254253392933
7	luctus.ut@euismod.com	Tariq Singh	P.O. Box 716, 3443 Metus Ave	+91 6777750639	5103138625325504

Figure 7.14 – Unmasked data in the electroniz lakehouse

Before making it available to end users, insecure data needs to be properly *masked* across all data consumption layers:

Important note

To protect the privacy of individuals, the **General Data Protection Regulation (GDPR)** mandatorily enforces data masking for every organization that collects, stores, and handles PII data.

The process of curating raw data

By this point, hopefully, it is easy to envision that the need for curating data is very real. Now, let's focus on the actual process to make this happen.

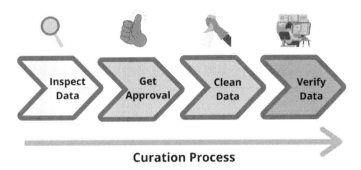

Figure 7.15 – Data curation process

Inspecting data

The process of data curation starts by inspecting sample data. Typically, this is a joint effort between the data engineers and the customer team members. You can start by visually inspecting data covering diverse data sources, although in many cases you may need to implement programming logic to discover data that is unstandardized, invalid, inconsistent, non-uniform, duplicate, or insecure.

Deliverable: A detailed report listing all the instances where data curation will be required, including a plan to fix each case. Within the report, feel free to include the pseudocode for the business logic that addresses the specific case, as follows:

```
IF raw_data.country IN ('USA', 'United States', 'United States
of America' THEN
    curated_data.country = 'USA'
```

Getting approval

The report created during the inspection phase should be formally submitted to the customer team for review and approval. This ensures that the customer is on board with the business logic that will be implemented to curate the data.

Deliverable: Formal approval by the customer team.

Cleaning data

Once the approval has been received, it is time to start the actual implementation of the business logic that implements data curation. As a data engineer, you are free to choose from a variety of frameworks, languages, and tools that can be used, although it is better to use something that the customer is comfortable with. Generally, the two most frequently used ones are **Apache Spark** and **SQL**. Once the curation logic has been developed, it is integrated within the curation pipeline.

Deliverable: Logic that implements the curation.

Verifying data

The final step of data curation is to verify that the curation logic worked as intended. Typically, this activity should be performed by customer team members because they are closer to the data and therefore more likely to understand it better than the data engineer.

Deliverable: Formal approval by the Customer Team.

> **Important note**
>
> Going from one project to another, a data engineer learns to spot common trends in data that require curation. In some cases, it is tempting to start fixing data right away, but it is equally important to follow a well-defined curation process.

Now that we have a fair understanding of the need for data curation and a sound understanding of the process, let's build an actual curation pipeline. For the sake of simplicity, we are going to assume that following the curation process, we diligently submitted a report to Electroniz with our findings as outlined in the *Need for Curating Raw Data* section. The Electroniz team has reviewed the report and given us a final approval to proceed with the next steps. Therefore, we are going to start developing the curation logic using Apache Spark on **Azure Databricks**.

Developing a data curation pipeline

We are ready to start the development of the Electroniz curation pipeline. The data will now take the journey from being in an unclean state to a more cleansed and usable state. I had previously promised to keep you updated with which area of the architecture diagram is being addressed, so here it is:

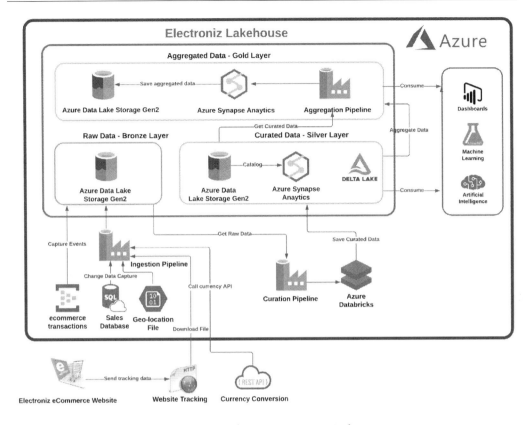

Figure 7.16 – Electroniz curation pipeline

In the following section, we will be creating the curation pipeline that is highlighted in the preceding figure.

Preparing Azure resources

We will begin by first preparing the required resources, as follows:

1. We will start by creating a new namespace in Azure data lake storage for the `silver` layer.

   I had mentioned earlier that storage account names in Azure are globally unique. Throughout this exercise, we are using the storage account name `traininglakehouse`. You will need to edit it as per the account name that you created:

```
SILVER_NAMESPACE="silver"
STORAGEACCOUNTNAME="traininglakehouse"
RESOURCEGROUPNAME="training_rg"
```

```
LOCATION="eastus"
az storage fs create -n $SILVER_NAMESPACE --account-
name $STORAGEACCOUNTNAME --metadata project=lakehouse
environment=development layer=bronze --only-show-errors
```

This results in the following output:

```
Azure> SILVER_NAMESPACE="silver"
Azure> STORAGEACCOUNTNAME="traininglakehouse"
Azure> RESOURCEGROUPNAME="training_rg"
Azure> LOCATION="eastus"
Azure> az storage fs create -n $SILVER_NAMESPACE --account-name
show-errors
{
  "client_request_id": "2235bb22-b42e-11eb-8c3c-0a580af46dd2",
  "date": "2021-05-13T20:59:39+00:00",
  "error_code": null,
  "etag": "\"0x8D916520671CA2A\"",
  "last_modified": "2021-05-13T20:59:40+00:00",
  "request_id": "1236c1f0-301e-0024-4f3a-48240f000000",
  "version": "2020-02-10"
}
```

Figure 7.17 – Azure data lake namespace for silver layer

If the above command is successful, you should be able to see the newly created container on the Azure portal by browsing to **Home** > **All Resources** > **traininglakehouse**:

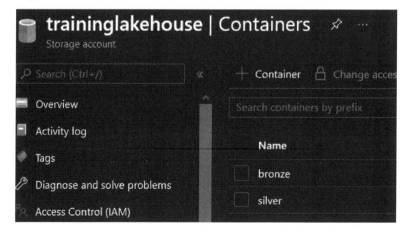

Figure 7.18 – Silver namespace in traininglakehouse

2. We also need an **Azure Data Factory** for this exercise. You may recall that we had previously created `traininglakehousedf` in *Chapter 5, Data Collection Stage – The Bronze Layer*. Hopefully, you still have it hanging around in your Azure subscription. If you accidentally deleted it, you will need to follow the steps to recreate it in the *Build Building a batch ingestion pipeline* section.

3. Once again, we will use Azure Databricks to read, perform curation, and write data in delta format. To read and write data, Azure Databricks requires the storage account keys for the Azure data lake storage. Invoke the following commands on the Azure Cloud Shell:

```
STORAGEACCOUNTNAME="traininglakehouse"
az storage account keys list --account-name
$STORAGEACCOUNTNAME
```

If the preceding commands worked as desired, you should see two storage keys as follows. Take note of the value for `key1` from the command shown. We will need it later for the Databricks workspace and Data Factory configuration:

Figure 7.19 – traininglakehouse storage account keys

4. To curate data and store it in the silver layer, we will create a new Azure Databricks workspace using the instructions as follows. Invoke the following commands on the Azure Cloud Shell. Azure Databricks workspace names are globally unique, so please edit the `WORKSPACE` name accordingly:

```
RESOURCEGROUPNAME="training_rg"
LOCATION="eastus"
WORKSPACE="trainingdatabricks"
az config set extension.use_dynamic_install=yes_without_
prompt
az databricks workspace create --resource-group
$RESOURCEGROUPNAME --name $WORKSPACE --location $LOCATION
--sku trial
```

If you do not have an Azure trial account, you need to use the `sku` standard:

```
training@Azure>RESOURCEGROUPNAME="training_rg"
training@Azure>LOCATION="eastus"
training@Azure>WORKSPACE="trainingdatabricks"
training@Azure>az config set extension.use_dynamic_install=yes_without_prompt
Command group 'config' is experimental and under development. Reference and support
training@Azure>az databricks workspace create --resource-group $RESOURCEGROUPNAME --
{| Finished ..
  "authorizations": [
    {
      "principalId": "9a74af6f-d153-4348-988a-e2672920bee9",
      "roleDefinitionId": "8e3af657-a8ff-443c-a75c-2fe8c4bcb635"
    }
  ],
  "createdBy": {
    "applicationId": "c44b4083-3bb0-49c1-b47d-974e53cbdf3c",
    "oid": "09a48665-df3d-42cd-b4d4-5b314a4cc3d4",
    "puid": "000300003AA12A41"
```

Figure 7.20 – Azure Databricks workspace creation

5. To validate the creation of the Azure Databricks workspace, go to the Azure portal:

    ▪ Click on **Home** > **All Resources** > **trainingdatabricks**

    ▪ Click on **Launch Workspace**:

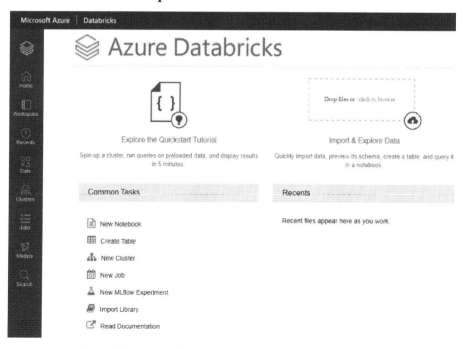

Figure 7.21 – Azure Databricks workspace on the Azure portal

6. We are now ready to create the Spark cluster. Using the menu on the left, click on **Compute**, and then click on **Create Cluster**:

    - Cluster name: `curationcluster`.

    - Cluster mode: `Single node`.

    - Edit the following command as per your Azure storage account name and key: `fs.azure.account.key.<storage-account-name>.blob.core.windows.net <storage-account-access-key>`.

    - Click on **Advanced options**:

    - Paste the edited command from the previous step in the **Spark Config** field as the last line. Now, click the **Create Cluster** button:

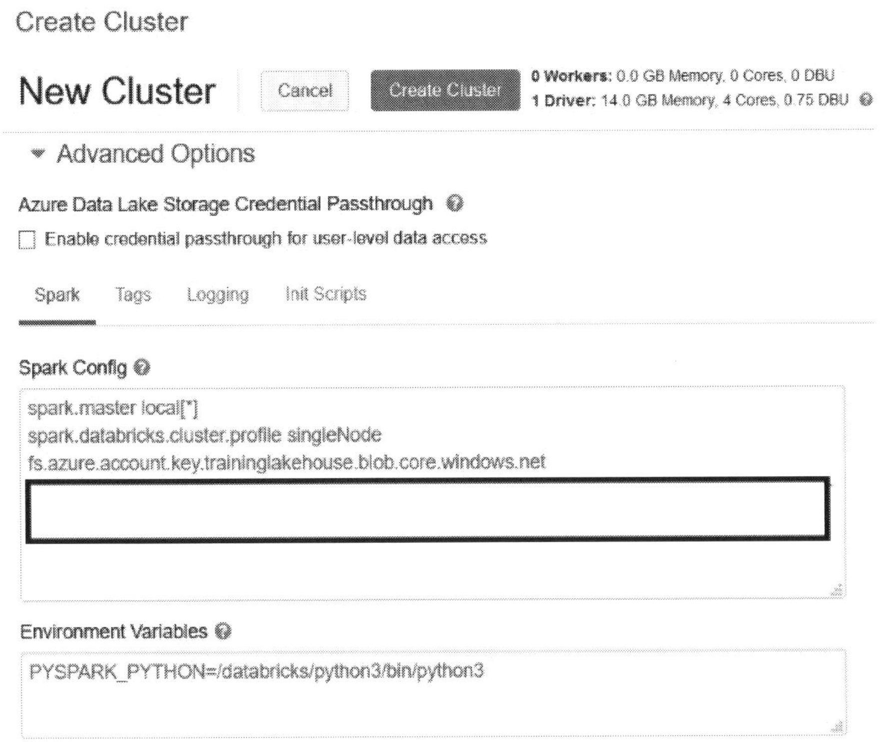

Create Cluster

New Cluster   Cancel   Create Cluster   **0 Workers:** 0.0 GB Memory, 0 Cores, 0 DBU
1 Driver: 14.0 GB Memory, 4 Cores, 0.75 DBU

▼ Advanced Options

Azure Data Lake Storage Credential Passthrough

☐ Enable credential passthrough for user-level data access

Spark   Tags   Logging   Init Scripts

Spark Config

```
spark.master local[*]
spark.databricks.cluster.profile singleNode
fs.azure.account.key.traininglakehouse.blob.core.windows.net
```

Environment Variables

```
PYSPARK_PYTHON=/databricks/python3/bin/python3
```

Figure 7.22 – Azure Databricks cluster creation option

This will spin up a small Apache Spark cluster that we will use for invoking Spark and Delta Lake commands.

7. Once the cluster creation has been completed, you should see a window that looks like this:

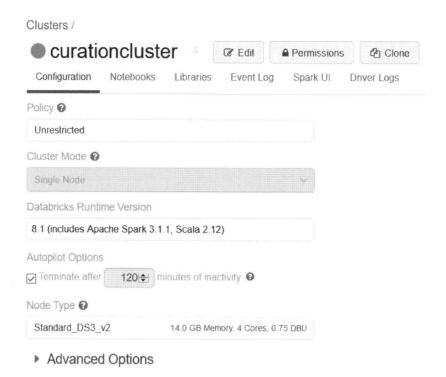

Figure 7.23 – Azure Databricks cluster creation

8. Now we need a notebook that will serve as our **interactive development environment (IDE)**. A notebook is a web-based interface to type and run code as well as create visualizations.

9. On the Databricks workspace, click on **Workspace**. Then, click on **Users**.

    Click on the arrow beside your username and then click on **Import**.

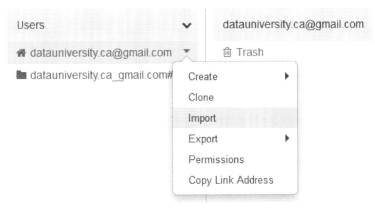

Figure 7.24 – Importing a notebook into the Azure Databricks workspace

Choose **URL**.

Use the following URL:

```
https://github.com/PacktPublishing/Data-Engineering-with-
Apache-Spark-Delta-Lake-and-Lakehouse/blob/main/project/
curation/delta_lake/electroniz_curation_notebook.ipynb
```

Click on **Import**.

10. Now, click on the cluster dropdown and choose **curationcluster**.

Figure 7.25 – Choosing a Spark cluster for the notebook

11. Now we need to get an access token from Azure Databricks that will allow the Azure Data Factory to connect to it. On the top-right corner, locate the Databricks workspace name and click on it.

Figure 7.26 – Accessing User Settings in Azure Databricks

12. Click on **User Settings**.

Under **Access Token**, click on **Generate New Token** and fill in the following field:

Comment: `Data Factory Connections`.

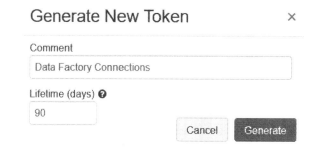

Figure 7.27 – Generating access token options in Azure Databricks

Click on **Generate**. A new window will open. Take note of this token, as you will need it later:

Figure 7.28 – Generating an access token in Azure Databricks

Now that we have created the required Azure resources, we are ready to move ahead with the creation of the curation pipeline.

Creating the pipeline for the silver layer

Perform the following steps to create the pipeline for the silver layer:

1. Using the Azure portal, connect to **Home** > **All Resources** > **traininglakehousedf**. Click on **Open** under **Open Azure Data Factory Studio**. This should open a new Azure Data Factory workspace window.

2. Navigate to the Azure Data Factory workspace window. Using the panel on the left, click on the menu on **Author**. In the **Factory Resources** panel, click on the **three dots** to the right of **Pipelines** and choose **New Pipeline**.

    In the **Properties** panel, input the following:

    - Name: electroniz_curation_pipeline.

    - Description: This pipeline will curate data for the sales database, currency conversion, geo-location, and e-commerce website tracking logs by fetching from the bronze layer and saving it in the silver layer.

3. Now, click on the empty white space in the **activities** section. In the panel below, under **Parameters**, create the following parameters:

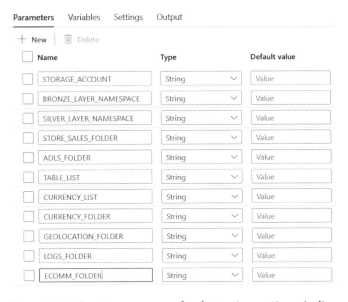

Figure 7.29 – Creating parameters for electroniz_curation_pipeline

4. In a previous chapter, we had stored the Azure data lake account key (`ADLSKEY`) in the secrets manager of the **Azure key vault**. The curation pipeline will fetch this secret *dynamically* at runtime so that we can read data from storage. This is how it is accomplished:

In the **Activities** panel, search for `Web`. Now, drag the **Web** activity to the right panel.

- Name: `Get Secret`.

- Click on **Settings**.

- URL: Enter the **Secret Identifier** value from the Azure key vault secret created previously.

5. Click on **Home** > **All Resources** > **trainingkv100**.

- Click on **Secrets** > **ADLSKEY**. Now, click on the entry under **CURRENT VERSION**.

- Note the value of the **Secret Identifier** value.

- Add `?api-version=7.0` at the end of the URL as follows: `https://trainingkv100.vault.azure.net/secrets/ADLSKEY/2d13f6f42ff14e53ae953e42c36c32c0?api-version=7.0`.

- **Authentication**: `Managed Identity`.

- **Resource**: `https://vault.azure.net`.

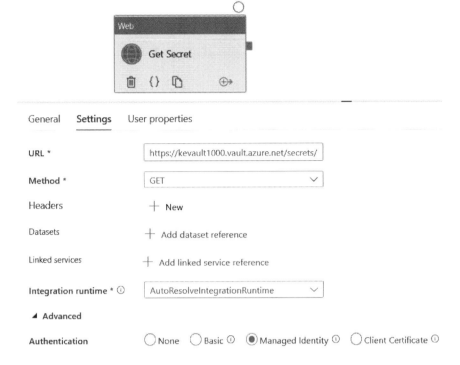

Figure 7.30 – Creating a Get Secret activity in electroniz_curation_pipeline

> **Important note**
>
> As per best practices, it is never a good idea to hardcode secrets within your
> pipelines and notebooks. Many times, developers push code into repositories
> with passwords and keys embedded in them. This is counted as a serious
> breach of security, so should be avoided at any cost.

6. Now that we have retrieved the storage secret, we need to pass the parameters and
    secret fetched previously to a notebook that will perform data curation:

    - In the **Activities** panel, search for `Notebook`. Now, drag the **Notebook** activity to
      the right panel.

    - Name: `Run Curation Notebook`.

    - Click on **Azure Databricks**. Click on **New**. A new window will open named **New
      linked service (Azure Databricks)**.

- Name: `Curation Spark Cluster`.

- Azure subscription: `Free Tier or Paid Subscription`.

- Databricks workspace: `trainingdatabricks`.

- Select cluster: `Existing interactive cluster`.

- Access token: Enter the Azure Databricks access token created previously.

- Choose from existing clusters: `curationcluster`.

Click **Create**. Click on **Settings**, followed by **Browse**. Navigate to **electroniz_curation_notebook** and then click **OK**.

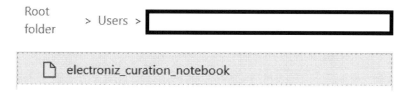

Figure 7.31 – Browsing to electroniz_curation_notebook in Azure Databricks

7. Click on **Settings**. Add the following base parameters by clicking **New**:

- Name: `STORAGE_ACCOUNT`.

- Value: `@pipeline().parameters.STORAGE_ACCOUNT`.

- Name: `BRONZE_LAYER_NAMESPACE`.

- Value: `@pipeline().parameters.BRONZE_LAYER_NAMESPACE`.

- Name: `SILVER_LAYER_NAMESPACE`.

- Value: `@pipeline().parameters.SILVER_LAYER_NAMESPACE`.

- Name: `STORE_SALES_FOLDER`.

- Value: `@pipeline().parameters.STORE_SALES_FOLDER`.

- Name: `ADLS_FOLDER`.

- Value: `@pipeline().parameters.ADLS_FOLDER`.

- Name: `TABLE_LIST`.

- Value: `@pipeline().parameters.TABLE_LIST`.

- Name: `CURRENCY_LIST`.

- Value: `@pipeline().parameters.CURRENCY_LIST`.

- Name: `CURRENCY_FOLDER`.

- Value: `@pipeline().parameters.CURRENCY_FOLDER`.

- Name: `GEOLOCATION_FOLDER`.

- Value: `@pipeline().parameters.GEOLOCATION_FOLDER`.

- Name: `LOGS_FOLDER`

- Value: `@pipeline().parameters.LOGS_FOLDER`

- Name: `ECOMM_FOLDER`.

- Value: `@pipeline().parameters.ECOMM_FOLDER`.

- Name: `ADLS_KEY`.

- Value: `@activity('Get Secret').output.value`.

Notice the use of the output value from the **Get Secret** activity. The **Get Secret** activity *dynamically* fetches the `ADLSKEY` key from the Azure key store at runtime and sends it to the curation notebook.

Chain activities by dragging the arrow from **Get Secret** to **Run Curation Notebook**.

8. Click on **Publish all**. The final pipeline will look like the following:

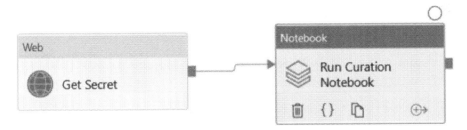

Figure 7.32 – Final look of electroniz_curation_pipeline

That was easy – the development curation pipeline is all done. We can now proceed with the steps to verify whether it works well at runtime.

Running the pipeline for the silver layer

In production, the curation pipeline will be invoked automatically after the ingestion pipeline completes successfully. Since we are still in the unit testing phase, we will trigger it manually using the following steps:

1. To invoke the pipeline for the silver layer, invoke the following commands on the Azure Cloud Shell. This pipeline run is counted as the first run of the pipeline. Notice we are sending `ADLS_FOLDER=2021/04/28/18` as a parameter to the pipeline. You may recall that this was the very first folder in which historical data was saved in the bronze layer:

```
RESOURCEGROUPNAME="training_rg"

DATAFACTORYNAME="traininglakehousedf"

PIPELINENAME="electroniz_curation_pipeline"

az datafactory pipeline create-run --factory-name
$DATAFACTORYNAME --name $PIPELINENAME --resource-group
$RESOURCEGROUPNAME \

--parameters "{\"STORAGE_
ACCOUNT\":\"traininglakehouse\",\"BRONZE_LAYER_
NAMESPACE\":\"bronze\", \

\"SILVER_LAYER_NAMESPACE\":\"silver\",\"STORE_SALES_
FOLDER\":\"sales\", \"ADLS_FOLDER\":\"2021/04/28/18\", \

\"TABLE_LIST\":\"products,store_customers,store_
orders\",\"CURRENCY_LIST\":\"CAD,INR,EUR\",\"CURRENCY_
FOLDER\":\"currency\", \

\"GEOLOCATION_FOLDER\":\"geolocation\",\"LOGS_
FOLDER\":\"logs\",\"ECOMM_FOLDER\":\"esalesns\/
esaleshub\/*\/*\/*\/*\/*\/*\" \

"}
```

2. Once the pipeline has been triggered, we can check the status of the pipeline by navigating to **Home** > **All Resources** > **traininglakehousedf**.

Click on **Monitor** > **Pipeline Runs**.

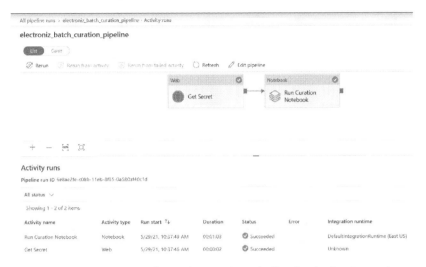

Figure 7.33 – Monitoring electroniz_curation_pipeline for the first invocation

If the pipeline completes successfully, you should see the following delta tables in the silver layer namespace of the Azure data lake storage account. Using the Azure portal, navigate to the following folder:

Home > **All Resources** > **traininglakehouse** > **Containers** > **silver**:

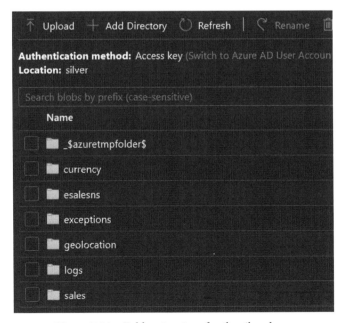

Figure 7.34 – Folder structure for the silver layer

3. You may recall that `electroniz_curation_pipeline` invokes `electroniz_curation_notebook` using the `Run Curation Notebook` activity.

Before we move ahead and verify the notebook run, it is important to understand at a high level what the notebook logic does. During the data curation process, the notebook performs the following steps:

-   Processes and reads incoming parameters passed by `electroniz_curation_pipeline`.

-   Reads raw data from the bronze layer of the lakehouse.

-   Invokes PySpark logic to curate data.

-   If it is the first run of the pipeline, new delta tables are created. Otherwise, incremental data is merged into existing delta tables in the silver layer of the lakehouse.

-   Catalogs the delta tables in the **Hive** metastore.

To check the status of the notebook run, navigate to the Azure Databricks workspace and click on **Data**. Since we invoked `electroniz_curation_pipeline` for the very first time, the following tables have been recently created and cataloged in Hive. They are now ready for querying.

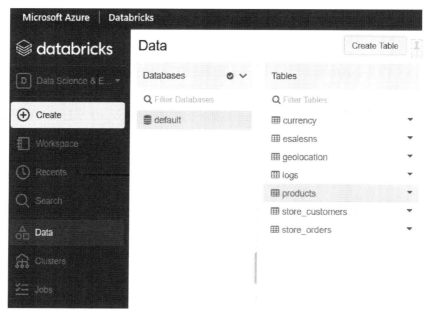

Figure 7.35 – Hive table definitions in Azure Databricks

> **Important note**
>
> Azure Databricks comes with a central Hive metastore built in. This metastore can persist table metadata and is available to all clusters within the Azure Databricks workspace.

4. To check the data and structure of a table, click on **products**. Notice the structure of the table, as well as the sample data rows:

Table: products

Size: 2.27 kB

Schema:

	col_name	data_type	comment
1	product_id	int	
2	product_name	string	
3	product_category	string	
4	updated_at	timestamp	
5			
6	# Partitioning		
7	Not partitioned		

Showing all 7 rows.

Sample Data:

	product_id	product_name	product_category	updated_at
1	1	Watch	Wearables	2021-06-16T15:40:00.000+0000
2	2	Vaccum	HomeAppliance	2021-06-16T15:40:00.000+0000
3	3	Airconditioner	HomeAppliance	2021-06-16T15:40:00.000+0000
4	4	Microwave	HomeAppliance	2021-06-16T15:40:00.000+0000
5	5	DVD	HomeEntertainment	2021-06-16T15:40:00.000+0000
6	6	TV	HomeEntertainment	2021-06-16T15:40:00.000+0000
7	7	Keyboard	Computers	2021-06-16T15:40:00.000+0000

Figure 7.36 – Structure and data of the products table

5. Now that we know the first invocation of `electroniz_curation_pipeline` was successful, we can invoke the pipeline for the hourly folders in the bronze layer. The hourly folders have incremental data in them. This time we will send `ADLS_FOLDER=2021/04/28/19`. Run the following commands on the Azure Cloud Shell:

```
RESOURCEGROUPNAME="training_rg"

DATAFACTORYNAME="traininglakehousedf"

PIPELINENAME="electroniz_batch_curation_pipeline"


az datafactory pipeline create-run --factory-name
$DATAFACTORYNAME --name $PIPELINENAME --resource-group
$RESOURCEGROUPNAME \

--parameters "{\"STORAGE_
ACCOUNT\":\"traininglakehouse\",\"BRONZE_LAYER_
NAMESPACE\":\"bronze\", \

\"SILVER_LAYER_NAMESPACE\":\"silver\",\"STORE_SALES_
FOLDER\":\"sales\", \"ADLS_FOLDER\":\"2021/04/28/19\", \

\"TABLE_LIST\":\"products,store_customers,store_
orders\",\"CURRENCY_LIST\":\"CAD,INR,EUR\",\"CURRENCY_
FOLDER\":\"currency\", \

\"GEOLOCATION_FOLDER\":\"geolocation\",\"LOGS_
FOLDER\":\"logs\",\"ECOMM_FOLDER\":\"esalesns\/
esaleshub\/*\/*\/*\/*\/*\/*\/*\" \

"}
```

6. Now, invoke the pipeline using `ADLS_FOLDER=2021/04/28/20`. Run the following commands on the Azure Cloud Shell:

```
RESOURCEGROUPNAME="training_rg"

DATAFACTORYNAME="traininglakehousedf"

PIPELINENAME="electroniz_batch_curation_pipeline"

az datafactory pipeline create-run --factory-name
$DATAFACTORYNAME --name $PIPELINENAME --resource-group
$RESOURCEGROUPNAME \

--parameters "{\"STORAGE_
ACCOUNT\":\"traininglakehouse\",\"BRONZE_LAYER_
NAMESPACE\":\"bronze\", \

\"SILVER_LAYER_NAMESPACE\":\"silver\",\"STORE_SALES_
FOLDER\":\"sales\", \"ADLS_FOLDER\":\"2021/04/28/20\", \
```

```
\"TABLE_LIST\":\"products,store_customers,store_
orders\",\"CURRENCY_LIST\":\"CAD,INR,EUR\",\"CURRENCY_
FOLDER\":\"currency\", \
```

```
\"GEOLOCATION_FOLDER\":\"geolocation\",\"LOGS_
FOLDER\":\"logs\",\"ECOMM_FOLDER\":\"esalesns\/
esaleshub\/*\/*\/*\/*\/*\/*\" \
```

```
"}
```

7. Finally, invoke the pipeline using ADLS_FOLDER=2021/04/28/21. Run the
    following commands on the Azure Cloud Shell:

```
RESOURCEGROUPNAME="training_rg"
```

```
DATAFACTORYNAME="traininglakehousedf"
```

```
PIPELINENAME="electroniz_batch_curation_pipeline"
```

```
az datafactory pipeline create-run --factory-name
$DATAFACTORYNAME --name $PIPELINENAME --resource-group
$RESOURCEGROUPNAME \
```

```
--parameters "{\"STORAGE_
ACCOUNT\":\"traininglakehouse\",\"BRONZE_LAYER_
NAMESPACE\":\"bronze\", \
```

```
\"SILVER_LAYER_NAMESPACE\":\"silver\",\"STORE_SALES_
FOLDER\":\"sales\", \"ADLS_FOLDER\":\"2021/04/28/21\", \
```

```
\"TABLE_LIST\":\"products,store_customers,store_
orders\",\"CURRENCY_LIST\":\"CAD,INR,EUR\",\"CURRENCY_
FOLDER\":\"currency\", \
```

```
\"GEOLOCATION_FOLDER\":\"geolocation\",\"LOGS_
FOLDER\":\"logs\",\"ECOMM_FOLDER\":\"esalesns\/
esaleshub\/*\/*\/*\/*\/*\/*\" \
```

```
"}
```

It is important to understand that at every subsequent run of electroniz_curation_
pipeline, electroniz_curation_notebook will merge incremental data into
existing delta tables that get created at the first invocation of electroniz_curation_
pipeline. Now that we have this understanding, we can move ahead and verify whether
electroniz_curation_notebook was able to curate data to our satisfaction.

Verifying curated data in the silver layer

In the previous section, we ran `electroniz_curation_pipeline` four times, each time with a different hourly folder. If everything worked correctly, we could safely infer that the silver layer of the Electroniz lakehouse is now functional.

As per the curation process, the last step is to verify the curated data. We will use another notebook that already contains the code that performs the validations. You simply need to run it step by step as follows:

1. The verification code is available in `curation_verification_notebook.ipynb`.

2. Import the `curation_verification_notebook.ipynb` notebook into Azure Databricks. The steps are very similar to what was done previously for the curation notebook (`electroniz_curation_notebook.ipynb`):

    -   On the Databricks workspace, click on **Workspace**. Then, click on **Users**.

    -   Click on the arrow beside your username and click on **Import**.

    -   Choose **URL**.

    -   Use the following URL: `https://github.com/PacktPublishing/ Data-Engineering-with-Apache-Spark-Delta-Lake-and- Lakehouse/blob/main/project/curation/delta_lake/curation_ verification_notebook.ipynb`.

    -   Click on **Import**.

3. In the following sections, I will be making references to certain code blocks (PySpark code) that are embedded within the curation notebook (`electroniz_ curation_notebook.ipynb`).

Verifying unstandardized data

During the inspection phase, we had discovered that the `store_orders` data has a column named `order_date` that uses the MM/DD/YYYY format. In the cell titled **Curate Sales Data - standardize, mask and merge**, notice the following code that converts `order_date` to a standard date field:

```
ORDERS_SCHEMA_1 =[('order_number', IntegerType()),('customer_id', IntegerType()),('product_id', IntegerType()),('order_
                  ('units', IntegerType()),('sale_price', FloatType()), ('currency', StringType()),
                  ('order_mode', StringType()), ('sale_price_usd', FloatType()), ('updated_at', TimestampType())
                  ]
fields = [StructField(*field) for field in ORDERS_SCHEMA_1]
schema_stores = StructType(fields)
df_table_incremental = spark.read.csv(bronze_table_path, schema=schema_stores )

df_currency=spark.sql('SELECT currency_name AS currency, currency_value from currency')

df_table_curated = df_table_incremental.join(df_currency, on=['currency'])
df_table_curated = df_table_curated.withColumn('sale_price_usd',curate_sales_price_udf('currency_value', 'sale_price'))
df_table_curated=df_table_curated.withColumn('updated_at', f.lit(UPDATED))
df_table_curated = df_table_curated.withColumn('order_date_new', to_date(df_table_curated.order_date, 'MM/dd
/yyyy')).drop('order_date').withColumnRenamed('order_date_new', 'order_date')
df_table_curated = df_table_curated.drop('currency_value')
```

Figure 7.37 – Code to standardize order_date in store_orders

Notice the `order_date` value has been converted to the Parquet native date type YYYY-MM-DD:

Verify Unstandardized Data in Store Orders

```
1   %sql
2   SELECT order_date FROM store_orders;
```

▶ (2) Spark Jobs

	order_date
1	2017-05-12
2	2020-08-14
3	2021-02-26
4	2019-12-21
5	2019-07-12
6	2019-06-29
7	2020-06-12

Figure 7.38 – Verify order_date in store_orders after standardization

We also discovered that the e-commerce transactions have an `order_date` column that uses the DD/MM/YYYY format. In the cell titled **Curate Sales Data - standardize, mask and merge,** notice the following code that addresses this issue:

```
deltaTable = DeltaTable.forPath(spark, ecomm_path)

bronze_ecomm_path="wasbs://"+BRONZE_LAYER_NAMESPACE+"@"+STORAGE_ACCOUNT+".blob.core.windows.net/"+ECOMM_FOLDER+"/"+ADLS_FOLDER+"/

try:
    df_ecomm=spark.read.format("avro").load(bronze_ecomm_path)

    df_ecomm_json = df_ecomm.select(df_ecomm.Body.cast("string")).rdd.map(lambda x: x[0])
    df_ecomm_data = spark.read.json(df_ecomm_json).select('data')
    df_data_values = df_ecomm_data.select('data.customer_name', 'data.address', 'data.city', 'data.country', 'data.currency', 'data
                                           'data.order_date', 'data.order_mode', 'data.order_number', 'data.phone','data.postalcode'

    df_data_values = df_data_values.withColumn('updated_at', f.lit(UPDATED))
    df_data_values = df_data_values.withColumn('phone_masked',mask_udf('phone')).drop('phone').withColumnRenamed('phone_masked', 'p
    df_data_values = df_data_values.withColumn('address_masked',mask_udf('address')).drop('address').withColumnRenamed('address_mas
    df_data_values = df_data_values.withColumn('order_date', from_unixtime(unix_timestamp('order_date', 'dd/MM/yyy')))

    df_data_values = df_data_values.withColumn('order_date_new', to_date(df_data_values.order_date, 'yyyy-MM-dd
HH:mm:ss')).drop('order_date').withColumnRenamed('order_date_new', 'order_date')
```

Figure 7.39 – Code to standardize order_date in e-commerce transactions

Once again, the `order_date` value has been converted to the Parquet native date type YYYY-MM-DD:

Verify Unstandardized Data in ecommerce Orders

```
1   %sql
2   SELECT order_date FROM esalesns;
```

▶ (2) Spark Jobs

	order_date ▲
1	2021-05-18
2	2021-05-18
3	2021-05-18

Figure 7.40 – Verify order_date in e-commerce transactions after standardization

Additionally, we had discovered that `store_customers` data has a column named `email` with a mix of lowercase and uppercase characters. In the cell titled **Define functions,** notice the use of a PySpark function that curates emails:

```
def curate_email(email):
    curated_value = email.lower()
    return curated_value
```

> **Important note**
>
> As per best practices, it is highly recommended to add a modular function for every specific curation algorithm. Having a modular function promotes code reusability.

In the cell titled **Curate Currency Data - standardize, mask and merge**, notice the following code that curates emails:

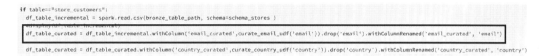

```
if table=="store_customers":
    df_table_incremental = spark.read.csv(bronze_table_path, schema=schema_stores )
    df_table_curated = df_table_incremental.withColumn('email_curated',curate_email_udf('email')).drop('email').withColumnRenamed('email_curated', 'email')

df_table_curated = df_table_curated.withColumn('country_curated',curate_country_udf('country')).drop('country').withColumnRenamed('country_curated', 'country')
```

Figure 7.41 – Code to standardize emails in store_customers

Note that email addresses now appear only in lowercase, as opposed to the previous mixed case:

Verify Store Customers Email

```
1   %sql
2   SELECT email FROM store_customers;
```

▶ (2) Spark Jobs

	email
1	sollicitudin@enimmitempor.ca
2	donec.non@dapibusrutrum.com
3	phasellus.ornare@antedictum.co.uk
4	nisl.nulla.eu@sed.net
5	magnis@tortoratrisus.co.uk
6	magna.phasellus@crasvulputate.org
7	sed@aeneangravidanunc.ca

Figure 7.42 – Verifying emails in store_customers after standardization

Verifying invalid data

You may recall that, during the inspection phase, we had discovered the following issues regarding invalid data:

- The `products` table has a `products_code` column that is the parent column for the `product_id` column in the `store_orders` table.

- The `products.products_code` column is of the *string* data type, yet it is supposed to join with `store_orders.products_id`, which is of the *integer* type.

In the following code, both issues were resolved by providing a schema to the Spark DataFrame at the time data is read from the bronze layer of the lakehouse.

> **Important note**
>
> The schema applies the structure (schema) to the data being read at the time of reading it. This principle drives modern-day analytics by enabling users to define the structure as per their unique requirements.

Let's find out how this was accomplished. In the cell titled **Define Schemas for all files**, notice the following code that enforces schemas. We have self-enforced a schema for the `orders` and `products` tables. This is a common way to control how PySpark interprets *type* definitions.

```python
ORDERS_SCHEMA =[
    ('order_number', IntegerType()),
    ('customer_id', IntegerType()),
    ('product_id', IntegerType()),
    ('order_date', DateType()),
    ('units', IntegerType()),
    ('sale_price', FloatType()),
    ('currency', StringType()),
    ('order_mode', StringType()),
    ('sale_price_usd', FloatType()),
    ('updated_at', TimestampType())
]

PRODUCTS_SCHEMA =[
    ('product_id', IntegerType()),
    ('product_name', StringType()),
    ('product_category', StringType()),
    ('updated_at', TimestampType())
]
```

Figure 7.43 – Code for enforcing schemas for products and store_orders

Now the schema of the *parent* and *child* delta tables matches both by *name* and *type*:

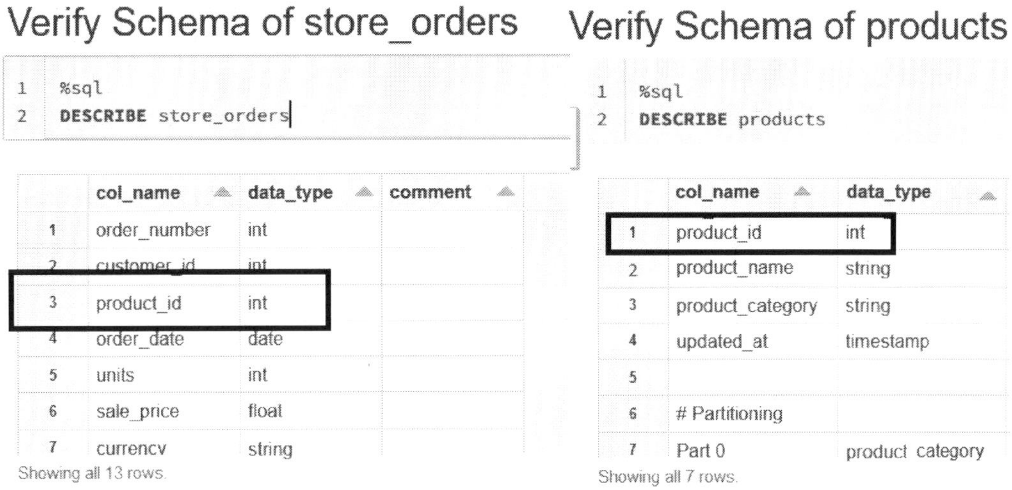

Verify Schema of store_orders

```
1   %sql
2   DESCRIBE store_orders
```

	col_name	data_type	comment
1	order_number	int	
2	customer_id	int	
3	product_id	int	
4	order_date	date	
5	units	int	
6	sale_price	float	
7	currency	string	

Showing all 13 rows.

Verify Schema of products

```
1   %sql
2   DESCRIBE products
```

	col_name	data_type
1	product_id	int
2	product_name	string
3	product_category	string
4	updated_at	timestamp
5		
6	# Partitioning	
7	Part 0	product category

Showing all 7 rows.

Figure 7.44 – Confirming the schema for products and store_orders after enforcing it

Additionally, we also discovered that two orders reference `product_id` rows that do not exist in the `products` table. This is how we located the *orphan* rows in the table.

Important note

In relational structures, an *orphan* row is a record that cannot be traced back to a parent. In database terms, this commonly signals data corruption.

In the cell titled **Find orphan store_orders**, notice the following code block that not only locates *orphan* rows, but additionally saves them to an `exceptions` folder in Azure data lake storage.

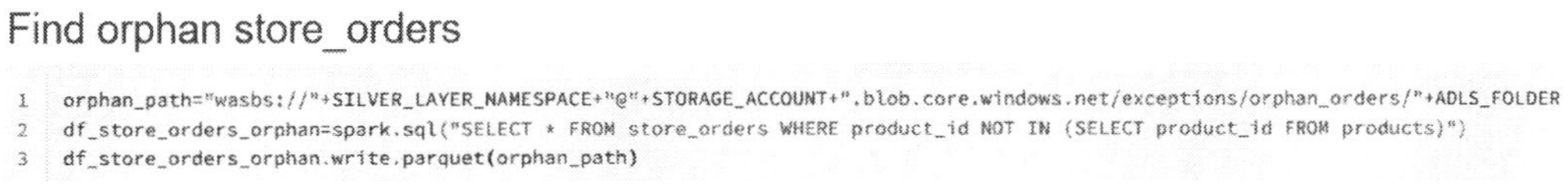

Find orphan store_orders

```
1   orphan_path="wasbs://"+SILVER_LAYER_NAMESPACE+"@"+STORAGE_ACCOUNT+".blob.core.windows.net/exceptions/orphan_orders/"+ADLS_FOLDER
2   df_store_orders_orphan=spark.sql("SELECT * FROM store_orders WHERE product_id NOT IN (SELECT product_id FROM products)")
3   df_store_orders_orphan.write.parquet(orphan_path)
```

Figure 7.45 – Finding orphan rows in store_orders

Periodically, the contents of the `exceptions` folder should be sent to the appropriate groups within the organization, such as the database group. It should be their responsibility to make *data adjustments* that can sufficiently deal with these kinds of issues.

It is important to note that it is better to make the adjustments to the data source than to make them in the lakehouse. Once the invalid data has been fixed, the same data can be resent through the regular channels as incremental data.

> **Important note**
>
> Dealing with exceptions arising due to invalid data is extremely time-consuming, as well as a painstaking process. A data engineer can easily locate invalid data, but fixing it could take many back-and-forth cycles.

Verifying non-uniform data

During the *inspection* phase, we discovered the following issues related to non-uniform data.

The `country` column in the `store_customers` table exists as a fully spelled-out value such as `United States`, whereas it exists as abbreviations in e-commerce transactions. The Electroniz team has decided to standardize `country` using the *abbreviated* form in their lakehouse. In the cell titled **Define functions**, notice the function to curate the `country` field:

```
def curate_country(country):
    if (country == 'USA' or country == 'United States'):
        curated_value = 'USA'
    elif (country == 'UK' or country == 'United Kingdom'):
        curated_value = 'UK'
    elif (country == 'CAN' or country == 'Canada'):
        curated_value = 'CAN'
    elif (country == 'IND' or country == 'India'):
        curated_value = 'IND'
    else:
        curated_value = country
    return curated_value
```

In the cell titled **Curate Currency Data - standardize, mask and merge**, notice the following code that curates `country`:

```
if table=="store_customers":
    df_table_incremental = spark.read.csv(bronze_table_path, schema=schema_stores )
    #display(df_table_incremental)
    df_table_curated = df_table_incremental.withColumn('email_curated',curate_email_udf('email')).drop('email').withColumnRenamed('email_curated', 'email')

    df_table_curated = df_table_curated.withColumn('country_curated',curate_country_udf('country')).drop('country').withColumnRenamed('country_curated', 'country')

    df_table_curated = df_table_curated.withColumn('phone_masked',mask_udf('phone')).drop('phone').withColumnRenamed('phone_masked', 'phone')
```

Figure 7.46 – Making country data uniform in store_customers

Note the `country` data in `store_customers` now exists in an abbreviated form:

Verify country in store_customers

```
1  %sql
2  select customer_name,country from store_customers
```

▶ (2) Spark Jobs

	customer_name	country
1	Aubrey Norris	UK
2	Bruno Hebert	UK
3	Serina Serrano	UK
4	Ivory Lester	UK
5	Tad Mcintyre	UK
6	Carson Gonzales	UK
7	Carly Yates	UK

Figure 7.47 – Verifying the uniform country data in store_customers

Notice how the same PySpark function is used to curate the `country` column in `e-commerce` transactions. In the cell titled **Curate e-commerce Sales Data - standardize, mask and merge**, notice the following code that curates country:

> **Important note**
>
> The idea of common functions not only promotes code re-usability but comes in extremely handy if data needs to be replayed from scratch using a modified logic within the function.

```
df_data_values = df_data_values.withColumn('phone_masked',mask_udf('phone')).drop('phone').withColumnRenamed('phone_masked', 'phone')
df_data_values = df_data_values.withColumn('address_masked',mask_udf('address')).drop('address').withColumnRenamed('address_masked', 'address')

df_data_values = df_data_values.withColumn('country_curated',curate_country_udf('country')).drop('country').withColumnRenamed('country_curated', 'country')
```

Figure 7.48 – Verifying the uniform country data in e-commerce transactions

Note the `country` data in `e-commerce` transactions now exists in an *abbreviated* form:

Verify country in ecommerce transactions

```
1  %sql
2  select customer_name,country from esalesns
```

▶ (2) Spark Jobs

	customer_name ▲	country ▲
1	Vera Russell	UK
2	Brynn Nelson	USA
3	Ignacia Price	UK
4	Beatrice Tucker	UK
5	Kenyon Daugherty	USA
6	Linda Pugh	CAN
7	Brenna Robles	CAN

Figure 7.49 – Verifying the uniform country data in e-commerce transactions

Previously, we also noticed that transactions in `store_orders` compared to `e-commerce` are done in varying currencies – USD, CAD, EUR, and INR. Electroniz had expressed a desire to covert all transactions to a common currency – USD.

In the cell titled **Define Functions**, notice the function to perform the appropriate currency conversion. Notice this function is using a currency *conversion factor* that converts the sale from the native currency to USD. You may recall that we fetch the currency conversion factory every hour as part of the Electroniz ingestion pipeline and store it in the `currency` table.

```
def curate_sales_price(currency, currency_value, sales_price):
  if (currency != 'USD'):
    curated_value = float(sales_price)/float(currency_value)
    return float(curated_value)
  else:
    return float(sales_price)
```

In the cell titled **Curate Sales Data** - **standardize, mask and merge**, notice the following code that creates a new column for currency conversion:

```
fields = [StructField(*field) for field in ORDERS_SCHEMA_1]
schema_stores = StructType(fields)
df_table_incremental = spark.read.csv(bronze_table_path, schema=schema_stores )

df_currency=spark.sql('SELECT currency_name AS currency, currency_value from currency')
columns = ['currency', 'currency_value']
df_currency_usd = spark.createDataFrame([{'USD','1'}], columns)
df_currency_final=df_currency_usd.union(df_currency)

df_table_curated = df_table_incremental.join(df_currency_final, on=['currency'], how="inner")
df_table_curated = df_table_curated.withColumn('sale_price_usd',curate_sales_price_udf('currency', 'currency_value', 'sale_price'))
df_table_curated = df_table_curated.withColumn('updated_at', f.lit(UPDATED))
df_table_curated = df_table_curated.withColumn('order_date_new', to_date(df_table_curated.order_date, 'MM/dd
/yyyy')).drop('order_date').withColumnRenamed('order_date_new', 'order_date')
df_table_curated = df_table_curated.drop('currency_value')
```

Figure 7.50 – Converting the sales price in USD

Note the new column below with the sales price converted to USD:

Verify currency conversion

```
1   %sql
2   select order_number, sale_price, sale_price_usd FROM store_orders WHERE currency='EUR'
```

▶ (2) Spark Jobs

	order_number	sale_price	sale_price_usd
1	2495	81.95	99.44362
2	2482	26.99	32.751476
3	2481	34.29	41.609787
4	2477	19.58	23.759686
5	2459	73.89	89.66308
6	2452	93.84	113.87174
7	2451	5.2	6.3100286

Figure 7.51 – Verifying the sales price in USD

> **Important note**
>
> Having uniform data in the silver layer of the lakehouse helps to establish the user's trust in the data.

Verifying duplicate data

You may recall that `electroniz_batch_ingestion_pipeline` ingested not only newly inserted data in the source but also data that has changed over time. In the previous chapter, *Understanding Delta Lake*, we learned how new and changed data can be merged into a common delta table to establish a single source of truth.

Even though data evolves and changes over time, end users are simply interested in querying the latest version. We need to understand this concept very clearly, so let me demonstrate it using the sequence of events for a customer name change as follows:

1. A new customer, `Prescott Barnes`, was created in the `stores` database at 17:56 on April 4, 2021.

2. This customer record was ingested into the Electroniz lakehouse during the run that happened at 18:00 on April 4, 2021.

3. The customer requested his name be changed to `Prescott Barnes Jr.` at 18:30 on April 4, 2021.

4. The customer record was re-ingested in the Electroniz lakehouse during the run that happened at 19:00 on April 4, 2021.

Now we have two records for the same customer in the bronze layer of the lakehouse – *duplicates*. Well, that's a problem, isn't it?

Fortunately, the magic of Delta Lake permits us to deal with such issues and deduplicate data with ease. In the cell titled **Curate Sales Data - standardize, mask and merge**, notice the following merge clause for Delta Lake:

```
deltaTable.alias("store_customers").merge(
df_table_curated.alias("store_customers_new"),
            "store_customers.email -store_customers_new.email") \
.whenMatchedUpdate(set = {"customer_id":      "store_customers_new.customer_id",    \
                          "customer_name":    "store_customers_new.customer_name",  \
                          "address":          "store_customers_new.address",        \
                          "city":             "store_customers_new.city",           \
                          "postalcode":       "store_customers_new.postalcode",     \
                          "country":          "store_customers_new.country",        \
                          "phone":            "store_customers_new.phone",          \
                          "email":            "store_customers_new.email",          \
                          "credit_card":      "store_customers_new.credit_card",    \
                          "updated_at":       "store_customers_new.updated_at" } )  \
.whenNotMatchedInsert(values =                                                      \
    {
                          "customer_id":      "store_customers_new.customer_id",    \
                          "customer_name":    "store_customers_new.customer_name",  \
                          "address":          "store_customers_new.address",        \
```

Figure 7.52 – Delta Lake merge of store_customers

This means if the customer record matches on a key (email), simply update the existing data of the customer by replacing it with the new version. So, if the Delta Lake merge process worked correctly, we should see the latest name change for this customer in the silver layer:

Verify customer name merge

```sql
1  %sql
2  SELECT customer_name FROM store_customers WHERE email = 'phasellus.vitae@vitae.co.uk'
```

▶ (2) Spark Jobs

	customer_name ▲
1	Prescott Barnes Jr.

Figure 7.53 – Result of the Delta Lake merge of store_customers

It looks like the customer's name merge process worked perfectly.

Let's verify the same process using another example. You may also recall that five orders were price adjusted. We should check whether the latest version of the delta table in the silver layer reflects the adjusted price. In the cell titled **Curate Sales Data - standardize, mask and merge**, notice the following merge clause for Delta Lake:

```
deltaTable.alias("store_orders").merge(
df_table_curated.alias("store_orders_new"),
        "store_orders.order_number = store_orders_new.order_number")       \
whenMatchedUpdate(set = {"order_number":      "store_orders_new.order_number",   \
                         "customer_id":       "store_orders_new.customer_id",    \
                         "product_id":        "store_orders_new.product_id",     \
                         "order_date":        "store_orders_new.order_date",     \
                         "units":             "store_orders_new.units",          \
                         "sale_price":        "store_orders_new.sale_price",     \
                         "sale_price_usd":    "store_orders_new.sale_price_usd", \
                         "currency":          "store_orders_new.currency",       \
                         "order_mode":        "store_orders_new.order_mode",     \
                         "updated_at":        "store_orders_new.updated_at" } )  \
whenNotMatchedInsert(values =
    {
                         "order_number":      "store_orders_new.order_number",   \
                         "customer_id":       "store_orders_new.customer_id",    \
                         "product_id":        "store_orders_new.product_id",     \
```

Figure 7.54 – Delta Lake merge of store_orders

If the Delta Lake merge process worked correctly, we should now see the latest price adjustments for these orders in the silver layer:

Verify store orders price adjustments

```
1   %sql
2   SELECT order_number, order_date,sale_price FROM store_orders WHERE order_number in (500, 1254, 1501, 2234, 2345)
```

▶ (2) Spark Jobs

	order_number ▲	order_date ▲	sale_price ▲
1	1254	2016-07-26	49.78
2	2234	2016-03-29	34.4
3	500	2016-02-16	93.77

Figure 7.55 – Result of the Delta Lake merge of store_orders

Indeed, the prices have been adjusted as desired. But why are a couple of orders missing from the table? This is because those orders were deleted from the `stores` database. We ingested the two deleted records in the `hour=21` run of `electroniz_batch_ ingestion_pipeline`. The following code was used to delete these orders:

```
deltaTable.delete("order_mode = 'DELETE'")
```

Figure 7.56 – Delta Lake deletion of store_orders

> **Important Note**
>
> You can further understand the issue of duplicates arising due to changed data by asking a simple question: *What do the end users want to query?* Undoubtedly, it's the latest version of data only. Fortunately, Delta Lake allows you to store, retrieve, and recover previous versions of data, but by default, it only supplies the latest version.

Verifying insecure data

Finally, we want to *validate* whether the data in the silver layer conforms to the security standards. During the discovery phase, a core security requirement was to *mask* all PII data. In the cell titled **Define functions**, notice the following function that masks a PII column:

```
def mask_value(column):
    mask_value = hashlib.sha256(column.encode()).hexdigest()
    return mask_value
```

In the cell titled **Curate Sales Data - standardize, mask and merge**, we used the same function to mask all PII columns as follows:

Figure 7.57 – Masking data for PII columns

If the masking worked correctly, all PII columns should be properly masked in the silver layer:

Verify Data Masking

```
1  %sql
2  select customer_name, address, phone, credit_card from store_customers
```

▸ (2) Spark Jobs

	customer_name	address	phone	credit_card
1	Hannah Ferrell	05897909ab6c663ef29d355955450f72617c9902883f71ea143c90f081266c11	73c857e4eb80dde212251499a01bc3d2c930dc741871b4447df5274a43474900d	0940976aa4def8d6a038d642c5abf8fb0
2	May Bentley	0500ea20e89af55a6fac0ef0bec4499e68b4141407af39c7ede5099d985b2d62	004ef30cb39b1ede61ac5d0ee87b6f89d1f895c1e2216770442789d642861ce	0c9c69f0e315de01f2074e6d77417be0e
3	Nelle Frost	258ea2462b43b6e4db568d480cc72d20ea3887b7b7798f09fde540444f50461	db693e6d5ab3a2d32d87b89dca3e1bfeb37733855fa6fc08dc5d3d0595dd10fe	517bdccaf00ad0146c4b9cd334850e1ae
4	Ayanna Morton	0358e5a17f7adf8e2e65123e40090402e8ff3cf4144335a7cc6659f7ac5e07c2	1e16545ab23f02231d393129e6bf570724c7ca0ca65c3014a82565965d9760eb	85adb57dda2675d6b6a2be0f1df6aa84
5	Faith Hooper	cb11233c9ebabec5ab5739d74eb75da22ac6a185a10bfc06f1326c1cbf655df8	727770f831c30684032f384c0f44f277659277c11329f2d3ab7c0701b657f5b4	62f70b8858dcf1090fa46648749e2517c
6	Sage Bauer	a42c76773611d4818fc1f2b09b4a0ede3ccf90eceed3e2e465b3cfa07b8db20b	fbcfda7b8f07af3a1c6f72d5842d6d37ce6ad63fa4bbb3ab3b7781fac3a4a070	a07e4417dd3fa177a863ac25606eb58ff
7	Lionel Dillon	940b40d3786bd962fb4o47a965ocf7bfc431fa8f3730351b6426c9e6487fb76f2	176253c995cdbe7408a72ef7c3e587fa0281393oacea32e38e3369dac977b84e	205bf4b6581fe6edf65983755547e191c

Showing the first 1000 rows

Figure 7.58 – Verifying the results of masking data for PII columns

In the preceding sections, we were able to verify that the various curation algorithms were able to transform unclean data and bring it to a state where it can be trusted and is ready to be consumed by end users. The single source of truth for the Electroniz lakehouse has been established.

Cleaning up Azure resources

To save on costs, you may want to clean up the following Azure resources:

Invoke the following commands in the Cloud Shell to delete the Azure Databricks workspace.

```
RESOURCEGROUPNAME="training_rg"
WORKSPACE="trainingdatabricks"
az config set extension.use_dynamic_install=yes_without_prompt
az databricks workspace delete --resource-group
$RESOURCEGROUPNAME --name $WORKSPACE
```

Summary

In this chapter, we learned how to build the silver layer of the lakehouse, which stores the cleansed version data. Data in the silver layer represents the single source of truth of data and is available to end users in a readily consumable state. During the chapter, we deep-dived into some of the reasons why data curation is required, discussed the curation process, and demonstrated how each case should be handled using code.

In *Chapter 8, Data Aggregation Stage – The Gold Layer*, we will use data from the silver layer of the Electroniz lakehouse and use it to perform data aggregations. These aggregations will help Electroniz users enhance their decision-making process using a combination of descriptive, diagnostic, and predictive analysis.

8
Data Aggregation Stage – The Gold Layer

Well done on making it this far! Your journey is fast approaching its final stage. I am happy to report that our skilled driver (data engineer) has successfully maneuvered the vehicle (data pipeline) through to its final leg of the journey. In the final leg of the journey, all the previously collected data that has been curated will be put to good use for descriptive, diagnostic, predictive, and prescriptive analysis.

In the previous chapter, we performed a deep dive into data curation. Using a variety of data curation examples, we successfully built the curation silver layer of the Electroniz lakehouse. In this chapter, we will continue building the next and final layer of the Electroniz lakehouse: the gold layer.

In this chapter, we will cover the following topics:

- The need to aggregate data
- The process of aggregating data
- Developing a data aggregation pipeline
- Running the data aggregation pipeline

- Understanding data consumption
- Verifying aggregated data in the gold layer
- Meeting customer expectations

The need to aggregate data

Before we deep dive into how to aggregate data and build the gold layer of the Electroniz lakehouse, we should quickly remind ourselves why we're building the lakehouse in the first place. During the discovery phase, Electroniz had put forth some key business requirements, as follows:

- They want to aim for a near-real-time sales analytics platform that can serve their customer needs faster and better.
- They want to streamline their advertising budgets through intelligent analytics based on the number of user hits on their e-commerce website.
- They want to decrease customer dissatisfaction because of interruptions in fulfilling orders due to inventory shortages.

Thus far, we have been able to identify, collect, and curate data from a variety of sources to help us perform intelligent decision-making using modern analytics. At this point, we have data in the silver layer that represents the state of the data that has been standardized, validated, de-duplicated, and secured. But does it provide the answers to all the business requirements that Electroniz wanted us to address? In short, the answer is not yet. So, how do we go about looking for the right answers?

> **Important**
> In data terms, the silver layer of every dataset is referred to as an "observation."
> Each dataset has multiple rows that are referred to as "variables."

The objective of creating the gold layer is to **aggregate** or **summarize** data. **Aggregation** is a technique that's used to identify patterns over a collection of observations using a set of variables. Some common examples of aggregations are the total sales over a given quarter, the total number of users per month who visited your website, and the average salary of your employees per department.

Largely, the structure (schema) of the data in the silver layer is very similar to the source where it was ingested from. On the contrary, the structure of aggregated data is either two-dimensional like a table or multi-dimensional like a cube:

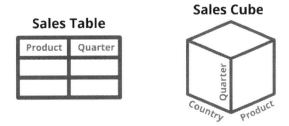

Figure 8.1 – Two-dimensional versus multi-dimensional data

Let's take a look at this in more detail:

- **Two-dimensional aggregations** summarize data over two given variables. For example, what is the aggregate sales per quarter for a given product?

- **Multi-dimensional aggregations** summarize data over multiple variables in the form of hierarchies. For example, you can find the aggregate sales per quarter for a given product by country.

Now that we know why data is useful and why aggregating data is helpful, let's look at the data aggregation process.

The process of aggregating data

Although the objective of data aggregation is largely straightforward, you should follow a definitive process. The data aggregation process is a co-shared responsibility between the customer and the data engineer. Each entity needs to contribute toward the objective through a combination of business and technical knowledge:

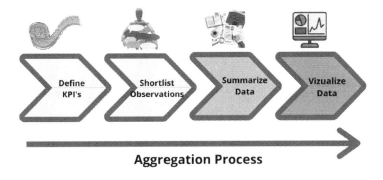

Figure 8.2 – Data aggregation process

This process can be explained as follows:

- **Define KPIs**: The process of data aggregation starts by defining the **key performance indicators** (**KPIs**). Data engineers are not the best resources for making such business-oriented decisions. Therefore, it is important to seek customer help on this one since they are closer to the business and can make these decisions more accurately.

> **Important**
>
> A quantifiable metric that's used to measure a company's success or failure is called a KPI. KPIs are often used to evaluate whether the company has met its objectives or not. These KPIs are best defined by people who know the business well enough to gauge whether a certain indicator can accurately define success or failure criteria.

- **Shortlist the Observations**: Once the KPIs have been well defined, the data engineer (with assistance from the customer) should shortlist the list of observations (datasets) that will participate in the aggregations. It is important to perform a detailed analysis of the datasets to fully understand the inter-dependencies, groupings, and filtering mechanisms.

- **Summarize the Data**: This is the stage where the data engineer will develop the logic to perform the necessary data aggregations. Aggregation logic can be developed in several coding languages, although these days, the two most common ones are SQL and Spark. Once the logic has been developed, it needs to be integrated into the overall pipeline, which runs on a scheduled basis.

- **Visualize the Data**: As humans, we relate well to visuals. Visualizing aggregated data in the form of colorful charts, maps, and dashboards is a common method that's used by modern-day decision-makers. In *Chapter 1, The Story of Data Engineering and Analytics*, we discussed the importance of data storytelling. Visualizing aggregated data narrates a well-crafted story regarding an organization's health and well-being.

I started this book by stating *"Every byte of data has a story to tell. The real question is whether the story is being narrated accurately, securely, and efficiently."* At this point, we are ready to narrate the story of Electroniz.

Developing a data aggregation pipeline

Before we start developing the aggregation pipeline, we need to deploy the following Azure resources:

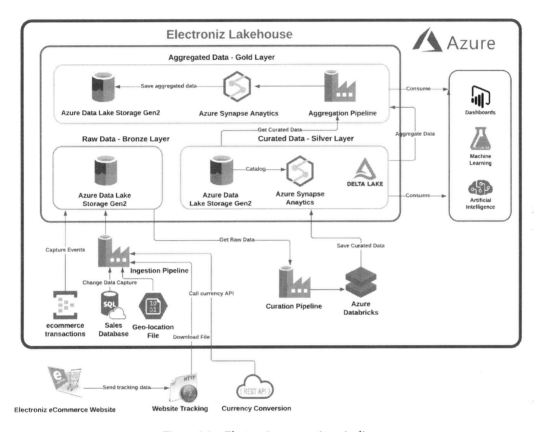

Figure 8.3 – Electroniz aggregation pipeline

In the following section, we will be creating the aggregation pipeline highlighted in the preceding diagram.

Preparing the Azure resources

Follow these steps to start the Azure resource deployment process:

1. We will start by creating a new namespace in Azure Data Lake Storage for the **gold** layer.

   I mentioned earlier that storage account names in Azure are globally unique. Throughout this exercise, we will be using `traininglakehouse` as the storage account name. You will need to edit it as per the account name that you created:

   ```
   STORAGEACCOUNTNAME="traininglakehouse"

   GOLDLAYER="gold"

   az storage fs create -n $GOLDLAYER --account-name
   $STORAGEACCOUNTNAME --only-show-errors
   ```

   This results in the following output:

   ```
   Azure> STORAGEACCOUNTNAME="traininglakehouse"
   Azure> GOLDLAYER="gold"
   Azure> az storage fs create -n $GOLDLAYER --account-name $STORAGE
   {
     "client_request_id": "e8d0df66-d385-11eb-b0e1-0a580af4683e",
     "date": "2021-06-22T18:16:04+00:00",
     "error_code": null,
     "etag": "\"0x8D935A9CD09653E\"",
     "last_modified": "2021-06-22T18:16:05+00:00",
     "request_id": "03a5b5c3-001e-0022-2f92-67f980000000",
     "version": "2020-02-10"
   }
   ```

   Figure 8.4 – Output of the gold container create command

2. If the preceding command is successful, you should be able to see the newly created container on the Azure portal by browsing to **Home** > **All Resources** > **traininglakehouse** > **Containers**:

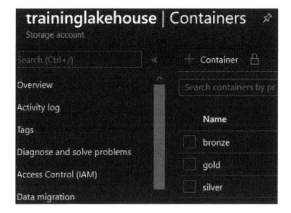

Figure 8.5 – Confirmation of the gold container's creation

3. Now, let's create a new Azure Synapse workspace that's pointing to the **gold** layer.
    Replace SQLPASSWORD with an actual password. Remember it as we will need it
    later. Also, the Azure Synapse workspace name is globally unique, so please edit the
    SYSNAPSEWORKSPACENAME variable accordingly:

```
SYSNAPSEWORKSPACENAME="trainingsynapse100"
RESOURCEGROUPNAME="training_rg"
LOCATION="westus"
SQLUSER="sqladminuser"
SQLPASSWORD="XXXXXXXX"
STORAGEACCOUNTNAME="traininglakehouse"
GOLDLAYER="gold"
az synapse workspace create \
  --name $SYSNAPSEWORKSPACENAME \
  --resource-group $RESOURCEGROUPNAME \
  --storage-account $STORAGEACCOUNTNAME \
  --file-system $GOLDLAYER \
  --sql-admin-login-user $SQLUSER \
  --sql-admin-login-password $SQLPASSWORD \
  --location $LOCATION
```

This results in the following output:

```
Azure> SYSNAPSEWORKSPACENAME="trainingsynapse100"
Azure> RESOURCEGROUPNAME="training_rg"
Azure> LOCATION="westus"
Azure> SQLUSER="sqladminuser"
Azure> SQLPASSWORD="▮▮▮▮▮▮▮▮"
Azure> STORAGEACCOUNTNAME="traininglakehouse"
Azure> GOLDLAYER="gold"
Azure> az synapse workspace create \
>    --name $SYSNAPSEWORKSPACENAME \
>    --resource-group $RESOURCEGROUPNAME \
>    --storage-account $STORAGEACCOUNTNAME \
>    --file-system $GOLDLAYER \
>    --sql-admin-login-user $SQLUSER \
>    --sql-admin-login-password $SQLPASSWORD \
>    --location $LOCATION
Command group 'synapse' is in preview and under development. R
{
  "adlaResourceId": null,
  "connectivityEndpoints": {
    "dev": "https://trainingsynapse100.dev.azuresynapse.net",
    "sql": "trainingsynapse100.sql.azuresynapse.net",
    "sqlOnDemand": "trainingsynapse100-ondemand.sql.azuresynap
    "web": "https://web.azuresynapse.net?workspace=%2fsubscrip
soft.Synapse%2fworkspaces%2ftrainingsynapse100"
```

Figure 8.6 – Output of the Azure Synapse workspace create command

4. Now, we must grant access to the new Azure Synapse workspace based on the original IP address. In a real production environment, it is suggested that the IP address list you use is very restrictive:

```
az synapse workspace firewall-rule create --name allowAll
--workspace-name $SYSNAPSEWORKSPACENAME \

--resource-group $RESOURCEGROUPNAME --start-ip-address
0.0.0.0 --end-ip-address 255.255.255.255
```

This results in the following output:

```
Azure> az synapse workspace firewall-rule create --name allowAll --work
> --resource-group $RESOURCEGROUPNAME    start-ip-address 0.0.0.0 --end-
Command group 'synapse' is in preview and under development. Reference
{
  "endIpAddress": "255.255.255.255",
  "id": "/subscriptions/0b35426c-85f3-45e8-9f96-577a13b738d5/resourceGr
es/allowAll",
  "name": "allowAll",
  "provisioningState": "Succeeded",
  "resourceGroup": "training_rg",
  "startIpAddress": "0.0.0.0",
  "type": "Microsoft.Synapse/workspaces/firewallRules"
}
```

Figure 8.7 – Output of the Azure Synapse workspace firewall rule command

5. If the preceding command is successful, you should be able to see the newly created **Azure Synapse** workspace in the Azure portal by browsing to **Home** > **All Resources** > **trainingsynapse100**:

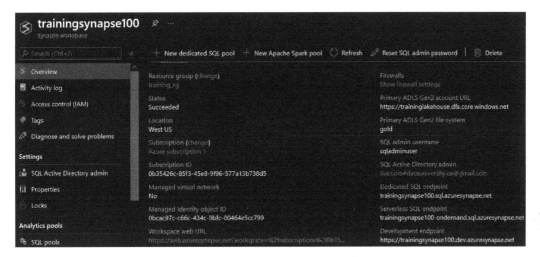

Figure 8.8 – Confirmation of Azure Synapse workspace creation

6. We are now ready to create a new Azure Synapse serverless database. Take note of the serverless SQL endpoint in your Azure Synapse workspace. The **username** and **password** properties are the same as the ones we used previously while creating the Azure synapse workspace:

```
SERVERLESS_SQL_ENDPOINT="trainingsynapse100-ondemand.sql.
azuresynapse.net"
```
```
SQLUSER="sqladminuser"
```
```
SQLPASSWORD="XXXXXXXXX"
```
```
sqlcmd -S $SERVERLESS_SQL_ENDPOINT -U $SQLUSER -P
$SQLPASSWORD -i Data-Engineering-with-Apache-Spark-Delta-
Lake-and-Lakehouse/project/aggregation/sql/create_db.sql
```

7. Now, create the stored procedures that will be used to create objects in the Azure Synapse serverless database. Make sure you edit SQLPASSWORD and SERVERLESS_SQL_ENDPOINT as per the serverless SQL endpoint you fetched in the previous step:

```
SERVERLESS_SQL_ENDPOINT="trainingsynapse100-ondemand.sql.
azuresynapse.net"
```
```
SQLUSER="sqladminuser"
```
```
SQLPASSWORD="XXXXXXXX"
```

```
sqlcmd -S $SERVERLESS_SQL_ENDPOINT -U $SQLUSER -P
$SQLPASSWORD -i Data-Engineering-with-Apache-Spark-
Delta-Lake-and-Lakehouse/project/aggregation/sql/create_
synapse_creds.sql
```

```
sqlcmd -S $SERVERLESS_SQL_ENDPOINT -U $SQLUSER -P
$SQLPASSWORD -i Data-Engineering-with-Apache-Spark-Delta-
Lake-and-Lakehouse/project/aggregation/sql/create_silver_
views.sql
```

```
sqlcmd -S $SERVERLESS_SQL_ENDPOINT -U $SQLUSER -P
$SQLPASSWORD -i Data-Engineering-with-Apache-Spark-Delta-
Lake-and-Lakehouse/project/aggregation/sql/drop_gold_
tables.sql
```

```
sqlcmd -S $SERVERLESS_SQL_ENDPOINT -U $SQLUSER -P
$SQLPASSWORD -i Data-Engineering-with-Apache-Spark-Delta-
Lake-and-Lakehouse/project/aggregation/sql/create_gold_
tables.sql
```

This results in the following output:

```
Azure> SERVERLESS_SQL_ENDPOINT="trainingsynapse100-ondemand.sql.azuresynapse.net"
Azure> SQLUSER="sqladminuser"
Azure> SQLPASSWORD="▮▮▮▮▮▮▮▮▮▮▮"
Azure> sqlcmd -S $SERVERLESS_SQL_ENDPOINT -U $SQLUSER -P $SQLPASSWORD -i Data-Engine
create_synapse_creds.sql
Changed database context to 'gold'.
Azure> sqlcmd -S $SERVERLESS_SQL_ENDPOINT -U $SQLUSER -P $SQLPASSWORD -i Data-Engine
create_silver_views.sql
Changed database context to 'gold'.
Azure> sqlcmd -S $SERVERLESS_SQL_ENDPOINT -U $SQLUSER -P $SQLPASSWORD -i Data-Engine
drop_gold_tables.sql
Changed database context to 'gold'.
Azure> sqlcmd -S $SERVERLESS_SQL_ENDPOINT -U $SQLUSER -P $SQLPASSWORD -i Data-Engine
create_gold_tables.sql
Changed database context to 'gold'.
Azure>
```

Figure 8.9 – Output of the stored procedure creation commands in an Azure Synapse database

8. We also need an Azure Data Factory for this exercise. You may recall that
    we created **trraininglakehousedf** in *Chapter 5, Data Collection Stage – The Bronze
    Layer*. Hopefully, you still have it hanging around in your Azure subscription.
    If you accidentally deleted it, then you will need to go back to the *Building the
    batch ingestion pipeline* section and follow the steps there.

At this point, you're ready to start developing the Electroniz aggregation pipeline.

Creating the pipeline for the gold layer

Once the Azure resources have been deployed, we can create the pipeline for building the gold layer:

1. Let's start by generating an Azure storage account **SAS** key that will be used by Azure Synapse to access data files.

   Using the Azure portal, navigate to **Home** > **All Resources** > **traininglakehouse**.

   Using the menu on the left, click on **Shared access signature**. Input the following options:

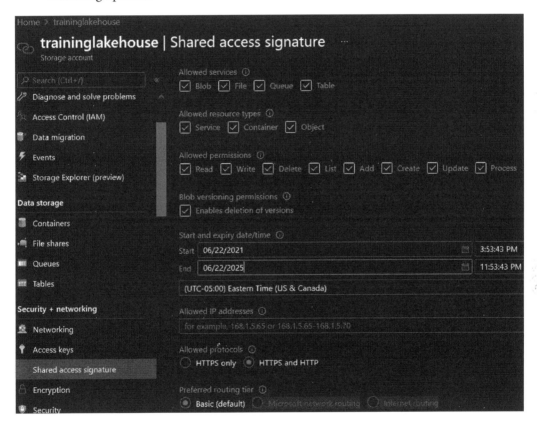

Figure 8.10 – Create options for an Azure storage account SAS token

Click on **Generate SAS and connection string**.

Take note of the **SAS token** property. You will need this token later when you start creating the gold pipeline:

Figure 8.11 – SAS token for authentication

Before we start crating the aggregation pipeline, let's understand what a **shared access signature (SAS)** is used for. A SAS is a **URI** that grants restricted access to Azure Data Lake Storage. A SAS may be configured to grant storage access with very limited permissions and for a specific period.

The following figure depicts the anatomy of a SAS URI. Note how each option maps to the URI to restrict the access of the user or application using it:

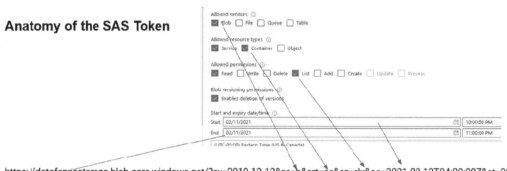

Figure 8.12 – The anatomy of a sample SAS token for authentication

> **Important**
>
> SAS keys provide delegated and limited access to Azure storage accounts. The SAS key options should be implemented with tighter controls and limited access in production.

2. Like using Azure storage keys, you should use the SAS URI with care. Instead of exposing the URI in code or deployment files, you should store it as a secret in the **Azure Key Vault** secrets manager. You may recall that we previously created an Azure Key Vault named **trainingkv100**:

    ▪ In the Azure portal, browse to **Home** > **All Resources** > **trainingkv100**.

    ▪ Using the left menu, click on **Secrets**.

    ▪ Click on **Generate/Import** and provide the following properties:

        ◆ **Name**: ADLSSASKEY

        ◆ **Value**: SAS token from the step above

3. Once the new secret has been created, click on **ADLSSASKEY**. After that, click on the entry below **current version** and note the **Secret Identifier** property. We will need this later.

4. At this point, we can start building the pipeline for the gold layer. Connect to the Azure portal and click on **Home** > **All Resources** > **trainingdatafactory100**.

    Using the panel on the left, click on **Manage**. We will start by creating the linked service for the Azure Synapse Serverless database. We want to create a **couple** of linked services for the aggregation pipeline.

5. To create the first linked service for **Azure Synapse**, click on **Create linked service**.

    In the **New linked service** window, choose the icon for **Azure SQL Database**. Click on **Continue**. A new window will open called **New linked service (Azure SQL Database)**. Provide the following properties:

    ▪ **Name**: Synapse Serverless.

    ▪ **Account selection method**: Enter manually

    ▪ **Fully qualified domain name**: trainingsynapse100-ondemand.sql. azuresynapse.net.

    ▪ Adjust the entry as per your **SERVERLESS_SQL_ENDPOINT**.

    ▪ **Database name**: gold.

    ▪ **Authentication type**: SQL authentication.

    ▪ **User name**: sqladminuser.

    ▪ **Password**: <SYNAPSE PASSWORD SET PREVIOUSLY>.

Click on **Test connection**. If the connection was successful, click on **Create**:

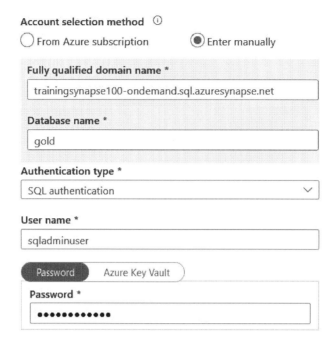

Figure 8.13 – Data factory linked service options for an Azure Synapse SQL serverless pool

6. Chances are that you may already have the second linked service, which is called **traininglakehouse**, because we created it while spinning up **electroniz_batch_ingestion_pipeline**.

    If you don't, click on **Create linked service**.

    Now, click on **New**. In the **New linked service** window, choose the icon for **Azure Data Lake Storage Gen2**. Click on **Continue**.

    A new window will open called **New linked service (Azure Data Lake Storage Gen2)**. Provide the following properties:

- **Name**: `traininglakehouse`
- **Authentication method**: `From Azure subscription`
- **Azure subscription**: `Free Tier or Paid Subscription`
- **Storage account name**: `traininglakehouse`

Click on **Test connection**. If the connection was successful, click on **Create**.

7. Now, we are ready to create the pipeline. Click on **Author & Monitor**.

Using the panel on the left, click on the **Author** menu. In the Azure Data Factory **Resources** panel, click on the three dots to the right of **Pipelines** and choose **New Pipeline**.

In the **Properties** panel, input the following:

- **Name**: `electroniz_aggregation_pipeline`

- **Description**: `This pipeline will aggregate data from the sales database, currency conversion, geo-location, and ecommerce website tracking.`

8. Now, click on the empty white space in the **Activities** section. In the panel under **Parameters**, create the following parameters:

Figure 8.14 – Creating parameters for electroniz_aggregation_pipeline

9. In the **Activities**, panel search for `Web`. Now, drag the **Web** activity to the right-hand panel and provide the following properties:

- **Name**: `Get Secret`.

- Click on **Settings**.

- **URL**: Enter the **Secret Identifier** property of **ADLSSASKEY** from the Azure Key Vault secret we created previously. Make sure you add `?api-version=7.0` to the end of the URL; for example, `https://trainingkv100.vault.azure.net/secrets/ADLSSASKEY/2d13f6f42ff14e53ae953e42c36c32c0?api-version=7.0`.

Make sure you adjust the name of the Azure Key Vault as per your settings:

- **Authentication**: Managed Identity

- **Resource**: https://vault.azure.net:

General   **Settings**   User properties

URL *   https://kevault1000.vault.azure.net/secrets/

Method *   GET   ⌄

Headers   + New

Datasets   + Add dataset reference

Linked services   + Add linked service reference

Integration runtime * ⓘ AutoResolveIntegrationRuntime   ⌄

◢ Advanced

Authentication   ○ None ○ Basic ⓘ ◉ Managed Identity ⓘ ○ Client Certificate ⓘ

Figure 8.15 – The Get Secret activity in electroniz_aggregation_pipeline

10. In the **Activities** panel, search for Stored Procedure. Now, drag the **Stored procedure** activity to the right-hand panel and provide the following properties:

- **Name**: Drop Gold Layer Tables.

- Click on **Settings**.

- **Linked service**: Synapse Serverless.

- **Stored procedure name**: [dbo].[drop_gold_tables].

- Under **Stored procedure parameters**: Add one parameter. Start by clicking **New**:

  - **Name**: goldns **Type**: String
    Value: @pipeline().parameters.GOLD_LAYER_NAMESPACE:

Figure 8.16 – Parameters of the stored procedure

11. Now, chain **Get Secret** to **Drop Gold Layer Tables**. Once you've done this, the pipeline should look like this:

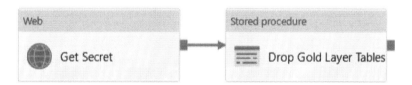

Figure 8.17 – Chaining activities – Get Secret to Drop Gold Layer Tables

12. In the **Activities** panel, search for Stored Procedure. Now, drag the **Stored procedure** activity to the right-hand panel and provide the following properties:

- **Name**: Create Synapse Credentials.

- Click on **Settings**.

- **Linked service**: Synapse Serverless.

- **Stored procedure name**: [dbo].[create_synapse_creds].

- Under **Stored procedure parameters**: Add five parameters. Start by clicking **New**:

  - **Name**: format **Type**: String
    Value: @pipeline().parameters.EXT_TAB_FILE_FORMAT

  - **Name**: extds   **Type**: String
    Value: @pipeline().parameters.EXT_DATA_SOURCE

- **Name**: `creds`   **Type**: `String`
  Value: `@pipeline().parameters.EXT_CREDENTIALS`

- **Name**: `secret`   **Type**: `String`
  Value: `@activity('Get Secret').output.value`

- **Name**: `location`   **Type**: `String`
  Value: `@pipeline().parameters.EXT_TAB_LOCATION:`

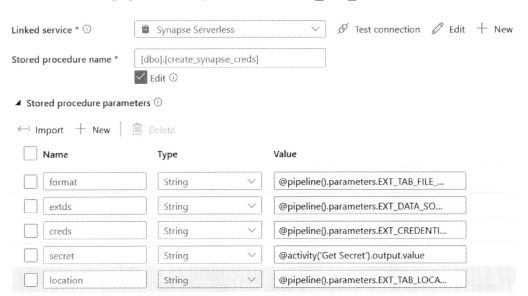

Figure 8.18 – Parameters of the create_synapse_creds stored procedure

13. Now, chain **Drop Gold Layer Tables** to **Create Synapse Credentials**. Once you've done this, the pipeline should look like this:

Figure 8.19 – Chaining activities – Drop Gold Layer Tables to Create Synapse Credentials

14. In the **Activities** panel, search for `Stored Procedure`. Now, drag the **Stored procedure** activity to the right-hand panel and provide the following properties:

- **Name**: `Create Silver Layer Views`.

- Click on **Settings**.

- **Linked service**: `Synapse Serverless`.

- **Stored procedure name**: `[dbo].[create_silver_views]`.

- Under **Stored procedure parameters**: Add two parameters. Start by clicking **New**:

  - **Name**: `silverns`   **Type**: `String`
    Value: `@pipeline().parameters.SILVER_LAYER_NAMESPACE`

  - **Name**: `location`   **Type**: `String`
    Value: `@pipeline().parameters.EXT_TAB_LOCATION:`

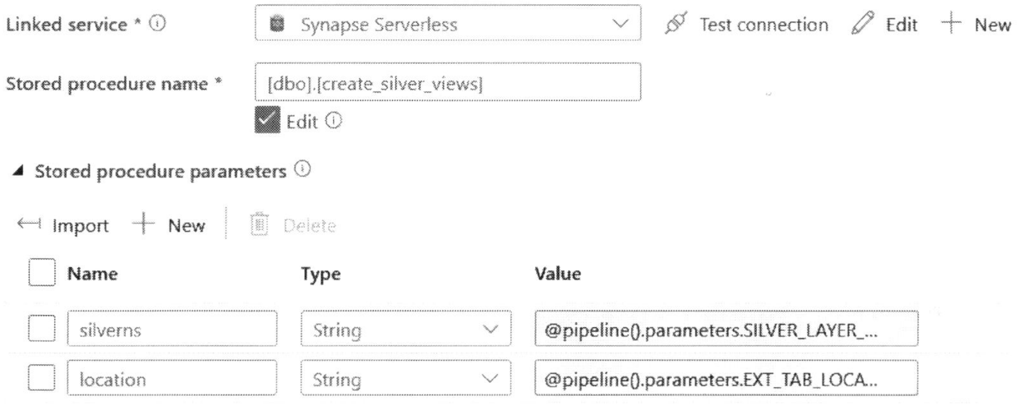

Linked service * ⓘ   🔲 Synapse Serverless   ∨   ✎ Test connection   ✏ Edit   ✛ New

Stored procedure name *   [dbo].[create_silver_views]
       ☑ Edit ⓘ

▲ Stored procedure parameters ⓘ

↤ Import   ✛ New | 🗑 Delete

	Name	Type	Value
☐	silverns	String ∨	@pipeline().parameters.SILVER_LAYER_...
☐	location	String ∨	@pipeline().parameters.EXT_TAB_LOCA...

Figure 8.20 – Parameters for the create_silver_views stored procedure

15. Now, chain **Create Synapse Credentials** to **Create Silver Layer Views**. Once you've done this, the pipeline should look like this:

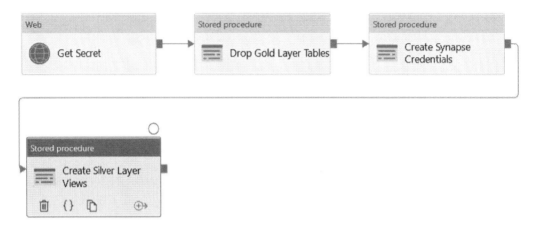

Figure 8.21 – Chaining activities – Create Synapse Credentials to Create Silver Layer Views

16. In the **Activities** panel, search for Delete. Now, drag the **Delete** activity to the right-hand panel and provide the following properties:

- **Name**: Cleanup Gold Data.
- Click on **Source**. Now, click on **New**.
- Choose **Azure Data Lake Storage Gen 2** and click **Continue**.
- **Name**: gold_data.
- **Linked service**: traininglakehouse.
- **File path**: gold/external:

Set properties

Name

```
gold_data
```

Linked service *

```
traininglakehouse            ∨    ⏐
```

File path

```
gold        /    external    /    File          ⏢  ∨
```

▷ Advanced

Figure 8.22 – Properties of the Delete activity

17. Click on **OK**. Click on the **Logging** setting and uncheck the **Enable Logging** box.

18. Now, chain **Create Silver Layer Views** to **Cleanup Gold Data**. Once you've done this, the pipeline should look like this:

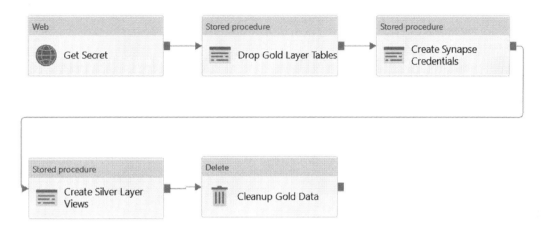

Figure 8.23 – Chaining activities – Create Silver Layer Views to Cleanup Gold Data

19. In the **Activities** panel, search for `Stored Procedure`. Now, drag the **Stored procedure** activity to the right-hand panel and provide the following properties:

- **Name**: `Create Gold Layer Tables`.

- Click on **Settings**.

- **Linked service**: `Synapse Serverless`.

- **Stored procedure name**: `[dbo].[create_gold_tables]`.

- Under **Stored procedure parameters**: Add three parameters. Start by clicking **New**:

  • **Name**: `goldns` **Type**: `String`
    Value: `@pipeline().parameters.GOLD_LAYER_NAMESPACE`

  • **Name**: `format`   **Type**: `String`
    Value: `@pipeline().parameters.EXT_TAB_FILE_FORMAT`

- **Name**: extds   **Type**: String
  Value: @pipeline().parameters.EXT_DATA_SOURCE:

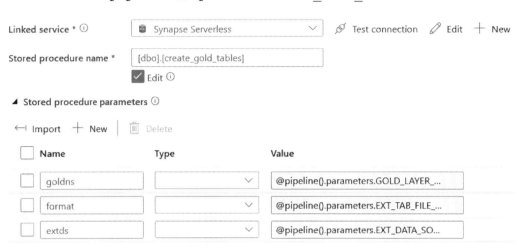

Figure 8.24 – Parameters of the create_gold_tables stored procedure

20. Now, chain **Cleanup Gold Data** to **Create Gold Layer Tables**. At this point, we've finished developing **electroniz_aggregation_pipeline**. Click on **Publish all**, followed by **Publish**.

This is what the final version of **electroniz_aggregation_pipeline** should look like:

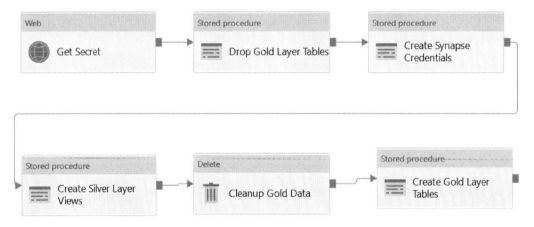

Figure 8.25 – Final electroniz_aggregation_pipeline

At this point, we are ready to unit test **electroniz_aggregation_pipeline**.

Running the aggregation pipeline

In production, the aggregation pipeline will be invoked automatically once the curation pipeline completes successfully. Since we are in the unit testing phase, we will trigger it manually for now. Let's get started:

1. You must invoke the following commands on Azure Cloud Shell. They will invoke **electroniz_aggregation_pipeline** based on the parameters we pass. Please make sure you edit **EXT_TAB_LOCATION** as per the instructions provided. Using the Azure portal, navigate to your Azure Data Lake Storage account by going to **Home** > **All Resources** > **traininglakehouse** > **Endpoints**.

    Note the URL of **Blob Service** and use this to edit EXT_TAB_LOCATION:

    ```
    RESOURCEGROUPNAME="training_rg"

    DATAFACTORYNAME="traininglakehousedf"

    PIPELINENAME="electroniz_batch_aggregation_pipeline"

    az datafactory pipeline create-run --factory-name
    $DATAFACTORYNAME --name $PIPELINENAME --resource-group
    $RESOURCEGROUPNAME \

    --parameters "{\"EXT_TAB_FILE_FORMAT\":\"parquetformat\",
    \"EXT_DATA_SOURCE\":\"trainingds\", \"EXT_
    CREDENTIALS\":\"trainingcreds\",

    \"EXT_TAB_LOCATION\":\"https://traininglakehouse.
    blob.core.windows.net\", \"SILVER_LAYER_
    NAMESPACE\":\"silver\",

    \"GOLD_LAYER_NAMESPACE\":\"gold\" "}
    ```

2. To verify whether the pipeline ran successfully, you can check the status of the pipeline:

    *   Using the Azure portal, navigate to **Home** > **All Resources** > **trainingdatafactorydf**.

    *   Click **Monitor** > **Pipeline Runs**.

- Click **electroniz_batch_aggregation_pipeline**:

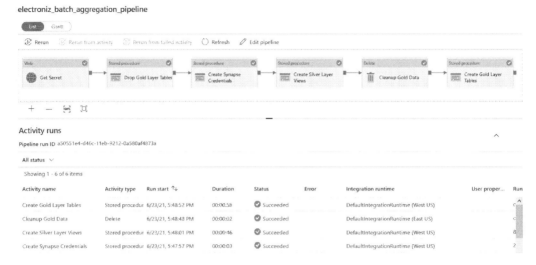

Figure 8.26 – Monitoring the run of electroniz_aggregation_pipeline

As you can see, we can safely infer that **electroniz_batch_aggregation_pipeline** has been completed successfully. However, this does not mean that it performed the job it was supposed to do. To be certain, we will need to verify the aggregated data in Azure Synapse.

Understanding data consumption

Before we start verifying the aggregated data, we should focus on how our end users will be able to consume data for dashboarding, ML, and AI purposes. As per the laid-out architecture of the **Electroniz** lakehouse, we decided to publish data from both the gold and silver layers.

Publishing data from the gold layer is necessary; otherwise, how would users be able to access aggregated data? But why do we need to publish data from the silver layer? You guessed it – analytics is an ongoing process. In the future, users may want to create new dashboards and ML models for the betterment of the company.

> **Important**
>
> Publishing data from the gold and silver layers is acceptable because they store data that is in a clean and secure state. But the same cannot be said for data in the bronze layer. Publishing raw/unclean data not only throws a lot of work around standardization, validation, and deduplication at end users, but it also ends up exposing classified information that should have been protected.

The following diagram shows the lakehouse's structure:

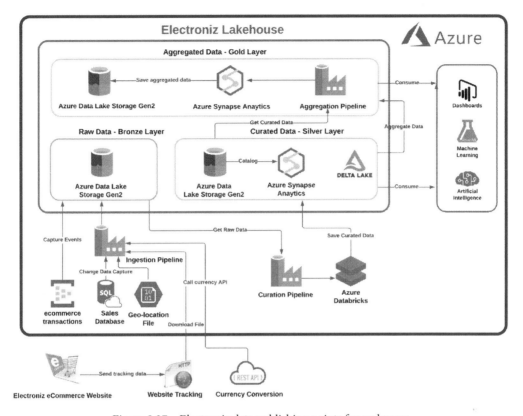

Figure 8.27 – Electroniz data publishing points for end users

Our promise to **Electroniz** was that by the end of the project, end users will not only be able to access the aggregated data in the gold layer but also have access to curated data in the silver layer for ad hoc access. Also, in the future, there will be new requirements for aggregations and ML models that will require access to the curated data.

You may have noticed that, while creating **electroniz_batch_aggregation_pipeline**, a series of activities were defined in the pipeline. These end up creating views and external tables in Azure Synapse. It is important to understand how the data in the lakehouse is published for end users. The following data has been provided:

- **Access to Silver Layer Data**: For access to curated data, we provided **EXTERNAL TABLES** and **VIEWS** in the **Azure Synapse serverless SQL pool**. As we mentioned previously, not all aggregations can be predicted initially in the project. Having access to the data in the silver layer will enable end users to perform ad hoc querying and create new aggregations in the future.

- **Access to Gold Layer Data**: We provided access to the aggregated tables in the gold layer by using **EXTERNAL TABLES** in the **Azure Synapse serverless SQL pool**. These external tables were created using **CREATE EXTERNAL TABLE AS SELECT (CETAS)**, and the query results were saved (persisted) in the gold layer in **Azure Data Lake Storage Gen2**. Since aggregated data is saved in the gold layer, this substantially improves query processing times:

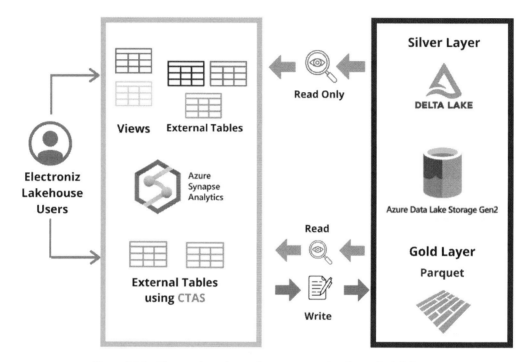

Figure 8.28 – Electroniz end user data consumption from the lakehouse

The preceding diagram shows how the external views and tables were created in **electroniz_batch_aggregation_pipeline**.

Accessing silver layer data

Create Silver Layer Views invokes a stored procedure named **create_silver_views** in Azure Synapse. The code for this stored procedure is available here:

```
https://github.com/PacktPublishing/Data-Engineering-with-
Apache-Spark-Delta-Lake-and-Lakehouse/blob/main/project/
aggregation/sql/create_silver_views.sql.
```

Look at the following SQL. You will notice how the combination of external tables and views works:

```
EXEC sp_executesql N'IF EXISTS ( SELECT * FROM sys.external_tables WHERE object_id = OBJECT_ID(''store_customers'') )
                    DROP EXTERNAL TABLE store_customers'
SET @sqlcmd = N'CREATE EXTERNAL TABLE store_customers ([customer_id] INTEGER ,[customer_name] VARCHAR(255) ,[address] VARCHAR(255) ,
                                                       [city] VARCHAR(255) ,[postalcode] VARCHAR(10) ,[country] VARCHAR(100) ,
                                                       [phone] VARCHAR(100) ,[email] VARCHAR(255) ,[credit_card] VARCHAR(255) ,
                                                       [updated_at] DATETIME)
   WITH (LOCATION = ''' + @silverns + '/sales/store_customers'',  data_source = trainingds, FILE_FORMAT = DeltaLakeFormat)';
   EXEC sp_executesql @sqlcmd

EXEC sp_executesql N'IF EXISTS ( SELECT * FROM sys.external_tables WHERE object_id = OBJECT_ID(''ecomm_customers'') )
                    DROP EXTERNAL TABLE ecomm_customers'
SET @sqlcmd = N'CREATE EXTERNAL TABLE ecomm_customers ([customer_id] INTEGER , [customer_name] VARCHAR(255) ,[address] VARCHAR(255) ,
                                                       [city] VARCHAR(255) ,[postalcode] VARCHAR(10) ,[country] VARCHAR(100) ,
                                                       [phone] VARCHAR(100) ,[email] VARCHAR(255), [updated_at] DATETIME )
   WITH (LOCATION = ''' + @silverns + '/esalesns'',  data_source = trainingds, FILE_FORMAT = DeltaLakeFormat)';
   EXEC sp_executesql @sqlcmd

EXEC sp_executesql N'DROP VIEW IF EXISTS customers'
   SET @sqlcmd = N'CREATE OR ALTER VIEW customers as
                   SELECT  [customer_id],[customer_name]  ,[address],[city],[postalcode],
                           [country],[phone],[email], NULL as credit_card,[updated_at]
               FROM [dbo].[ecomm_customers]
               UNION
               SELECT  [customer_id],[customer_name],[address],[city],[postalcode],
                       [country],[phone],[email],[credit_card],[updated_at]
               FROM [dbo].[store_customers]'
   EXEC sp_executesql @sqlcmd
```

Figure 8.29 – External tables and views in the silver layer of the lakehouse

store_customers (customers in the **stores** database) is an external table that's declared in the /sales/store_customers directory in the silver layer of the traininglakehouse Azure Data Lake Storage account. Since the silver layer is using the Delta format, FILE_FORMAT has been set to DeltaLakeFormat.

ecomm_customers (the customer who brought a product online) is an external table that's declared in the /esalesns directory in the silver layer of the traininglakehouse Azure Data Lake Storage account. Since the silver layer is using the Delta format, FILE_FORMAT has been set to DeltaLakeFormat.

Notice how we cleverly combined the two types of customers in a common **view** named customers. This gives our end users the flexibility to query customers separately from stores versus e-commerce or have a common aggregated version.

Accessing gold layer data

Create Gold Layer Tables invokes a stored procedure named **create_gold_tables** in Azure Synapse. The code for this stored procedure is available here:

https://github.com/PacktPublishing/Data-Engineering-with-Apache-Spark-Delta-Lake-and-Lakehouse/blob/main/project/aggregation/sql/create_gold_tables.sql.

Look at the following SQL. You will notice how the external tables have been created using CTAS:

```
EXEC sp_executesql N'IF EXISTS ( SELECT * FROM sys.external_tables WHERE object_id = OBJECT_ID(''ext_aggregated_sales'') )
                    DROP EXTERNAL TABLE ext_aggregated_sales'
    SET @sqlcmd = N'CREATE EXTERNAL TABLE ext_aggregated_sales
                    WITH (
                                        LOCATION = ''' + @goldns + '/external/ext_aggregated_sales/'',
                                        DATA_SOURCE = ' + @extds + ',
                                        FILE_FORMAT = ' + @format + '
                    )
    AS   SELECT YEAR(order_date) AS year, DATEPART(QUARTER, order_date) as quarter,
                            round(sum(sale_price_usd),2) as aggregated_sales_price
                    FROM orders
              GROUP BY YEAR(order_date), DATEPART(QUARTER, order_date) '
EXEC sp_executesql @sqlcmd
```

Figure 8.30 – External tables in the gold layer of the lakehouse

Notice how ext_aggregated_sales was created using CTAS. The query fetches aggregated data by quarter from the orders view and the result is persisted in the gold layer in Parquet format.

Important

Having a solid data consumption strategy is critical for the overall success of data lake projects. After all, this is the point of entry for end users for their data usage scenarios.

Now that we have a solid understanding of the data consumption patterns used by end users, we can verify the actual data.

Verifying aggregated data in the gold layer

Assuming the previous invocation of **electroniz_batch_aggregation_pipeline** was successful, you should see the following external tables and views in the silver container of the Azure Data Lake Storage account:

1. Using the Azure portal, navigate to **Home** > **All Resources** > **trainingsynapse100**.

Now, click on **Open** in the **Open Synapse Studio** section:

Figure 8.31 – The Open Synapse Studio section

2. Using the menu on the left, click on **Data**. Now, keep clicking on the arrow beside **Database**, then **gold (SQL)** and **External Tables**.

You should now see the following pane:

Figure 8.32 – Silver layer external tables in the Synapse serverless SQL pool

3. Similarly, the following external tables and views represent the aggregated data in the gold layer:

Figure 8.33 – Gold layer external tables and views in the Synapse serverless SQL pool

4. Let's go even further and fetch data from a view. To query the view, click on the three-dotted line beside the view name, followed by **New SQL script**, and then **Select TOP 100 rows**:

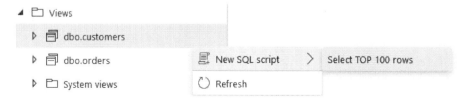

Figure 8.34 – Querying a view in the Synapse serverless SQL pool

Now, click on **Run**:

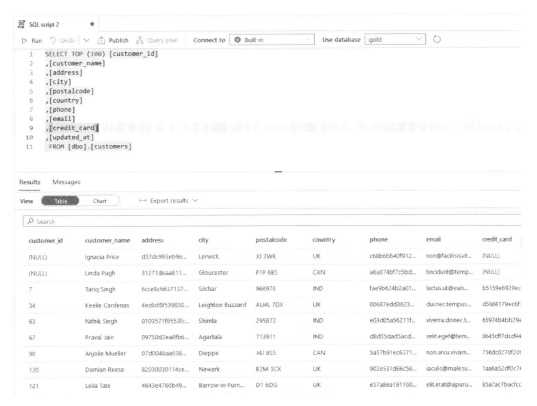

Figure 8.35 – Data from the customers view in the Synapse serverless SQL pool

You should see data displayed for the **customers** view. You may notice that the **orders** view aggregates data from two external tables called **store_customers** and **ecomm_customers**.

5. Let's do another one but this time, we will choose an external table that was created using CTAS. Using the menu on the left, click **External Tables**.

    To query the view, click on the three-dotted line beside the view name, followed by **New SQL script**, and then **Select TOP 100 rows**:

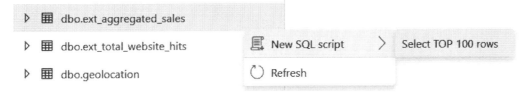

Figure 8.36 – Query an external table in the Synapse serverless SQL pool

Now, click on **Run**:

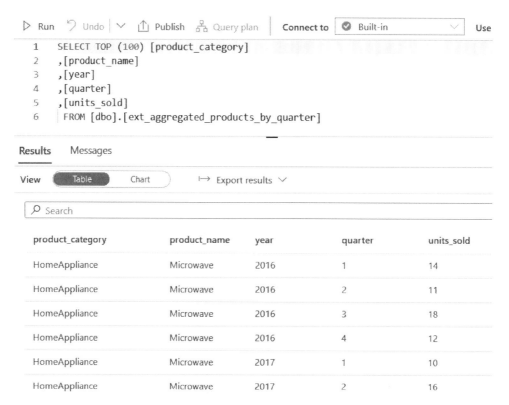

Figure 8.37 – Data from ext_aggregated_products_by_quarter

6. As you may have noticed, the performance of the **ext_aggregated_products_by_quarter** fetch from Azure Synapse was drastically faster than the fetch for the **customers** view. The reason for this is that the data for **ext_aggregated_products_by_quarter** has been persisted in the following directory in the gold layer of the lakehouse:

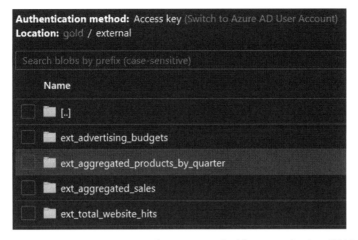

Figure 8.38 – Data persistence for aggregated tables created using CTAS

You may want to query a few more external tables and views yourself to gain further confidence. At this stage, we can infer that the data in Azure Synapse is ready for querying by end users. But one question remains unanswered: does the data in the lakehouse serve Electroniz's end user needs? Did we meet the customer's expectations? We are about to find out!

Meeting customer expectations

Based on the results shown in the preceding section, we can safely infer that we can query data successfully from the silver and gold layers of the **Electroniz** lakehouse. This is certainly a huge technical win; however, the real question is whether we meet customer expectations from a business standpoint.

Before we deep dive into validating the business requirements, we need to ascertain if we provided sufficient access to our end users, such as **data analysts**, **data scientists**, and **business intelligence engineers**. Ultimately, the end users will be using the lakehouse for their diverse analytical requirements, so their needs should be addressed properly.

Let's focus on validating the business requirements that were put forth by **Electroniz** at the start of the project:

1. First, Electroniz aimed for a near-real-time sales analytics platform that can serve their customer needs faster and better.

   You may recall that **Electroniz** sells products both in-store and online. While building the bronze layer, we ingested sales data from both sources. To provide near-real-time analytics that includes both **in-store** and **online** sales data, we aggregated the sales data into one common view named **orders**. This view was created as part of the **create_silver_views** stored procedure, which is invoked using the **Create Silver Layer Views** activity in **electroniz_aggregation_pipeline**:

```
EXEC sp_executesql N'DROP VIEW IF EXISTS store_orders'
SET @sqlcmd = N'CREATE OR ALTER VIEW store_orders AS
            SELECT * FROM openrowset(
                BULK ''' + '/' + @silverns +'/sales/store_orders/'', data_source = ''trainingds'', FORMAT = ''delta'')
            AS rows'
EXEC sp_executesql @sqlcmd

EXEC sp_executesql N'DROP VIEW IF EXISTS ecomm_orders'
SET @sqlcmd = N' CREATE OR ALTER VIEW ecomm_orders AS
            SELECT order_number, email, product_name, order_date, order_mode, sale_price, sale_price_usd, updated_at
            FROM openrowset(
                BULK ''' + '/' + @silverns +'/sales/store_orders/'', data_source = ''trainingds'', FORMAT = ''delta'')
            WITH { order_number INT, product_name NVARCHAR(MAX), order_date DATE, order_mode NVARCHAR(MAX),
                    email NVARCHAR(MAX), sale_price FLOAT, sale_price_usd FLOAT, updated_at DATETIME
                } AS rows'
EXEC sp_executesql @sqlcmd

EXEC sp_executesql N'DROP VIEW IF EXISTS orders'
SET @sqlcmd = N' CREATE OR ALTER VIEW orders AS
            SELECT order_number, email, product_name, order_date, units, sale_price,
                    order_mode, sale_price_usd, dbo.store_orders.updated_at
            FROM dbo.store_orders
            JOIN dbo.customers ON dbo.customers.customer_id = dbo.store_orders.customer_id
            JOIN dbo.products ON dbo.products.product_id = dbo.store_orders.product_id
            UNION
            SELECT order_number, email, product_name, order_date, 1 AS units, sale_price,
                    order_mode, sale_price_usd, updated_at
            FROM dbo.ecomm_orders'
EXEC sp_executesql @sqlcmd
```

Figure 8.39 – SQL for creating the orders view

The same view is also used to aggregate sales data by quarters and published as **ext_aggregated_sales**. This table is created as part of the **create_gold_tables** stored procedure, which is invoked using the **Create Gold Layer Tables** activity in **electroniz_aggregation_pipeline**:

```
SET @sqlcmd = N'CREATE EXTERNAL TABLE ext_aggregated_sales
                WITH (
                    LOCATION = ''' + @goldns + '/external/ext_aggregated_sales/'',
                    DATA_SOURCE = ' + @extds + ',
                    FILE_FORMAT = ' + @format + '
                )
            AS  SELECT YEAR(order_date) AS year, DATEPART(QUARTER, order_date) as quarter,
                    round(sum(sale_price_usd),2) as aggregated_sales_price
                FROM orders
            GROUP BY YEAR(order_date), DATEPART(QUARTER, order_date) '
EXEC sp_executesql @sqlcmd
```

Figure 8.40 – SQL for the ext_aggregated_sales external table

The following query from `ext_aggregated_sales` will show aggregated sales data per quarter:

```
SELECT [year], [quarter], [aggregated_sales_price]
FROM [dbo].[ext_aggregated_sales]
ORDER BY 1 DESC, 2 ASC
```

This results in the following output:

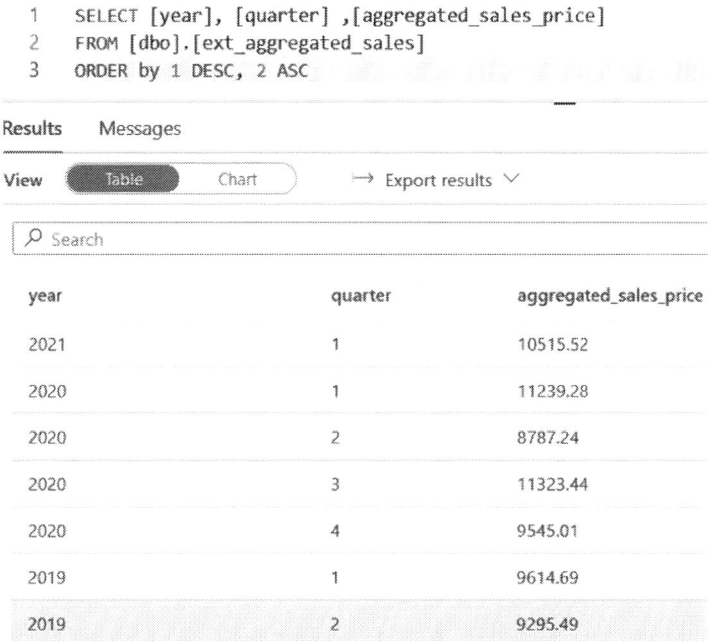

```
1   SELECT [year], [quarter] ,[aggregated_sales_price]
2   FROM [dbo].[ext_aggregated_sales]
3   ORDER by 1 DESC, 2 ASC
```

Results   Messages

View   Table   Chart   ⟼ Export results ∨

🔍 Search

year	quarter	aggregated_sales_price
2021	1	10515.52
2020	1	11239.28
2020	2	8787.24
2020	3	11323.44
2020	4	9545.01
2019	1	9614.69
2019	2	9295.49

Figure 8.41 – Aggregated sales per quarter

2. Let's have some fun and visualize this as a bar chart. Click on **Chart** and change the variables, as per the following screenshot. As you can see, the end users at **Electroniz** can now easily visualize aggregated sales figures by year/quarter to enhance their decision-making in near real time:

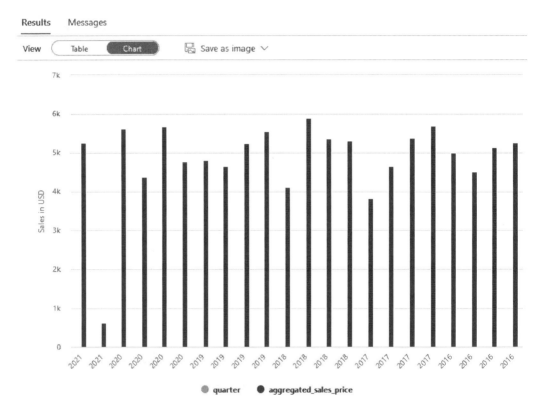

Figure 8.42 – Chart of sales per quarter

3. **Electroniz** also wanted to streamline advertising budgets through intelligent analytics based on the number of user hits on their e-commerce website. They wanted **advertising** and **marketing** dollars to be allocated country wise and backed by the user hits that were received on their e-commerce website.

We created a couple of external tables for this business requirement. The first external table is named **ext_total_website_hits**, which aggregates the number of hits per country where at least 1,000 hits were received. **Electroniz** has decided that anything less than 1,000 hits is not a substantial figure that will impact their decision making:

> **Important**
>
> Having input from a customer like this is extremely critical for the overall success of the project. This is why I previously mentioned that the aggregation process is a shared responsibility between customers and data engineers.

```
SET @sqlcmd = N'CREATE EXTERNAL TABLE ext_total_website_hits
                WITH (
                        LOCATION = ''' + @goldns + '/external/ext_total_website_hits/'',
                        DATA_SOURCE = ' + @extds + ',
                        FILE_FORMAT = ' + @format + '
                )
                AS      SELECT SUM(hits) AS total_hits FROM
                        (SELECT country_name, count(*) AS hits
                        FROM logs
                        GROUP BY country_name
                        HAVING count(*) > 1000) as webhits '
EXEC sp_executesql @sqlcmd

SET @sqlcmd = N'CREATE EXTERNAL TABLE ext_advertising_budgets
                WITH (
                        LOCATION = ''' + @goldns + '/external/ext_advertising_budgets/'',
                        DATA_SOURCE = ' + @extds + ',
                        FILE_FORMAT = ' + @format + '
                )
                AS  SELECT country_name, hits, (hits*100/total_hits) AS advtg_budget
                FROM
                (SELECT country_name, count(*) as hits, (SELECT total_hits from ext_total_website_hits) AS total_hits
                FROM logs
                GROUP BY country_name
                HAVING count(*) > 1000) AS agg_hits '
```

Figure 8.43 – SQL for aggregated advertising budgets

The second external table, named **ext_advertising_budgets**, aggregates website hits by country from the **log** view. These external tables are created as part of the **create_gold_tables** stored procedure, which is invoked using the **Create Gold Layer Tables** activity in **electroniz_aggregation_pipeline**:

```
SELECT TOP (100) [country_name]
,[hits]
,[advtg_budget]
  FROM [dbo].[ext_advertising_budgets]
  ORDER BY 3 DESC
```

In the future, end users can use the preceding query to easily allocate the percentage of advertising and marketing budgets that are backed by user hits:

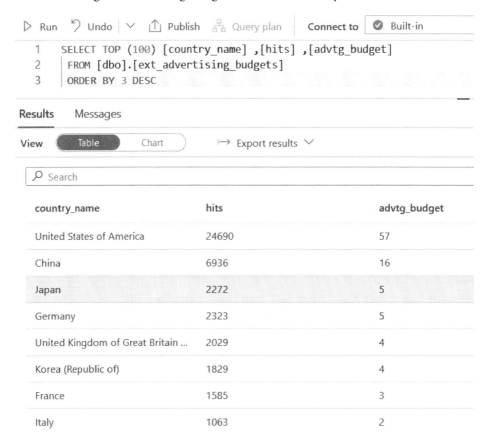

Figure 8.44 – Aggregated website hits and budget allocation

Click on **Chart** and change the variables provided, as per the following screenshot. By doing this, the end users at **Electroniz** can easily visualize the country-wise allocation of **advertising** and **marketing** dollars:

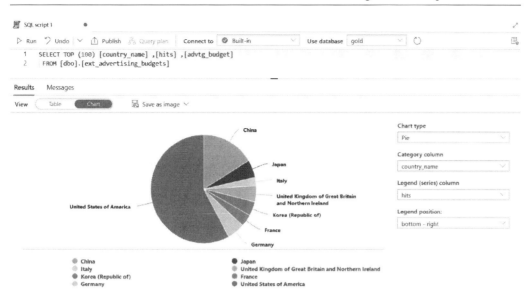

Figure 8.45 – Chart of advertising budget allocation per country

4. The final core requirement put forth by **Electroniz** was to decrease customer dissatisfaction arising due to interruptions in fulfilling orders due to inventory shortages. They wanted a near-real-time view of **products** sold so that they have a clear idea about falling inventory levels and could stock appropriately.

    To satisfy this requirement, we created an aggregated external table named **ext_aggregated_products_by_quarter**. This table reports the number of products sold per quarter. This information provides decision-makers with a clear idea of depleted inventory levels at any given time so that they can take appropriate action regarding future procurements and stocking. This table was created as part of the **create_gold_tables** stored procedure, which is invoked using the **Create Gold Layer Tables** activity in **electroniz_aggregation_pipeline**.

The end users at Electroniz can invoke the following query to show the current state of their inventory levels:

```
SELECT TOP (100) [product_category]
,[product_name]
,[year]
,[quarter]
,[units_sold]
  FROM [dbo].[ext_aggregated_products_by_quarter]
  WHERE year=2021
  ORDER BY 3 DESC, 2 ASC
```

This results in the following output:

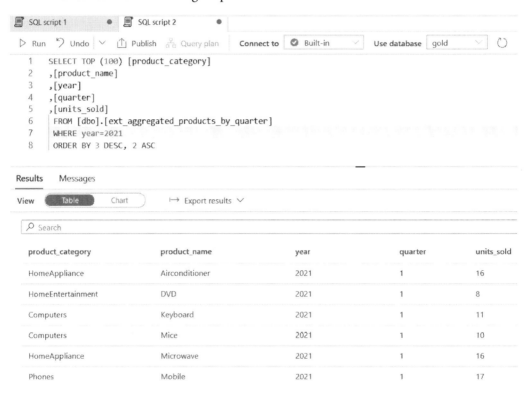

Figure 8.46 – Aggregated products sold in the recent quarter

Click on **Chart** and change the variables provided, as per the following screenshot. The end users at **Electroniz** can easily visualize the required inventory per product:

Figure 8.47 – Chart of products sold in the recent quarter

I think we did our job very well; you may celebrate, Mr Data Engineer! The preceding reports and visuals are proof enough that we did well in meeting customer expectations. These results should be shared with the customer management team in the form of a live demo. We can certainly celebrate this win, but our work is not done yet.

Now, we need to make sure the ingestion, curation, and aggregation pipelines work as a single unit. This means that our focus now will be on infrastructure and code deployments.

Summary

In this chapter, we learned how to build the gold layer of the lakehouse, which stores aggregated data. We also learned that data aggregation is a collaborative effort between the customer and the data engineer, each part providing a specialized set of skills that are essential for the overall success of the project. Toward the end of this chapter, we tried to validate whether we successfully addressed the **Electroniz** business requirements for building a lakehouse.

In *Chapter 9, Deploying and Monitoring Pipelines in Production*, we will deploy the three pipelines we created in this chapter – namely **electroniz_ingestion_pipeline**, **electroniz_curation_pipeline**, and **electroniz_aggregation_pipeline** – in succession. This will ensure that at every invocation, they can work as a single unit to contribute toward the overall objective.

Section 3:
Data Engineering Challenges and Effective Deployment Strategies

This part of the book educates you on the challenges faced by data engineering professionals. The concepts of Delta Lake are introduced. Lastly, a number of data engineering challenges will be highlighted with real-life examples of how Delta Lake can help deal with these issues effectively.

This section also educates you on effective deployment strategies for a data lake. Once the individual code components dealing with the various stages of data engineering have been built, these strategies play an important role in provisioning the cloud resources and deploying the data pipelines in a repeatable and continuous fashion.

This section contains the following chapters:

- *Chapter 9, Deploying and Monitoring Pipelines in Production*
- *Chapter 10, Solving Data Engineering Challenges*
- *Chapter 11, Infrastructure Provisioning*
- *Chapter 12, Continuous Integration and Deployment (CI/CD) of Data Pipelines*

9
Deploying and Monitoring Pipelines in Production

The journey of data is fast approaching its destination. In the previous chapter, we learned about data aggregation and how to build the gold layer of a lakehouse. Data in the gold layer is the representation of summary data, which keeps changing every time new data gets ingested. Therefore, it is a cyclical process. Now that we have built and tested all of the necessary pieces of the **Electroniz** lakehouse, we need to start thinking about deploying the pipeline in production. This is so that it can serve the needs of the end users in the most timely and durable fashion.

In this chapter, we will cover the following topics:

- The deployment strategy
- Developing the master pipeline
- Testing the master pipeline
- Scheduling the master pipeline
- Monitoring pipelines

The deployment strategy

We have worked extremely hard to get to the point where we have three functional pipelines, as follows:

- **The Electroniz ingestion pipeline**: `electroniz_batch_ingestion_pipeline`
- **The Electroniz curation pipeline**: `electroniz_curation_pipeline`
- **The Electroniz aggregation pipeline**: `electroniz_aggregation_pipeline`

Just as a recap, in the last few chapters, we followed multiple steps in order to create these pipelines. After their creation, we invoked each one manually to unit test their functionality. Finally, we validated the data that each one produced to make sure it matched the expectation of the **Electroniz** use cases. That's a lot of work, so we should be proud to have reached this far.

Assuming we are happy with the outcomes of the unit tests performed on the preceding pipelines, it is time to start thinking about the best way to deploy these pipelines in production. As per best practices, the three pipelines should run as one complete unit. Each pipeline run, which is also referred to as a job, should work by invoking the ingestion pipeline to pull incremental data from various sources. This is followed by invoking the curation pipeline, which cleanses the data and merges it in **Delta Lake** tables. Finally, the aggregation pipeline summarizes data for use by end users.

Typically, pipelines are deployed in two ways, as described next.

The time-based method

In the **time-based method**, each pipeline is deployed separately and invoked according to a time-based approach. For example, you can invoke the ingestion pipeline at 12:00 a.m., invoke the curation pipeline at 12:20 a.m., and invoke the aggregation pipeline at 12:30 a.m. The following is a list of some of the pros and cons of this method:

- **The overall deployment is simple**: You simply need to schedule each pipeline at a designated time.
- **It requires time precision**: The invocation time of each pipeline needs to be carefully calculated; otherwise, they might overlap each other. You do not want the second pipeline to start before the first one has finished.

- **There is less control**: Overall, there is little control over the success of the pipeline because each one runs separately without any dependencies on each other:

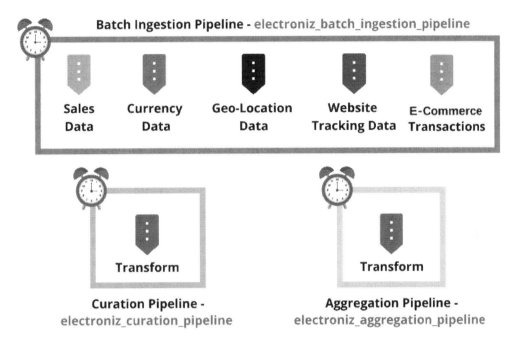

Figure 9.1 – The time-based method of deploying pipelines

The event-based approach

In the **event-based method,** a master pipeline is created that runs all other pipelines bases on success and failure events. For example, first, invoke the ingestion pipeline. Then, on success, invoke the curation pipeline. Then, on success, invoke the aggregation pipeline. The following is a list of some of the pros and cons of this method:

- **It requires a master pipeline**: In this method, a master pipeline is required that orchestrates the run of all other pipelines.

- **Time precision is less of a concern**: In this method, only the master pipeline schedules other pipelines. Once invoked, the master pipeline controls the run of all other pipelines in a controlled manner that is driven using events.

- **Enhanced control**: This method offers more control in comparison to the time-based method. The subsequent pipeline does not start until the predecessor has completed:

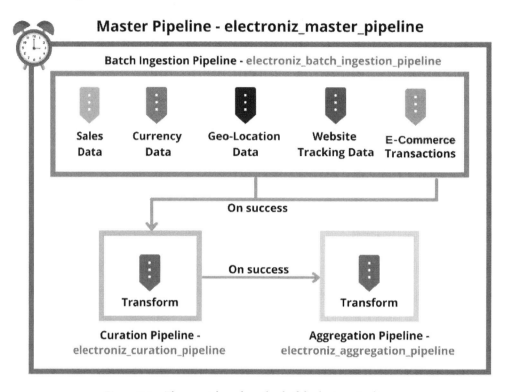

Figure 9.2 – The event-based method of deploying pipelines

The event-based method is preferable since it offers greater control over the eventual success of the pipelines. For the reasons stated earlier, let's use this approach to deploy the **Electroniz** pipeline. In the next section, we will start creating a master pipeline that will invoke the rest of the pipelines.

Developing the master pipeline

To start the creation of the master pipeline, make sure you have the `electroniz_batch_ingestion_pipeline`, `electroniz_curation_pipeline`, and `electroniz_aggregation_pipeline` pipelines installed and in working condition in the Azure data factory:

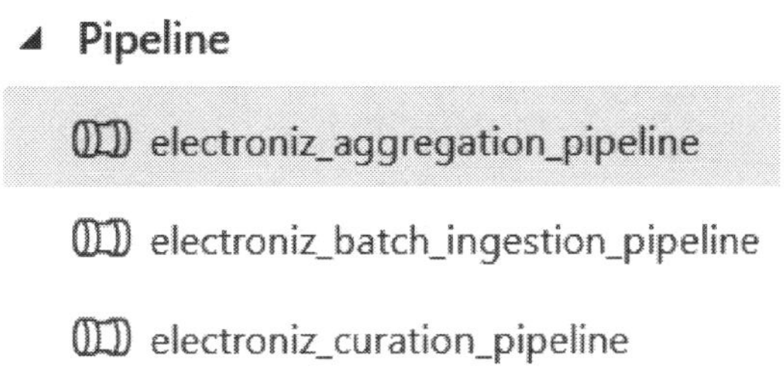

▲ Pipeline

    (◯◯◯) electroniz_aggregation_pipeline

    (◯◯◯) electroniz_batch_ingestion_pipeline

    (◯◯◯) electroniz_curation_pipeline

Figure 9.3 – The Electroniz ingestion, curation, and aggregation pipelines

We will get started by performing the following steps:

1. Using the Azure portal, navigate to **Home** > **All Resources** >
    trainingdatafactory100. Click on **Open** underneath **Open Azure Data
    Factory Studio**.

2. Using the panel on the left-hand side, from the menu, click on **Author**. In the
    Factory Resources panel, click on the three dots to the right of **Pipelines** and
    choose **New Pipeline**.

    In the **Properties** panel, input the following:

    - **Name**: electroniz_master_pipeline

    - **Description**: This pipeline runs the ingestion, curation, and
      aggregation pipeline.

    Using the bottom panel, click on **Parameters** and add the following parameters:

    - **Name:** STORAGE_ACCOUNT **Type:** String

    - **Name:** BRONZE_LAYER_NAMESPACE **Type:** String

    - **Name:** STORE_SALES_FOLDER **Type:** String

    - **Name:** TABLE_LIST   **Type:** String

    - **Name:** CURRENCY_LIST   **Type:** String

    - **Name:** CURRENCY_FOLDER **Type:** String

    - **Name:** GEOLOCATION_FOLDER **Type:** String

    - **Name:** LOGS_FOLDER   **Type:** String

    - **Name:** ECOMM_FOLDER **Type:** String

    - **Name:** EXT_TAB_FILE_FORMAT **Type:** String

- **Name:** EXT_DATA_SOURCE **Type:** String

- **Name:** EXT_CREDENTIALS **Type:** String

- **Name:** EXT_TAB_LOCATION **Type:** String

- **Name:** SILVER_LAYER_NAMESPACE **Type:** String

- **Name:** GOLD_LAYER_NAMESPACE **Type:** String:

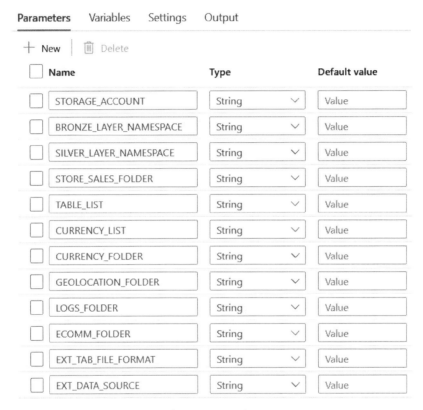

Figure 9.4 – The master pipeline parameters

3. Now, click on the empty white space in the **Activities** section. In the **Activities** panel, search for Execute. Now, drag the **Execute Pipeline** activity to the panel on the right-hand side:

- **Name**: Run electroniz_batch_ingestion_pipeline.

- Click on **Settings**.

- For **Invoked Pipeline**, choose electroniz_batch_ingestion_pipeline from the drop-down menu.

- **Wait on completion**: Checked:

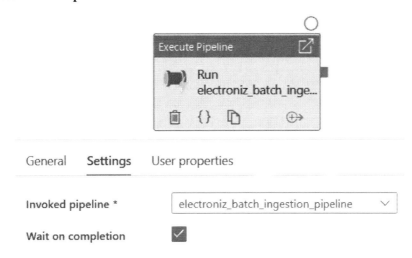

Figure 9.5 – Configuring Run electroniz_batch_ingestion_pipeline

4. In the **Activities** panel, search for Execute. Now, drag the Execute Pipeline activity to the panel on the right-hand side:

- **Name**: Run electroniz_curation_pipeline

- Click on **Settings**.

- For **Invoked Pipeline**, choose electroniz_curation_pipeline from the drop-down menu.

- **Wait on completion**: Checked

In the **Parameters** section, add the following parameters:

- **Name:** STORAGE_ACCOUNT **Type:** String
  Value: @pipeline().parameters.STORAGE_ACCOUNT

- **Name:** BRONZE_LAYER_NAMESPACE **Type:** String
  Value: @pipeline().parameters.BRONZE_LAYER_NAMESPACE

- **Name:** SILVER_LAYER_NAMESPACE **Type:** String
  Value: @pipeline().parameters.SILVER_LAYER_NAMESPACE

- **Name:** STORE_SALES_FOLDER **Type:** String
  Value: @pipeline().parameters.STORE_SALES_FOLDER

- **Name:** ADLS_FOLDER **Type:** String
  Value: @{formatDateTime(utcnow(),'yyyy')}/@{formatDateTime(utcnow(),'MM')}/@

```
{formatDateTime(utcnow(),'dd')}/@
{formatDateTime(utcnow(),'HH')}
```

- **Name:** TABLE_LIST **Type:** String
  Value: @pipeline().parameters.TABLE_LIST

- **Name:** CURRENCY_LIST **Type:** String
  Value: @pipeline().parameters.CURRENCY_LIST

- **Name:** CURRENCY_FOLDER **Type:** String
  Value: @pipeline().parameters.CURRENCY_FOLDER

- **Name:** GEOLOCATION_FOLDER **Type:** String
  Value: @pipeline().parameters.GEOLOCATION_FOLDER

- **Name:** LOGS_FOLDER **Type:** String
  Value: @pipeline().parameters.LOGS_FOLDER

- **Name:** ECOMM_FOLDER **Type:** String
  Value: @pipeline().parameters.ECOMM_FOLDER:

Parameters

Name	Type	Value	Default value
STORAGE_ACCOUNT	string	@pipeline().parameters.STORAGE_ACC...	
BRONZE_LAYER_NAMESPACE	string	@pipeline().parameters.BRONZE_LAYE...	
SILVER_LAYER_NAMESPACE	string	@pipeline().parameters.SILVER_LAYER_..	
STORE_SALES_FOLDER	string	@pipeline().parameters.STORE_SALES_...	
ADLS_FOLDER	string	@{formatDateTime(utcnow(),'yyyy')}/...	
TABLE_LIST	string	@pipeline().parameters.TABLE_LIST	
CURRENCY_LIST	string	@pipeline().parameters.CURRENCY_LIST	
CURRENCY_FOLDER	string	@pipeline().parameters.CURRENCY_FO..	
GEOLOCATION_FOLDER	string	@pipeline().parameters.GEOLOCATIO...	
LOGS_FOLDER	string	@pipeline().parameters.LOGS_FOLDER	
ECOMM_FOLDER	string	@pipeline().parameters.ECOMM_FOLD..	

Figure 9.6 – Running the electroniz_curation_pipeline parameters

5. Now, chain **Run electroniz_batch_ingestion_pipeline** to **Run electroniz_ curation_pipeline**. The pipeline should look like this:

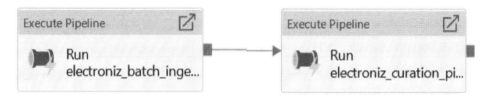

Figure 9.7 – Chaining the Electroniz ingestion and curation pipelines

6. In the **Activities** panel, search for Execute. Now, drag the **Execute Pipeline** activity to the panel on the right-hand side:

- **Name:** Run electroniz_aggregation_pipeline.

- Click on **Settings**.

- From **Invoked Pipeline**, choose electroniz_aggregation_pipeline from the drop-down menu.

- **Wait on completion:** Checked.

In the **Parameters** section, add the following parameters:

- **Name:** EXT_TAB_FILE_FORMAT **Type:** String
  Value: @pipeline().parameters.EXT_TAB_FILE_FORMAT

- **Name:** EXT_DATA_SOURCE **Type:** String
  Value: @pipeline().parameters. @pipeline().parameters.EXT_
  DATA_SOURCE

- **Name:** EXT_CREDENTIALS **Type:** String
  Value: @pipeline().parameters.EXT_CREDENTIALS

- **Name:** EXT_TAB_LOCATION **Type:** String
  Value: @pipeline().parameters.EXT_TAB_LOCATION

- **Name:** SILVER_LAYER_NAMESPACE **Type:** String
  Value: @pipeline().parameters.SILVER_LAYER_NAMESPACE

- **Name:** GOLD_LAYER_NAMESPACE **Type:** String
  Value: @pipeline().parameters.GOLD_LAYER_NAMESPACE:

Parameters

Name	Type	Value
EXT_TAB_FILE_FORMAT	string	@pipeline().parameters.EXT_TAB_FILE_...
EXT_DATA_SOURCE	string	@pipeline().parameters.EXT_DATA_SO...
EXT_CREDENTIALS	string	@pipeline().parameters.EXT_CREDENTI...
EXT_TAB_LOCATION	string	@pipeline().parameters.EXT_TAB_LOCA...
SILVER_LAYER_NAMESPACE	string	@pipeline().parameters.SILVER_LAYER_...
GOLD_LAYER_NAMESPACE	string	@pipeline().parameters.GOLD_LAYER_...

Figure 9.8 – Running the electroniz_aggregation_pipeline parameters

7.   Now, chain **Run electroniz_curation_pipeline** to **Run electroniz_aggregation_ pipeline**.

Click on **Publish all**, followed by **Publish**.

The final pipeline will look as follows:

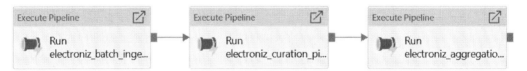

Figure 9.9 – Chaining the Electroniz ingestion, curation, and aggregation pipelines together

The development of the **electroniz_master_pipeline** pipeline is now complete. Next, we will move on to unit test the pipeline.

Testing the master pipeline

Now that the development of the master pipeline is complete, we should validate whether the pipeline runs successfully or not. Let's invoke it manually and check the outcome of the run:

1. Connect to the Azure Cloud Shell and invoke the following commands:

```
DATAFACTORYNAME="trainingdatafactory100"

RESOURCEGROUPNAME="training_rg"

PIPELINENAME="electroniz_master_pipeline"

az datafactory pipeline create-run --factory-name
$DATAFACTORYNAME --name $PIPELINENAME --resource-group
$RESOURCEGROUPNAME \

--parameters "{\"STORAGE_
ACCOUNT\":\"traininglakehouse\",\"BRONZE_LAYER_
NAMESPACE\":\"bronze\", \

\"SILVER_LAYER_NAMESPACE\":\"silver\",\"STORE_SALES_
FOLDER\":\"sales\",   \

\"TABLE_LIST\":\"products,store_customers,store_
orders\",\"CURRENCY_LIST\":\"CAD,INR,EUR\",\"CURRENCY_
FOLDER\":\"currency\", \

\"GEOLOCATION_FOLDER\":\"geolocation\",\"LOGS_
FOLDER\":\"logs\",\"ECOMM_FOLDER\":\"esalesns\/
esaleshub\/*\/*\/*\/*\/*\/*\", \

\"EXT_TAB_FILE_FORMAT\":\"parquetformat\",
\"EXT_DATA_SOURCE\":\"trainingds\", \"EXT_
CREDENTIALS\":\"trainingcreds\", \

\"EXT_TAB_LOCATION\":\"https://traininglakehouse.blob.
core.windows.net\", \"GOLD_LAYER_NAMESPACE\":\"gold\" "}
```

2. Using the Azure portal, navigate to **Home** > **All Resources** > **trainingdatafactory100**. Click on **Open** underneath **Open Azure Data Factory Studio**.

Now, click on the **Monitor** menu and then click on **Pipeline runs**. Notice how the master pipeline successfully ran the other three pipelines:

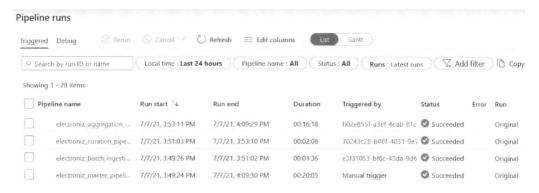

Figure 9.10 – The status of the master pipeline manual run

During the preceding pipeline run, all layers of the **Electroniz** lakehouse, namely, bronze, silver, and gold have been populated. In a single run, the latest data is ingested from sources, merged into the silver layer (**Delta Lake**), and, finally, aggregated inside the gold layer.

Let me remind you that during the discovery phase of the project, **Electroniz** had expressed a desire to have near real-time data ingestion in the lakehouse with a maximum delay of **1 hour**. This means we should run the master pipeline on an hourly schedule. Let's figure out how this can be done next.

Scheduling the master pipeline

Scheduling a pipeline for **automated** execution at a given time requires you to create a **trigger** in the Azure data factory. Let's find out how to do this:

1. Using the panel on the left-hand side, click on **Manage**. Then, click on **Triggers**. Finally, click on **New**:

    -   **Name**: `electroniz_master_trigger`

    -   **Start date**: Choose a date and time

    -   **Time Zone**: Choose your time zone

    -   **Recurrence**: `Every 1 hour`

    -   **Activated**: `Yes`.

Finally, click on **OK**:

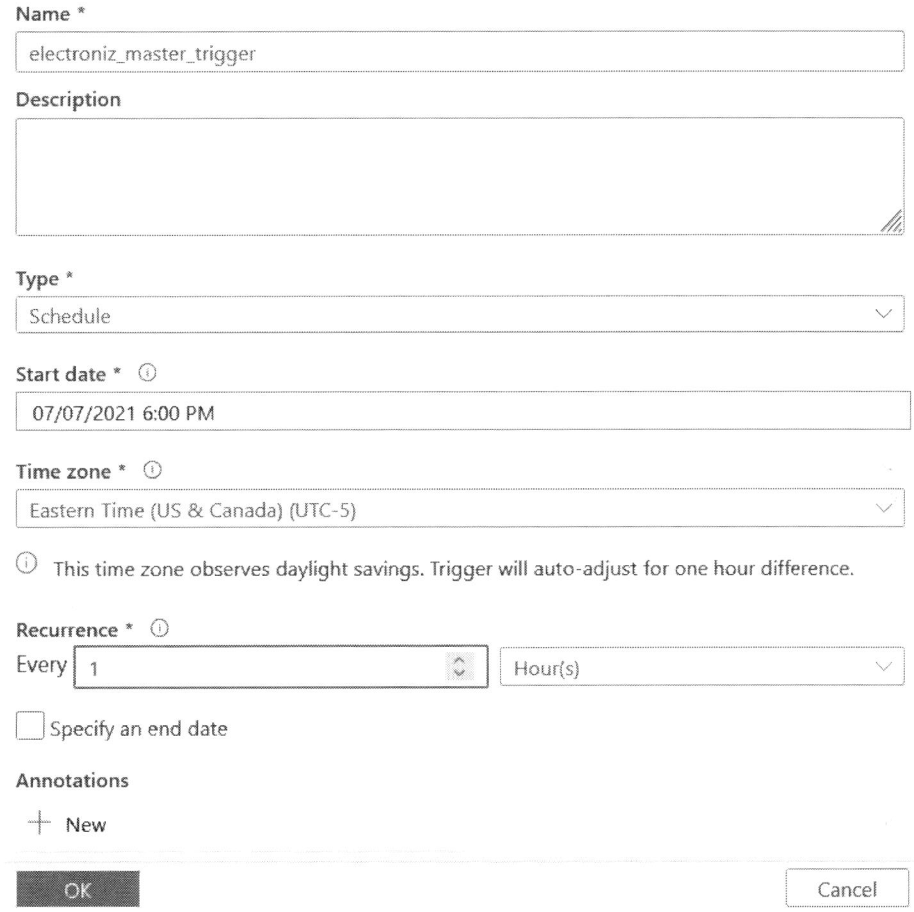

Name *

electroniz_master_trigger

Description

Type *

Schedule

Start date * ⓘ

07/07/2021 6:00 PM

Time zone * ⓘ

Eastern Time (US & Canada) (UTC-5)

ⓘ This time zone observes daylight savings. Trigger will auto-adjust for one hour difference.

Recurrence * ⓘ

Every 1   ⌃⌄   Hour(s)

☐ Specify an end date

Annotations

+ New

OK   Cancel

Figure 9.11 – Trigger for the Electroniz master pipeline

2. Using the pane on the left-hand side, click on **Author**. Click on the **electroniz_master_pipeline** underneath **Pipeline**:

- Click on **Add Trigger**. Then, click on **New/Edit**.
- Choose the following trigger: electroniz_master_trigger.
- Click on **OK**.

In the **Edit trigger** panel, add the **Trigger Run** parameters as follows:

- **Name:** STORAGE_ACCOUNT   **Type:** String
  Value: traininglakehouse

- **Name:** BRONZE_LAYER_NAMESPACE   **Type:** String
  Value: bronze

- **Name:** SILVER_LAYER_NAMESPACE   **Type:** String
  Value: silver

- **Name:** STORE_SALES_FOLDER   **Type:** String
  Value: sales

- **Name:** TABLE_LIST   **Type:** String
  Value: products,store_customers,store_orders

- **Name:** CURRENCY_LIST   **Type:** String
  Value: CAD,INR,EUR

- **Name:** CURRENCY_FOLDER   **Type:** String
  Value: currency

- **Name:** GEOLOCATION_FOLDER   **Type:** String
  Value: geolocation

- **Name:** LOGS_FOLDER   **Type:** String
  Value: logs

- **Name:** ECOMM_FOLDER   **Type:** String
  Value: esalesns/esaleshub/*/*/*/*/*/*/*

- **Name:** EXT_TAB_FILE_FORMAT   **Type:** String
  Value: parquetformat

- **Name:** EXT_DATA_SOURCE   **Type:** String
  Value: trainingds

- **Name:** EXT_CREDENTIALS   **Type:** String
  Value: trainingcreds

- **Name:** EXT_TAB_LOCATION   **Type:** String
  Value: https://traininglakehouse.blob.core.windows.net

Please edit the preceding parameter as per your Azure data lake storage account. The final parameters are as follows:

- **Name:** GOLD_LAYER_NAMESPACE **Type:** String
  Value: gold:

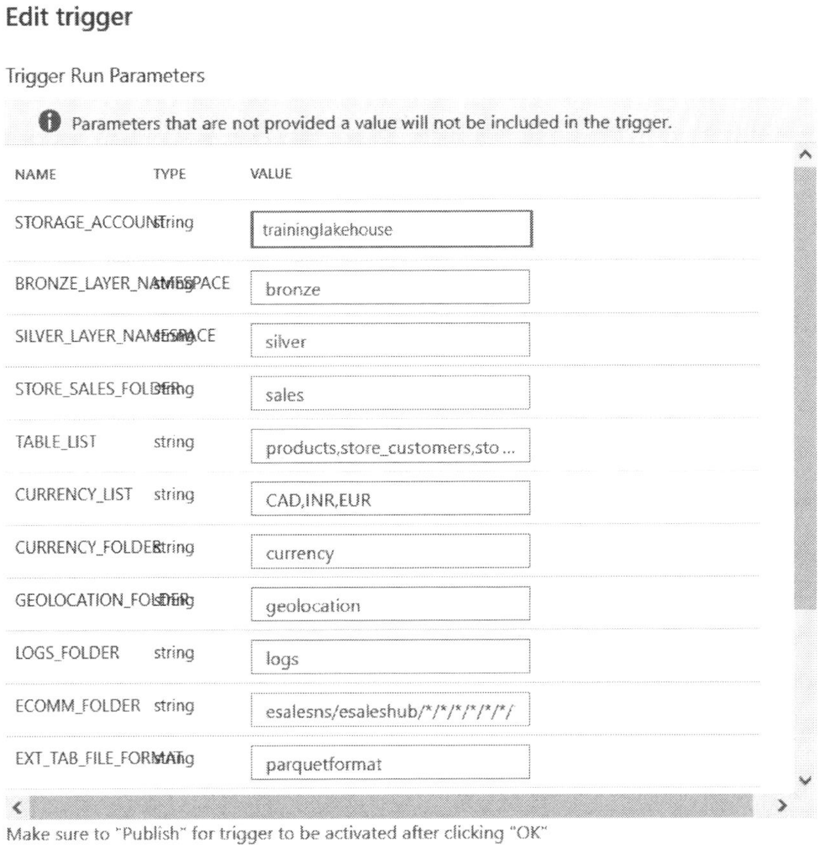

Edit trigger

Trigger Run Parameters

ⓘ Parameters that are not provided a value will not be included in the trigger.

NAME	TYPE	VALUE
STORAGE_ACCOUNT	String	traininglakehouse
BRONZE_LAYER_NAMESPACE	String	bronze
SILVER_LAYER_NAMESPACE	String	silver
STORE_SALES_FOLDER	String	sales
TABLE_LIST	string	products,store_customers,sto ...
CURRENCY_LIST	string	CAD,INR,EUR
CURRENCY_FOLDER	String	currency
GEOLOCATION_FOLDER	String	geolocation
LOGS_FOLDER	string	logs
ECOMM_FOLDER	string	esalesns/esaleshub/*/*/*/*/*/*/
EXT_TAB_FILE_FORMAT	String	parquetformat

Make sure to "Publish" for trigger to be activated after clicking "OK"

Figure 9.12 – The trigger parameters

3. Now, click on **Publish all** from the top menu followed by the **Publish** button.

4. From here onward, the master pipeline will be invoked every hour.

> **Important**
>
> For a data engineer, successfully creating a functional pipeline is a major accomplishment. However, the job is not completely done yet. We need to deploy the pipelines in such a fashion that they are durable, secure, and reactive.

Next, we will learn how to monitor pipelines properly.

Monitoring pipelines

To monitor the hourly runs using the panel on the left-hand side, click on **Monitor**. Then, click on **Trigger runs**:

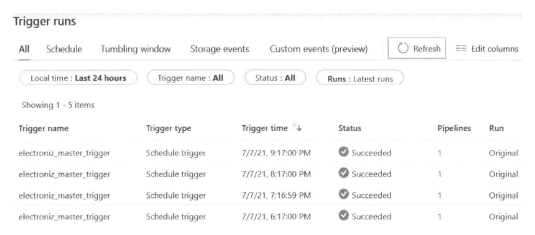

Figure 9.13 – The first trigger run for the Electroniz master pipeline

Notice how the master pipeline successfully runs every hour to ingest the incremental data and recompute the aggregations. Hopefully, this should make **Electroniz** a very happy customer. As a data engineer, you should be proud of your achievements. Getting this far involves a lot of work.

In an ideal world after the deployment, pipelines should run automatically and seamlessly. The reality is that failures will happen, so you need to be prepared for them well in advance. After all, your pipelines ingest data from varying sources that may or may not be under your direct control. One day, the database that your pipeline ingests from might be down for maintenance, or a REST API that you subscribe to might go offline.

> **Important**
> A smart data engineer develops their pipeline for the best-case scenarios but also prepares them well for the worst-case scenarios.

In other cases, the problem might be transient. The pipeline could not connect to the database or the API due to a network hiccup. Naturally, as a data engineer, it is impossible to predict these sorts of failures. However, there are ways in which to make your pipelines react and handle errors gracefully. Let's examine some ways in which this can be done.

Adding durability features

While creating the **Electroniz** pipelines, we created several types of activities to perform specific actions. Looking closely at the properties of each activity, you will notice three important ones that can add durability to your pipelines:

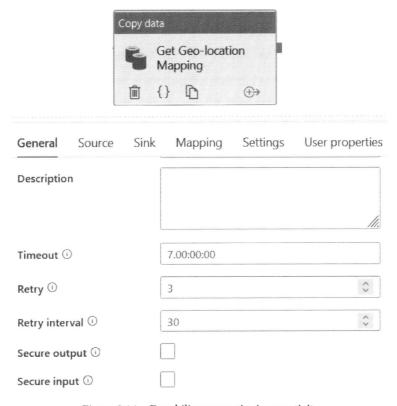

Figure 9.14 – Durability properties in an activity

The following list explains the parameters:

- **Timeout**: This property represents the maximum amount of time a particular activity should run for. In the Azure data factory, the value is set to 7 days by default. After the timeout expires, the activity is terminated whether it was successful or not. Now that might sound very bad, but it is not. On the contrary, it is highly advisable to set a timeout value to a safe value. With some initial monitoring performed during the development and testing phases, it is easy to predict how much time a particular activity usually takes. For instance, you might have a notebook activity in your pipeline that usually takes 5 minutes to finish. If you add a buffer, you might want to set the value to 15-30 minutes.

I am sure you will be wondering what has been achieved by doing that. Well, the simple answer is conserving cloud resource costs. In instances where a program unexpectedly hangs around, would you rather accumulate for 7 days of cloud resource costs or just 15–30 minutes? In this case, it might be better to let the activity terminate and separately investigate the reason for any unexpected hangs.

> **Important**
>
> A hallmark of a smart data engineer is to effectively choose between the bad and the worse. In some scenarios, it is better to choose a fast-fail mechanism in the long term because the latter could end up costing a lot of unnecessary cloud resources.

- **Retry**: As the name suggests, adding retries means the number of times the activity will be retried before calling it quits. The default for this value is set to 0 in the Azure data factory, which, in other words, means trying the activity only once. Setting a higher value for retries covers against transient failures that are, typically, related to network glitches and unavailability. In most cases, a value of 3 might be a good start. However, the behavior of retires is directly impacted by the retry interval.

- **Retry interval**: The retry mechanism adds a delay between each retry attempt. The default for this value is 30 seconds in the Azure data factory. As mentioned earlier, this property is frequently paired with the number of retires.

These parameters can certainly add durability to your pipelines; however, they don't cover you against all failure scenarios. Some day, the failure is bound to happen.

> **Important**
>
> Anticipating and gracefully dealing with failure conditions in your pipelines should be well planned and exercised. After all, after your job is done as a data engineer, you will hand over the system to the operational team for future monitoring and support.

Dealing with failure conditions

As discussed earlier, a well-designed pipeline should be able to handle failure conditions gracefully. But the question is how? Let's illustrate this using the following failure scenario.

As part of the **Electroniz** pipeline, we added activities that ingest incremental data from the stores database. One fine day, the stored database went down for maintenance. As a result, the hourly triggered pipeline failed to run due to database unavailability. In this scenario, the Azure data factory reports the error as follows:

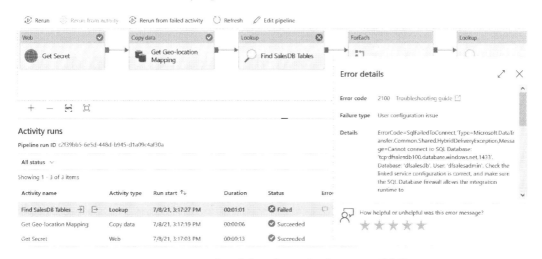

Figure 9.15 – Pipeline failure due to database unavailability

Overall, this is expected behavior. But the real question is how to deal with such a situation? Well, we have a few options – bypass the failed activity and let the remainder of the pipeline proceed as usual or terminate the entire pipeline and deal with the failure separately. Let's explore both options in greater detail next.

Bypassing failed activities

In some cases, it is advisable to let the rest of the pipeline proceed even though an activity ran into a problem. This is how it is done:

1. Within every activity in the Azure data factory, you will notice **Add output icon** in the lower-right corner. Clicking on it will reveal a **Conditions** menu, as follows:

Figure 9.16 – Adding activity conditions

2. Click on **Failure**. Now, chain the **Failure** condition from **Find SalesDB Tables** to **Find Currencies**. In this way, if the sales database is down, the failure condition will not terminate the entire job; instead, it will bypass **For Each Table** and proceed to **Find Currencies**:

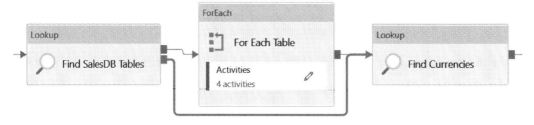

Figure 9.17 – Bypassing failed activities

> **Important**
>
> The decision to bypass failed activities needs to be planned very carefully. In some scenarios, data ingested down the line might be directly dependent on the failed activity. In that case, it would be better to terminate the entire pipeline when any activity fails.

Rerunning failed activities

Another way to deal with failures is to let the entire pipeline fail as soon as any single activity runs into a problem. This method is frequently chosen over the bypassing activities method if there are strong data dependencies between the pipeline activities. In this method, the error messages and logs from failed activity runs are carefully evaluated. Once the error is discovered and fixed, the failing pipeline is rerun as follows:

electroniz_batch_ingestion_pipeline

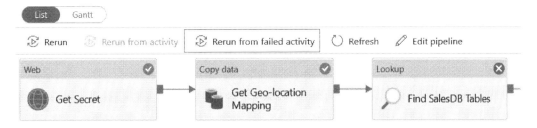

Figure 9.18 – Rerunning failed activities

The following list demonstrates the activities:

1. **Rerun**: The entire pipeline can be rerun using the **Rerun** option. Since some activities might be run more than once, this method has a drawback because it can duplicate data in the bronze layer.

2. **Rerun from failed activity**: Alternatively, if using this option, you will only run from the failed activity onward. While this method is safe from getting duplicates, it tends to ingest inconsistent data because parts of the data might be ingested at different time intervals.

> **Important**
> The decision to rerun the entire pipeline versus run from a failed activity needs to be carefully planned and well tested. The data engineer should seek their customer's approval on the chosen method.

Adding alerting features

In the preceding section, we carefully planned and executed our approach regarding pipeline failures and restart mechanisms. To add greater durability to the pipelines, we should configure some alerting mechanisms. Without proper alerting mechanisms, administrative users might not be able to react and recover from failures in time. This can be catastrophic because delays in recovering from pipeline failures have been known to cause huge customer dissatisfaction, delays in real-time decision making, or, even worse, data corruption:

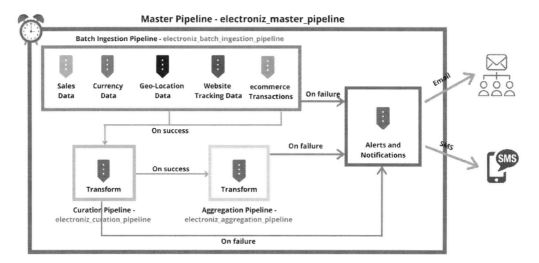

Figure 9.19 – Adding alerts to a pipeline

Here are the steps for creating real-time alerts:

1. Consult the customer regarding the user(s) who should receive the alerts. Emails and SMS are two commonly chosen mechanisms. Instead of sending alerts to individual emails addresses, it is highly advisable that you send alerts to email groups such as administrators@site.com.

2. In the Azure data factory, click on **Monitor**. Now click on **Alerts and metrics**. Then, click on **New alert rule**:

    -   **Alert rule name**: Error Alerts

    -   **Description**: Alert for pipeline failures

    -   **Severity**: Sev1

3. Click on **+ Add criteria**. From the **Add criteria** screen, choose **Failed pipeline runs metrics**:

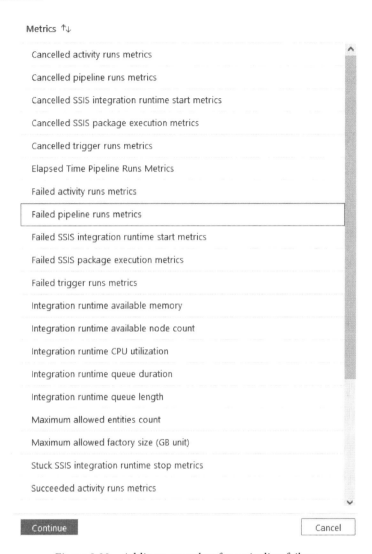

Figure 9.20 – Adding a new alert for a pipeline failure

4. Click on **Continue**:

- Navigate to the **Configure alert logic** screen.

- Underneath **Dimension**, input the following:

- **Name**: Click on **Select all**

- **FailureType**: Click on **Select all**:

Figure 9.21 – Configure alert logic

5. Click on **Update criteria**.

Now, click on the + **Configure** notification. Choose **Create new**:

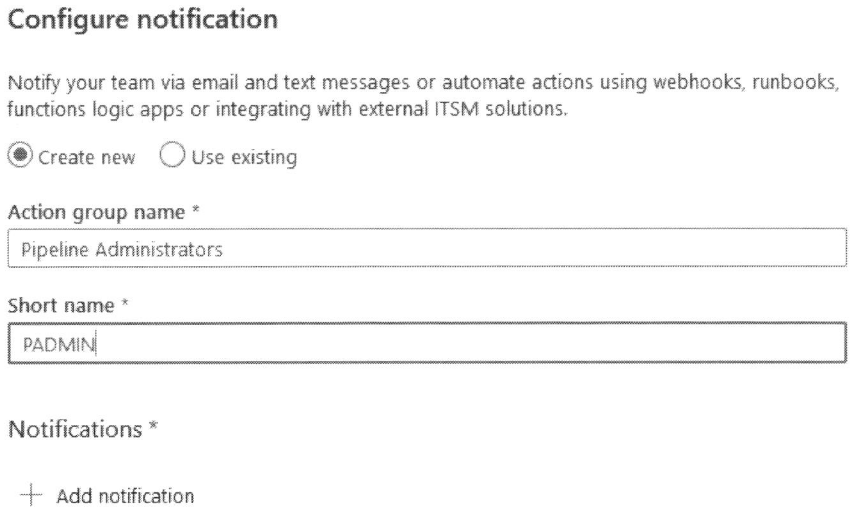

Configure notification

Notify your team via email and text messages or automate actions using webhooks, runbooks, functions logic apps or integrating with external ITSM solutions.

⦿ Create new   ○ Use existing

Action group name *

| Pipeline Administrators |

Short name *

| PADMIN |

Notifications *

+ Add notification

Figure 9.22 – Configure notification

6. Click on + **Add notification**.

7. Click on the **Email** checkbox and add the email ID of the alerting group.

8. Click on the **SMS** checkbox and add a phone number to receive alerts:

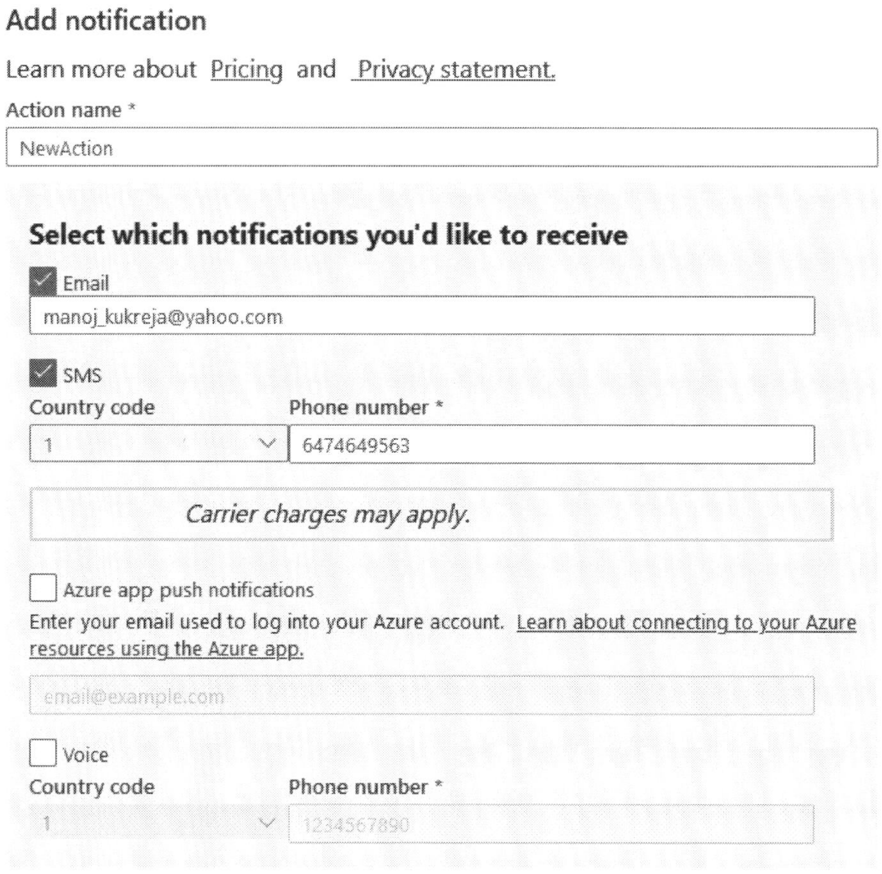

Add notification

Learn more about Pricing and   Privacy statement.

Action name *

NewAction

Select which notifications you'd like to receive

☑ Email

manoj_kukreja@yahoo.com

☑ SMS

Country code   Phone number *

1   6474649563

Carrier charges may apply.

☐ Azure app push notifications

Enter your email used to log into your Azure account. Learn about connecting to your Azure resources using the Azure app.

email@example.com

☐ Voice

Country code   Phone number *

1   1234567890

Figure 9.23 – Adding an email and SMS to receive alerts

9. Click on **Add notification**:

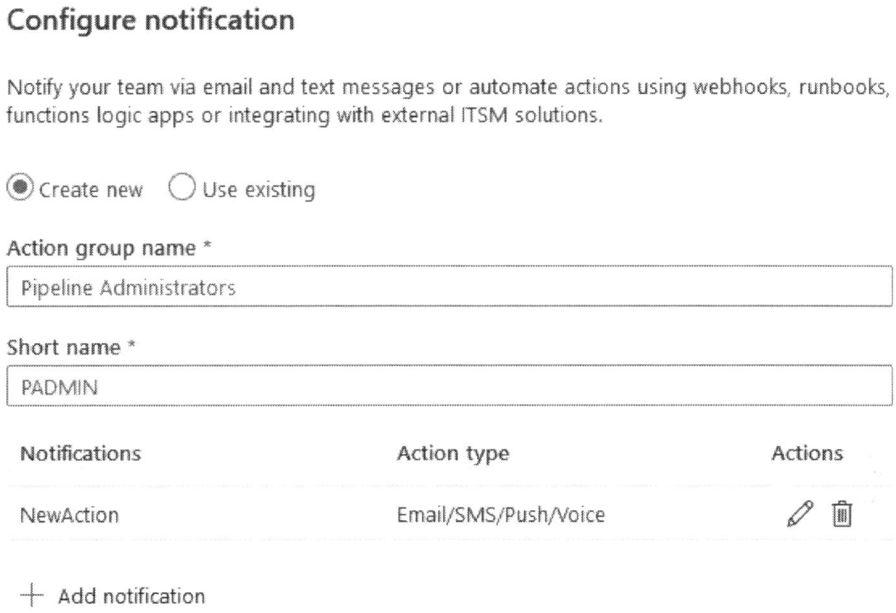

Configure notification

Notify your team via email and text messages or automate actions using webhooks, runbooks, functions logic apps or integrating with external ITSM solutions.

◉ Create new   ◯ Use existing

Action group name *

| Pipeline Administrators |

Short name *

| PADMIN |

Notifications	Action type	Actions
NewAction	Email/SMS/Push/Voice	✎ 🗑

+ Add notification

Figure 9.24 – The Add action group confirmation screen

10. Click on **Add action group**:

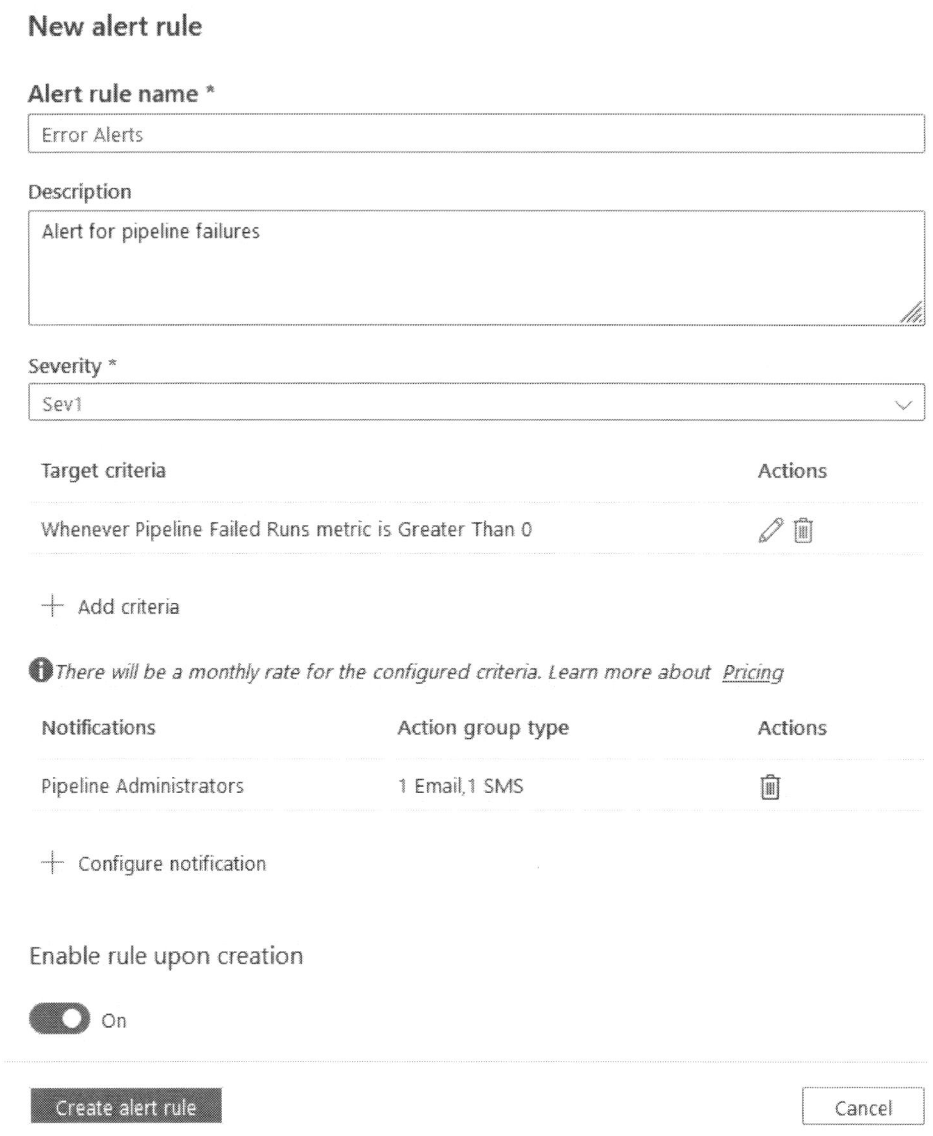

New alert rule

Alert rule name *

> Error Alerts

Description

> Alert for pipeline failures

Severity *

> Sev1   ⌄

Target criteria	Actions
Whenever Pipeline Failed Runs metric is Greater Than 0	✏ 🗑

+ Add criteria

🛈 *There will be a monthly rate for the configured criteria. Learn more about* *Pricing*

Notifications	Action group type	Actions
Pipeline Administrators	1 Email,1 SMS	🗑

+ Configure notification

Enable rule upon creation

◖◗ On

Create alert rule   Cancel

Figure 9.25 – The creating the alert rule confirmation screen

11. Click on **Create alert rule**.

Once the rule has been created, you will receive a confirmation in an email:

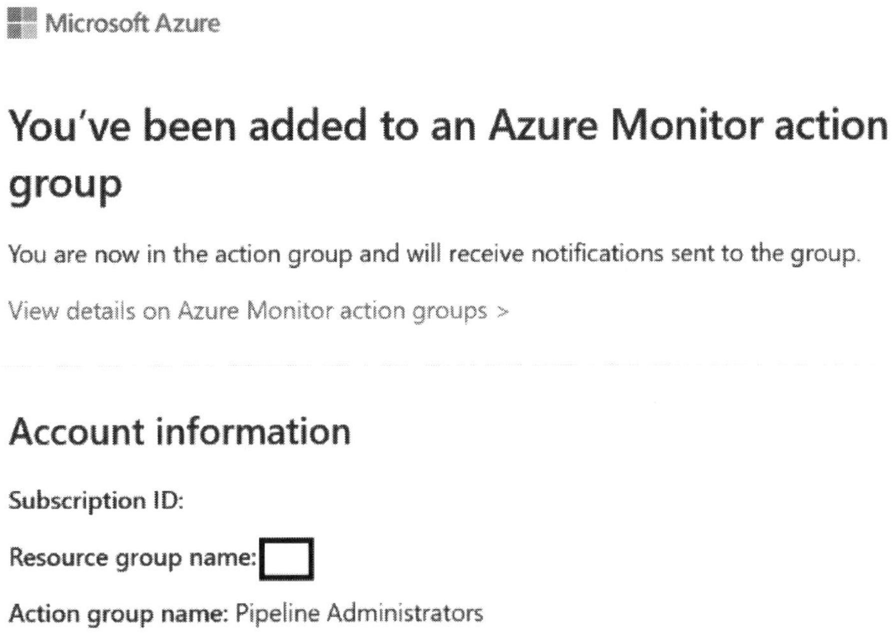

Microsoft Azure
You've been added to an Azure Monitor action group
You are now in the action group and will receive notifications sent to the group.
View details on Azure Monitor action groups >
Account information
Subscription ID:
Resource group name:
Action group name: Pipeline Administrators

Figure 9.26 – An example email confirming the alert subscription

You will also receive an alert on the mobile device, as follows:

5:07
29873 >
Text Message
Today 5:02 PM
All done. You're in PADMIN group. Reply 'STOP' to stop all, 'Disable PADMIN' to stop grp, 'HELP' for info. Msg&data rates apply

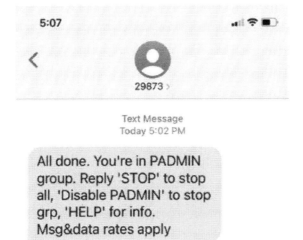

Figure 9.27 – An example SMS confirming the alert subscription

This confirms that the alert rule is now **active**. From here onward, if the pipelines encounter failures, you should expect to receive alerts that look like this:

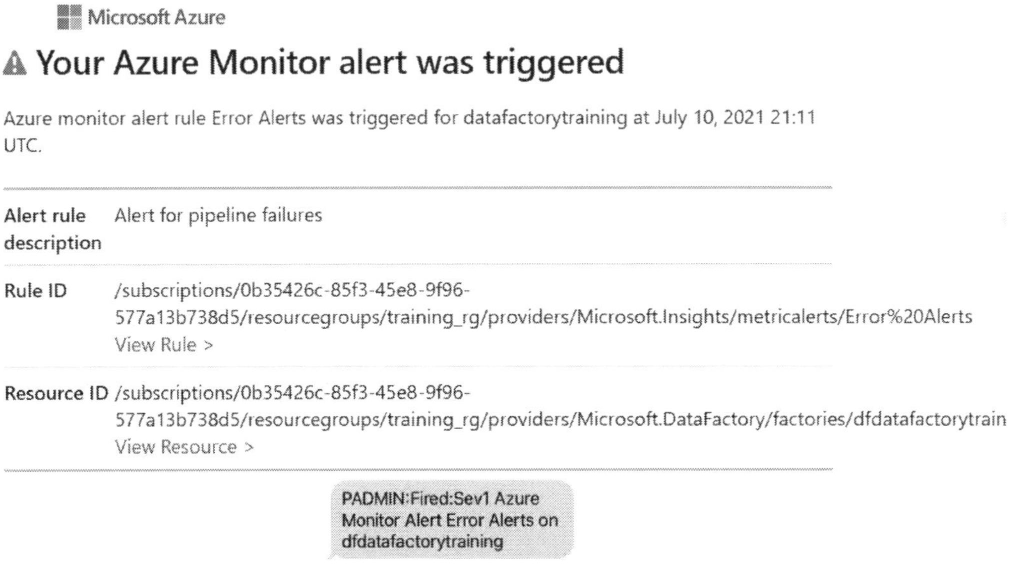

Microsoft Azure

⚠ Your Azure Monitor alert was triggered

Azure monitor alert rule Error Alerts was triggered for datafactorytraining at July 10, 2021 21:11 UTC.

Alert rule description	Alert for pipeline failures
Rule ID	/subscriptions/0b35426c-85f3-45e8-9f96-577a13b738d5/resourcegroups/training_rg/providers/Microsoft.Insights/metricalerts/Error%20Alerts View Rule >
Resource ID	/subscriptions/0b35426c-85f3-45e8-9f96-577a13b738d5/resourcegroups/training_rg/providers/Microsoft.DataFactory/factories/dfdatafactorytrain View Resource >

PADMIN:Fired:Sev1 Azure Monitor Alert Error Alerts on dfdatafactorytraining

Figure 9.28 – An example email and SMS alert sent after a pipeline failure

> **Important**
>
> When implementing alerting mechanisms, a data engineer should carefully shortlist important scenarios that warrant alerts being sent. Having too much noise from alerts is frequently perceived negatively by customers.

Therefore, we have learned how to monitor pipelines, add durability, and also alert features that can warn us when a pipeline fails.

Summary

In this chapter, we learned about various deployment strategies such as time-based and event-based mechanisms. Additionally, using the event-based mechanism, we created the **Electroniz** master pipeline. After manually testing the master pipeline, we scheduled it to run every hour. We also learned how to monitor pipelines, add durability features, and deal with failure conditions. Finally, we examined how to add alerts to pipelines so that the administrative groups of users are alerted to failures.

The next chapter is very critical because it equips the data engineer with some critical skills. In *Chapter 10, Solving Data Engineering Challenges*, we will learn about some common challenges faced by modern-day data engineers along with the recommended ways in which to deal with them.

10
Solving Data Engineering Challenges

In the past few chapters, we learned about the data lakehouse architecture. After covering several exercises, we learned how a data engineer builds and deploys the bronze, silver, and gold layers of the lakehouse. Data in the lakehouse increases and changes over time. As new data sources get added and the previous ones undergo modifications, the data engineering practice needs to keep up with this growth. Just like anything else in the industry, the role of the data engineer needs to evolve as well. In addition to building and deploying data pipelines, they need to cover several other complicated aspects of data engineering that were not covered previously. They must learn to deal with these new challenges.

In this chapter, we will cover the following topics:

- Schema evolution
- Sharing data
- Data governance

Schema evolution

Schema evolution can be described as a technique that's used to adapt to ongoing structural changes to data. As systems mature and add more functionality, schema evolution is inevitable. Therefore, adapting to schema evolution is an extremely important requirement of modern-day pipelines.

It is customary to start developing pipelines so that they have base schemas for tables at the start of the project. Frequently, by the time things move into production, there is a very high likelihood that the schema for some incoming file or table has changed. But why is this such a big problem?

> **Important**
>
> A data engineer should never make the mistake of assuming that the schema of incoming data will never change. Instead, prepare the pipelines so that they auto-adjust to this evolution.

Let's discuss an example scenario to illustrate this point. Let's assume your pipelines have been deployed in production and that, for a while, you have been ingesting an inventory file in the bronze layer that contains three columns: **inventory_date**, **product**, and **inventory**. In the silver layer, a Delta table for the same file exists called `inventory`. The very next day, when the inventory file was ingested, it was discovered that it contained not three but four columns. The schema for the inventory file had evolved. Now, the problem is how this new column can be effectively reflected in the lakehouse, as shown here:

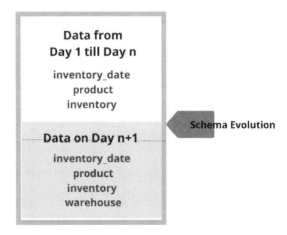

Figure 10.1 – Schema evolution

The real challenge is that prior data for the inventory file had fewer columns than the new file that was received today. How can we accommodate the new column in the future while preserving the sanity of the previous data? In the past, we dealt with this problem in one of two ways:

- We would create multiple versions of the inventory table, where a new version of the table will be created each time the schema changes. To get aggregate results, we can create a **VIEW** on top of all versions. This method has serious drawbacks. Not only do you need to create a new version of the table each time the schema changes, but the encompassing view needs to be changed as well.

- A simpler method is to rewrite the old data files with a dummy column that has a value of **NULL**. After that, you can simply alter the schema of the table and add a new column to it. This method is a little better than the multi-version approach, but it could be a problem if the prior data is extremely large.

A similar situation could arise if a previously existing column gets deleted from the new incoming file. The method of dealing with this delete scenario is very similar to what we've just talked about, except the treatment is reversed. In this case, the previous data stays as-is but the data with the missing column gets defaulted to **NULL** for future data.

> **Important**
>
> Before developing the pipelines, make sure the customer is in complete agreement with the method that's been chosen for dealing with schema evolution. Changing this method after the project is in production could prove to be very costly.

Fortunately, there is a simpler method we can implement here, and that involves using Delta Lake. **Delta Lake** can not only safeguard your data by enforcing **schema validation** but it can also adjust the schema, without the need for table versioning or rewriting prior data with the dummy column. Delta Lake automatically compares the schema of the incoming data against prior data. If a discrepancy is detected in Delta Lake, an exception is raised by default. You can override this default behavior and force the schema changes to be merged into the table, without the need to rewrite prior data. Let's take a look at schema validation and evolution in Delta tables with the following example:

1. Upload some sample inventory files to the `bronze` layer of the lakehouse. Copy each command shown here, line by line, paste them into the Azure Cloud Shell window, and press *Enter*:

```
STORAGEACCOUNTNAME="traininglakehouse"
STORAGECONTAINER="bronze"
```

```
RESOURCEGROUPNAME="training_rg"

LOCATION="eastus"

KEY=`az storage account keys list -g $RESOURCEGROUPNAME
-n $STORAGEACCOUNTNAME | jq .[0].value`

az storage blob upload --container-name $STORAGECONTAINER
--account-name $STORAGEACCOUNTNAME --name inventory/1/
inventory.csv --file ~/Data-Engineering-with-Apache-
Spark-Delta-Lake-and-Lakehouse/project/prep/inventory/1/
inventory.csv --account-key $KEY

az storage blob upload --container-name $STORAGECONTAINER
--account-name $STORAGEACCOUNTNAME --name inventory/2/
inventory.csv --file ~/Data-Engineering-with-Apache-
Spark-Delta-Lake-and-Lakehouse/project/prep/inventory/2/
inventory.csv --account-key $KEY

az storage blob upload --container-name $STORAGECONTAINER
--account-name $STORAGEACCOUNTNAME --name inventory/3/
inventory.csv --file ~/Data-Engineering-with-Apache-
Spark-Delta-Lake-and-Lakehouse/project/prep/inventory/3/
inventory.csv --account-key $KEY
```

We just uploaded three inventory files to Azure Data Lake. Before we move on, lets's understand what each file represents:

- **File**: `inventory/1/inventory.csv`:
    - **Received on Day 1**: `2021-04-18`
    - **Schema**: `inventory_date`, `product`, `inventory`:

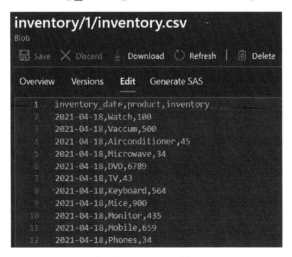

Figure 10.2 – Data for the inventory file sent on 2021-04-18

- **File**: `inventory/2/inventory.csv`:

  - **Received on Day 2**: `2021-04-19`

  - **Schema**: `inventory_date, product, inventory, warehouse`

  - **The schema has evolved**: A fourth column (warehouse) was added to the source:

Figure 10.3 – Data for the inventory file sent on 2021-04-19

- **File**: `inventory/3/inventory.csv`:

  - **Received on Day 3**: `2021-04-20`

  - **Schema**: `inventory_date, product, inventory, city`

- **Schema has evolved even further**: A new column (city) was added but a previous column was deleted (warehouse):

Figure 10.4 – Schema for the inventory file sent on 2021-04-20

2. Let's find out how to effectively deal with this evolving schema scenario. Once again, for this exercise, we will use **Azure Databricks** to read and write data from Azure Data Lake Storage. If you have dropped the Azure Databricks workspace we created previously, you can perform the following steps to recreate it.

3. Get the storage account keys for Azure Data Lake Storage. Invoke the following commands in Azure Cloud Shell:

```
STORAGEACCOUNTNAME="traininglakehouse"
az storage account keys list --account-name
$STORAGEACCOUNTNAME
```

If the preceding commands worked as desired, you should see two storage keys. Take note of the value for **key1**. We will need it later in the Databricks workspace configuration:

```
training@Azure>STORAGEACCOUNTNAME="traininglakehouse"
training@Azure>az storage account keys list --account-name $STORAGEACCOUNTNAME
[
  {
    "keyName": "key1",
    "permissions": "FULL",
    "value": "                                                        "
  },
  {
    "keyName": "key2",
    "permissions": "FULL",
    "value": "                                                        "
  }
]
```

Figure 10.5 – traininglakehouse keys

4. Create the Azure Databricks workspace using the following code. Invoke the following commands on Azure Cloud Shell:

```
RESOURCEGROUPNAME="training_rg"

LOCATION="eastus"

WORKSPACE="trainingdatabricks"

az config set extension.use_dynamic_install=yes_without_
prompt

az databricks workspace create --resource-group
$RESOURCEGROUPNAME --name $WORKSPACE --location $LOCATION
--sku trial
```

If you do not have an Azure trial account, you need to use an SKU of standard:

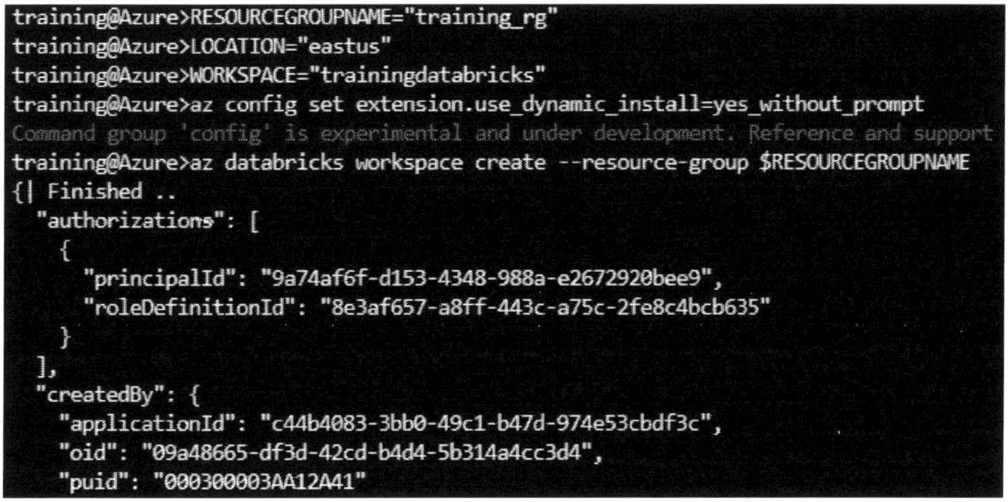

```
training@Azure>RESOURCEGROUPNAME="training_rg"
training@Azure>LOCATION="eastus"
training@Azure>WORKSPACE="trainingdatabricks"
training@Azure>az config set extension.use_dynamic_install=yes_without_prompt
Command group 'config' is experimental and under development. Reference and support
training@Azure>az databricks workspace create --resource-group $RESOURCEGROUPNAME
{| Finished ..
  "authorizations": [
    {
      "principalId": "9a74af6f-d153-4348-988a-e2672920bee9",
      "roleDefinitionId": "8e3af657-a8ff-443c-a75c-2fe8c4bcb635"
    }
  ],
  "createdBy": {
    "applicationId": "c44b4083-3bb0-49c1-b47d-974e53cbdf3c",
    "oid": "09a48665-df3d-42cd-b4d4-5b314a4cc3d4",
    "puid": "000300003AA12A41"
```

Figure 10.6 – Azure Databricks workspace creation

5. To validate the creation of the Azure Databricks workspace, navigate to the Azure portal.

    To do so, click on **Home** > **All Resources** > **trainingdatabricks**, and then click on **Launch Workspace**:

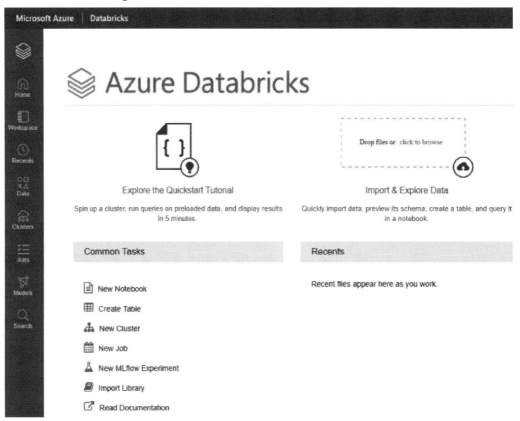

Figure 10.7 – Azure Databricks workspace on the Azure portal

Using the menu on the left, click on **Compute**. Then, click on **Create Cluster**. Make the following changes:

- **Cluster name**: curationcluster.

- **Cluster mode**: Single node.

- Edit the `fs.azure.account.key.<storage-account-name>.blob.core.windows.net <storage-account-access-key>` command as per your Azure storage account name and key.

- Click on **Advanced options**.

Paste the edited command into Spark Config as the last line. Now, press the **Create Cluster** button:

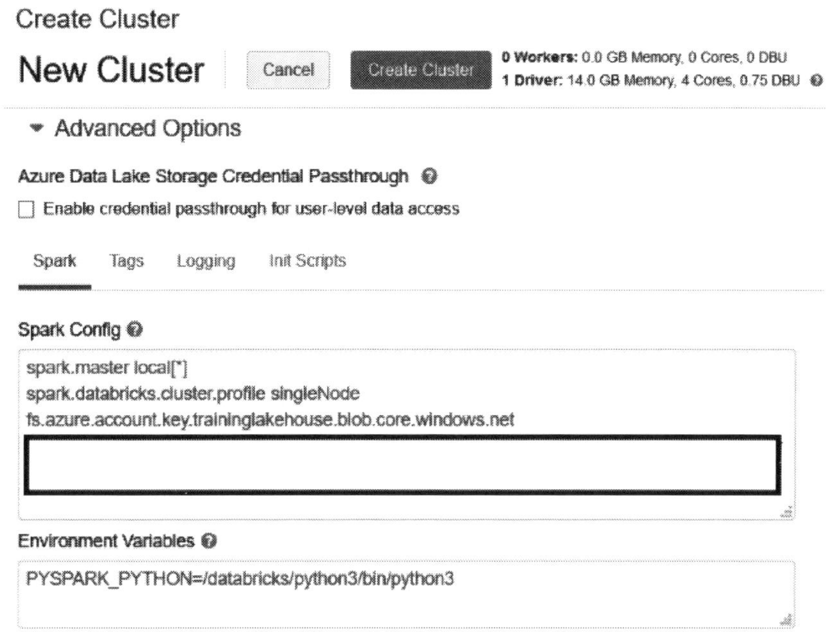

Create Cluster

New Cluster   Cancel   Create Cluster   **0 Workers:** 0.0 GB Memory, 0 Cores, 0 DBU
1 Driver: 14.0 GB Memory, 4 Cores, 0.75 DBU

▾ Advanced Options

Azure Data Lake Storage Credential Passthrough

☐ Enable credential passthrough for user-level data access

Spark   Tags   Logging   Init Scripts

Spark Config

```
spark.master local[*]
spark.databricks.cluster.profile singleNode
fs.azure.account.key.traininglakehouse.blob.core.windows.net
```

Environment Variables

```
PYSPARK_PYTHON=/databricks/python3/bin/python3
```

Figure 10.8 – Azure Databricks Create Cluster button

6. This will spin up a small Apache Spark cluster, which will be required for this exercise. Once the cluster has been created, you should see a window that looks like this:

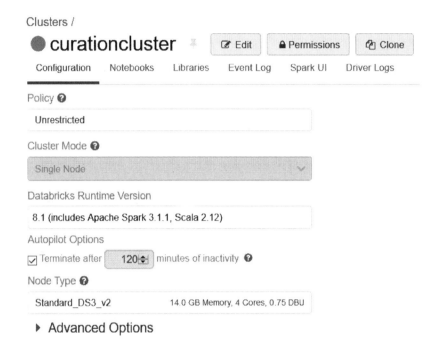

Figure 10.9 – Azure Databricks cluster creation

7. Now, we need a notebook that will serve as our **interactive development environment (IDE)**.

On the Databricks workspace, click on **Workspace**, and then **Users**.

Then, click on the arrow beside your username and click on **Import**:

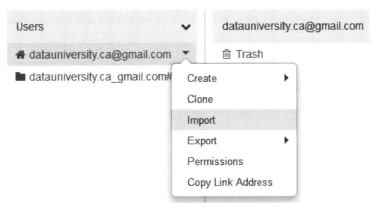

Figure 10.10 – Importing a notebook into the Azure Databricks workspace

- Choose **URL**.

- Use the following URL: `https://github.com/PacktPublishing/Data-Engineering-with-Apache-Spark-Delta-Lake-and-Lakehouse/blob/main/project/challenges/schema_evolution/inventory_notebook.ipynb`.

Click on **Import**.

Now, click on the cluster dropdown and choose **curationcluster**:

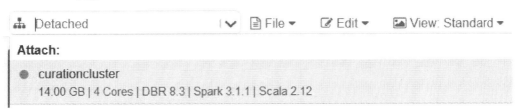

Figure 10.11 – Choosing a Spark cluster for the notebook

8. For the next set of commands, you should be on the notebook interface. Before running the notebook cells, make sure you edit STORAGE_ACCOUNT and ADLS_KEY in the **Cmd 2** notebook cell, as per your Azure account.

9. Run **Cmd1**, **Cmd2**, and **Cmd3**. These instructions will create a Spark DataFrame named **df_read_inventory1** using the **Day 1=2021-04-18** inventory file from the bronze layer:

Cmd 2
```
1  STORAGE_ACCOUNT="traininglakehouse"
2  ADLS_KEY="pk4WsKke/E5unihwlzpGpV3fIX5WIiQSTJvjIuE2r7R2ktxlf2Crgfa+IyceY8uq1tfDExUPodpKLT3R3ddPkg=="
3  BRONZE_LAYER_NAMESPACE="bronze"
4  SILVER_LAYER_NAMESPACE="silver"
5  INVENTORY_FOLDER="inventory"
6  spark.conf.set("fs.azure.account.key."+STORAGE_ACCOUNT+".blob.core.windows.net", ADLS_KEY)
```
Command took 0.04 seconds -- by datauniversity.ca@gmail.com at 2021-07-12, 9:01:52 p.m. on curationcluster

Cmd 3
```
1  BRONZE_TABLE_PATH="wasbs://"+BRONZE_LAYER_NAMESPACE+"@"+STORAGE_ACCOUNT+".blob.core.windows.net/"+INVENTORY_FOLDER+"/1"
2  df_read_inventory1 = spark.read.csv(BRONZE_TABLE_PATH, header='True', inferSchema='True' )
3  display(df_read_inventory1)
```

▶ (3) Spark Jobs

▶ 🖿 df_read_inventory1 pyspark.sql.dataframe.DataFrame = [inventory_date: string, product: string ... 1 more fields]

	inventory_date	product	inventory
1	2021-04-18	Watch	100
2	2021-04-18	Vaccum	500
3	2021-04-18	Airconditioner	45
4	2021-04-18	Microwave	34
5	2021-04-18	DVD	6789
6	2021-04-18	TV	43
7	2021-04-18	Keyboard	564

Showing all 11 rows.

Figure 10.12 – Reading the 2021-04-18 inventory file

Notice that **df_read_inventory1** has three columns: **inventory_date**, **product**, and **inventory**.

• Now, run **Cmd4**, **Cmd5**, **Cmd6**, and **Cmd7**. These instructions will create a Delta table using the **Day 1=2021-04-18** inventory file:

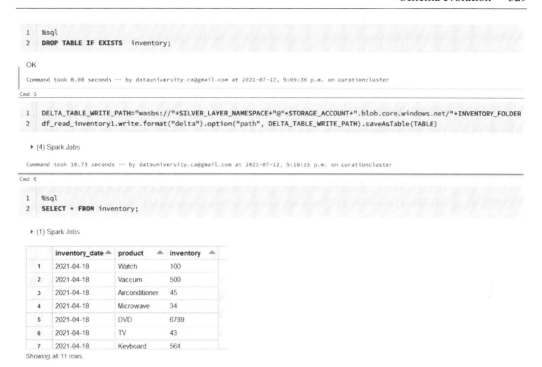

Figure 10.13 – Creating the inventory Delta table using the 2021-04-18 file

10. Notice that the **inventory** table schema in Delta Lake now has three columns; that is, **inventory_date**, **product**, and **inventory**:

Figure 10.14 – Checking the inventory Delta table's schema

- Next, run **Cmd8**. These instructions will create a Spark DataFrame named **df_read_inventory2** using the **Day 2=2021-04-19** inventory file:

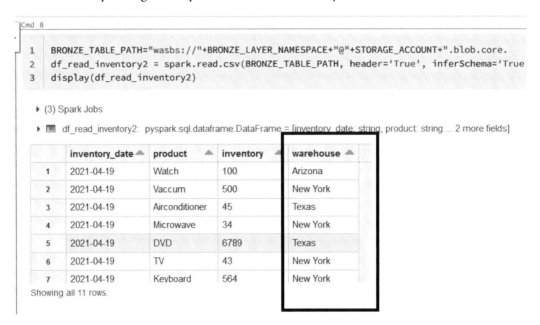

Figure 10.15 – Reading the 2021-04-19 inventory file

Notice that **df_read_inventory2** has four columns: **inventory_date**, **product**, **inventory**, **warehouse**.

- Run **Cmd9**. This instruction will try to merge **df_read_inventory2** into the existing **inventory** Delta table:

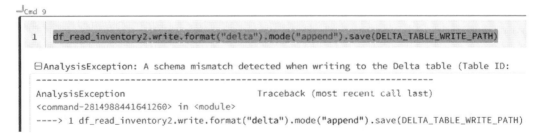

Figure 10.16 – Schema mismatch exception

Here, the instruction ran into an exception. If you scroll down the error window, you will see the following output:

```
⊟AnalysisException: A schema mismatch detected when writing to the Delta table (Table ID: 2990042c-3e69-4a50-b75c-70f8d2d9ef25).
To enable schema migration using DataFrameWriter or DataStreamWriter, please set:
'.option("mergeSchema", "true")'.
For other operations, set the session configuration
spark.databricks.delta.schema.autoMerge.enabled to "true". See the documentation
specific to the operation for details.

Table schema:
root
-- inventory_date: string (nullable = true)
-- product: string (nullable = true)
-- inventory: integer (nullable = true)

Data schema:
root
-- inventory_date: string (nullable = true)
-- product: string (nullable = true)
-- inventory: integer (nullable = true)
-- warehouse: string (nullable = true)
```

Figure 10.17 – Schema mismatch between the 2021-04-18 and 2021-04-19 inventory files

This is the expected behavior. The Delta table has correctly detected a schema mismatch between the incoming data and the pre-existing Delta table. By default, Delta Lake will throw an exception if such a mismatch is detected. The real question is how to deal with such a situation.

11. Now, run **Cmd10** and **Cmd11**. Notice that a new option has been added in the merge command. mode=append overrides the default behavior and instructs Delta Lake to proceed with the data merge by adjusting the schema:

Figure 10.18 – Creating the inventory Delta table using the 2021-04-19 file using mode=append

Notice that this time, an exception was not raised. Instead, Delta Lake calmly adjusted the schema of the pre-existing table by adding a new column to it.

> **Important**
>
> The decision to either raise an exception or use `mode=append` in the Delta table's merge commands should be discussed and agreed upon with the customer.

12. Run **Cmd12**. Note how Delta Lake has adjusted the data after merging the data and schema. All data before **Day 2=2021-04-19** has been marked as **NULL** because the new column warehouse did not exist before:

```
Cmd 12

1   %sql
2   SELECT * FROM inventory;
```

▶ (2) Spark Jobs

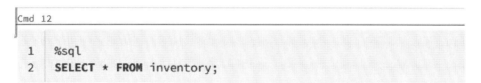

	inventory_date ▲	product ▲	inventory ▲	warehouse ▲
9	2021-04-19	Monitor	435	Texas
10	2021-04-19	Mobile	659	New York
11	2021-04-19	Phones	34	Arizona
12	2021-04-18	Watch	100	null
13	2021-04-18	Vaccum	500	null
14	2021-04-18	Airconditioner	45	null
15	2021-04-18	Microwave	34	null

Showing all 22 rows.

Figure 10.19   Checking the data in the inventory Delta table

Now, let's see what happens when we try to merge the **Day 3=2021-04-20** inventory file with the **inventory** table. You may recall that on this day, a new column (**city**) was added but a previous column was deleted (**warehouse**).

Run **Cmd13**. These instructions will create a Spark DataFrame named **df_read_inventory3** using the **Day 2=2021-04-120** inventory file:

```
Cmd 13

1   BRONZE_TABLE_PATH="wasbs://"+BRONZE_LAYER_NAMESPACE+"@"+STORAGE_ACC
2   df_read_inventory3 = spark.read.csv(BRONZE_TABLE_PATH, header='True
3   display(df_read_inventory3)
```

▶ (3) Spark Jobs

▶ 🖼 df_read_inventory3: pyspark.sql.dataframe.DataFrame = [inventory_date: string, product

	inventory_date	product	inventory	city
1	2021-04-20	Watch	100	Phoenix
2	2021-04-20	Vaccum	500	New York
3	2021-04-20	Airconditioner	45	Dallas
4	2021-04-20	Microwave	34	New York
5	2021-04-20	DVD	6789	Dallas
6	2021-04-20	TV	43	New York
7	2021-04-20	Keyboard	564	New York

Showing all 11 rows.

Figure 10.20 – Reading the 2021-04-20 inventory file

13. Run **Cmd14**. This instruction will try to merge **df_read_inventory3** in the existing **inventory** Delta table.

Run Cmd15. Notice how Delta Lake was able to adjust the schema once again. Even though the warehouse column was deleted in the incoming file, it remains in the Delta table:

```
Cmd 14

1   df_read_inventory3.write.format("delta").mode("append").option("mergeSchema", "true").save(DELTA_TABLE_WRITE_PATH)
```

▶ (4) Spark Jobs

Command took 3.66 seconds -- by datauniversity.ca@gmail.com at 2021-07-12, 9:43:51 p.m. on curationcluster

```
Cmd 15

1   %sql
2   DESCRIBE inventory;
```

	col_name	data_type	comment
1	inventory_date	string	
2	product	string	
3	inventory	int	
4	warehouse	string	
5	city	string	
6			
7	# Partitioning		

Showing all 8 rows.

Figure 10.21 – Creating the inventory Delta table using the 2021-04-20 file using mode=append

14. Run **Cmd16**:

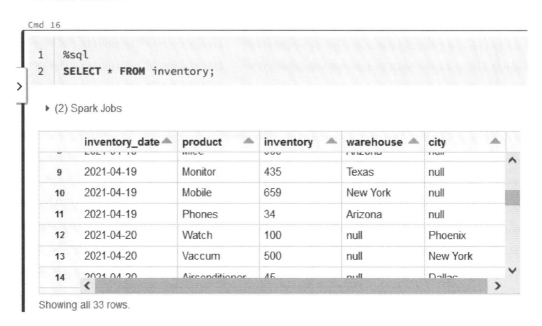

Figure 10.22 – Checking the data in the inventory Delta table

This time, after merging data from **Day 3=2021-04-20**, the **warehouse** column gets defaulted to **NULL**, and the new **city** column has been added to the **inventory** table.

With that, you've seen how Delta Lake can transparently adjust the data and schema each time a schema change is detected. Hopefully, this example was able to effectively highlight how schema evolution can be managed in modern data engineering pipelines. We will now look at sharing data. This is quickly becoming a necessity for organizations who are wanting to harness the power of data in monetary terms.

Sharing data

In *Chapter 1, The Story of Data Engineering and Analytics*, we discussed the power of data. This has enabled organizations to realize **revenue diversification** using **data monetization**. But this dream cannot be effectively realized without sharing data with external parties. In the past, organizations used several data-sharing mechanisms such as emails, SFTP, APIs, cloud storage, and hard drives:

Figure 10.23 – State of data sharing currently

Unfortunately, there are several problems related to these data-sharing methods:

- **Complex**: These data sharing mechanisms can be complex to set up and use because they may require exchanging keys/passwords and using a variety of different tools.

- **Insecure**: These mechanisms may not be secure for data-at-rest or data-in-transit. This means the classic **man-in-the-middle** attack could expose data in cleartext.

- **Tracking**: There is no clear method available for effectively tracking who shared data with whom and using which mechanism.

- **Control**: You can't control over who is using the shared data.

- **Updates**: Sharing data is a continuous process, and using the mechanisms mentioned previously does not provide a simple way to share updates.

Fortunately, there is an effective alternative. Azure allows organizations to share data both internally and externally using a simple and secure service named **Azure Data Share**. Using Azure Data Share, users sharing data (**providers**) can easily invite users they wish to share data with (**consumers**). Before the data is shared with the consumers, they are required to accept the data usage terms. Updates to data can also be shared on a set frequency that's been configured by the provider. Data sharing can happen in one of two ways. We will look at both in the following subsections.

In-place sharing

In this case, data always stays in the provider's Azure subscription, and a symbolic link is sent to the consumer's Azure subscription. Consumers can read the data using this symbolic link, as shown here:

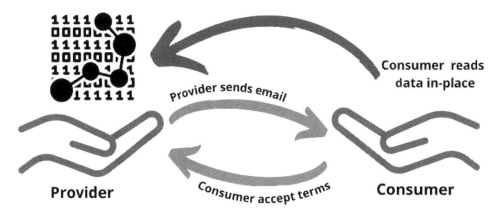

Figure 10.24 – In-place sharing using Azure Data Share

Snapshot sharing

In this case, data moves from the data provider's Azure subscription and lands in the data consumer's Azure subscription:

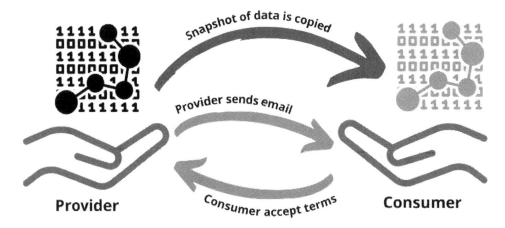

Figure 10.25 – Snapshot sharing using Azure Data Share

Let's learn more about sharing data by performing a simple exercise. For this exercise, you will need a sharing buddy to act as the consumer. Your buddy should have an operational Azure account. If they don't, they can create a new one.

Preparing the Azure resources

We will start by preparing the Azure resources that are required for sharing data:

1. On the Azure portal, search for Data Shares and navigate to it.

2. On the **Data Shares** page, click **Create**.

3. On the **Create Data Share** page, enter the following details:

    Subscription: Free Tier or Paid Subscription

    Resource group: training_rg

    Location: East US 2

    Name: trainingshare

Click on **Review + create**:

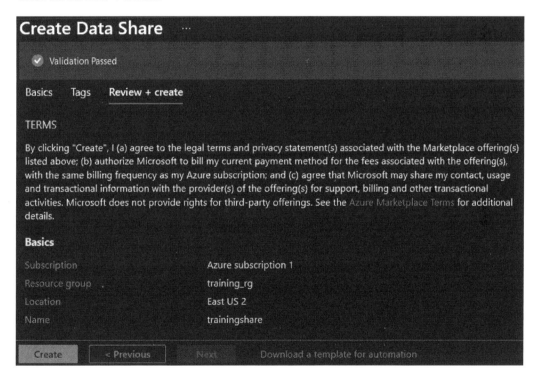

Figure 10.26 – Creating a new data share

4. Notice the **Validation Passed** message at the top. Press **Create**.

5. The newly created data share will now be deployed. After the deployment finishes, you should receive a message stating **Your deployment is complete**.

6. Click on **Go to resource**. This should take you to the newly created data share page:

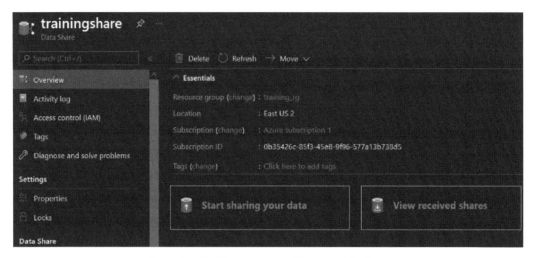

Figure 10.27 – Home screen of the new data share

> **Important**
> The decision of sharing data internally or externally is extremely sensitive.
> As a data engineer, you should mandatorily seek written approval from the
> customer before proceeding with the data share.

Creating a data share

Now that we have created a new data share account, we can proceed with sharing the data:

1. Click on **Start sharing your data**. Now, click on **Create** and provide the
    following values:

    - **Share name**: golddata

    - **Share type**: Snapshot

    Click **Continue**. This should take you to the **Datasets** tab. From here, click on **Add
    datasets** and choose **Azure Data Lake Gen2**:

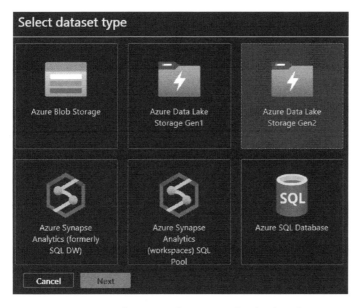

Figure 10.28 – Choosing a dataset type for the data share

2. Click **Next** and provide the following values:

    - **Subscriptions**: Free Tier or Paid Subscription
    - **Resource groups**: training_rg
    - **Storage accounts**: traininglakehouse:

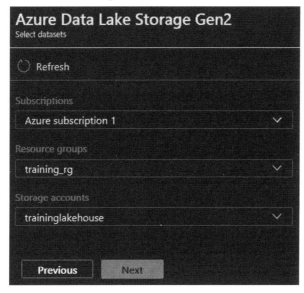

Figure 10.29 – Choosing an Azure Data Lake Storage account for the data share

3.   Click **Next**.

On the **Select datasets** page, choose **gold** and click **Next**:

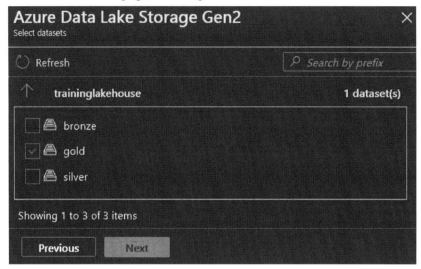

Figure 10.30 – Choosing the gold dataset for the data share

4.   On the **Rename datasets** page, leave the name as is or change it as required:

Figure 10.31 – Renaming the dataset for the data share

5.   Click **Add datasets** and then **Continue**.

Now, we will add the email address value of the consumer (buddy) who will receive the share.

6. Click on **Add recipient**. Enter the email address of the recipient and click **Add**, followed by **Send invitation**:

Figure 10.32 – Adding the email address of the consumer

7. Azure will now send an email to the consumer, who will need to accept the invitation and execute a series of steps to download data from the newly created data share.

    Please note that the next series of steps are from the point of view of the consumer. Some screenshots displayed hereafter will reflect what the consumer will see after they receive the email. To show this difference, all the screenshots with a **white background** are from the consumer's Azure account.

8. The consumer will receive an email that looks like this:

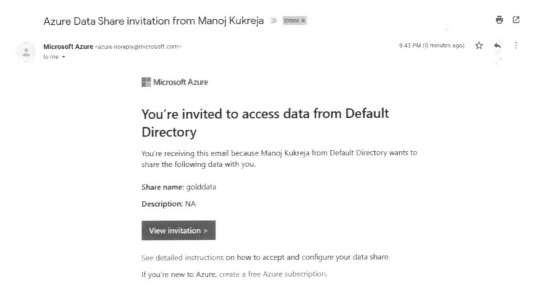

Figure 10.33 – Invitation email for the consumer

9. After clicking **View Invitation**, the request will be forwarded to the consumer's Azure portal. After logging into the portal, the following screen will appear:

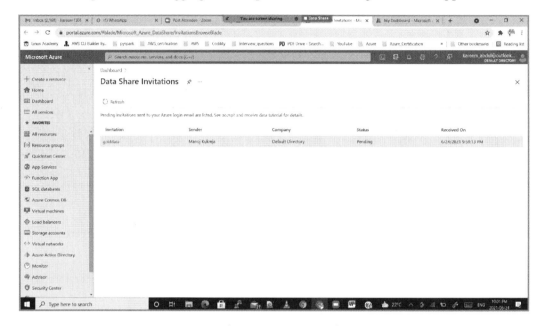

Figure 10.34 – The customer viewing the invitation

Click on **golddata** and provide the following values:

- **Data share account name**: golddatashare

- **Subscription**: Free Tier or Paid Subscription

- **Resource group**: training_rg

- **Location**: East US 2

Click on **Create**. You will receive the following error:

The subscription is not registered to use namespace 'Microsoft.DataShare'. See https://aka.ms/rps-not-found for how to register subscriptions.

There's no need to panic – Azure subscriptions do not enable **Data Sharing** by default.

10. Navigate to the **Subscriptions** page and click on your Azure subscription:

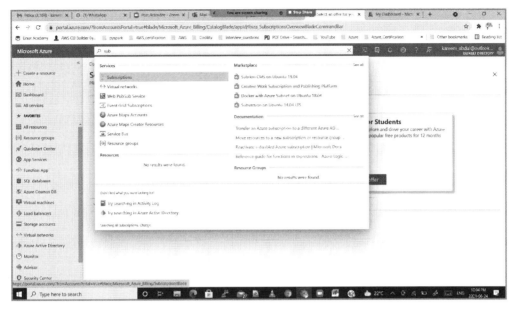

Figure 10.35 – Enabling data sharing in the consumer's subscription

11. Now, click on **Resource providers** using the menu on the left:

Figure 10.36 – Navigating to the resource providers in the consumer's subscription

12. Using the search bar at the top, type `datashare`. Notice that **Microsoft.Datashare** is currently not registered:

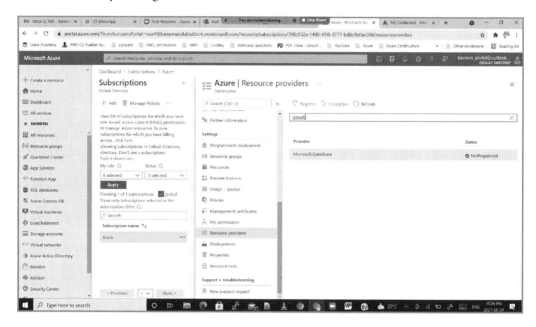

Figure 10.37 – Checking the state of Microsoft.Datashare in the consumer's subscription

13. Choose **Microsoft.Datashare** and click on **Register**. **Microsoft.Datashare** will now be registered for the consumer's Azure subscription. Please note that this step may take a few minutes to complete:

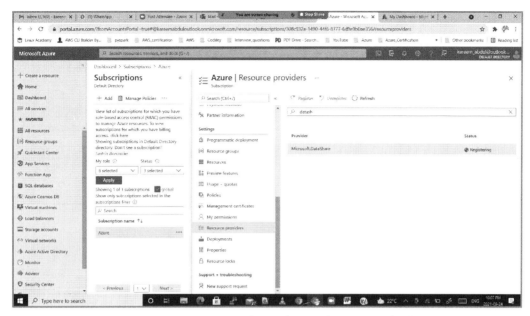

Figure 10.38 – Registering Microsoft.Datashare in the consumer's subscription

14. Once the status changes to **Registered**, navigate back to the data share account tab and click on **Create** again. Hopefully, this time, the process will run without any errors:

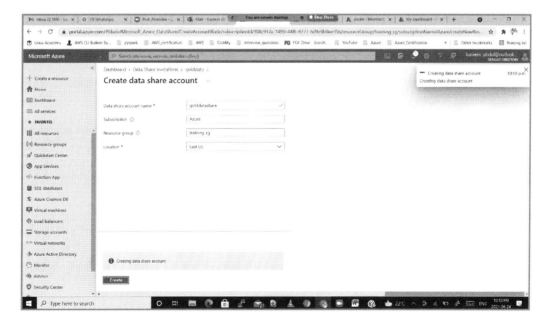

Figure 10.39 – Creating a new data share in the consumer's subscription

15. The data share invitation will now be displayed. Enter the details shown in the following screenshot, and then click **Accept and configure**:

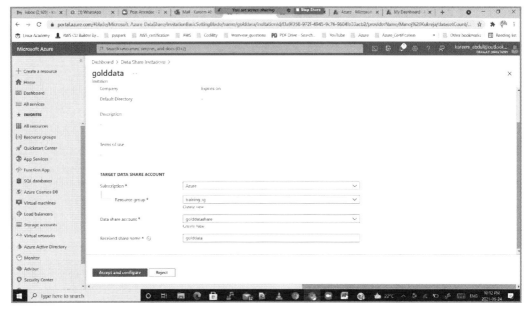

Figure 10.40 – Setting the data share parameters in the consumer's subscription

16. The confirmation screen for a successful data share should look like this:

Figure 10.41 – Home screen of the data share in the consumer's subscription

17. Now, click on **Datasets**. Notice that the data share is *not* mapped to a storage account on the recipient's side:

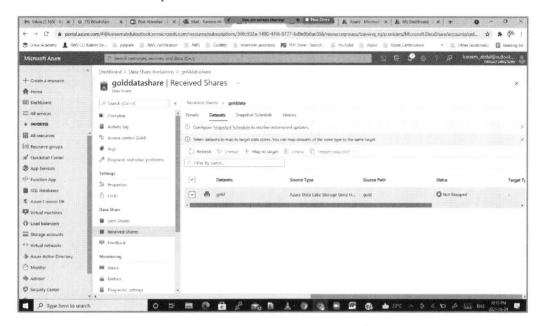

Figure 10.42 – Checking the received shares in the consumer's subscription

18. Click on **Map to target** and supply the following values:

- **Target data type**: Azure data lake storage Gen2

- **Subscription**: Free Tier or Paid Subscription

- **Resource group**: training_rg

- **Storage accounts**: <Consumers Storage Account>

The consumer is free to choose any storage account in their subscription to receive the shared data.

- **Path**: `goldshared`:

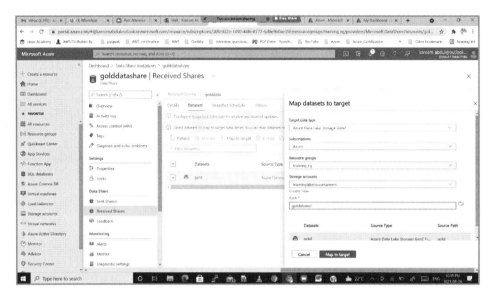

Figure 10.43 – Mapping datasets to the target in the consumer's subscription

19. Click on **Map to target**. The confirmation screen should look like this:

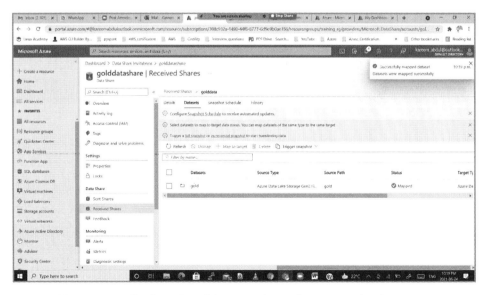

Figure 10.44 – Confirmation of data mapping in the consumer's subscription

20. Now, we are all set to **trigger** a full snapshot, which will copy the shared data from the **provider** account to the **consumer** storage account.

Before we trigger a **full snapshot**, we need to grant a role to the storage account.

Using a new browser tab, navigate to the Azure portal.

Click on **Home** > **All Resources** > <**Consumers Storage Account**>.

Then, using the menu on the left, click on **Access Control (IAM)**.

From here, click on **Add role assignment**.

Now, choose **Owner** and click on **Next**.

Choose **User, group, or service principal**, and then click on **Select members**.

Choose the Azure **principal** where the name starts with the same account name that the user logs into the Azure portal with. Click **Select** and then **Next**:

Figure 10.45 – Adding a role assignment to the consumer's subscription

Finally, click **Review + assign**.

21. Navigate back to the **Data share** tab. Click on **Trigger snapshot** and choose **Full copy**:

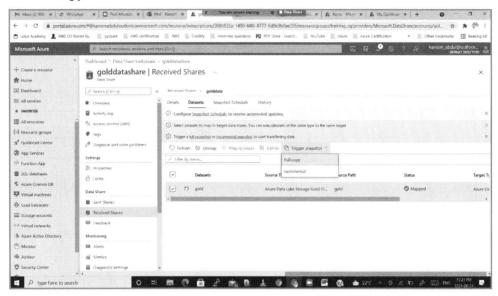

Figure 10.46 – Triggering a new snapshot in the consumer's subscription

22. This will **trigger** a full snapshot copy from the **provider** account to the **consumer** account. Notice the messages in the notification area. This area should display the status of the snapshot being copied:

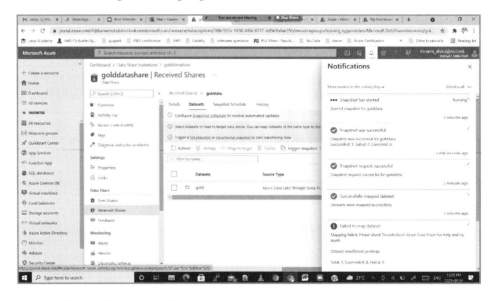

Figure 10.47 – Checking notifications for snapshot creation in the consumer's subscription

23. After a few minutes, navigate back to the storage account. You should see a new container called **goldshared** in the storage account, as follows:

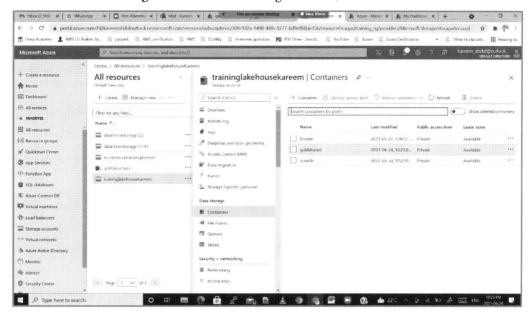

Figure 10.48 – Checking the new snapshot in the consumer's subscription

24. Now, if you click on **goldshared**, you should see the following folders:

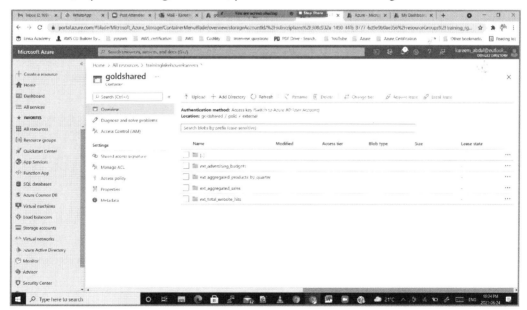

Figure 10.49 – Checking the contents of the data share in the consumer's subscription

25. Now, click on any folder and check that the files have been successfully copied, as follows:

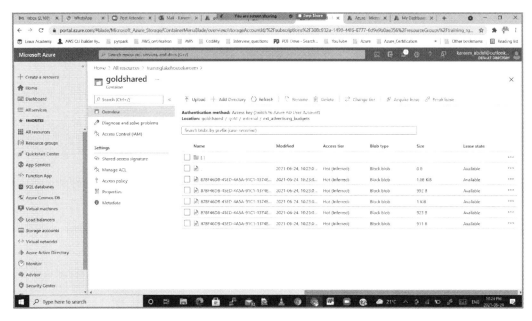

Figure 10.50 – Checking the blobs in the consumer's subscription

Here, we were able to successfully share data between the provider and the consumer with simplicity, security, and accountability. Next, we will look at another critical challenge that's faced by organizations dealing with sensitive data.

Data governance

I started this book by stating *"Every byte of data has a story to tell. The real question is whether the story is being narrated accurately, securely, and efficiently."* While organizations are busy harnessing the true power of data, data governance and security frequently get neglected. But it cannot be neglected for too long. Regulations such as **GDPR** and many others are enforcing legal accountability and strict penalties on organizations failing to meet governance policies related to data privacy, retention, and portability.

An effective path to data governance often starts with an effective method for data discovery, classification, and tracking lineage. This can be a daunting task, considering the vast variety, volumes, and velocity of data. **Azure Purview** is a new, unified governance service that automates tasks such as discovery, classification, and lineage.

Using Azure Purview, the registered data sources can be automatically discovered once or regularly on a schedule. The discovered data is classified based on predefined or custom rules. Once the data has been cataloged, users can manually enhance the metadata by providing descriptions, tags, and access rules. Let's explore how Azure Purview can effectively handle this.

Preparing the Azure resources

We will start by preparing the Azure Purview account:

1. On the Azure portal search, for `Purview accounts` and navigate to it.

2. On the **Purview accounts** page, click on **Create Purview account** and provide the following values:

   - **Subscription**: `Free Tier or Paid Subscription`

   - **Resource group**: `training_rg`

   - **Purview account name**: `trainingcatalog`

   - **Location**: `East US 2`:

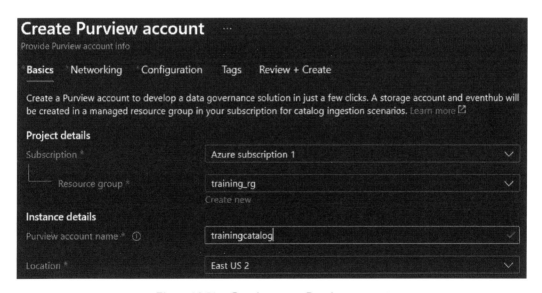

Figure 10.51 – Creating a new Purview account

Click on **Review + Create**:

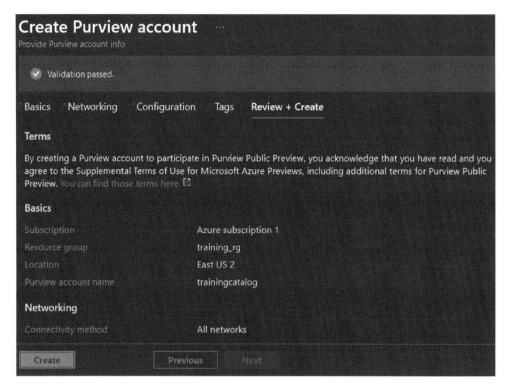

Figure 10.52 – Specifying the parameters for the new Purview account

Click on **Create**. Once the deployment has finished, click on **Go to Resource**:

Figure 10.53 – Home screen of the new Purview account

Now that we have an Azure Purview account, we are ready to create the data catalog.

Creating a data catalog

A data catalog is a collection of data assets and their relationships. It promotes effective governance by enabling end users to discover relevant data using terms, classifications, and sensitivity labels. Follow these steps to create one:

1. Click on **Open Purview Studio**:

Figure 10.54 – Purview Studio home screen for trainingcatalog

2. To register a data source, click on **Register Sources**, then **Register**:

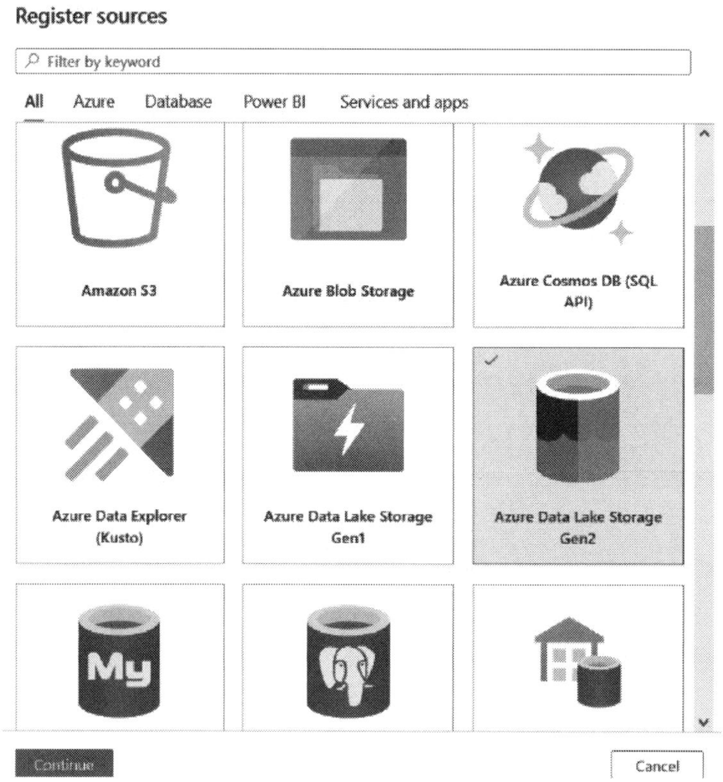

Figure 10.55 – Choosing Azure Data Lake Storage Gen2 in trainingcatalog

Select **Azure Data Lake Storage Gen2**.

Click **Continue** and provide the following values:

- **Name**: trainingsource
- **Subscription**: Free Tier or Paid Subscription
- **Storage account name**: traininglakehouse
- **Endpoint**: Automatically populated based on evious choices

- **Select a collection**: **None**:

Register sources (Azure Data Lake Storage Gen2)

Name *

```
trainingsource
```

Azure subscription

```
Azure subscription 1 (0b35426c-85f3-45e8-9f96-577a13b738d5)        ∨
```

Storage account name *

```
traininglakehouse                                                 ∨
```

Endpoint

```
https://traininglakehouse.dfs.core.windows.net/                   🗅
```

Select a collection

```
None                                                              ∨
```

Figure 10.56 – Registering a new source in trainingcatalog

3.   Click on **Register**:

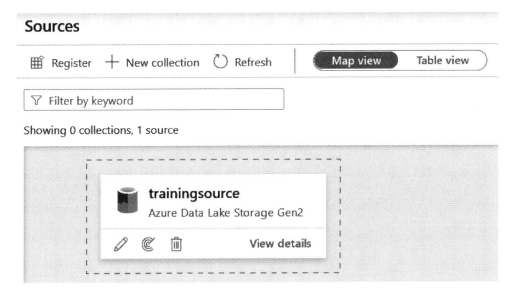

Figure 10.57 – Confirming the creation of trainingsource

4. We are now ready to scan the data source we have created. Before proceeding, we need to make sure that **trainingsource** has the appropriate permissions to scan **traininglakehouse**.

    Using the Azure portal, navigate to **Home** > **All resources** > **traininglakehouse**.

5. Using the menu on the left, click on **Access Control (IAM)**:

Figure 10.58 – Access Control (IAM) for traininglakehouse

Click on + **Add**, and then **Add role assignment**. Provide the following values:

- **Role: Storage Blob Data Reader**

- **Assign access to**: **User, group, or service principal**

- **Select**: `trainingcatalog`:

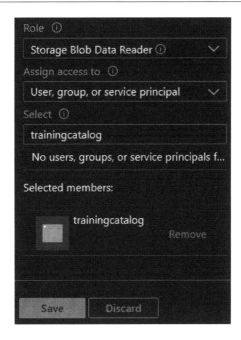

Figure 10.59 – Granting a role to trainingcatalog

Click on **Save**.

6.   Now, navigate back to **Azure Purview Studio**:

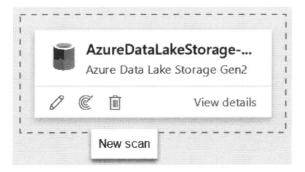

Figure 10.60 – Invoking a new scan

7.   To start the scan, click on the **New Scan** icon. Provide the following values:

- **Name**: Scan Data
- **Connect via integration runtime**: Use default value

- **Credential**: Use default value:

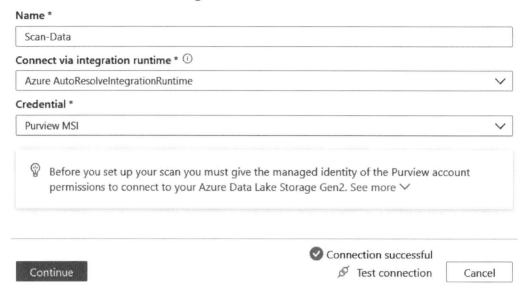

Figure 10.61 – New scan details

Click on **Test Connection**, then **Continue**.

8. On the **Scope your scan** screen, choose **bronze**, as follows:

Figure 10.62 – Choosing the bronze layer for the new scan

Click on **Continue**.

> **Important**
>
> The bronze layer is the first entry of data in the lakehouse. For this reason, it is a good candidate for scanning data that may contain classified information, such as PII.

9. For **Select a scan rule set**, choose **AdlsGen2**. AdlsGen2 is the default scan rule set and includes all the supported file types for schema extraction and classification, as well as all the supported system classification rules:

Select a scan rule set

+ New scan rule set   ○ Refresh

Select one scan rule set to be used by your scan.

> **AdlsGen2** SYSTEM DEFAULT
>
> Microsoft default scan rule set that includes all supported file types for schema extraction and classification, and all supported system classification rules View detail

Continue   Back   Cancel

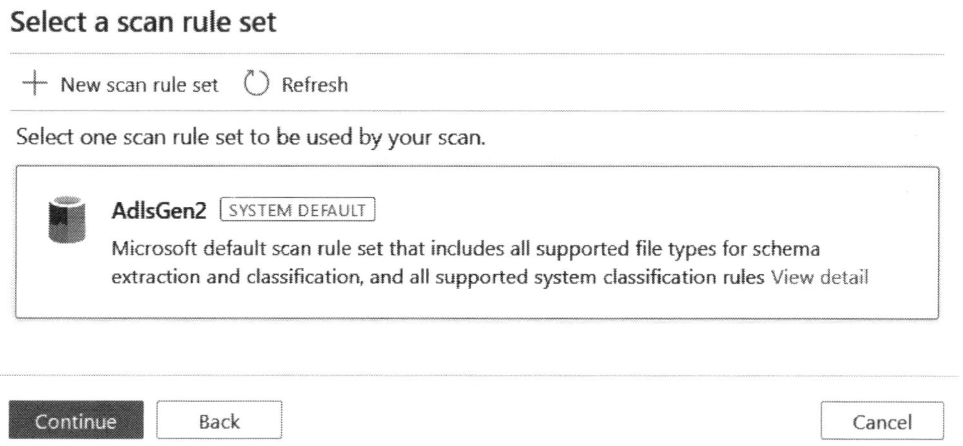

Figure 10.63 – Choosing a scan rule for the new scan

10. Click on **Continue**. On the **Set a scan trigger** screen, you can set up a scan that is recurring or happens only once:

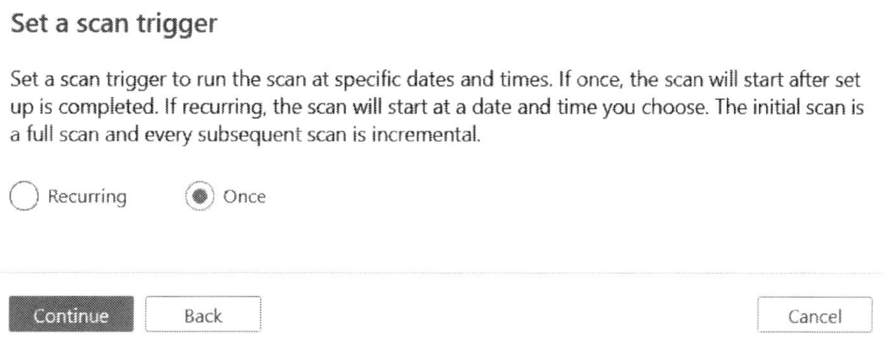

Set a scan trigger

Set a scan trigger to run the scan at specific dates and times. If once, the scan will start after set up is completed. If recurring, the scan will start at a date and time you choose. The initial scan is a full scan and every subsequent scan is incremental.

○ Recurring   ◉ Once

Continue   Back   Cancel

Figure 10.64 – Setting a scan trigger for the new scan

For now, we will choose **Once**. Click on **Continue**:

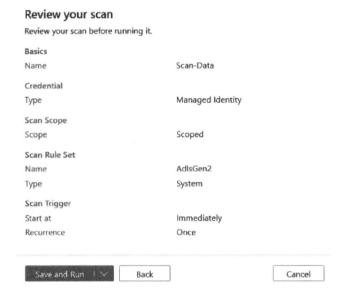

Review your scan

Review your scan before running it.

Basics

Name	Scan-Data

Credential

Type	Managed Identity

Scan Scope

Scope	Scoped

Scan Rule Set

Name	AdlsGen2
Type	System

Scan Trigger

Start at	Immediately
Recurrence	Once

Save and Run | Back | Cancel

Figure 10.65 – Reviewing the scan settings for the new scan

11. Click on **Save and Run**. You should now be back on the **Sources** screen:

AzureDataLakeStorage-...

Azure Data Lake Storage Gen2

View details

Figure 10.66 – Viewing the new scan details

12. At this point, the data in the bronze layer is being scanned. Wait for a few minutes for the scan to finish. To check the status of the run, click on **View Details**:

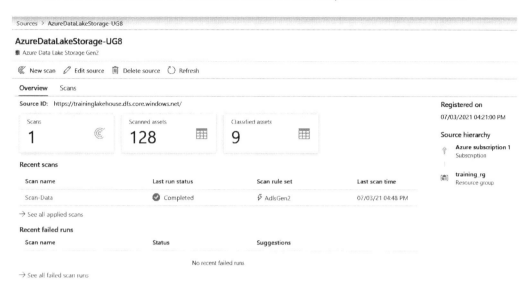

Figure 10.67 – New scan status

Once the scan has been completed, its status will be **Completed**.

Important

In production, you are bound to receive new data every time the ingestion pipelines are run. Therefore, it is advisable to use the recurring option so that incremental data is scanned regularly.

---

13. We are now ready to browse the assets that were scanned previously. Using the menu on the left, click on **Home**:

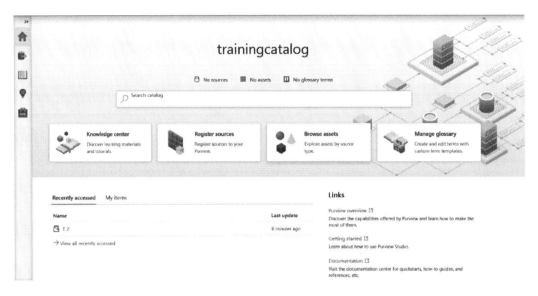

Figure 10.68 – Browsing the scanned assets

14. Click on **Browse Assets**, then **Azure Data Lake Storage Gen2**.

15. Browse the directory structure by going to **traininglakehouse** > **bronze** > **sales** > **[dbo].[store_customers]** > **T Z**.

You will see **Schema classifications**, as shown here:

Figure 10.69 – Checking classifications

Note how the scan in Azure Purview has automatically discovered **Classifications** for two columns: **Email Address** and **Credit Card Number**. As you may recall from previous chapters, we have these columns in the store customer table. So, why is classifying data that important?

Data classification is an important first step for meeting compliance requirements and data governance. Defining proper tags, labels, and metadata based on the sensitivity of data helps define data confidentiality at query time.

> **Important**
> Depending on the type of business data, classification is usually performed based on data content, context, and user levels.

Cleaning up Azure resources

To save on costs, you may want to clean up the following Azure resources:

1. Delete the Azure Purview account; that is, `trainingcatalog`.
2. Delete the Azure Data Share account; that is, `trainingshare`.

Now, let's summarize this chapter.

Summary

This was an extremely important chapter for several reasons. Using a few examples, we learned about the common challenges that are faced in the world of data engineering. Dealing with challenges such as schema evolution and governance are critical in modern data engineering projects. These challenges have evolved over time, and so have the techniques and tools that make the job of the data engineer a little easier.

In the next chapter, we will look at DevOps essentials for data engineers. DevOps is quickly becoming an essential add-on skill for data engineers, so we will learn how to automatically provision cloud resources using the **Infrastructure as Code (IaC)** paradigm. Using the power of IaC, data engineers can spin up data pipelines that use cloud resources in a fast, repeatable, and secure fashion.

11
Infrastructure Provisioning

While the demand for data analytics grows, data engineers are becoming an expensive and hard-to-find commodity in the marketplace. On the other hand, organizations that hire data engineers are finding innovative methods to do more with less so that they can justify the high resource costs. In a recent trend, most of these organizations have started to use automated infrastructure provisioning as a means to streamline cloud deployments. Until recently, infrastructure provisioning work has typically been handled by the **DevOps** group, but not anymore.

In the previous chapter, we talked about the dynamic nature of the data engineer's job profile. The modern data engineer needs to keep up with this latest trend and train themselves in a few DevOps skills. This chapter and the next are designed to teach the data engineer a few critical DevOps skills.

> **Important Note**
> In today's job market, a data engineer who knows DevOps is a lethal combination. Modern organizations would rather hire one resource who has both of these skills than hire two.

In this chapter, we will cover the following topics:

- Infrastructure as code
- Deploying infrastructure using **Azure Resource Manager**
- Deploying multiple environments using IaC

Infrastructure as code

Until recently, infrastructure deployment has been an extremely time-consuming and expensive process. In a typical organization, a team of system administrators would be responsible for deploying hardware and software on several environments using a series of manually executed steps. Due to its manual nature, this process has major deficiencies:

- **Unique settings per environment**: Every individual environment can have unique settings. To meet these requirements, the manual steps need to be documented for each environment.
- **Time-consuming**: The documentation and execution of manual steps are very time-consuming.
- **Inconsistent and error-prone**: Following manual steps for infrastructure deployments can lead to inconsistencies and errors.

Infrastructure as Code (**IaC**) is a practice to deploy and manage infrastructure components using source code. Using IaC, the system administration teams (also known as DevOps) are no longer bound by manual practices and documented processes. Instead, they can now perform automated and repeatable deployments using configuration files.

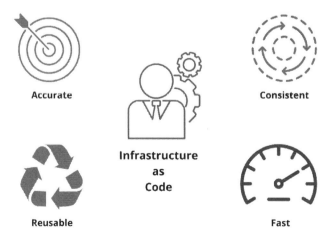

Figure 11.1 – Benefits of using IaC

Infrastructure that is deployed using the IaC practice is accurate, consistent, reusable, and fast. DevOps teams create, manage, and version control infrastructure configuration files in a similar way to how application teams create application code. The IaC practice follows the same set of protocols for bug-fixing, testing, and code promotions.

There are several open source and commercially available IaC tools available on the market such as **Ansible**, **Terraform**, **Chef**, and **Puppet**. For infrastructure provisioning, **Azure Resource Manager** (**ARM**) is the native platform in Azure. Modern organizations are using the power of ARM to organize and standardize their cloud deployments for uniformity, security, and performance.

Deploying infrastructure using Azure Resource Manager

Before ARM came into existence in 2014, **Azure Service Manager** (**ASM**) was used for infrastructure deployments. However, there were some serious drawbacks with the ASM approach arising due to inter-dependencies of resources. Before deploying resources, you had to carefully understand dependencies and sequence the operations accordingly in scripts.

Thankfully, ARM has taken care of the inter-dependency problem to deploy Azure resources easily, uniformly, and seamlessly. ARM uses **resource groups** as the logical grouping of cloud assets. Using a resource group ensures a consistent life cycle for resource provisioning, security, and tear-offs. ARM uses resource groups as the single unit of deployment and management.

ARM uses templates to deploy IaC. Once created, these templates become part of an enterprise code repository like other types of application code.

Creating ARM templates

An ARM template is simply a **JSON** format file that embeds the configuration of the resource within itself. ARM templates use declarative syntax, which means that you can deploy multiple Azure resources within one template. During runtime, ARM automatically sequences the operations in the correct order and fires them parallelly if possible.

Before we create a new template for the IaC deployment, we need to understand the format of an ARM template.

```
{
  "$schema": "https://schema.management.azure.com/schemas/2019-04-
01/deploymentTemplate.json#", << Version of template language
  "contentVersion": "", << Version of template
  "apiProfile": "",       << Collection of API versions
  "parameters": {  },     << External values provided to template
  "variables": {  },      << Internal values created using expressions
  "functions": [  ],      << User defined functions
  "resources": [  ],      << Resource types to be deployed
  "outputs": {  }         << Output values returned by deployment
}
```

Figure 11.2 – Anatomy of an ARM template

Every element in the template has several properties that can be set within it. Let me demonstrate this using examples as follows. Throughout this chapter, we will be referencing ARM templates from the following location in the **Packt** Git repository:

```
https://github.com/PacktPublishing/Data-Engineering-with-
Apache-Spark-Delta-Lake-and-Lakehouse/tree/main/project/infra
```

For the following example, let's understand a simple template that deploys the Electroniz Azure Data Lake Storage account.

Parameters

The `parameters` section of the ARM template is reserved for input values. Parameters are extremely important to enforce the reusability of ARM templates. You may notice two parameters named `environment` and `project` here. These parameters can be used to spin up varying environments such as `dev`, `test`, or `prod` on varying projects.

```json
{
    "$schema": "https://schema.management.azure.com/schemas/2019-04-01/deploymentTemplate.json#",
    "contentVersion": "1.0.0.0",
    "parameters": {
        "environment": {
            "type": "string"
        },
        "project": {
            "type": "string"
        },
        "storageAccountName": {
            "type": "string",
            "metadata": {
                "description": "The name of the storage account"
            }
        },
        "bronzeLayer": {
            "type": "string"
        },
        "silverLayer": {
            "type": "string"
        },
        "goldLayer": {
            "type": "string"
        },
        "location": {
            "type": "string",
            "defaultValue": "[resourceGroup().location]",
            "metadata": {
                "description": "The location in which the resources should be deployed."
            }
        }
```

Figure 11.3 – Parameters in an ARM template

Variables

The variables section of the ARM template is reserved for creating custom values that can be used throughout the template. The custom values are created using expressions denoted by two square brackets ([ ]). Within the expression, you can use several predefined functions provided by ARM, such as CONCAT, MIN, and MAX.

```json
        }
    },
    "variables": {
        "storageAccountName": "[concat(parameters('environment'), parameters('project'), parameters('storageAccountName'))]"
    },
    "resources": [
        {
```

Figure 11.4 – Variables in an ARM template

Notice the use of the CONCAT function in the storageAccountName variable. This expression is adding the name of project and environment to the storageAccountName parameter. This makes it easier to identify the Azure resource.

Resources

The resources section of the ARM template is reserved for defining the resources (one or many) required. In the following example, a new storage account needs to be created using the storageAccountName variable. Notice that isHnsEnabled is set to true, which means this is **Azure Data Lake Storage Gen2**.

```
"resources": [
    {
        "name": "[variables('storageAccountName')]",
        "type": "Microsoft.Storage/storageAccounts",
        "apiVersion": "2021-02-01",
        "sku": {
            "name": "Standard_LRS"
        },
        "kind": "StorageV2",
        "location": "[parameters('location')]",
        "properties": {
            "isHnsEnabled": true
        },
        "tags": {
            "owner":"data engineering",
            "project":"lakehouse",
            "environment":"production"
        },
        "resources": [
            {
                "name": "[concat('default/', parameters('bronzeLayer'))]",
                "type": "blobServices/containers",
                "apiVersion": "2019-06-01",
                "dependsOn": [
                    "[variables('storageAccountName')]"
                ],
                "properties": {
                    "publicAccess": "None"
                }
            }
```

Figure 11.5 – Resource definitions in an ARM template

Also, notice there is a new sub-resource embedded within the outer resource. The sub-resource is used to create a resource within the parent. In this instance, we are creating a container within the given storage account. Notice the use of the dependsOn property that is used to establish the parent-child relationship.

Deploying ARM templates using the Azure portal

Like many other services in Azure, ARM templates can be deployed both from the **Azure portal** and the **Azure client**. Initially in the project, using the Azure portal provides a convenient method for developing, testing, and deploying infrastructure code. Once the templates are in working order, they may be deployed through scripts using the Azure client. To start, we will deploy a template using the Azure portal:

1. On the Azure portal, navigate to **Home**. Now click on the **Create a resource** icon.

2. In the search box, type Templates, and press *Enter*.

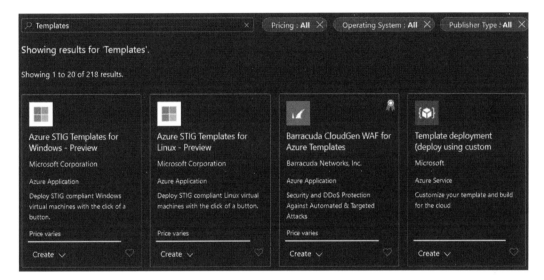

Figure 11.6 – Creating resources using ARM templates on the Azure portal

3. Choose **Template deployment (deploy using custom templates)**.

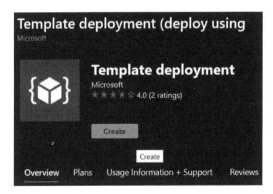

Figure 11.7 – Creating custom ARM templates

Click on **Create**.

4.   We are now ready to create a new template.

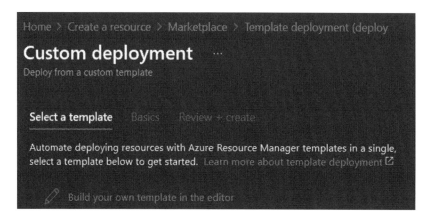

Figure 11.8 – Building a custom ARM template

Click on **Build your own template in the editor**.

5.   Copy the contents of the following file and paste it into the textbox. This is the same
     template that was in the previous section:

```
https://raw.githubusercontent.com/PacktPublishing/Data-
Engineering-with-Apache-Spark-Delta-Lake-and-Lakehouse/
main/project/infra/storage_accounts/storage_accounts.json
```

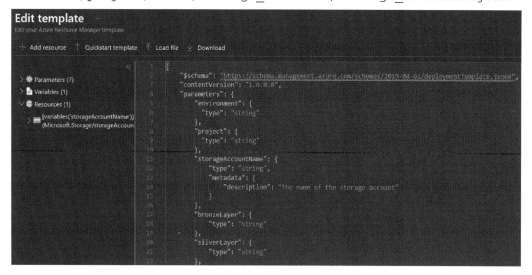

Figure 11.9 – Adding code for a custom ARM template

Notice how the template was read and ARM successfully identified the correct number of parameters, variables, and resources created by this template. Click on **Save**.

6. On the **Custom deployment** screen, input the following values:

   - **Subscription**: **Free Tier** or **Paid Subscription**.

   - **Resource group**: Click **Create new**.

   - **Name**: elz_prod.

   Click **OK**.

   Now input the following values:

   - **Region**: East US 2

   - **Environment**: prod

   - **Project**: dlake

   In many cases, Azure resource names are globally unique. Try to make the project name as unique as possible. Since a lot of readers will be using the same instructions, having uniqueness will eliminate unnecessary errors related to unique resource names:

   - **Storage Account Name**: elz

   - **Bronze Layer**: bronze

   - **Silver Layer**: silver

   - **Gold Layer**: gold

   - **Location**: [resourceGroup().location]

   Click on **Review + create**.

7. Check for the **Validation Passed** message.

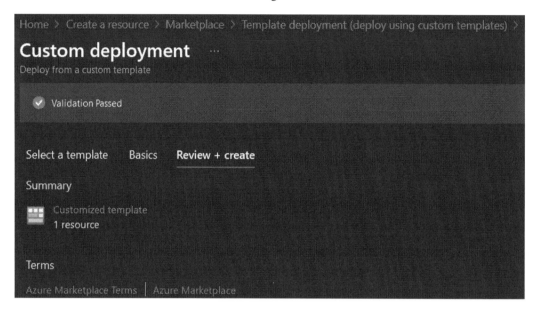

Figure 11.10 – Validating the custom ARM template

Click on **Create**.

8. ARM will now start the deployment. You should now see the **Deployment is in progress** screen as follows:

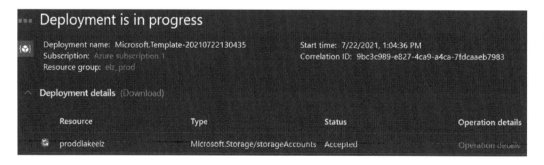

Figure 11.11 – Deploying the custom ARM template

9. Once the deployment is finished, you should see the **Your deployment is complete** screen as follows:

Figure 11.12 – Deployment completed confirmation message

Click on **Go to resource group**.

10. Check that a new storage account has been created. Notice the name of the storage account embeds the environment and project name.

Figure 11.13 – Azure resources in the newly created resource group

Click on the **storage account name (proddlakeelz)**.

11. Now click on **Containers**. Notice the three newly created containers as sub-resources in the ARM template.

Figure 11.14 – Azure resources in the newly created resource group

12. Navigate back to **Home | Resource group | elz_prod**.

Using the menu on the left, click on **Deployments**. Notice that ARM maintains a log of all deployments that were performed.

Figure 11.15 – Checking the deployments in the newly created resource group

Deploying ARM templates using the Azure CLI

Once the template has been developed and tested using the Azure portal, it is essential to run it using the Azure client. This will provide us with the assurance that the template is ready for use in the future using deployment scripts.

> **Important Note**
> Even though deploying an ARM template using the Azure portal is a relatively simple process, a lot of administrators prefer automated deployments using the **Azure CLI**.

This is how the `Lakehouse_Storage_Account` template can be deployed using Bash. Invoke the following commands using Azure Cloud Shell:

```
RESOURCEGROUPNAME="elz_prod"

LOCATION="eastus"

IAC_ENVIRONMENT=prod

FILE_PATH=~/Data-Engineering-with-Apache-Spark-Delta-Lake-and-
Lakehouse/project/infra

TEMPLATE_FILE=$FILE_PATH/storage_accounts/storage_accounts.json

PARAMETERS_FILE=$FILE_PATH/parameters/$IAC_ENVIRONMENT/storage_
accounts_parameters.json

az group create --name $RESOURCEGROUPNAME --location $LOCATION

az deployment group create --name Lakehouse_Storage_Account
--resource-group $RESOURCEGROUPNAME --template-file $TEMPLATE_
FILE --parameters $PARAMETERS_FILE
```

As we can see, it is pretty straightforward and easy to do.

Deploying ARM templates containing secrets

In the previous section, we deployed a relatively simple ARM template. The complexity of the template increases if the Azure resources require administrator credentials to be set while creating the resource itself. Since we are creating the infrastructure using code, it is unsafe and against security practices to leave exposed reference passwords in configuration files. In such cases, the security aspect of the template needs to be properly addressed. This security issue is frequently encountered when spinning up resources such as **Azure SQL** and **Azure Synapse**. Fortunately, Azure ARM can easily accommodate this requirement. It can retrieve secrets from **Azure Key Vault** at runtime during the deployment process. The process starts by creating the infrastructure secrets in Azure Key Vault. This is how it is done:

1. Run the following commands in Azure Cloud Shell:

    ```
    RESOURCEGROUPNAME="elz_prod"

    LOCATION="eastus"

    KEYVAULTNAME="deploykvelz"

    az group create --name $RESOURCEGROUPNAME --location
    $LOCATION

    az keyvault purge -n $KEYVAULTNAME

    az config set extension.use_dynamic_install=yes_without_
    prompt
    ```

```
az keyvault create --location $LOCATION --name
$KEYVAULTNAME --resource-group $RESOURCEGROUPNAME
--enabled-for-template-deployment true
```

If run correctly, you should see the following output:

```
    "softDeleteRetentionInDays": 90,
    "tenantId": "3292c8fb-83df-4e46-a195-da02380f8f5c",
    "vaultUri": "https://deploykvelz.vault.azure.net/"
},
"resourceGroup": "elz_prod",
"systemData": {
    "createdAt": "1970-01-19T20:14:05.765000+00:00",
    "createdBy": "                              ",
    "createdByType": "User",
    "lastModifiedAt": "1970-01-19T20:14:05.765000+00:00",
    "lastModifiedBy": "                              ",
    "lastModifiedByType": "User"
},
"tags": {},
"type": "Microsoft.KeyVault/vaults"
```

Figure 11.16 – Output of the new Azure Key Vault creation

2. We will now add secrets to the newly created Azure Key Vault. Using the Azure portal, navigate to **Home | Resource group | elz_prod | deploykvelz**.

    Click on **Secrets**. Then create two new secrets using **Generate/Import**:

    - **Name**: SQLUSER   **Value**: salesadmin

    - **Name**: SQLPASSWORD   **Value**: <password for Azure SQL administrator>

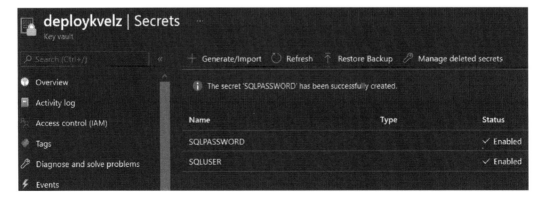

Figure 11.17 – Checking newly created secrets in Azure Key Vault

> **Important Note**
>
> Even though the creation of secrets in Azure Key Vault can be automated,
> it is highly recommended to perform this step manually. You can request the
> customer's IT team to create the secrets for you. Using this method ensures
> confidentiality at their end.

3. We are now ready to deploy the `Stores_Azure_SQL_Database` template. Run
    the following commands using Azure Cloud SQL. These commands will deploy an
    Azure SQL Database template while dynamically fetching database credentials using
    secrets from Azure Key Vault created previously:

```
SERVERNAME="elzsql"
DATABASENAME="salesdb"
VAULTNAME="deploykvelz"
PASSWORDSECRETNAME="SQLPASSWORD"
USERSECRETNAME="SQLUSER"
RESOURCEGROUPNAME="elz_prod"
LOCATION="eastus"
TEMPLATE_FILE="~/Data-Engineering-with-Apache-Spark-
Delta-Lake-and-Lakehouse/project/infra/azure_sql/azure_
sql.json"
az deployment group create --name Stores_Azure_
SQL_Database --resource-group $RESOURCEGROUPNAME
--template-file $TEMPLATE_FILE --parameters
vaultName=$VAULTNAME databaseName=$DATABASENAME
adminPasswordsecretName=$PASSWORDSECRETNAME
sqlServerName=$SERVERNAME
adminLoginUsersecretName=$USERSECRETNAME
vaultResourceGroupName=$RESOURCEGROUPNAME
```

4. Navigate to **Home | Resource group | elz_prod**. If the preceding commands are successful, you should be able to see a new SQL server and database created as follows:

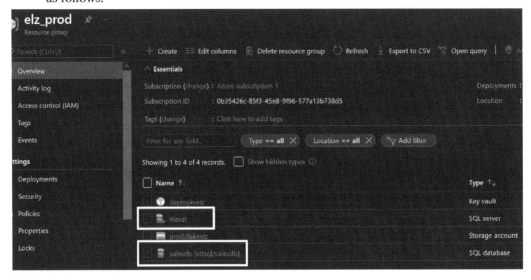

Figure 11.18 – Checking the creation of the Azure SQL database

5. It would be interesting to find out how the dynamic fetch of secrets was achieved within ARM.

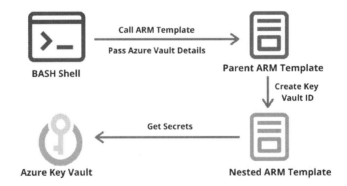

Figure 11.19 – Process of ARM fetching secrets from Azure Key Vault

ARM allows for the use of nested templates. Using the parameters passed from the command line (`vaultName`, `adminLoginUsersecretName`, `adminPasswordsecretName`), the parent template generates the Azure Key Vault resource ID for the secrets.

```
"adminLoginUser": {
  "reference": {
    "keyVault": {
      "id": "[resourceId(parameters('vaultSubscription'), parameters('vaultResourceGroupName'), 'Microsoft.KeyVault/vaults', parameters
    },
    "secretName": "[parameters('adminLoginUsersecretName')]"
  }
},
"adminPassword": {
  "reference": {
    "keyVault": {
      "id": "[resourceId(parameters('vaultSubscription'), parameters('vaultResourceGroupName'), 'Microsoft.KeyVault/vaults', parameters
    },
    "secretName": "[parameters('adminPasswordsecretName')]"
  }
}
```

Figure 11.20 – Parent ARM templates generating the Azure vault resource ID

These resource IDs are used by the nested template to retrieve the actual value of the secret from Azure Key Vault.

> **Important Note**
>
> On highly secure projects, it is not becoming a standard practice to hide production secrets from data engineers. In such cases, the secrets are created by the customer's security teams. Once created, these secrets are dynamically retrieved during runtime without exposing them to unauthorized entities.

Deploying multiple environments using IaC

In the previous section, we learned that once the IaC assets have been created by the DevOps team, they can be deployed repeatedly to create different environments, each time achieving consistent results.

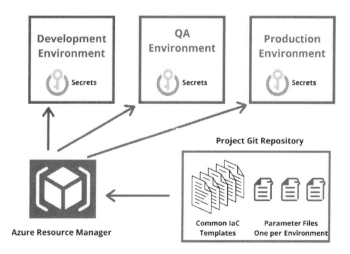

Figure 11.21 – Process of deploying multiple environments using IaC

Let's get started with the following steps:

1. If both of your templates worked as desired, there is no need to create the next set of resources one at a time. Let's do what the professionals do by running a script that will spin up the rest of the resources for us.

2. Here is what the deployment script (`electroniz_isc.sh`) looks like. There is a section for every Azure resource that is required to be created. Notice the use of the template file and parameter files in the deployment script. The paths for template and parameter files are sent as arguments to this script. This means we can reuse the same script to deploy multiple environments.

Figure 11.22 – IaC deployment script

3. It's the moment of truth. Invoke the following command in Azure Cloud Shell and watch it roll. The script will spin up the entire infrastructure in a matter of minutes. This is the magic of IaC. Make sure you replace the value of `<HOME_DIR>` in the following command as per your environment:

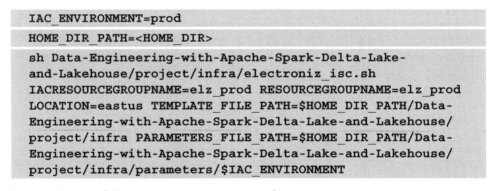

Notice the use of the `IAC_ENVIRONMENT` and `PARAMETERS_FILE_PATH` arguments in the preceding command can enforce the reusability aspect of the IaC scripts. To build multiple environments, you simply need to create one folder per environment in source control and reference it in the preceding command. Yet the ARM template files remain the same for every build. The following is an example `parameters` folder for the production environment:

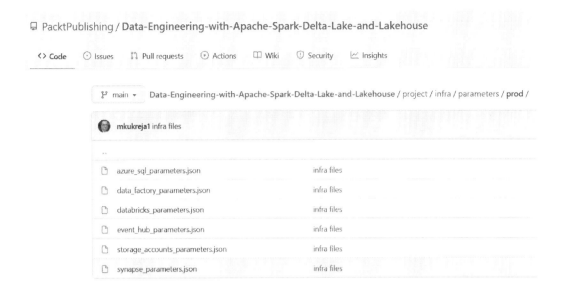

Figure 11.23 – IaC environment parameters

Sit back, relax, and let the deployment script do its job. The script will take a few minutes to complete.

4. It's time to verify whether the script has done what it was supposed to do.
    Let's check by navigating back to **Home | Resource group | elz_prod**.

Figure 11.24 – Listing Azure resources after deployment

5. The deployment script seems to have worked as desired. We can see several Azure resources deployed under the `ez_prod` resource group. Additionally, we can check the status of deployments by navigating to **Home | Resource group | elz_prod | Deployments**.

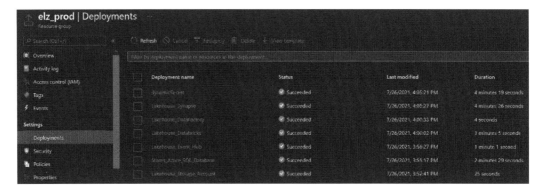

Figure 11.25 – Checking current deployments

Creating cloud resources using IaC is the first step toward faster, consistent, and repeatable deployments. The IaC process can be easily integrated with the existing enterprise software development cycle. In the long run, it has been proven not only to save time but also a lot of costs related to unnecessary repetition from using manual deployments.

However, a huge question is still left unanswered… *is being fast and consistent enough?* Like anything else, cloud resources and pipelines evolve with time. Without automation, we still need someone to invoke these scripts anytime there is a change. Wouldn't it be cool if changes were to be deployed automatically? We will explore what can be done regarding this in a future chapter.

Cleaning up Azure resources

Before leaving, make sure you clean up the `ez_prod` resource group using the following command. There is no point in leaving the resources hanging around and incurring a large bill at the end of the month:

```
RESOURCEGROUPNAME="elz_prod"
az group delete --name $RESOURCEGROUPNAME
```

This results in the following output:

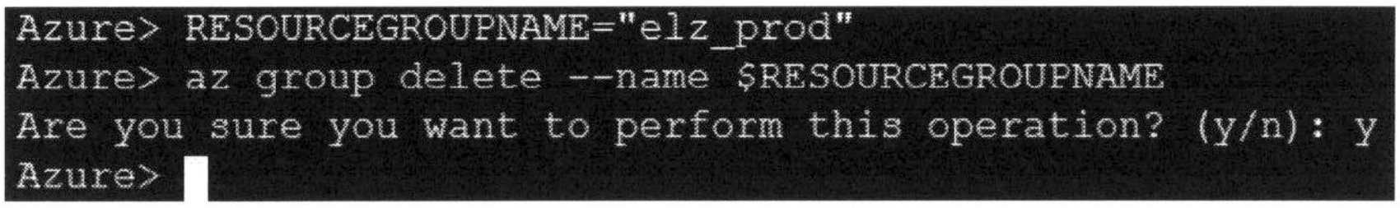

```
Azure> RESOURCEGROUPNAME="elz_prod"
Azure> az group delete --name $RESOURCEGROUPNAME
Are you sure you want to perform this operation? (y/n): y
Azure>
```

Figure 11.26 – Confirmation screen while deleting a resource group

Summary

In this chapter, we got our first taste of deploying cloud resources using the principle of IaC. The overall deployment process can be hugely accelerated using this principle. This process can be further improved and streamlined by introducing automation.

In the final chapter, *Chapter 12, Continuous Integration and Deployment (CI/CD) of Data Pipelines*, we will learn how to automate pipeline deployments. Using **CI/CD** is a hallmark practice of mature cloud deployments. CI/CD can dramatically accelerate code delivery while maintaining a high level of efficiency. In the next chapter, we will find out how to automate infrastructure deployment and code delivery using CI/CD.

12
Continuous Integration and Deployment (CI/CD) of Data Pipelines

Our data journey is finally approaching its destination. As the new era of analytics takes over, the demand for data engineers will continue to grow, and so will the amount of code that they will produce. The ever-increasing demand for developing, managing, and deploying large code sets is already testing the limits of modern data engineers.

Luckily, a modern trend is fast emerging that has the potential of taking a lot of burden off poor data engineers. In this chapter, we will learn about code delivery automation using CI/CD pipelines. In short, CI/CD is a collection of practices that's used to integrate and deliver code faster using small atomic changes.

In this chapter, we will cover the following topics:

- Understanding CI/CD
- Designing CI/CD pipelines
- Developing CI/CD pipelines

Understanding CI/CD

The process of data transformation is continuous. In every modern organization, the volume and variety of data is increasing at a very high pace. As a result, the need for creating new or modifying existing data pipelines is very high. This sudden growth in data pipeline code is testing the limits of the traditional software delivery cycle.

As a result, organizations are eagerly looking forward to adopting viable methods that can accelerate product delivery, using a combination of best practices and automation. After all, streamlining the software cycle creates a clear path to success. Before we try to understand how CI/CD works, there is merit in understanding the traditional software delivery cycle.

Traditional software delivery cycle

Before we start talking about the modern approach to software delivery, let's understand how the traditional method has worked so far:

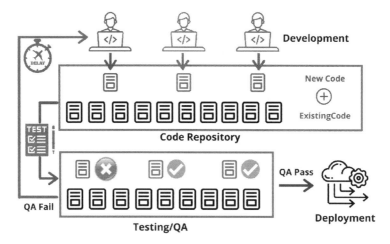

Figure 12.1 – Traditional software delivery cycle

The traditional software development process for a data pipeline typically undergoes the following phases:

- **Development**: In this phase, developers (data engineers) either create new pipelines or modify existing ones. Changes in existing pipelines may be attributed to schema evolution or changes in functionality. On completion, the developer merges their piece of code into the existing code repository. The same process is repeated by other developers who may be dealing with other pipelines.

- **Code Packaging**: On a pre-agreed schedule, likely at the end of the agile sprint cycle, the code package is released to QA for testing.

- **QA Deployment**: The release is deployed in the testing/QA environment.

- **Testing/QA**: The QA group performs testing for all new or modified code. If successful, the code is released for production deployment; otherwise, the release is rejected and put on hold until the pending bugs have been fixed.

- **Production Deployment**: All the code that passes QA is deployed to production.

Although **simple** by nature, there is an inherent **problem** with this process. In the preceding diagram, code sets from multiple developers are merged in the repository to formulate a **release**. During the quality assurance testing phase, code from all developers may successfully pass unit testing but fails one of them. Unfortunately, the entire release needs to be rejected due to the failure of only one code component. Cases like these can cause unnecessary **delays** and customer **dissatisfaction**. Needless to say, a better method needs to be devised.

Modern software delivery cycle

The theme of the modern software delivery process is very simple – **develop**, **test**, and **integrate** small pieces of code frequently. Using the practice of **continuous integration (CI)**, developers are encouraged to make small code adjustments, merge their code into the main code branch, and validate it by using automated tests. Doing this provides developers with a quick and easy feedback mechanism regarding inter-dependency between code components. It helps us detect errors quickly, making the lives of developers easier in many ways.

Once the code is successfully validated, the practice of **continuous deployment** (**CD**) automatically deploys the code to either the testing or production environment. Doing this provides a quick and easy feedback mechanism for developers regarding the **validity** of code in a particular environment:

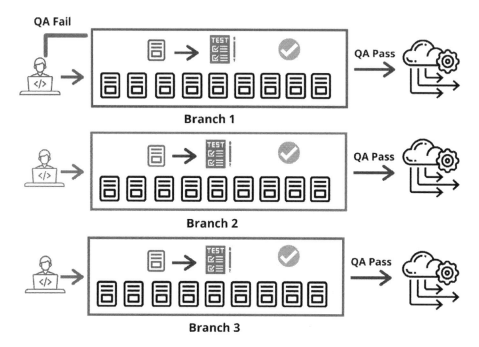

Figure 12.2 – Modern software delivery cycle

CI/CD is known to streamline and improve, as well as accelerate, software delivery. These days, it is common for organizations to follow the **DevOps** practice. DevOps promotes a culture shift, one that has a tight collaboration between the development and operation groups within an organization.

Traditionally, creating and managing CI/CD pipelines has been handled by the DevOps group. But with the changing landscape of the industry, data engineers are being strongly **encouraged** (more like mandated) to add this skill set to their existing job profiles. As a result, it is now becoming increasingly important for data engineers to carry some DevOps skills.

> **Important**
>
> DevOps, short for **Developer** and **Operations**, is a practice that aims to accelerate software delivery using a combination of tools, best practices, and automation.

There are several DevOps tools available that can implement CI/CD pipelines, such as **Jenkins**, **Chef**, and **CircleCI**. **Azure DevOps** is the native SaaS platform in Azure that supports modern developers with planning, inter-team collaboration, and seamless delivery of code. In this chapter, we are going to use Azure DevOps to create CI/CD pipelines.

Designing CI/CD pipelines

Before we deep dive into the actual development and implementation of CI/CD pipelines, we should try to design their layout. In typical data analytics projects, the focus of development revolves around two key areas:

- **Infrastructure Deployment**: As discussed in the previous chapter, these days, it is recommended to perform cloud deployments using the **Infrastructure as Code (IaC)** practice. Infrastructure code used to be developed by DevOps engineers, although recently, data engineers are being asked to share this responsibility.

- **Data Pipelines**: The development of data pipelines is likely handled entirely by data engineers. The code that's developed includes functionality to perform data collection, ingestion, curation, aggregations, governance, and distribution.

Following the continuous development, integration, and deployment principles, the recommended approach is to create two CI/CD pipelines that we will refer to as the **Electroniz infrastructure CI/CD pipeline** and **Electroniz code CI/CD pipeline**.

> **Important**
>
> Adopting CI/CD is more of a cultural shift than a technical one. Before implementation, it is essential to seek the confidence of the development team and senior management.

At a high level, the **Electroniz infrastructure CI/CD pipeline** will be utilized for deploying Azure resources such as Azure Key Vault, Azure Data Lake Storage, and Azure Synapse. Typically, the core responsibility of creating and managing this pipeline lies with the DevOps group.

The **Electroniz code CI/CD pipeline** will be used to deploy pieces of code such as SQL scripts, data factory pipelines, and Spark notebooks. In all likelihood, the core responsibility of creating and managing this pipeline lies with the data engineering group.

Having both these pipelines running under the same workspace promotes collaboration between the DevOps and data engineering teams. Instead of working in their independent shell, it allows both teams to work together, share ideas, and, most importantly, grow their **skill set**. These two pipelines are depicted in the following diagram:

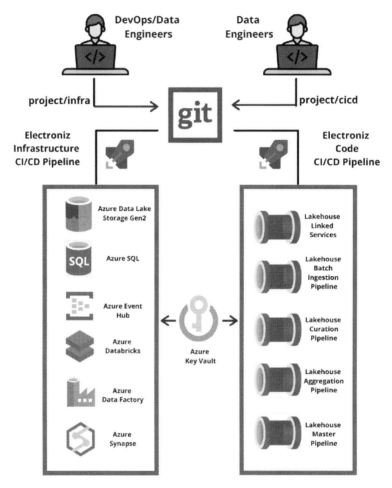

Figure 12.3 – Recommended design of CI/CD pipelines

Important

In the preceding diagram, notice how both pipelines store and fetch **secrets** from a common Azure Key Vault. Securely storing secrets such as database passwords and API keys at creation time and dynamically fetching them at runtime goes a long way in controlling unauthorized exposures.

The Electroniz infrastructure CI/CD pipeline

DevOps/data engineers will develop code to spin up the necessary Azure resources required for the Electroniz lakehouse. You may recall that in *Chapter 11*, *Infrastructure Provisioning*, we used IaC to spin up the infrastructure. That was one step in the right direction but still not automated enough. In this chapter, we will learn how to automate the deployment process using the same set of code we created previously. The following is the structure of the code for the infrastructure pipeline:

main
Data-Engineering-with-Apache-Spark-Delta-Lake-and-Lakehouse / project / infra /
Go to file
Add file
mkukreja1 changes to deployment files
69bc2af 2 days ago
History
azure_sql infra files 11 days ago
data_factory infra files 11 days ago
databricks infra files 11 days ago
event_hubs infra files 11 days ago
keyvault infra files 16 days ago
parameters/prod changes to deployment files 3 days ago
storage_accounts infra files 11 days ago
synapse changes to deployment files 2 days ago
azure-infra-pipeline.yml changes to deployment files 3 days ago
electroniz_isc.sh changes to deployment files 3 days ago

Figure 12.4 – The code structure of the Electroniz infrastructure CI/CD pipeline

Let's take a look at this structure in more detail:

- **azure-infra-pipelines.yml**: This file contains the configuration of the Azure resources, defined in stages. Each stage creates a new resource by referencing the JSON file in each resource folder.
- **Azure resource folders**: Each resource folder contains the definition of the resource defined as a JSON file.
- **Parameters**: The global parameters for resources such as names, locations, and the environment are stored in the **electroniz_infra_variables** variable group in the Azure DevOps pipeline library.

The Electroniz code CI/CD pipeline

Data engineers develop code to implement the various stages of the data pipeline. This is done using a variety of development tools, including Azure Data Factory, Azure Synapse SQL scripts, and Databricks Spark notebooks. Progressively, all this code is integrated and deployed on different environments using the code CI/CD pipeline:

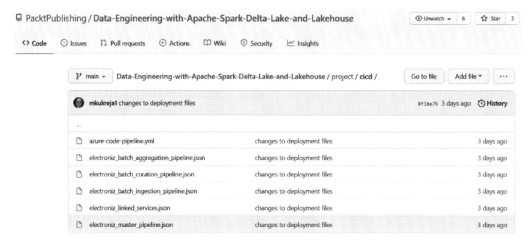

Figure 12.5 – The code structure of the Electroniz code CI/CD pipeline

Let's take a look at this structure in more detail:

- **azure-code-pipelines.yml**: This file contains the configuration of the Azure data pipelines, defined in stages. Each stage deploys code using a JSON file.

- **Pipeline JSON files**: These files contain the definitions of each pipeline as a separate file stored in JSON format.

- **Parameters**: The global parameters for resources such as names, locations, and the environment are stored under the **electroniz_code_variables** variable group in the Azure DevOps pipeline library.

Both these pipelines work independently of each other. **Azure Pipeline** includes functionality to trigger independent pipelines using path include switches in the deployment files. Using this approach, multiple teams can concurrently develop code simultaneously, without interfering or depending on other teams.

With this understanding, we are now ready to start developing CI/CD pipelines.

Developing CI/CD pipelines

In this section, we will learn how to create and deploy the two CI/CD pipelines we mentioned previously. We will create these CI/CD pipelines using **Azure DevOps**. Azure DevOps is a collection of developer services for planning, collaborating, developing, and deploying code. Although Azure DevOps supports a variety of developer services, for this exercise, we will primarily focus on **Azure Repos** and **Azure Pipelines**.

I know we are eager to proceed with creating the pipelines, but there is a fair bit of preparation required before we can get started. The process starts with creating the Azure DevOps organization, which can be done in a few simple steps. However, to use the free tier of Azure Pipelines, you need to fill in a **free parallelism request form** for your newly created Azure DevOps organization. The approval process may take 2-3 days to complete.

Creating an Azure DevOps organization

Follow these steps to create an Azure DevOps organization:

1. Connect to the Azure portal. Search for `Azure DevOps` and click on **Azure DevOps Organizations**:

Figure 12.6 – Azure DevOps Organizations main page

2. Now, click on **My Azure DevOps Organizations**. This will open a new
    browser window:

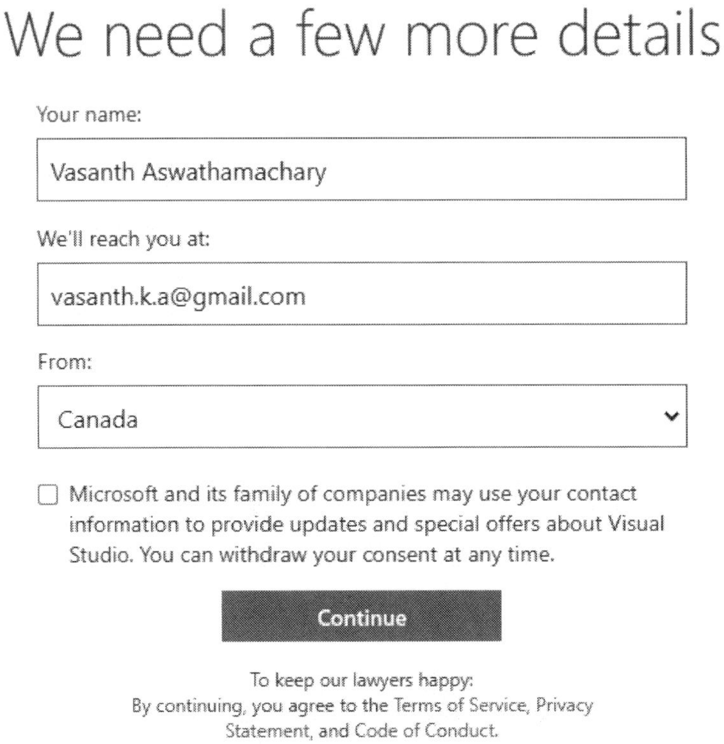

We need a few more details

Your name:

Vasanth Aswathamachary

We'll reach you at:

vasanth.k.a@gmail.com

From:

Canada ⌄

☐ Microsoft and its family of companies may use your contact
information to provide updates and special offers about Visual
Studio. You can withdraw your consent at any time.

Continue

To keep our lawyers happy:
By continuing, you agree to the Terms of Service, Privacy
Statement, and Code of Conduct.

Figure 12.7 – Details of the new Azure DevOps organization

Fill in your details and press **Continue**.

3. Click on **Create new organization**:

Get started with Azure DevOps

Plan better, code together, ship faster with Azure DevOps

Create new organization

Figure 12.8 – Creating a new Azure DevOps organization

4. You will be presented with the **Get started with Azure DevOps** window:

Figure 12.9 – Getting started with a new Azure DevOps organization

Click **Continue**.

5. On the next screen, enter details for **Name your Azure DevOps organization** and choose the region that's the closest to you:

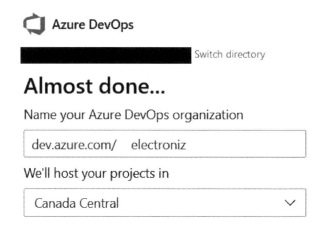

Figure 12.10 – Naming the new Azure DevOps organization

Add **Captcha** and click **Continue**.

6. Provide a **Project name**

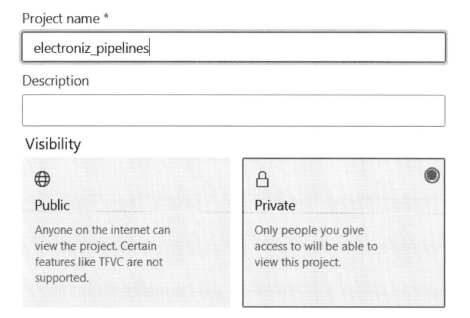

Figure 12.11 – Creating a new project in the new Azure DevOps organization

Click on + **Create project**.

7. The home screen for the new project should look like this:

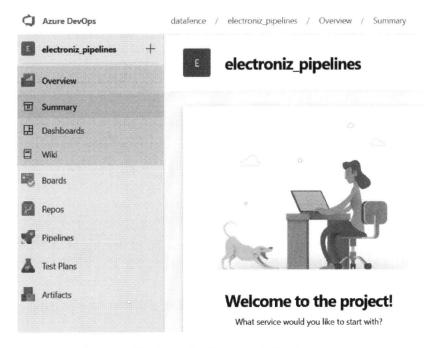

Figure 12.12 – Azure DevOps organization home screen

8. At the bottom-left corner of the screen, click on **Project Settings** > **Service connections**:

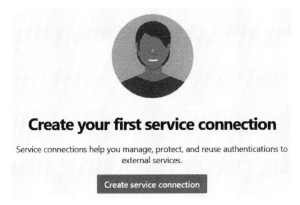

Figure 12.13 – Creating a new service connection

Click on **Create service connection**.

9. Choose **Azure Resource Manager** and click **Next**:

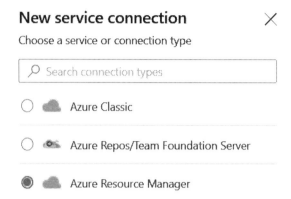

Figure 12.14 – Choosing the connection type of the new service connection

10. On the **New Azure service connection** screen, choose **Service principal (automatic)** and click **Next**:

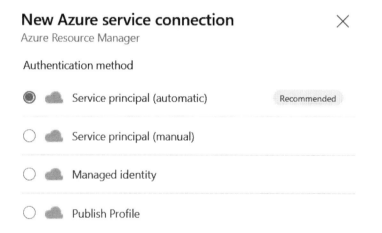

Figure 12.15 – Choosing the authentication method of the new service connection

11. On the **New Azure service connection** page, choose **Subscription**. The **Subscription** box should refresh automatically and show you the Azure subscription in use. Provide a value for **Service connection name** and click **Next**:

New Azure service connection   ✕

Azure Resource Manager using service principal (automatic)

Scope level

⦿ Subscription

◯ Management Group

◯ Machine Learning Workspace

Subscription

| Azure subscription 1 (0b35426c-85f3-45e8-9f96-577a13b738... ⌄ |

Resource group

| ⌄ |

Details

Service connection name

| electroniz_connection |

Description (optional)

| |

Figure 12.16 – Naming the new service connection

Click on **Save**.

12. The Azure service connection confirmation screen should look like this:

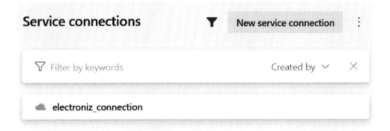

Figure 12.17 – New service connection confirmation

13. Now, we need to import the **Packt** Git repository.

Using the menu on the left, click on **Repos**.

Under **Import a repository**, click on the **Import** button. Provide the following values:

- **Repository type**: Git

- **Clone URL**: https://github.com/PacktPublishing/Data-Engineering-with-Apache-Spark-Delta-Lake-and-Lakehouse:

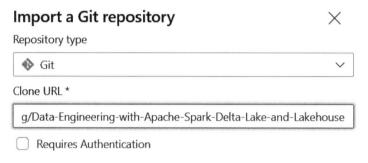

Figure 12.18 – Importing the Packt Git repository

14. Click on **Import**. After a few seconds, the project's Packt Git repository will be imported, as shown here:

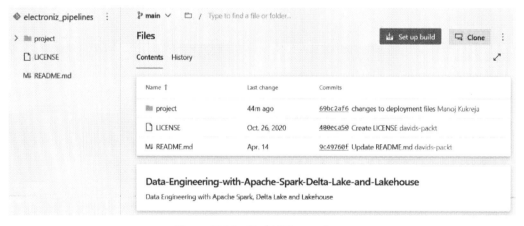

Figure 12.19 – Packt Git repository

15. You can use the free tier of Azure DevOps for this exercise. After creating the new Azure DevOps organization, you need to fill in the **free parallelism request form** by going to

https://aka.ms/azpipelines-parallelism-request:

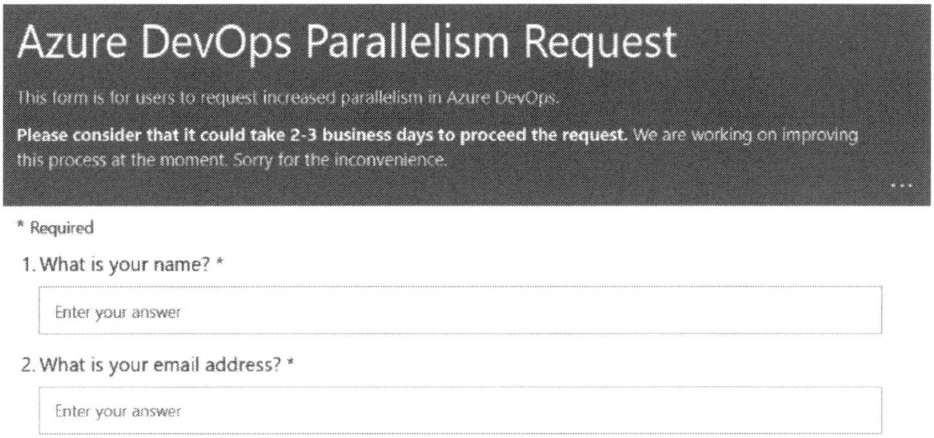

Azure DevOps Parallelism Request

This form is for users to request increased parallelism in Azure DevOps.

Please consider that it could take 2-3 business days to proceed the request. We are working on improving this process at the moment. Sorry for the inconvenience.

. . .

* Required

1. What is your name? *

> Enter your answer

2. What is your email address? *

> Enter your answer

Figure 12.20 – Azure DevOps Parallelism Request page

Please note that it may take Azure 2-3 business days to review and respond to your request. Once your request has been approved, you will get an email, like this:

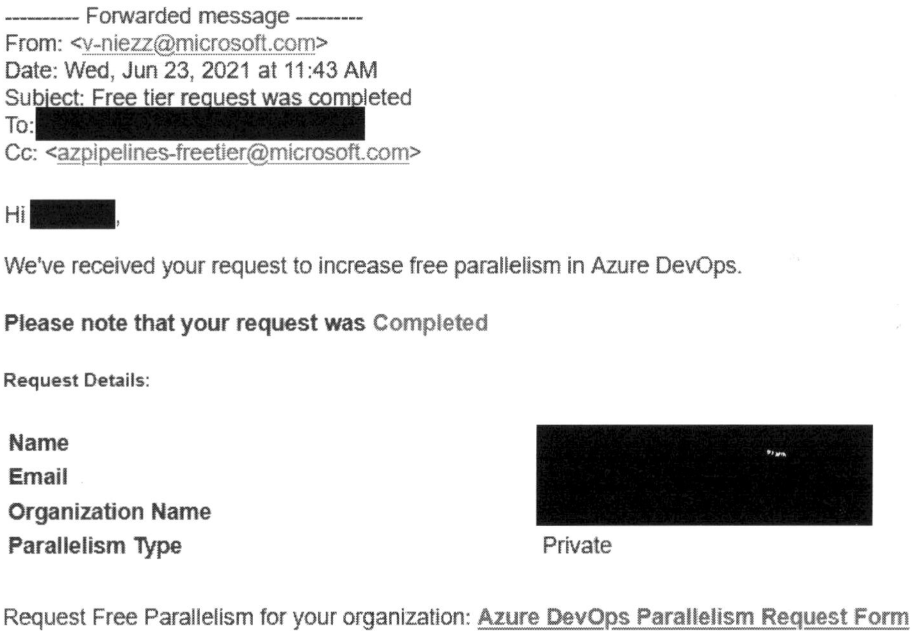

---------- Forwarded message ---------
From: <v-niezz@microsoft.com>
Date: Wed, Jun 23, 2021 at 11:43 AM
Subject: Free tier request was completed
To: ███████████████████
Cc: <azpipelines-freetier@microsoft.com>

Hi ██████,

We've received your request to increase free parallelism in Azure DevOps.

Please note that your request was Completed

Request Details:

Name	
Email	
Organization Name	
Parallelism Type	Private

Request Free Parallelism for your organization: **Azure DevOps Parallelism Request Form**

Figure 12.21 – Azure DevOps parallelism request confirmation email

Once you've received this email, you can start creating the necessary CI/CD pipelines.

Creating the Electroniz infrastructure CI/CD pipeline

Finally, we can start developing our first CI/CD pipeline. For obvious reasons, we have chosen to develop the infrastructure pipeline first. The reason for this is that the code pipeline directly depends on the Azure resources that are created by the infrastructure pipelines. Let's get started:

1. You may recall that the recommended pipeline design included an Azure Key Vault to store the secrets for the CI/CD pipelines. Run the following commands in Azure Cloud Shell to create one:

```
RESOURCEGROUPNAME="elz_prod"
LOCATION="eastus"
IAC_ENVIRONMENT=prod
KEYVAULTNAME="deploykvelz"
az group create --name $RESOURCEGROUPNAME --location
$LOCATION
az keyvault purge -n $KEYVAULTNAME
az config set extension.use_dynamic_install=yes_without_
prompt
az keyvault create --location $LOCATION --name
$KEYVAULTNAME --resource-group $RESOURCEGROUPNAME
--enabled-for-template-deployment true
```

2. We will now add a couple of secrets to the newly created Azure Key Vault. Using the Azure portal, navigate to **Home** > **Resource groups** > **elz_prod** > **deploykvelz**.

    Click on **Secrets**. Then, create two new secrets using **Generate/Import**, as follows:

    - **Name**: SQLUSER **Value**: salesadmin

    - **Name**: SQLPASSWORD **Value**: <password for Azure SQL
      administrator>:

Figure 12.22 – Creating secrets in the deploykvelz Azure Key Vault

> **Important**
>
> Notice that in the preceding step, we forced ourselves to create the secrets manually. The process of creating secrets in the Azure Key Vault can easily be scripted, but then you will need to go against best practices and store passwords in configuration files.

3. Click the **Pipelines** menu on the left and choose **Library**:

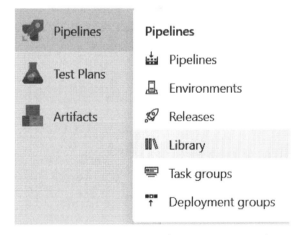

Figure 12.23 – Navigating to Library in Azure Pipelines

4.   Create a **New variable group**:

New variable group

Create groups of variables that you can share
across multiple pipelines.

Learn more about variable groups. ⌞⌝

Figure 12.24 – Creating a new variable group in Azure Pipelines

Click + **Variable group**.

5.   Create a new variable group using the following details:

- **Variable group name**: electroniz_infra_variables

- **Description**: These variables are used by the infrastructure
deployment files

Now, add the following variables each time by pressing the + **Add** button:

- **Name**: DATABRICKS_WORKSPACE_NAME **Value**: elzdbws

- **Name**: DATAFACTORY_NAME **Value**: elzdf

- **Name**: ENVIRONMENT **Value**: prod

- **Name**: EVENTHUB_CONTAINER **Value**: ecommlogs

- **Name**: EVENTHUB_NAME **Value**: esaleshub

- **Name**: EVENTHUB_NAMESPACE **Value**: esalesns

- **Name**: EVENTHUB_STORAGE_ACCOUNT **Value**: elzlogs

- **Name**: EVENTHUB_SUBSCRIPTION **Value**: esalesevent

- **Name**: EVENTHUB_TOPIC_NAME **Value**: esales

- **Name**: KEY_VAULT_NAME **Value**: deploykvelz

- **Name**: KEY_VAULT_RESOURCE_GROUP **Value**: elz_prod
- **Name**: LAKEHOUSE_BRONZE_LAYER **Value**: bronze
- **Name**: LAKEHOUSE_SILVER_LAYER **Value**: silver
- **Name**: LAKEHOUSE_GOLD_LAYER **Value**: gold
- **Name**: LAKEHOUSE_STORAGE_ACCOUNT **Value**: elz
- **Name**: PROJECT **Value**: dlake

In many cases, Azure resource names are globally unique. Try to make the project name as unique as possible. Since a lot of you will be using the same instructions, having uniqueness will eliminate unnecessary errors related to unique resource names.

Now add the following variables:

- **Name**: REGION **Value**: East US
- **Name**: RESOURCE_GROUP **Value**: elz_prod
- **Name**: SERVICE_CONNECTION **Value**: electroniz_connection

Make sure the following entries match with the **service connection** you created previously:

- **Name**: SQL_DB_NAME **Value**: salesdb
- **Name**: SQL_PASSWORD_SECRET **Value**: SQLPASSWORD

> **Important**
>
> Note that this parameter is not the actual password; it is simply the name of the password secret that's stored in the Azure Key Vault we created previously.

- **Name**: SQL_SERVERNAME **Value**: elzsql
- **Name**: SQL_USERNAME_SECRET **Value**: SQLUSER
- **Name**: SQL_USERNAME **Value**: salesadmin
- **Name**: SUBSCRIPTION_ID **Value**: XXXXX-XXX-XXX-XXX-XXXXXXXX

To fetch the value of **SUBSCRIPTION_ID**, use the Azure portal and navigate to **Home** > **Subscriptions**. Take note of the Subscription ID and use it here, like so:

- **Name**: SYNAPSE_WORKSPACE_NAME **Value**: elzsyn

Click **Save**:

Library > ⬚ electroniz_infra_variables

Variable group | 🖫 Save   🗗 Clone   ♡ Security   ♡ Pipeline permissions

Properties

Variable group name

electroniz_infra_variables

Description

These variables are used by the infrastructure deployment files

🔘   Link secrets from an Azure key vault as variables   ⓘ

Variables

Name ↑	Value
DATABRICKS_WORKSPACE_NAME	elzdbws
DATAFACTORY_NAME	elzdf
ENVIRONMENT	prod
EVENTHUB_CONTAINER	ecommlogs

Figure 12.25 – The electroniz_infra_variables variable group in Azure Pipelines

6. We are now ready to create the infrastructure pipeline. Using the menu on the left, click on **Pipelines**:

Create your first Pipeline

Automate your build and release processes using our wizard, and go from code to cloud-hosted within minutes.

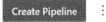

Figure 12.26 – Creating a new Azure pipeline

Click on **Create Pipeline**.

7. At this point, you will see the **Where is your code?** screen:

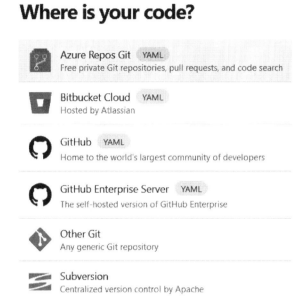

Figure 12.27 – Configuring the code repository for the Azure pipeline

Choose **Azure Repos Git**.

8. You will now see the **Select a repository** screen:

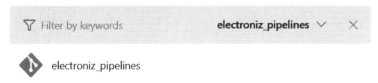

Figure 12.28 – Selecting the code repository for the Azure pipeline

Click on **electroniz_pipelines**.

9. Next up is the **Configure your pipeline** screen:

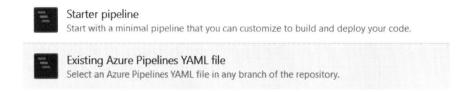

Figure 12.29 – Choosing an existing YAML file for the Azure pipeline

Choose **Existing Azure Pipelines YAML File**.

10. On the **Select an existing YAML file** screen, provide the following values:

- **Branch**: `main`

- Click on **Path**; the value will be auto-populated: `/project/infra/azure-infra-pipeline.yml`:

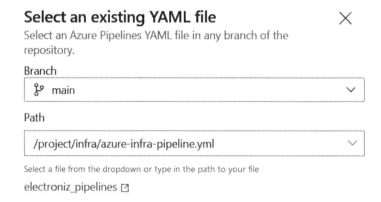

Figure 12.30 – Choosing the infrastructure YAML file for the Azure pipeline

Click on **Continue**.

11. On the **Review your pipeline YAML** screen, you should see the following:

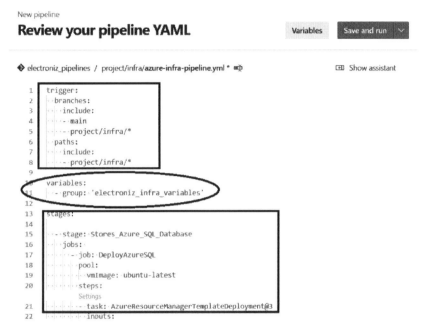

Figure 12.31 – Anatomy of the infrastructure YAML file

Let's briefly look at the structure of the YAML file:

- **Trigger**: Specifies the branch that will be invoked for CI/CD.

- **Variables**: Configuration data for the CI/CD pipeline. This can be pointed to a named group of variables in a library.

- **Stage, Job, and Steps**: A collection of jobs that are run sequentially. A job is a series of steps, and steps are the actual tasks and scripts that do a certain function.

Click on the arrow beside the **Save and run** button and click **Save**.

12. Using the menu on the left, click on **Pipelines**. Toward the right-hand side of the screen, click on the three dots and click **Rename/move**:

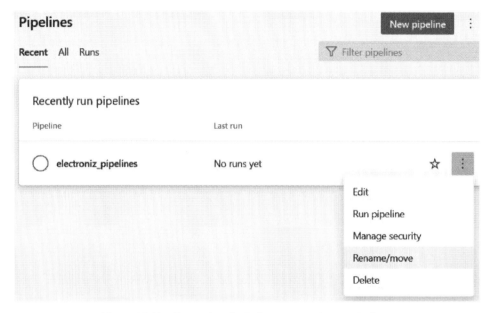

Figure 12.32 – Renaming the infrastructure Azure pipeline

13. Change the name of the pipeline, as follows:

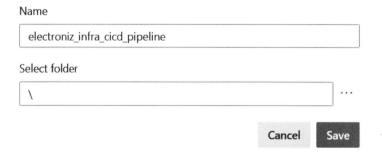

Figure 12.33 – Naming the infrastructure Azure pipeline

Click on **Save**.

14. Click on the three dots once again but this time, click **Run pipeline**:

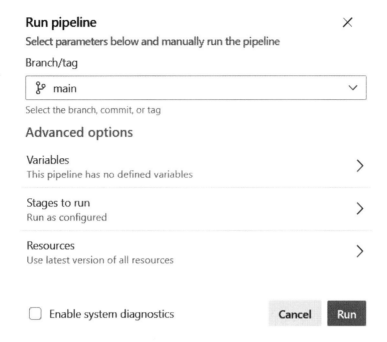

Figure 12.34 – Running the infrastructure Azure pipeline

Click on **Run**.

15. **electroniz_infra_cicd_pipeline** will now be triggered:

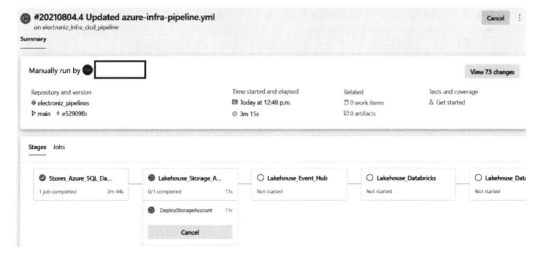

Figure 12.35 – Triggering the infrastructure Azure pipeline

16. Monitor the pipeline as it goes through the various stages of infrastructure deployment:

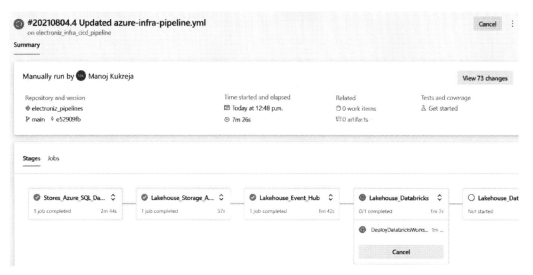

Figure 12.36 – Monitoring the infrastructure Azure pipeline

17. On completion of the CI/CD pipeline, check the status of all the stages, as follows. A green checkmark for each stage means that the job is done:

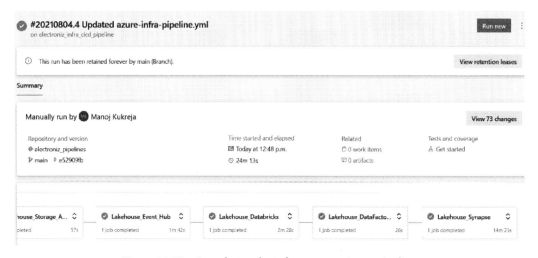

Figure 12.37 – Completing the infrastructure Azure pipeline

18. In another tab on your browser, navigate to the Azure portal by going to **Home** > **Resource Groups** > **elz_prod**.

Notice the creation of Azure resources while the pipeline is **running**. You may need to refresh the browser window multiple times to check for new items:

Figure 12.38 – Confirmation of the resources that were created by the infrastructure Azure pipeline

19. Eventually, after the pipeline finishes, the pipeline window will look like this:

Figure 12.39 – Completion confirmation of the infrastructure Azure pipeline

20. So far, so good. However, you may have noticed that we triggered this CI/CD pipeline manually. Triggering pipelines manually is only acceptable in development and testing mode. In production, we should aim to trigger pipelines **automatically**.

21. In the next few steps, we are going to edit the existing template so that code changes are automatically applied as soon as the code gets committed to the main branch.

You may recall that as part of **electroniz_infra_cicd_pipeline**, we created an Azure Data Lake account. Notice the three tags that were implemented originally:

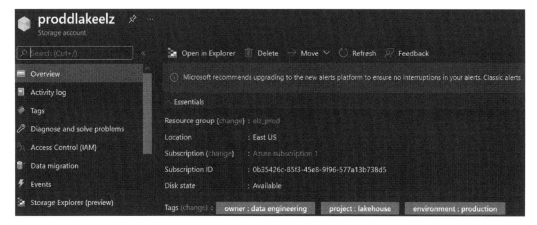

Figure 12.40 – Tags information of the proddlakeelz Azure Data Lake Storage account

To simulate a code change, we are going to edit the **storage_accounts.json** template file and add a new tag.

Navigate to **Repos** > **project** > **infra** > **storage_accounts** > **storage_accounts.json**.

Add a new tag called `"group":"finance"`, like so:

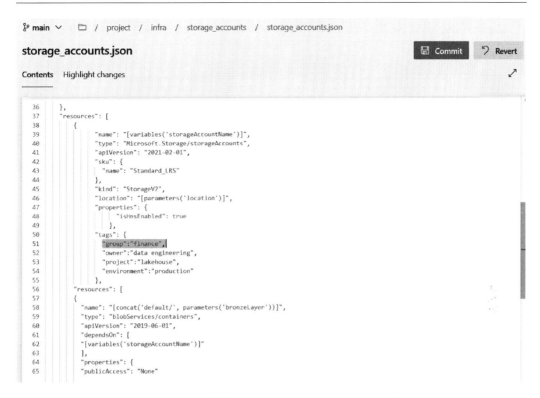

Figure 12.41 – Adding a new tag in storage_accounts.json

Click on **Commit**:

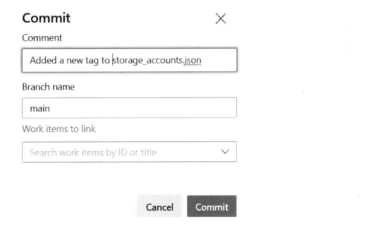

Figure 12.42 – Committing storage_accounts.json

Once again, click on **Commit**.

22. Now, navigate back to **Pipelines**. This time, **electroniz_infra_cicd_pipeline** should auto-trigger. The CI/CD pipeline should only pick up the incremental changes from last time and apply them to the Azure resources:

Figure 12.43 - electroniz_infra_cicd_pipeline auto-trigger

You will then see the confirmation of the newly added tag after deployment:

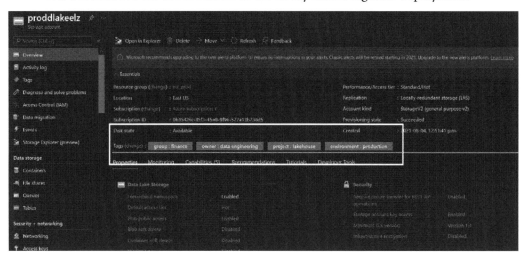

Figure 12.44 – Confirmation of the newly added tag after deployment

With that, we can celebrate – the first CI/CD pipeline is working as desired! From here on, incremental changes to the Azure resources can be automatically pushed to Azure. Our focus moves to the second pipeline now.

Creating the Electroniz code CI/CD pipeline

Now that the base resources have been created by the infrastructure pipeline, we can kickstart the development of the code pipeline. This process is very similar to the infrastructure pipelines we created previously, but with one exception: while creating the code pipeline, we will learn how the process of **building**, **approving**, **deploying**, and **merging** code works:

1. During the development of the **Electroniz** pipelines, we created a few additional secrets to store storage account keys. We are going to start by adding them to the existing Azure Key Vault:

    ```
    STORAGEACCOUNTNAME="proddlakeelz"
    az storage account keys list --account-name
    $STORAGEACCOUNTNAME
    ```

    If the preceding commands worked as desired, you should see two storage keys. Take note of the value of `key1` here:

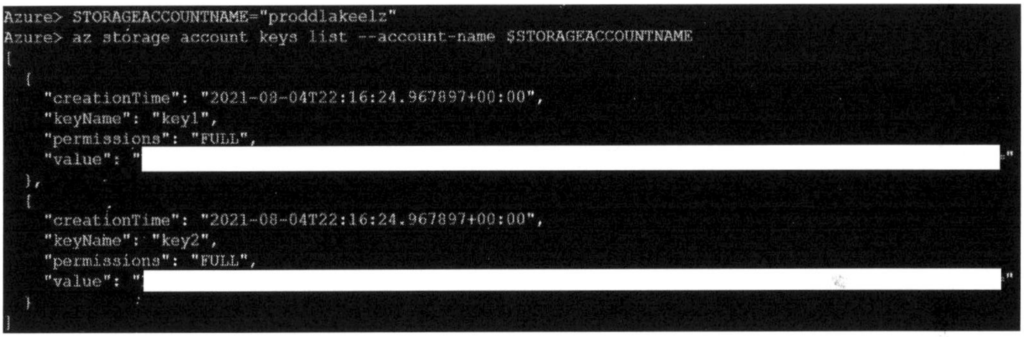

Figure 12.45 – Azure storage account keys

Browse to **Home** > **All Resources** > **proddlakeelz**.

Using the menu on the left, click on **Shared access signature.**

Input the options shown in the following screenshot:

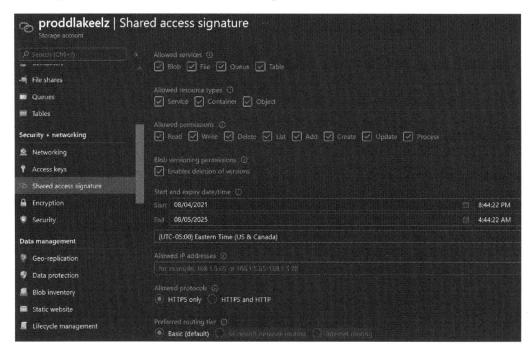

Figure 12.46 – Create options for the Azure storage account SAS token

Click on **Generate SAS and connection string**.

Take note of the **SAS token** value, as shown in the following screenshot:

Figure 12.47 – Azure storage account SAS token

2. We will now add secrets to the newly created Azure Key Vault. Using the Azure portal, navigate to **Home** > **Resource groups** > **clz_prod** > **dcploykvclz**.

    Click on **Secrets**. Then, create two new secrets using **Generate/Import**, like so:

    ▪ **Name**: ADLSKEY **Value**: Use the value of key1 from the preceding command

    ▪ **Name**: ADLSSASKEY **Value**: Use the value of SAS token from the preceding command:

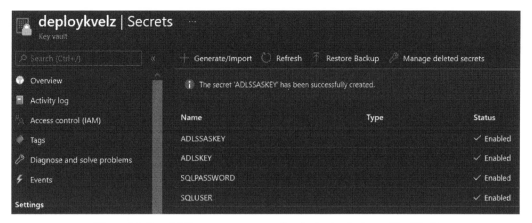

Figure 12.48 – Adding new secrets to the deploykvelz Azure Key Vault

3. As a strong security measure, we want to reference **Secret Identifier** (and not the secret itself) in the code. For that, we need to note down the secret identifiers for **ADLSKEY** and **ADLSSASKEY**, as follows:

    - **ADLSKEY Secret Identifier**: Navigate to **Home** > **Resource groups** > **elz_prod** > **deploykvelz** > **elz_prod** > **ADLSKEY**. Click on the entry under **CURRENT VERSION** and take note of the **Secret Identifier** property:

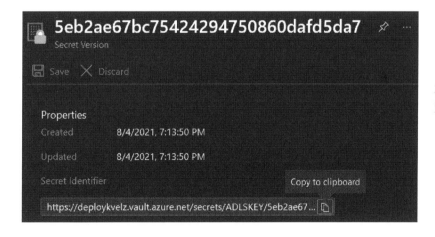

Figure 12.49 – Fetching the secret identifier for ADLSKEY

- **ADLSSASKEY Secret Identifier**: Navigate to **Home** > **Resource groups** > **elz_prod** > **deploykvelz** > **elz_prod** > **ADLSSASKEY**. Click on the entry under **CURRENT VERSION** and take note of the **Secret Identifier** property:

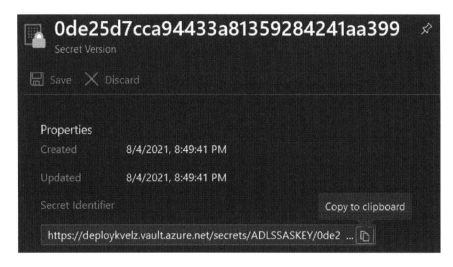

Figure 12.50 – Fetching the secret identifier for ADLSSASKEY

4. Click on the **Pipelines** menu on the left and choose **Library**:

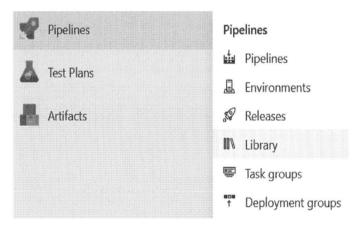

Figure 12.51 – Navigating to Library in Azure Pipelines

Click on + **Variable group**.

5. Create a new variable group using the following details:

- **Variable group name**: `electroniz_code_variables`
- **Description**: `These variables are used by the code deployment files`

Now, add the following variables each time by pressing the **+ Add** button:

- **Name**: `ADLS_SAS_SECRET`
- **Value**: `ADLSSASKEY Secret Identifier +?api-version=7.0`

Example:

`https://deploykvelz.vault.azure.net/secrets/ADLSSASKEY/a1a9e84038e548c0a3a03c6d696c4dc3?api-version=7.0`

- Name: `ADLS_SECRET`
- Value: `ADLSKEY Secret Identifier +?api-version=7.0`

Example:

`https://deploykvelz.vault.azure.net/secrets/ADLSKEY/0de25d7cca94433a81359284241aa399?api-version=7.0`

- **Name**: `CURATION_CLUSTER` **Value**: `Curation Spark Cluster`
- **Name**: `DATABRICKS_CLUSTER` **Value**: `curationcluster`
- **Name**: `DATABRICKS_NAME`
- **Value**: `https://adb-7285613526976736.16.azuredatabricks.net`

The value of this parameter can be fetched from the Azure Databricks workspace page. To do so, go to **Home** > **Resource groups** > **elz_prod** > **prod-dlake-elzdbws**:

- **Name**: `DATAFACTORY_NAME` **Value**: `prod-dlake-elzdf`
- **Name**: `KEY_VAULT_NAME` **Value**: `deploykvelz`
- **Name**: `LAKEHOUSE_GOLD_LAYER` **Value**: `gold`
- **Name**: `LAKEHOUSE_HTTP_LINK`
- **Value**: `https://raw.githubusercontent.com/mkukreja1/datafenceazure/master/datafactory/prep/iplocation/IP2LOCATION-LITE-DB1.CSV`
- **Name**: `LAKEHOUSE_HTTPSOURCE` **Value**: `httpsource`
- **Name**: `LAKEHOUSE_RESTSOURCE` **Value**: `restsource`

- **Name**: LAKEHOUSE_SALESDBSOURCE **Value**: salesdbsource
- **Name**: LAKEHOUSE_SOURCE **Value**: traininglakehouse
- **Name**: LAKEHOUSE_STORAGE_ACCOUNT **Value**: proddlakeelz
- **Name**: LAKEHOUSE_WEBTRACKING **Value**: proddlakeelzlogs
- **Name**: REGION **Value**: East US
- **Name**: RESOURCE_GROUP **Value**: elz_prod
- **Name**: SERVICE_CONNECTION **Value**: electroniz_connection
- **Name**: SPARK_CLUSTER_TOKEN **Value**: XXXXXXXXXXXXXXXXXXXXXX

You may recall that we created this token while developing the silver layer. For more information regarding creating the access token, you may refer to *Chapter 7, Data Curation Stage – The Silver Layer*:

- **Name**: SQL_CON_STRING **Value**: elzsql.database.windows.net
- **Name**: SQL_DATABASE **Value**: salesdb
- **Name**: SUBSCRIPTION_ID **Value**: XXXXX-XXX-XXX-XXX-XXXXXXXX

To fetch the value of **SUBSCRIPTION_ID**, use the Azure portal and navigate to **Home** > **Subscriptions**. Note down the subscription ID and use it here:

- **Name**: SYNAPSE_CON_STRING
- **Value**: elzsyn-ondemand.sql.azuresynapse.net

Click on **Save**:

Library > 🖾 electroniz_code_variables

Variable group   🖫 Save   🗗 Clone   ♡ Security   ♡ Pipeline permissions   🗒 Approvals and checks   ⑦ Help

Properties

Variable group name

electroniz_code_variables

Description

These variables are used by the code deployment files

(●) Link secrets from an Azure key vault as variables   ⓘ

Variables

Name ↑	Value	🔒
ADLS_SAS_SECRET	https://deploykvelz.vault.azure.net/secrets/ADLSSASKEY/0de25d7cca94...	
ADLS_SECRET	https://deploykvelz.vault.azure.net/secrets/ADLSKEY/0de25d7cca94433...	
CURATION_CLUSTER	Curation Spark Cluster	
DATABRICKS_CLUSTER	https://adb-7285613526976736.16.azuredatabricks.net	
DATAFACTORY_NAME	prod-dlake-elzdf	

Figure 12.52 – The electroniz_code_variables variable group in Azure Pipelines

6. We are now ready to create the code pipeline. Using the menu on the left, click on **Pipelines**, and then click on **New Pipeline**.

7. You will see the **Where is your code?** screen:

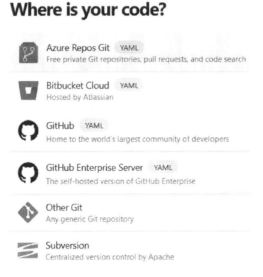

New pipeline

Where is your code?

Azure Repos Git YAML
Free private Git repositories, pull requests, and code search

Bitbucket Cloud YAML
Hosted by Atlassian

GitHub YAML
Home to the world's largest community of developers

GitHub Enterprise Server YAML
The self-hosted version of GitHub Enterprise

Other Git
Any generic Git repository

Subversion
Centralized version control by Apache

Figure 12.53 – Configuring the code repository for the Azure pipeline

Choose **Azure Repos Git**.

8. You will now see the **Select a repository** screen:

Select a repository

    electroniz_pipelines

Figure 12.54 – Selecting the code repository for the Azure pipeline

Click on **electroniz_pipelines**.

9. Now, you will be taken to the **Configure your pipeline** screen:

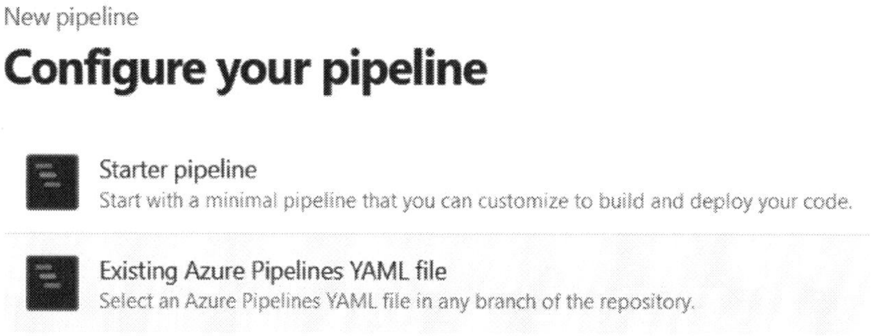

New pipeline

Configure your pipeline

Starter pipeline
Start with a minimal pipeline that you can customize to build and deploy your code.

Existing Azure Pipelines YAML file
Select an Azure Pipelines YAML file in any branch of the repository.

Figure 12.55 – Choosing an existing YAML file for the Azure pipeline

Choose **Existing Azure Pipelines YAML File**.

10. On the **Select an existing YAML file** screen, provide the following values:

- **Branch**: `main`

- Click on **Path**; the value will be auto-populated: `/project/cicd/azure-code-pipeline.yml`

Click on **Continue**.

11. You will now see the **Review your pipeline YAML** screen:

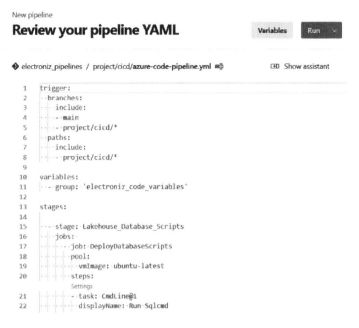

Figure 12.56 – Structure of the code YAML file

Click on the arrow beside the **Save** button and click **Run**. Then, click **Save**.

12. Using the menu on the left, click **Pipelines**, then **All**. Toward the right-hand side of the screen, click on the three dots beside **electroniz_pipelines** and click **Rename/move**:

Figure 12.57 – Renaming the code Azure pipeline

13. Change the name of the pipeline, as follows:

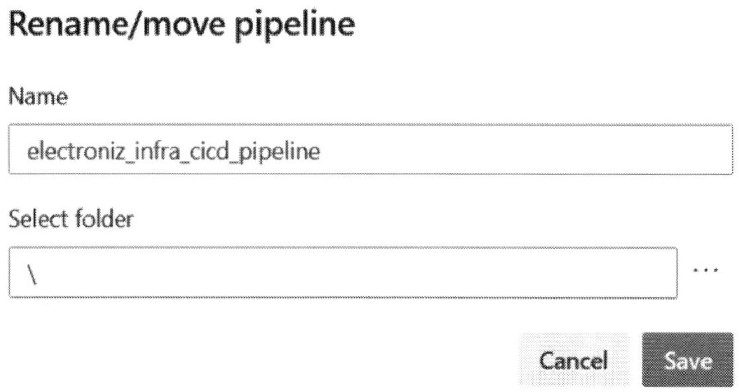

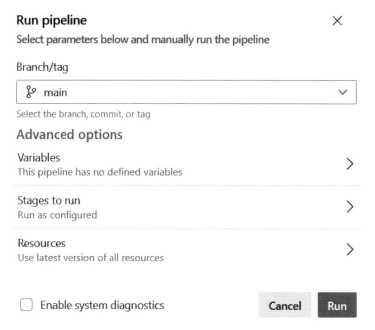

Figure 12.58 – Naming the code Azure pipeline

Click on **Save**.

14. Click on the three dots once again and this time, click **Run pipeline**:

Figure 12.59 – Running the code Azure pipeline

15. **electroniz_code_cicd_pipeline** will now be triggered:

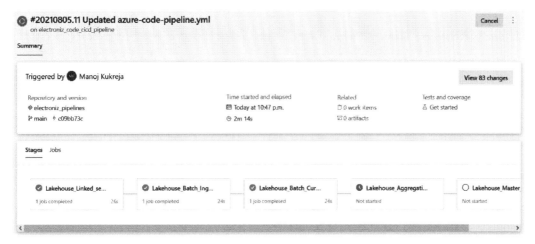

Figure 12.60 – Triggering the code Azure pipeline

16. Monitor the pipeline as it goes through the various stages of code deployment. The stage is marked with a green check sign once the deployment is complete:

Figure 12.61 – Monitoring the code Azure pipeline

17. In another tab, navigate to the following Azure portal link: **Home** > **Resource Groups** > **elz_prod** > **prod-dlake-elzdf**

Click on **Open** under **Open Azure Data Factory Studio**:

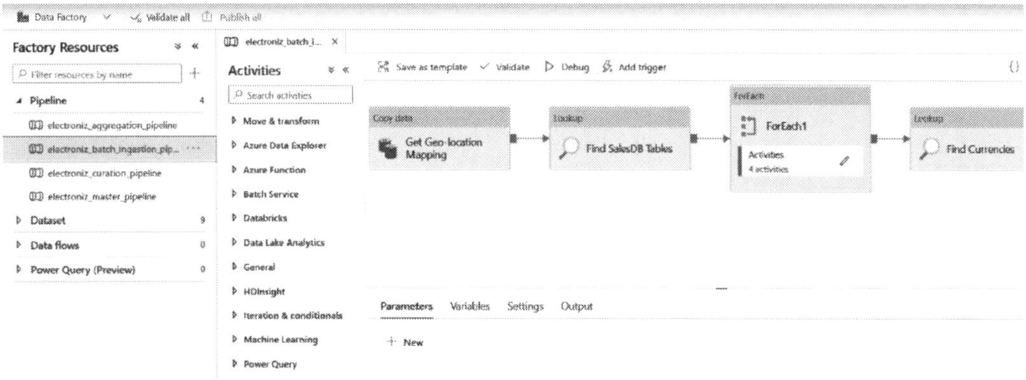

Figure 12.62 – Confirming the data pipelines created in Azure Data Factory

The fact that we can see the four data pipelines we created in **Azure Data Factory** is enough to prove that **electroniz_code_cicd_pipeline** worked well. But the job is not completely done yet. We just created a CI/CD pipeline for existing code. Now, we need to make it work for future changes and additions.

Creating the CI/CD life cycle

Hopefully, we all agree that the development of new code is a continuous process. Previously, we discussed the drawbacks of the traditional approach of committing several changes to the code repository, followed by a combined testing process. CI/CD mitigates some of these issues by integrating code continuously and deploying changes automatically. At a high level, the code merge cycle for the CI/CD pipeline looks like this:

- **Build**: After changes, developers commit code in the shared repository, usually under a feature branch.

- **Approve**: A pull request is generated by the developer for team approval. If the code fails approval, the reviewers either suggest fixes or approve the code for merge.

- **Merge**: After a successful review, the feature branch is merged with the main branch.

- **Deploy**: A process automatically deploys the code to production:

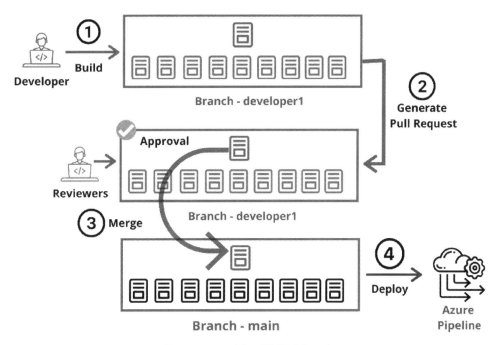

Figure 12.63 – The CI/CD life cycle

In the following steps, we'll find out how all of this works practically. The following steps will walk us through an example scenario:

1. A developer commits a code change and creates a pull request for the reviewer(s) for approval.

2. The reviewer(s) approve the change and merge it in the main branch.

3. An automated CI/CD pipeline deploys the code.

Please note that the following steps will be performed by multiple team members, so the owner is mentioned in each step.

Build – developer

This can be done by performing the following steps:

1. Navigate to **Repos** > **Branches**. Click on **New Branch** and create a new branch, as follows:

Figure 12.64 – Creating a new code branch

Click on **Create**:

Figure 12.65 – developer1 branch creation

2. Now, click on **developer1**. You are now connected to the **developer1** branch:

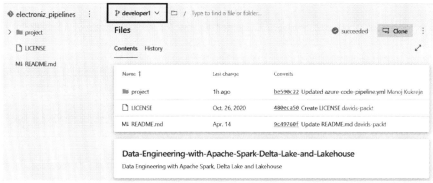

Figure 12.66 – Confirming the switch to the developer1 branch

3. Navigate to **project/cicd/azure-code-pipeline.yml**. Click on **Edit**. Now, paste the following code toward the end of the file:

```
- stage: Lakehouse_Database_Scripts
  jobs:
    - job: DeployDatabaseScripts
      pool:
        vmImage: ubuntu-latest
      steps:
      - task: AzureKeyVault@1
        inputs:
          azureSubscription: '$(SERVICE_CONNECTION)'
          keyVaultName: '$(KEY_VAULT_NAME)'
          secretsFilter: '*'
      - task: CmdLine@1
        displayName: Run Sqlcmd
        inputs:
          filename: sqlcmd
          arguments: '-S $(SYNAPSE_CON_STRING) -U
$(SQLUSER) -P $(SQLPASSWORD) -i project/aggregation/sql/
create_db.sql'
      - task: CmdLine@1
        displayName: Run Sqlcmd
        inputs:
          filename: sqlcmd
```

```
           arguments: '-S $(SYNAPSE_CON_STRING) -U
$(SQLUSER) -P $(SQLPASSWORD) -i project/aggregation/sql/
create_synapse_creds.sql'
        - task: CmdLine@1
          displayName: Run Sqlcmd
          inputs:
            filename: sqlcmd
            arguments: '-S $(SYNAPSE_CON_STRING) -U
$(SQLUSER) -P $(SQLPASSWORD) -i project/aggregation/sql/
create_silver_views.sql'
        - task: CmdLine@1
          displayName: Run Sqlcmd
          inputs:
            filename: sqlcmd
            arguments: '-S $(SYNAPSE_CON_STRING) -U
$(SQLUSER) -P $(SQLPASSWORD) -i project/aggregation/sql/
drop_gold_tables.sql'
        - task: CmdLine@1
          displayName: Run Sqlcmd
          inputs:
            filename: sqlcmd
            arguments: '-S $(SYNAPSE_CON_STRING) -U
$(SQLUSER) -P $(SQLPASSWORD) -i project/aggregation/sql/
create_gold_tables.sql'
```

Make sure that the code indentations have been set appropriately. After editing the file, it should look like this:

```
106            action: 'Create Or Update Resource Group'
107            resourceGroupName: '$(RESOURCE_GROUP)'
108            location: '$(REGION)'
109            templateLocation: 'Linked artifact'
110            csmFile: 'project/cicd/electroniz_master_pipeline.json'
111            overrideParameters: '-factoryName $(DATAFACTORY_NAME)'
112            deploymentMode: 'Incremental'
113            deploymentName: 'dataFactoryDeployment'
114
115  - stage: Lakehouse_Database_Scripts
116    jobs:
117      - job: DeployDatabaseScripts
118        pool:
119          vmImage: ubuntu-latest
120        steps:
121        - task: AzureKeyVault@1
122          inputs:
123            azureSubscription: '$(SERVICE_CONNECTION)'
124            keyVaultName: '$(KEY_VAULT_NAME)'
125            secretsFilter: '*'
126        - task: CmdLine@1
127          displayName: Run Sqlcmd
128          inputs:
129            filename: sqlcmd
130            arguments: '-S $(SYNAPSE_CON_STRING) -U $(SQLUSER) -P $(SQLPASSWORD) -i project/aggregation/sql/create_db.sql'
131        - task: CmdLine@1
132          displayName: Run Sqlcmd
133          inputs:
134            filename: sqlcmd
135            arguments: '-S $(SYNAPSE_CON_STRING) -U $(SQLUSER) -P $(SQLPASSWORD) -i project/aggregation/sql/create_synapse_creds.sql'
```

Figure 12.67 – Adding a new stage to azure-code-pipeline.yml

Press **Commit**.

On the next screen, make sure that the branch is set to **developer1**. Press **Commit**. Now, press the **Create a pull request** button. Create a new pull request, as follows:

Figure 12.68 – Creating a new pull request

Click on **Create**.

Approve – reviewers

This can be done by performing the following steps:

1. The reviewers are notified (usually via email) about the new pull request. Reviewers, either individually or as a group, may review the changes and add their comments. Once the code has been reviewed, add a new comment, as follows:

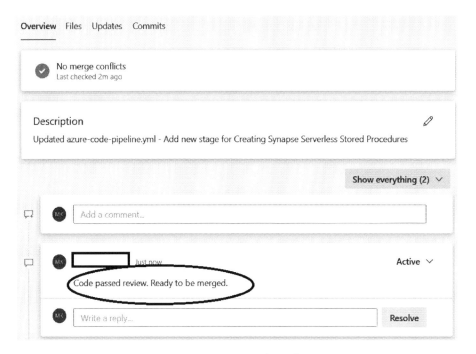

Figure 12.69 – Reviewing the pull request

Merge – team lead

This can be done by performing the following steps:

1. Once all the reviewers have entered their comments, the team leader may either reject or approve the changes. In our case, we are going to assume the review process was positive. Click on **Approve**:

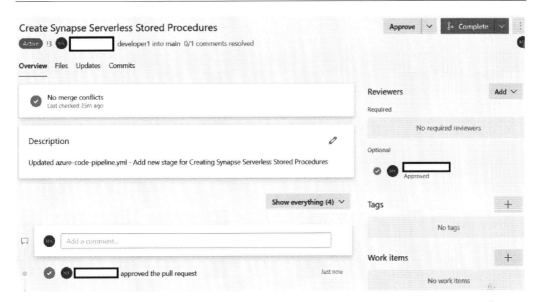

Figure 12.70 – Approving the pull request

2. Notice **No merge conflicts**. This means that the new code is ready to be merged:

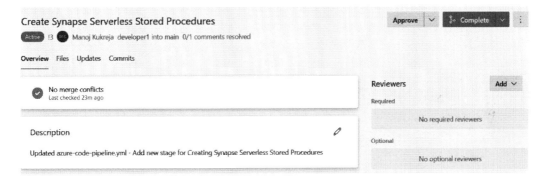

Figure 12.71 – Checking for merge conflicts

Deploy – automated

This can be done by performing the following steps:

1. After the code merge from the **developer1** branch to the main branch, the trigger section in the YAML deployment file deploys the code to the specified environment. Click on **Complete**:

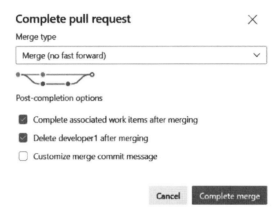

Figure 12.72 – Merging the developer1 branch into the main branch

2. The following confirmation message is received once the merge process is successful:

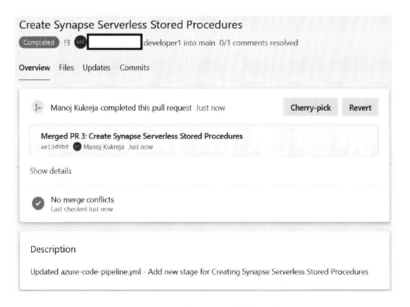

Figure 12.73 – Confirmation of the code merge

3. These code merges trigger the CI/CD pipeline automatically. Navigate back to **Pipelines** via the **Azure DevOps** portal. Click on **electroniz_code_cicd_pipeline**. Now, click on the latest entry in the list. You should see the following confirmation regarding the automated deployment:

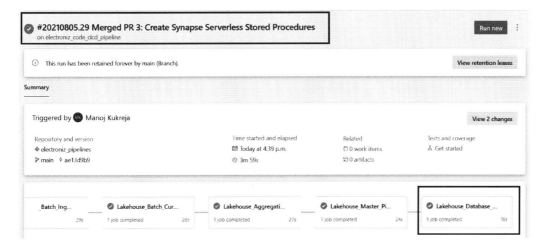

Figure 12.74 – Confirmation of the automated pipeline run

Notice how the automated run has correctly identified, created, and deployed the **Lakehouse_Database_Scripts** stage.

> **Important**
>
> Deploying atomic code changes allows us to find and fix faults faster. CI/CD promotes a transparent method for code integrations and deployment that is known to increase efficiency and enhance customer satisfaction.

That's it for this chapter. Using the preceding steps, we were able to successfully automate infrastructure creation and code delivery using CI/CD pipelines. We also learned how to implement the CI/CD life cycle in a team environment. From here onward, Electroniz can safely rely on these pipelines to deliver future code additions and changes in their environment with minimal effort and risk.

Summary

In an era where organizations are aiming to do more with less, automation is quickly gaining a lot of attention. As CI/CD continues to grow and gain strength, it is set to become one of the most critical skills for modern data engineers. In most cases, the high cost of data engineers can only be justified if their skill set includes automation.

In many respects, adopting automation practices such as CI/CD is proving to be a lifesaver. Not only does automation take a lot of work off the data engineers' shoulders, but it also lowers costs by predictably performing repetitive iterations. On top of that, the built-in approval and fail fast mechanisms in CI/CD ensure team accountability and collaboration. If used wisely, adopting automation can ensure the predictable and seamless delivery of code and infrastructure components.

This is the last chapter of this book. I must admit that in the last 12 chapters, we have covered a lot of ground. We undertook the journey of data – one that contains a lot of twists and turns. I am glad that, in the end, we successfully overcame these obstacles and navigated our way to success. Our journey started by collecting and storing data before curating and aggregating it in the various layers of the lakehouse. We also learned how to design, develop, monitor, and automatically deploy data pipelines. Toward the end, we covered some challenges that are faced by data engineers by providing some suggestions of how to overcome them. But all in all, in the end, it was all worth it.

Every byte of data has a story to tell, and I am confident that we narrated this story accurately, securely, and efficiently.

`Packt.com`

Subscribe to our online digital library for full access to over 7,000 books and videos, as well as industry leading tools to help you plan your personal development and advance your career. For more information, please visit our website.

Why subscribe?

- Spend less time learning and more time coding with practical eBooks and Videos from over 4,000 industry professionals

- Improve your learning with Skill Plans built especially for you

- Get a free eBook or video every month

- Fully searchable for easy access to vital information

- Copy and paste, print, and bookmark content

Did you know that Packt offers eBook versions of every book published, with PDF and ePub files available? You can upgrade to the eBook version at `packt.com` and as a print book customer, you are entitled to a discount on the eBook copy. Get in touch with us at `customercare@packtpub.com` for more details.

At `www.packt.com`, you can also read a collection of free technical articles, sign up for a range of free newsletters, and receive exclusive discounts and offers on Packt books and eBooks.

Other Books You May Enjoy

If you enjoyed this book, you may be interested in these other books by Packt:

Data Engineering with Python

Paul Crickard

ISBN: 9781839214189

- Understand how data engineering supports data science workflows

- Discover how to extract data from files and databases and then clean, transform, and enrich it

- Configure processors for handling different file formats as well as both relational and NoSQL databases

- Find out how to implement a data pipeline and dashboard to visualize results

- Use staging and validation to check data before landing in the warehouse

- Build real-time pipelines with staging areas that perform validation and handle failures

- Get to grips with deploying pipelines in the production environment

Azure Data Engineering Cookbook

Ahmad Osama

ISBN: 9781800206557

- Use Azure Blob storage for storing large amounts of unstructured data

- Perform CRUD operations on the Cosmos Table API

- Implement elastic pools and business continuity with Azure SQL Database

- Ingest and analyze data using Azure Synapse Analytics

- Develop Data Factory data flows to extract data from multiple sources

- Manage, maintain, and secure Azure Data Factory pipelines

- Process streaming data using Azure Stream Analytics and Data Explorer

Packt is searching for authors like you

If you're interested in becoming an author for Packt, please visit `authors.packtpub.com` and apply today. We have worked with thousands of developers and tech professionals, just like you, to help them share their insight with the global tech community. You can make a general application, apply for a specific hot topic that we are recruiting an author for, or submit your own idea.

Share Your Thoughts

Now you've finished, we'd love to hear your thoughts! Scan the QR code below to go straight to the Amazon review page for this book and share your feedback or leave a review on the site that you purchased it from.

`https://packt.link/r/1-801-07774-6`

Your review is important to us and the tech community and will help us make sure we're delivering excellent quality content.

Index

A

access control 25
access control lists (ACLs) 25
ACID transactions 49, 163
aggregated data
  about 102
  verifying, in gold layer 268-273
aggregation pipeline 104
Amazon Kinesis 44
Amazon Redshift Spectrum 51
Ambari 58
analytics units 71
Ansible 369
Apache Flink 40, 41, 44
Apache Hadoop 40
Apache Hive 41
Apache Kafka 44
Apache Spark 40, 66, 164, 206
Apache Spark Streaming 41, 44
Apache Storm 39, 41
application programming interfaces
      (APIs) 16, 23, 83
ARM template
  creating 369, 370
  deploying, with Azure CLI 378
  deploying, with Azure portal 373-378

deploying, with secrets 379-383
  parameters 370
  resources 372
  variables 371
artificial intelligence (AI) engineers 23
authorization 26
automated failure detection 63
automatic pause mechanism 74
Azure
  data engineering 53-55
  data processing services 65
  data storage services 60
Azure Active Directory 60
Azure Active Directory integration 66
Azure Blob storage
  about 60, 66, 67, 99
  data, organizing 61
Azure CLI 378
Azure client 373
Azure Cloud Shell 111
Azure Cosmos DB 64, 66
Azure Databricks 66, 67, 70,
      101, 166, 206, 322
Azure Databricks SQL Analytics 68
Azure Databricks workspace 68

Azure Data Factory
  about 66, 67, 69, 83, 100
      103, 104, 209, 432
  data control activity 70
  data movement activity 70
  data transformation activity 70
Azure Data Factory service, components
  control flow 70
  data flow 70
  ingest 70
  monitor 70
  schedule 70
Azure Data Lake Analytics
  about 71
  phases 71
Azure Data Lake Storage 100, 102, 103
Azure Data Lake Storage
      Gen 2 61, 62, 66, 67, 266, 372
Azure Data Share
  about 76, 335
  in-place sharing 76
  snapshot-based sharing 76
Azure DevOps 393, 397
Azure DevOps organization
  creating 397-405
Azure event grid 111, 155
Azure event hub namespace 155
Azure Event Hubs 44, 63, 67, 103
Azure HDInsight 66, 70
Azure Key Vault 216, 253, 379
Azure Kubernetes Service (AKS) 59
Azure-managed data engineering
      services (PAAS) 59
Azure Monitor 66
Azure Pipelines 104, 397
Azure portal
  about 373

used, for deploying ARM
      template 373-378
Azure Purview 75, 352
Azure Repos 397
Azure Resource Manager (ARM)
  about 59, 104
  used, for infrastructure deployment 369
Azure resources
  cleaning up 194, 240, 365, 386
  preparing 164-174
  preparing, for data aggregation
      pipeline 246-250
  preparing, for data curation
      pipeline 207-215
Azure Service Manager (ASM) 369
Azure SQL 379
Azure Stream Analytics
  about 72
  case scenarios 72
Azure Stream Analytics Cluster 72
Azure Stream Analytics job 72
Azure Synapse 66, 67, 101,
      102, 249, 253, 379
Azure Synapse Analytics
  about 51, 73
  data processing services 73, 74
Azure Synapse Link 74
Azure Synapse serverless SQL pool 265
Azure Traffic Manager 64
Azure Virtual Machines (Azure VMs)
  features 57

B

Bash 111
batch collection 38
batch ingestion pipeline
  building 119-141

inserts 145-154

testing, for historical data 142-144

testing, for incremental data 145

updates 149-151

batch pipeline 103

batch processing 38

batch workflow 38

block storage

about 27

versus object storage 27

business insights 5

business intelligence (BI) 23, 88

business intelligence (BI) engineers 4

business requirements

validating 273-281

C

CAP theorem

about 34, 37

availability 36

consistency 36

partition tolerance 36

trade-offs 37

central processing unit (CPU) 29

change data capture (CDC) 40, 83, 203

Chef 369, 393

chief technology officer (CTO) 95

CIA triad 25, 26

CI/CD 392

CI/CD life cycle

creating 432

CI/CD pipeline, code merge cycle

Approve 432, 438

Build 432-437

Deploy 432, 440, 441

CI/CD pipelines

designing 393

developing 397

CircleCI 393

cloud architecture

about 100

aggregated data 102

curated data 101

raw data 100

cloud computing

adopting 10, 11

cloud data storage 44

cloud data warehouses 44

Cloudera 58

Cloudera Manager 58

cloud storage 27

code-to-data paradigm shift 9

Comma-separated values (CSV) 21

compute

about 29

versus storage 30, 31

compute costs

preserving 33

concurrency control 193, 194

constraints, types 199

containerization 59

containers 29

continuous deployment (CD) 390, 392

continuous integration (CI) 390, 391

continuous integration/continuous

deployment (CI/CD) 91

control plane 68

curated data

about 101

duplicate data, verifying 236-238

insecure data, verifying 238, 239

invalid data, verifying 229-231

non-uniform data, verifying 232-235

unstandardized data, verifying 226-229
verifying, in silver layer 226
curation pipeline 104
currency conversion data 99

D

data
  changing, in Delta Lake table 180, 181
  journey to effective data analysis 4, 5
data aggregation
  need for 242
  process 243, 244
data aggregation pipeline
  Azure resources, preparing 246-250
  creating, for gold layer 251-262
  developing 245
  running 263, 264
data analysts 4
data analytics
  about 22
  evolution 5, 6
data-at-rest 26
Databricks Community Edition
  reference link 67
Databricks Delta Lake 50
data classification 365
data consumption
  about 264, 265
  gold layer data, accessing 266-268
  silver layer data, accessing 265-267
data curation
  about 163
  need for 198
data curation pipeline
  Azure resources, preparing 207-215
  creating, for silver layer 215-219
  developing 206

running, for silver layer 220-225
data curation process
  about 205
  approval, obtaining 205
  data, cleaning 206
  data, inspecting 205
  data, verifying 206
data curation, reasons
  duplicate data 203, 204
  inconsistent data 202
  insecure data 204
  invalid data 199, 201
  non-uniform data 201, 202
  unstandardized data 198, 199
data destination
  about 84
  configuring 117, 118
  final 84
  intermediate 84
data engineer 4
data engineering 4
Data engineering as a service (SAAS) 68
data engineering, in Azure
  about 53-55
  performing 56
data engineering practice,
    reasons for business
  about 6
  cloud computing, adoption 10, 11
  datasets, availability 7, 8
  data storytelling 11-13
  paradigm shift, to distributed
    computing 8-10
  storage and compute resources,
    core capabilities 7
data exchange formats 21
data governance
  about 352

Azure resources, preparing 353-355
data catalog, creating 355-365
data-in-motion 26
data lake architectures
about 33, 34
Kappa architecture 44
Lambda architecture 39
traditional architecture 38
data lakes
about 20
adhering, to compliance
frameworks 24, 25
characteristics 20
data lakes, benefits
about 21
data, storing in zones 22, 23
varying data characteristics,
accommodating 23, 24
varying data formats,
accommodating 21, 22
data lake zones
about 22
curated 22
raw 22
transformed 22
data lineage 101, 181
data masking 104
data monetization 16, 334
data movement service (DMS) 73
data pipeline, methods
event-based 94
manually 93
scheduled 93
data pipelines
about 393
creating, process 85
exploring 82

monitoring, benefits 85
running 93, 94
data pipelines, components
about 82
destination 84
ingestion 83
monitoring 85
sources 83
transformation 83, 84
workflow 84
data pipelines design process
deployment phase 93
design phase 88
development phase 92
discovery phase 86
data plane 68
data preparation
about 106
source data, preparing for
database stores 107-111
source data, preparing for e-commerce
transactions 111-116
data processing services, Azure
about 65
Azure Databricks 66, 67
Azure Databricks SQL Analytics 68
Azure Databricks workspace 68
Azure HDInsight 66
data provider 21
data scientists 4
datasets
availability 7
data sharing
about 334
Azure resources, preparing 337
creating 338-352
in-place sharing 336
snapshot sharing 336

data sharing, methods
  complex 335
  control 335
  insecure 335
  tracking 335
  updates 335
data sources
  configuring 106
data standardization 104
data storage services, Azure
  about 60
  Azure Blob storage 60
  Azure Cosmos DB 64
  Azure Data Lake Storage Gen 2 61, 62
  Azure Event Hubs 63
data storytelling 11-13
data streams 7
data-to-code processing
  about 8
  disadvantages 8
data transformation 83
data warehouses 23, 44
data warehouse units (DWUs) 73
dedicated SQL pools 73
delta 101
Delta Lake
  about 66, 101, 162-164, 286, 319
  Azure resources, preparing 164-174
  lakehouse, enabling 162, 163
Delta Lake table
  creating 174-179
  data, changing 180, 181
deployment phase 93
deployment strategy 104
descriptive analysis 5
design phase
  about 88
  automation, designing 91

cloud architecture, designing 90
  costing 91
  data pipeline monitoring, designing 91
  datasets, shortlisting 89
  pipeline, designing with parent-
    child approach 89, 90
development phase 92
DevOps 392, 393
diagnostic analysis 5
direct-attached storage (DAS) 26
discovery phase
  about 86
  discovery sessions, conducting 87, 88
  product owner, identifying 86, 87
  use cases, shortlisting 87
distributed computing
  about 9, 35
  advantages, over traditional
    processing approach 9
distributed query processing (DQP) 74
duplicate data
  about 203, 204
  verifying 236-238

E

e-commerce transactions 99
e-commerce website tracking 99
electronic sensors 14
Electroniz 95, 98
Electroniz code CI/CD pipeline
  about 393, 396
  code structure 396
  creating 421-432
Electroniz data lake
  architecting 98-100
  cloud architecture 100
  deployment strategy 104

pipeline design 103
Electroniz infrastructure CI/CD pipeline
    about 393, 395
    code structure 395
    creating 406-420
encryption 26
end-of-life (EOL) cycle 15
entity-relationship diagram (ERD) 200
event-based method 94, 287, 288
Extensible Markup Language (XML) 21
Extract, Load, Transform (ELT) 69
extract, transform, load (ETL) 20, 69, 87

F

fault tolerance (FT) 44
filtering Internet Protocol
        (IP) addresses 25
Flume 38
free parallelism request form 397

G

General Data Protection Regulation
        (GDPR) 24, 204
geo-location data 99
globally unique identifier (GUID) 27
gold layer
    aggregated data, verifying 268-273
    pipeline, creating for 251-262
gold layer data
    accessing 267, 268
Google BigQuery 51
Google Pub/Sub 44

H

Hadoop 56, 66
Hadoop cluster 58
Hadoop Distributed File
        System (HDFS) 23
Hadoop/Spark/Kafka distributions 58
hard disk drive/solid-state
        drive (HDD/SSD) 26
Health Insurance Portability and
        Accountability Act (HIPAA) 24
high availability (HA) 44
Hive 38, 66, 175, 222
horizontal scalability 35, 36
Hortonworks 58
Hortonworks Data Platform (HDP) 66
HyperText Transfer Protocol (HTTP) 28

I

inconsistent data 202
indexing 163
Infrastructure as a Service (IaaS) layer
    use cases 57
Infrastructure as Code (IaC)
    about 58, 368, 369, 393
    used, for deploying multiple
        environments 383-386
infrastructure deployment
    with Azure Resource Manager
        (ARM) 369
Infrastructure Deployment 393
ingestion pipeline
    batch ingestion pipeline,
        building 119-141
    batch ingestion pipeline, testing
        for historical data 142-144

batch ingestion pipeline, testing
    for incremental data 145
building 119
streaming ingestion pipeline,
    building 155-159
testing 141
in-place sharing 336
insecure data
about 204
verifying 238, 239
interactive development environment
    (IDE) 67, 169, 212, 326
Internet of Things (IoT) 21
invalid data
about 199-201
verifying 229-231
isolation level 191, 192

J

Java 38
Java Database Connectivity (JDBC)/Open
    Database Connectivity (ODBC) 51
JavaScript Object Notation
    (JSON) 21, 177, 369
Jenkins 393

K

Kafka 56, 66
Kafka Streams 44
Kappa architecture
about 44
case scenarios 47
cons 46
functionality 44, 45
pros 46
serving layer 44

streaming layer 44
key performance indicators (KPIs) 244
Kubernetes 59

L

lakehouse
about 162
enabling, with Delta Lake 162, 163
Lakehouse architecture
about 48
features 50, 51
give-and-take struggle 48, 49
lakehouse project
building 95, 96
Lambda architecture
about 39
advantages 43
batch layer 39
drawbacks 43
layers 42
serving layer 40, 41
speed layer 41
usage scenarios 43
linked service 69
locally redundant data (LRS) 77
logical partitions 65
loosely coupled data lake 32

M

machine learning (ML) 6
machine learning (ML) engineers 23
man-in-the-middle attack 335
MapR 58
MapReduce engine 38
massively parallel processing
    (MPP) 10, 50

master data management (MDM) 89
master dataset
  characteristics 39
  file structure 40
master pipeline
  developing 288-294
  scheduling 296-300
  testing 295, 296
Microsoft Azure
  about 30
  data catalogs and data
    sharing services 75
  free account, opening 76, 77
Microsoft Azure calculator
  reference link 30
Microsoft SQL server 99
MLFlow 66
modern software delivery cycle 391, 392
monetary power of data
  about 13
  organic growth 13
multi-dimensional aggregations 243
multi-factor authentication (MFA) 25, 87
multiple environments
  deploying, with Infrastructure
    as Code (IaC) 383-386

N

natural language processing (NLP) 16
network-attached storage (NAS) 26
non-uniform data
  about 201, 202
  verifying 232-235
notebook commands
  reference link 171

O

object storage
  about 27
  advantages 28
  data 27
  drawbacks 28
  Identifier (id) 27
  metadata 27
  versus block storage 27
observations 242
online analytical processing
    (OLAP) 7, 28, 87
online transaction processing
    (OLTP) 7, 28, 87, 198
Oozie 38
optical character recognition (OCR) 16
optimistic concurrency control 194
orchestration 38
organic growth
  about 14
  customer retention 14
  data monetization 16, 17
  fraud prevention 14
  problem detection 14, 15

P

PagerDuty 68
paradigm shift 9
parent-child approach
  benefits 90
  used, for designing pipeline 89
Parquet 175
partitioning 65
Payment Card Industry (PCI) 24, 96

perimeter security 25
Perl 38
personally identifiable
        information (PII) 26, 88
Pig 38
pipeline design 103
pipeline design, components
    aggregation pipeline 104
    batch pipeline 103
    curation pipeline 104
    streaming pipeline 103
pipelines
    alerting features, adding 306-314
    dealing, with failure conditions 303
    deployment strategy 286
    durability features, adding 301, 302
    monitoring 300
pipelines, deployment strategy
    event-based method 287, 288
    time-based method 286
pipelines, failure conditions
    failed activities, bypassing 304
    failed activities, rerunning 305
platform as a service (PaaS) layer
    use cases 60
PowerShell 111
prediction models 14
predictive analysis 6
prescriptive analysis 6
Presto 41
Puppet 369
PySpark 169
Python 38

R

random-access memory (RAM) 29
raw/curation layer 84
raw data
    about 100, 105, 106
    advantages 105
    features 105
real-time views 41
relational databases 44
REpresentational State Transfer (REST) 93
resource groups 369
REST API calls 99
revenue diversification 13, 334
role-based access control (RBAC) 25, 60

S

SAAS use case
    Azure Data Factory 69, 70
    Azure Data Lake Analytics 71
    Azure Stream Analytics 72
    Azure Synapse Analytics 73
sales database 99
Sarbanes-Oxley Act (SOX) 24
scalability 34
schedule 94
scheduler 93
schema evolution 318-334
schema validation 319-334
secrets
    about 394
    used, for deploying ARM
        template 379-383
self-managed data engineering
        services (IAAS) 56

self-managed services
  cons 58
  pros 58
self-service model 23
semi-structured data 21
serializers/deserializers (SerDes) 24
serverless SQL pools 74
service-level agreements (SLAs) 85
shared access signatures (SASes) 60, 252
silver layer
  curated data, verifying 226
  pipeline, creating for 215-219
  pipeline, running for 220-225
silver layer data
  accessing 266, 267
single-sign-on (SSO) 25
site-to-site virtual private
     networks (VPNs) 25
skill set 394
Slack 68
snapshot sharing 336
Snowflake 51
software as a service (SaaS) layer
  use cases 69
Spark 56, 66
Spark cluster 58
Spark DataFrame 174
SQL 169, 206
SQL endpoints 68
Sqoop 38
storage
  about 26
  block storage 27
  object storage 27
  versus compute 30, 31
storage area network (SAN) 26
Storm 66

streaming ingestion pipeline
  building 155
streaming pipeline 103
streaming units (SUs) 72
stream processing 7
stream-processing engine 44
structured data 21
Synapse Spark 74
Synapse SQL 73

T

Terraform 369
tightly coupled data lake 31
time-based method 286
time travel
  performing 181-184
traditional architecture
  about 38
  issues 39
traditional software delivery cycle
  about 390
  Code Packaging 391
  Development 391
  Production Deployment 391
  QA Deployment 391
  Testing/QA 391
transformation layer 84
two-dimensional aggregations 243

U

unstandardized data
  about 198, 199
  verifying 226-229
unstructured data 21

upsert operation
  performing 184-190
U-SQL runtime engine 71

V

variables 242
versioning 163
vertexes 71
vertical scalability 34, 35
virtual CPU (vCPU) 29

W

watermark approach 119
workflow
  about 84
  control actions 84
  input and output (I/O) actions 84
  transformation actions 84

Y

Yet Another Resource Negotiator
      (YARN) 29

Made in the USA
Las Vegas, NV
03 February 2022

42999836R00265